Pope Clement I, Joseph Barber Lightfoot

The two epistles to the Corinthians

Pope Clement I, Joseph Barber Lightfoot

The two epistles to the Corinthians

ISBN/EAN: 9783337728847

Printed in Europe, USA, Canada, Australia, Japan

Cover: Foto ©Lupo / pixelio.de

More available books at **www.hansebooks.com**

S. CLEMENT OF ROME.

THE TWO EPISTLES

TO THE

CORINTHIANS.

*A REVISED TEXT
WITH INTRODUCTION AND NOTES.*

BY

J. B. LIGHTFOOT, D.D.

HULSEAN PROFESSOR OF DIVINITY,
AND FELLOW OF TRINITY COLLEGE, CAMBRIDGE.

London and Cambridge:
MACMILLAN AND CO.
1869.

THIS Volume is the first part of a complete edition of the Apostolic Fathers. The second part is intended to include the Ignatian Epistles (genuine, interpolated, and spurious) together with the Epistle of Polycarp.

The preface and indices will be issued with the second part; and the present title-page, which is only temporary, will then be superseded by another.

The preface will give me an opportunity of stating my obligations to others; but I cannot delay the expression of my thanks to the authorities of the British Museum for allowing me free access to the Alexandrian MS, and to Mr A. A. Vansittart as well for collating the MS as for much valuable assistance in correcting the proof sheets of this edition.

J. B. LIGHTFOOT.

TRINITY COLLEGE,
July 31, 1869.

THE EPISTLES

OF

S. CLEMENT OF ROME.

THE EPISTLE OF CLEMENT

TO THE

CORINTHIANS.

I.

THE FIRST EPISTLE ascribed to S. Clement is addressed by the Church of Rome to the Church of Corinth. Though the writer's name is not mentioned either in the address or in the body of the letter, there can be no reasonable doubt about the authorship. Not only have we very wide and very early testimony to the fact that Clement held the first place in the Roman Church about this time; but the direct proofs of his being the writer are numerous. His contemporary Hermas, the author of the Shepherd, represents himself as directed by the angelic messenger to deliver a copy of the book with which he is charged to Clement, that he may communicate it to foreign churches, 'for this function belongs to him' (*Vis.* ii. 4 πέμψει οὖν Κλήμης εἰς τὰς ἔξω πόλεις, ἐκείνῳ γὰρ ἐπιτέτραπται). Not long after the middle of the second century testimony is borne to the authorship from two independent quarters. Dionysius, bishop of Corinth, writing to the Roman Christians during the episcopate of Soter (c. A.D. 165—175) in reply to a letter received from them, says: 'This day, being the Lord's day, we kept as a holy-day; when we read your epistle, which we shall ever continue to read for our edification, as also the former epistle which you wrote to us by Clement' (ὡς καὶ τὴν προτέραν ἡμῖν διὰ Κλήμεντος γραφεῖσαν, Euseb. *H. E.* iv. 23). About the same time Hegesippus, a native of Palestine, who had visited both Rome and Corinth, alludes to the feuds which had disturbed the latter Church, and (as reported by Eusebius) mentions in connexion therewith 'some particulars about the letter of Clement to the Corinthians' (Euseb. *H. E.* iv. 22; comp. *H. E.* iii. 16). A few years later Irenæus writes thus: 'In the time of this

1—2

Clement (ἐπὶ τούτου τοῦ Κλήμεντος), no small dissension having arisen among the brethren in Corinth, the Church in Rome sent a very able (ἱκανωτάτην) letter to the Corinthians, urging them to peace, etc.' (*Hær.* iii. 3. 3; comp. Euseb. *H. E.* v. 6). Again about the close of the century the writer's namesake, Clement of Alexandria, repeatedly quotes the letter; citing it most commonly as 'Clement in the Epistle to the Corinthians' (e.g. *Strom.* i. 7, p. 339; iv. 17, p. 609; vi. 8, p. 773), but in one passage as the 'Epistle of the Romans to the Corinthians' (*Strom.* v. 12, p. 693). Either designation is equally appropriate; for, though addressed in the name of the Roman Church, it would be written and forwarded by Clement. In the next generation again Origen more than once quotes it as the work of Clement (*de Princ.* ii. 6, I. p. 82; *Select. in Ezech.* viii. 3, III. p. 422; *in Joann.* vi. § 36, IV. p. 153). And Eusebius, while mentioning the Second Epistle as *ascribed* to Clement, states that he was universally recognised as the author of the First (τοῦ Κλήμεντος ἐν τῇ ὁμολογουμένῃ παρὰ πᾶσιν), which was written by him to the Corinthians 'in the person of the Roman Church' (ἣν ἐκ προσώπου τῆς Ῥωμαίων ἐκκλησίας τῇ Κορινθίων διετυπώσατο, *H. E.* iii. 38). In short it may fairly be said that very few writings of Classical or Christian antiquity are so well authenticated as this letter.

About its date some difference of opinion exists. The troubles mentioned in the opening chapter must refer to some persecution of the Roman Christians. The persecution of Trajan, to which Clement has been supposed by some recent critics to allude, is too late for the notices found elsewhere in the epistle (see the notes on §§ 5, 44); nor indeed is there any reason for thinking that the Roman Christians especially were sufferers during this reign. It must be added also that the only positive argument urged in favour of this very late date is unsound (see the note on § 55). We are therefore limited to the persecutions of Nero and Domitian. Those who maintain the earlier of these two epochs appeal to the fact that Clement, when referring to the temple services, uses the present tense, as though the temple were still standing and the services regularly performed: but parallel instances show that this mode of speaking was common long after the destruction of Jerusalem (see the notes on §§ 40, 41). On the other hand the notices in other passages of the epistle seem to require a greater lapse of time since the foundation of the Corinthian Church and the death of the chief Apostles (see §§ 5, 44, 47, with the notes); and the language in which the troubles of the Roman Church are described in the opening chapter accords better with the persecution of Domitian than with that of Nero (see the notes, § 1). Again the manifest quotations from the New Testament, more especially from the Epistle to the Hebrews, are hardly reconcilable with a date so early as the time of Nero. Thus the balance of internal evidence points clearly to the later of the two persecutions. And this result is confirmed by the direct statement of Hegesippus, who according to Eusebius referred the dissensions of the Corinthian Christians, which prompted the letter, to the time of Domitian (Euseb. *H. E.* iii. 16 καὶ ὅτι γε κατὰ τὸν δηλούμενον τὰ τῆς Κορινθίων κεκίνητο στάσεως ἀξιόχρεως μάρτυς ὁ Ἡγήσιππος). As Hegesippus visited both churches in succession about half a century after the letter was written, the greatest weight must be assigned to his testimony. This date moreover is confirmed by the fact, that the most trustworthy accounts place the episcopate of Clement late in the century, making him third in the succession of Roman bishops. Thus the letter will have been written about the year 95.

A fuller discussion of the nature of the feuds, which prompted the Roman Church to address this letter to the Corinthians, will be found in the notes (§§ 1, 40—47, 54). It is sufficient to say here that they had led to the expulsion of some faithful and honoured presbyters. But besides these social dissensions, it would appear that the old difficulty about the resurrection, which had troubled the Corinthian Church in St Paul's day, was again revived. At all events Clement takes some pains to argue the matter with his readers, as though it were a question of dispute among them (see § 24 sq. with the notes). Beyond these two points the letter contains no strictly argumentative matter, but is chiefly hortatory and didactic.

The effect of this interposition of the Roman Church may be inferred from the fact that Hegesippus immediately after his mention of the letter sent to heal these dissensions adds; 'And the Church of Corinth remained in the right doctrine till the episcopate of Primus in Corinth' (Euseb. *H. E.* iv. 22), this being the date of his own visit. At all events we find the Corinthian Christians not long after the middle of the second century communicating with their Roman brethren in the most friendly and cordial manner; for Dionysius of Corinth, writing in the name of his Church, loudly praises the 'hereditary liberality' of the Romans by which all the brethren had profited (Euseb. *H. E.* iv. 23); and the fact, already mentioned on his authority, that they continued in his time to read the letter of Clement in their religious assemblies, shows that the remonstrances of the Roman brotherhood had been received by them in a right spirit.

2.

The following is an analysis of the letter:

'THE CHURCH OF ROME TO THE CHURCH OF CORINTH. Greeting in Christ Jesus.'

'We regret that domestic troubles have prevented our writing before: we deplore the feuds which have gained ground among you; for your present unhappy state reminds us by contrast of the past, when such breaches of brotherly love were unknown among you, and your exemplary concord and charity were known far and wide (§§ 1, 2). Now all is changed. Like Jeshurun of old, you have waxed fat and kicked. Envy is your ruling passion (§ 3). Envy, which led Cain to slay his brother; which sent Jacob into exile; which persecuted Joseph; which compelled Moses to flee; which drove Aaron and Miriam out of the camp; which threw Dathan and Abiram alive into the pit; which incited Saul against David (§ 4); which in these latest days, after inflicting countless sufferings on the Apostles Peter and Paul, brought them to a martyr's death (§ 5); which has caused numberless woes to women and girls, has separated wives from their husbands, has destroyed whole cities and nations (§ 6). We and you alike need this warning. Let us therefore repent, as men repented at the preaching of Noah, at the preaching of Jonah (§ 7). The Holy Spirit, speaking by the prophets, again and again calls to repentance (§ 8). Let us not turn a deaf ear to the summons; let us supplicate God's mercy; let us follow the example of Enoch who was translated, of Noah who was saved from the flood (§ 9), of Abraham whose faith was rewarded by repeated blessings and by the gift of a son (§ 10). Call to mind the example of Lot whose hospitality saved him from the fate of Sodom, when even his wife perished (§ 11); of Rahab whose faith and protection of the spies rescued her from the general destruction (§ 12). Pride and passion must be laid aside; mercy and gentleness cherished; for the promises in the Scriptures are reserved for the merciful and gentle (§§ 13, 14). We must not call down denunciations upon our heads, like the Israelites of old (§ 15): but rather take for our pattern the lowliness of Christ as portrayed by the Evangelical Prophet and by the Psalmist (§ 16); and copy also the humility of the ancient worthies, Elijah, Elisha, Ezekiel, Abraham, and Job; of Moses the most highly favoured and yet the meekest of men (§ 17); of David the man after God's heart, who nevertheless humbled himself in the dust (§ 18). Nay, let us have before our eyes the long-suffering of God himself, the

Lord of the Universe, whose mind can be read in His works (§ 19). Harmony prevails in heaven and earth and ocean; day and night succeed each other in regular order; the seasons follow in due course; all created things perform their functions peacefully (§ 20). Let us therefore act as becomes servants of this beneficent Master. He is near at hand, and will punish all unruliness and self-seeking. In all relations of life behave soberly. Instruct your wives in gentleness, and your children in humility (§ 21). For the Holy Spirit in the Scriptures commends the humble and simple-hearted, but condemns the stubborn and double-tongued. The Lord will come quickly (§§ 22, 23).'

'All nature bears witness to the resurrection; the dawn of day; the growth of the seedling (§ 24); above all the wonderful bird of Arabia (§ 25). So too God Himself declares in the Scriptures (§ 26). He has sworn, and He can and will bring it to pass (§ 27).'

'Let us therefore cleanse our lives, since before Him is no concealment (§ 28). Let us approach Him in purity, and make our election sure (§ 29). As His children, we must avoid all lust, contention, self-will, and pride (§ 30). Look at the example of the patriarchs, Abraham, Isaac, and Jacob (§ 31). See how the promise was granted to their faith, that in them all the nations of the earth should be blessed (§ 32). To their *faith;* but we must not therefore be slack in works. The Creator Himself rejoices in His works, and we are created in His image. All righteous men have been rich in good works (§ 33). If we would win the reward, we must not be slothful but ever diligent, as the angels in heaven are diligent (§ 34). And how glorious is the hope held out to us! Well may we strive earnestly to attain this bright promise: well may we school ourselves to lay aside all bitterness and strife, which, as the Scriptures teach us, are hateful in God's sight (§ 35). Nor shall we be unaided in the struggle. Christ our High-Priest is mightier than the angels, and by Him we are ushered into the presence of God (§ 36).'

'Subordination of rank and distinction of office are the necessary conditions of life. Look at the manifold gradations of order in an army, at the diverse functions of the members in the human body (§ 37). We likewise are one body in Christ, and members in particular (§ 38). They are fools and mad, who thirst for power; men whom the Scriptures condemn in no measured terms (§ 39). Are not the ordinances of the Mosaic law—where the places, the seasons, the persons, are all prescribed—a sign that God will have all things done decently and in order (§§ 40, 41)? The Apostles were sent by Jesus Christ, as Jesus Christ was sent by the Father. They appointed presbyters in all churches, as the prophet had foretold (§ 42). Herein they followed the precedent of Moses. You will remember how the murmuring against Aaron was quelled by the budding of Aaron's rod (§ 43). In like manner the Apostles, to avoid dissension, made provision for the regular succession of the ministry. Ye did wrongly therefore to thrust out presbyters who had been duly appointed according to this Apostolic order, and had discharged their office faithfully (§ 44). It is an untold thing, that God's servants should thus cast out God's messengers. It was by the enemies of God that Daniel and the three children were persecuted of old (§ 45). There is one body and one Spirit. Whence then these dissensions (§ 46)? Did not the Apostle himself rebuke you for this same fault? And yet you had the excuse then, which you have not now, that they whom you constituted your leaders—Cephas and Paul and Apollos—were Apostles and Apostolic men (§ 47). Away with these feuds. Reconcile yourselves to God by humility and righteousness in Christ (§ 48). Love is all-powerful, love is beyond praise, love is acceptable to God. Seek love before all things, and ye shall be blessed indeed; for so the Scriptures declare (§§ 49, 50). Ask pardon for your offences, and do not harden your hearts like Pharaoh. Else, like Pharaoh, ye will also perish (§ 51). God asks nothing from us, but contrition and prayer and praise (§ 52). Moses spent forty days and nights in prayer, entreating God that he himself might be blotted out and the people spared (§ 53). Let the same spirit be in you. Let those who are the causes of dissension sacrifice themselves and retire, that strife may cease (§ 54). Nay, have not heathen kings and rulers been ready to offer themselves up for the common weal? Even women have perilled their lives, like men, for the public good. So did Judith; so also did Esther (§ 55). Let us intercede for one another; let us admonish one another (§ 56). And you especially, who were the first to stir up this feud, be the first to repent. Remember the stern threats, which the Scriptures pronounce against the stubborn and impenitent (§ 57).'

[Here a leaf of the manuscript is torn out, but we are enabled from quotations in different authors to supply the lacuna, as follows:

'The end is near, when all things shall be burnt up by fire. So the Prophets and Apostles testify: so also the Sibyl has declared. Prepare for this great and terrible day. God is tempting you, as He tempted Abraham. But be not dismayed. He is a living God'.]

'Finally, may He grant all graces and blessings to them that call upon His name, through Jesus Christ our High Priest (§ 58).'

'Ephebus and Bito and Fortunatus are the bearers of this letter.

Despatch them speedily, that they may return with the glad tidings of your peace and concord.'

'The grace of our Lord Jesus Christ be with you and with all men (§ 59).'

3.

The Epistle to the Corinthians was widely known and highly esteemed at a very early date. POLYCARP, who wrote early in the second century, appears to have been acquainted with it, for his extant Epistle presents many striking coincidences of language (see the notes on Polyc. *Phil.* 1, 2, 4, 7, 9; the parallels are collected by Hefele *Patr. Apost.* p. xxvi.). It is less certain whether the passage in IGNATIUS *Polyc.* 5, εἴ τις δύναται ἐν ἁγνείᾳ μένειν εἰς τιμὴν τῆς σαρκὸς τοῦ Κυρίου, ἐν ἀκαυχησίᾳ μενέτω, is a reminiscence of a passage in Clement's Epistle (§ 38); though this is not improbable (see Hilgenfeld p. xxi). The language of the PSEUDO-IGNATIUS also, *Ephes.* 15 οὐδὲν λανθάνει τὸν Κύριον ἀλλὰ καὶ τὰ κρυπτὰ ἡμῶν ἐγγὺς αὐτῷ ἐστιν, closely resembles a passage of Clement (§ 27). Many parallels to the Epistle of BARNABAS have also been produced (Hilgenfeld p. xix sq.), but these are unconvincing; and, even if they were so close as to suggest a historical connexion, it would still remain a question whether Clement was not indebted to the Epistle of Barnabas rather than conversely. The reputation of Clement as a letter writer among his contemporaries may be inferred from the passage in the Shepherd of HERMAS already quoted (p. 3).

The testimonies in the ages immediately following are more precise and definite, and come from the most diverse quarters. We have seen in what manner this epistle is mentioned and quoted by HEGESIPPUS of Palestine, by DIONYSIUS of Corinth, by IRENÆUS of Asia Minor and Gaul, and by CLEMENT and ORIGEN of Alexandria. To these witnesses we should probably add TERTULLIAN of Carthage; for in one passage (*de Resurr. carn.* 12, 13) where he is speaking of the resurrection, he uses the same arguments as Clement (§§ 24, 25), appealing first to the succession of night and day, of winter and summer, and then to the marvellous resuscitation of the phœnix. THEOPHILUS of ANTIOCH also (*ad Autol.* i. 13) seems to have copied from the earlier part of this same passage (see the notes §§ 24, 25). In like manner a coincidence of expression with Clement's epistle (§ 43) in JUSTIN MARTYR (*Dial.* 56), where Moses is called ὁ μακάριος καὶ πιστὸς θεράπων Θεοῦ, suggests that it was known to this writer also; (see again the note on § 12). And again the treatise of CYPRIAN, *de Zelo et Livore*, seems to betray the influence of the corresponding passage in Clement (§ 4 sq.).

Three false Clements also, who wrote during the second century, seem to have been acquainted with the genuine Epistle. The so-called SECOND EPISTLE TO THE CORINTHIANS offers more than one parallel to this letter (see the notes on § 11 of the Second Epistle). The EPISTLES TO VIRGINS also (see below, p. 14) seem to aim at reproducing the style of the true Clement by repeating his favourite words and expressions (see the parallels collected by Beelen, p. lx sq.). And lastly, the EPISTLE OF CLEMENT TO JAMES, prefixed to the Clementine Homilies, presents one coincidence at least with the genuine writing, which is probably not accidental (§ 1 ὁ τῆς δύσεως τὸ σκοτεινότερον μέρος κ.τ.λ.: see § 5.of the Epistle to the Corinthians with the note).

Early in the third century PETER of ALEXANDRIA (Routh's *Rel. Sacr.* III. p. 34) in his account of the Apostles Peter and Paul treads closely in the footsteps of Clement (§ 5). The testimony of EUSEBIUS who wrote a few years later has been quoted already. Not long after him S. BASIL quotes a passage from 'Clement's Epistle to the Corinthians,' which is not found in the MS but may have occurred in the lacuna (see the note at the end of § 57). His selection of examples also in his homily *de Invidia* (II. p. 91) may have been suggested by the parallel passage in Clement (§ 4 sq.). About the same time CYRIL OF JERUSALEM refers to Clement by name as an authority for the story of the phœnix (*Catech.* xviii. 8). The writer of the APOSTOLIC CONSTITUTIONS too (v. 7), when describing this bird, though he does not mention his authority, obviously has the passage of Clement in his mind, as the coincidence of language shows. In the same way the descriptions of the phœnix in S. AMBROSE (*Hexaem.* v. 23, I. p. 110; *in Ps.* cxviii. *Expos.* xix. § 13, I. p. 1212; *de Fide resurr.* 59, II. p. 1149) so closely resemble the account of Clement, that they must be derived from this father directly or indirectly. On the other hand, when EPIPHANIUS handles the same subject (*Ancorat.* 85, II. p. 86), he presents no striking parallels, and his account of the marvellous bird would seem to be derived from some other source. It will be seen presently that, when he refers to the genuine epistle, he does so at second hand, and betrays no personal knowledge of it. A little later JEROME quotes this letter more than once (see below, p. 16). We are thus brought to the beginning of the fifth century. If the PSEUDO-JUSTIN (*Quæst. et Resp. ad Orthod.* 74) may be assigned to this age, we have another witness of about the same date; for he also alleges the authority of 'the blessed Clement in the Epistle to the Corinthians' (see the note after § 57).

About the close of the sixth century it is quoted by LEONTIUS and JOHN (*Sacr. Rer.* lib. II. 5 in Mai's *Script. Vet. Nov. Coll.* VII. p. 84), and in the seventh by MAXIMUS the CONFESSOR (*Sermon.* 49). It is a wrong inference however (in Hilgenfeld p.'xxv, and others), that a passage of ANTIOCHUS PALÆSTINENSIS (*Hom.* xliii. in *Bibl. Vet. Patr.* I. p. 1097, Paris 1624) is founded on the language of Clement (§ 13), for the words of Antiochus are much nearer to the original LXX (1 Sam. ii. 10) than to Clement's quotation. In the eighth century JOHN of DAMASCUS more than once quotes this epistle (see the notes on §§ 33, 57), and in the ninth PHOTIUS (*Bibl.* 126; comp. 113) mentions having read both Epistles to the Corinthians, and criticises them at some length (see the notes on §§ 2, 17, 20, 25, 36). In the eleventh century the genuine letter is cited by NICON of RHÆTHUS (see §§ 14, 46), and in the twelfth by ANTONIUS MELISSA (see § 48).

But more important than the fact of its being quoted with respect by individual writers is the liturgical position which it held. I use this word rather than canonical, because there is no evidence to show that it was ever placed by any respectable writer in the same category or invested with the same authority as the canonical books of Scripture. The Church of Corinth to which it was addressed, soon after the middle of the second century, and probably earlier, read it from time to time in the congregation, as they also read another letter which they had just recently received from the same Church of Rome (see p. 3): nor is there any reason for supposing that they attached more weight to the one document than to the other. This use however seems soon to have extended beyond the Church of Corinth. In the fourth century Eusebius (*H. E.* iii. 16) speaks of it from personal knowledge (ἔγνωμεν) as 'read publicly in very many churches both in former times and in his own day' (ἐν πλείσταις ἐκκλησίαις ἐπὶ τοῦ κοινοῦ δεδημοσιευμένην πάλαι τε καὶ καθ' ἡμᾶς αὐτούς). A generation or two later S. Jerome, speaking more cautiously and perhaps without any direct knowledge, says (*Vir. ill.* 15) that it is 'read publicly in some places (in nonnullis locis publice legitur).' At all events, when Photius wrote, the practice was a thing of the past; for he describes the letter as 'a notable epistle which among many *was* deemed worthy of reception so as even to be read in public' (ἥτις παρὰ πολλοῖς ἀποδοχῆς ἠξιώθη ὡς καὶ δημοσίᾳ ἀναγινώσκεσθαι, *Bibl.* 113).

For this purpose however, it was sometimes for convenience bound up with the books of the Canon. So we find it in the Alexandrian MS of the Greek Bible. But the position which it there occupies separates it from the canonical Scriptures; for it comes after the Apocalypse, itself followed by the so-called Second Epistle of Clement and this Second Epistle by the spurious Psalms of Solomon; whereas its proper place, if regarded as strictly canonical, would have been with the Apostolic Epistles and before the Apocalypse. When moreover it is remembered that in this MS even Christian hymns are appended to the Psalms of David in the Old Testament for ecclesiastical purposes, it will be seen that no canonical authority is implied by the fact that the Epistles of Clement are added to the sacred volume. On the other hand it must be remarked, that in the enumeration of the books of the *New Testament* in this MS these two epistles are comprised, while the Psalms of Solomon are excluded (see below, p. 22). There is no evidence that Dionysius of Corinth who first mentions the public reading of the genuine epistle, or Clement of Alexandria who quotes it so often, regarded it as canonical. The language of the former is against any such supposition; and the latter cites so freely from all writings, Heathen as well as Christian, that the mere fact of his quoting it frequently implies nothing. He cites the 'Apostle Clement,' as he cites the 'Apostle Barnabas,' one of whose interpretations he nevertheless criticises and condemns with a freedom which he would not have allowed himself in dealing with writings regarded by him as strictly canonical (see the notes on Barnab. § 10). It is remarkable too that Eusebius, while he calls Clement's epistle 'great and marvellous,' and (as quoted above, p. 11) speaks of its being publicly read in very many churches, yet in the two passages where he discusses the Canon of Scripture and distinguishes the acknowledged from the disputed and spurious books (*H. E.* iii. 3, and iii. 24, 25) does not allude to it; though elsewhere (*H. E.* vi. 13) he names it with several others among the ἀντιλεγόμενα quoted by Clement of Alexandria. We may infer from this silence that its claims to a place in the New Testament were not very seriously entertained in his day (see Westcott *History of the Canon* pp. 371, 373, 2nd ed.). The same remark applies to the canon of Athanasius (*Epist. Fest.* 39, I. p. 767) who, after giving a list of the veritable Scriptures, at the close expressly excludes the Doctrine of the Apostles ascribed to our Clement and the Shepherd of Hermas, but does not mention the Epistles of Clement; and to other later lists (e.g. Bibl. Bodl. *Barocc.* 206; see Westcott *Canon* p. 500). The catalogue in the Canons attached to the eighth book of the Apostolic Constitutions, which probably dates from the sixth century, is an exception; for there the Two Epistles of Clement are included together with the Apostolic Constitutions themselves (Κλήμεντος ἐπιστολαὶ δύο καὶ αἱ διαταγαὶ ὑμῖν τοῖς ἐπισκόποις δι' ἐμοῦ Κλήμεντος ἐν ὀκτὼ βιβλίοις προσπεφωνημέναι); but this manifest forgery never carried any authority. It is however commented upon (*c*. A.D. 1165) by Alexius Aristenus *de Can. Apost.* 85 (Beveridge *Synodicon* I. p. 53, Oxon. 1672) and (*c*. A.D. 1335) by Matthæus Blastaris *Syntagma* B. 11 (*ib.* II. ii. p 56), of whom the former accepts and the latter rejects the Epistles of Clement as Scripture (see Credner's *Gesch des N. T. Kanon*, ed. Volkmar pp. 252, 254).

Early in the ninth century Nicephorus of Constantinople († A.D. 828) includes the two Epistles of Clement, not among the disputed books, among which he places the Epistle of Barnabas, but among the apocryphal with the Itinerary of Peter, the Gospel of Thomas, etc. (Westcott *Canon* p. 503). Altogether a perusal of these lists leaves the impression that these two Epistles of Clement had not the same quasi-canonical place which was given to the Shepherd of Hermas in the West, and to the Epistle of Barnabas in Alexandria and some Eastern Churches. In the Latin Church they were necessarily unknown, except to the learned few, if (as seems to have been the case) they were never translated. Their absence from the numerous Latin lists of canonical and apocryphal books confirms this opinion. Thus, if they had been generally known in the West, they could hardly have failed to be included in the very miscellaneous and comprehensive list of apocryphal works condemned in the Gelasian decree. The two Epistles of Clement mentioned in the *Liber Pontificalis* are probably not our Epistles to the Corinthians (as Cotelier and others suppose), but the two spurious Epistles to James (see below, p. 19).

4.

The works ascribed to Clement of Rome fall into four groups; (1) The *Apostolic Constitutions*, etc.; (2) The *Liturgy*; (3) The *Homilies*, *Recognitions*, and other works professing to give a narrative of St Peter's preaching; (4) The *Letters*. The most complete collection of the Clementine works, genuine and spurious, will be found in Migne's *Patrologia Græca*, Tom. I, II.

With the first three groups we are not concerned here: but a short account of the *Letters* will not be out of place, since the notices and references to them are sometimes perplexing. The extant letters, which bear the name of this father, are nine in number.

1. *The First Epistle to the Corinthians*, a genuine work, to which this introduction refers and of which the text is given below. I cannot

find any indications that it was ever translated into Latin before the seventeenth century; and, if so, it must have been a sealed book to the Western Church[1]. This supposition is consistent with the facts already brought forward; for no direct quotation from it is found in any Latin father who was unacquainted with Greek. When the Church of Rome ceased to be Greek and became Latin, it was cut off perforce from its earliest literature. The one genuine writing of the only illustrious representative of the early Roman Church was thus forgotten by his spiritual descendants, and its place supplied by forgeries written in Latin or translated from spurious Greek originals. In the same way the genuine Epistles of Ignatius were supplanted first by spurious and interpolated Greek letters, and ultimately by a wretched and transparent Latin forgery, containing a correspondence with the Virgin, by which chiefly or solely this father was known in the Western Church for some generations.

2. *The Second Epistle to the Corinthians*, a spurious but very early work, perhaps written as soon as the middle of the second century. It is printed below, and its date and character will be discussed in the introduction. I need only say here that it early obtained a place after the genuine Epistle (though not without being questioned), as appears from the notice of Eusebius (*H. E.* iii. 38) and from its position in the Alexandrian MS.

---

[1] A quotation or rather a paraphrastic abridgment of Clement's account of the institution of the ministry (§ 44) is given by one Joannes (6th cent.?) a Roman deacon with the heading *In Epistola Sancti Clementis ad Corinthios* (*Spicil. Solesm.* 1. p. 293). Pitra, the learned editor, (pp. lvii, 293) suggests that this John must have got the quotation from a Latin translation of the epistle by Paulinus of Nola, adding 'A Paulino Nolano conditam fuisse Clementinam versionem tam Paulinus ipse (*Epist.* xlvi) quam Gennadius (*Catal.* xlviii) diserte testatur.' I do not understand the reference to Gennadius, who says nothing which could be construed into such a statement. The reference in the passage of Paulinus' own letter addressed to Rufinus (*Epist.* xlvi. § 2, p. 275) is obscure. He says that he has no opportunity of getting a more thorough knowledge of Greek, as Rufinus urges him; that, if he saw more of Rufinus, he might learn from him; and that in his translation of S. Clement he had guessed at the sense where he could not understand the words. His commentator Rosweyd supposes him to allude to the *Recognitions*, which Rufinus himself afterwards translated, not being satisfied with his friend's attempt. It seems to me more probable that Paulinus had rendered only an extract or extracts from some Clementine writing for a special purpose; for he calls Greek an 'ignotus sermo' to himself, and with this little knowledge he would hardly have attempted a long translation. Among the extracts so translated may have been this very passage, which is quoted by Joannes in illustration of the narrative in Numbers xvii. But we do not even know whether the Clement meant by Paulinus is the Alexandrian or the Roman, and all speculation must therefore be vague. At all events the loose quotation of a single very prominent passage is not sufficient evidence of the existence of a Latin version.

These two epistles generally went together and had the widest circulation in the Greek Church to very late times.

3, 4. *The Two Epistles on Virginity*, extant only in Syriac. They were first published, as an appendix to his Greek Testament, by J. J. Wetstein (Lugd. Bat. 1752), who maintained their genuineness. They have found champions also in their two latest editors, Villecourt (Paris 1853) whose preface and translation are reprinted with the text in Migne's *Patrologia* I. p. 350 sq., and Beelen (Louvain 1856) whose edition is in all respects the most complete: and other Roman Catholic divines have in like manner held them to be genuine. The lame arguments urged in many cases by their impugners have given to their advocates almost the appearance of a victory; but weighty objections against them still remain, unanswered and unanswerable. To say nothing of the style, which differs from that of the true Clement, the manner and frequency of the quotations from the New Testament, and the picture presented of the life and development of the Church, do not accord with the genuine epistle and point to a later age. For these reasons the Epistles to Virgins can hardly have been written before the middle of the second century. At the same time they bear the stamp of high antiquity, and in the opinion of some competent writers (e.g. Westcott *Canon* p. 162, Hefele in *Wetzer u. Welte's Kirchen-Lexicon* II. p. 586) cannot be placed much later than this date. As they seem to have emanated from Syria, and the Syrian Church changed less rapidly than the Greek or the Western, it is perhaps safer to relax the limits of the possible date to the beginning of the third century.

The MS which contains them is now in the Library of the Seminary of the Remonstrants at Amsterdam (no. 184) and is fully described by Beelen. It forms the second volume of a copy of the Syriac New Testament, bears the date 1781 (i. e. A.D. 1470), and was brought to Europe from Aleppo in the last century. It is written in Syriac and Carshunic, and includes other books of the New Testament besides those which have a place in the Peshito Canon. After the books comprised in this Canon, of which the Epistle to the Hebrews stands last, the scribe has added a doxology and a long account of himself and the circumstances under which the MS was written. Then follow in the same handwriting 2 Peter, 2, 3 John, and Jude, from the Philoxenian version; and immediately after these in succession '*The First Epistle of the blessed Clement, the disciple of Peter the Apostle*,' and '*The Second Epistle of the same Clement.*' Thus the two Epistles on Virginity hold the same position in this late

Syrian copy which is held by the two Epistles to the Corinthians in the ancient Greek MS. This is possibly due to a mistake. A Syrian transcriber, finding the 'Two Epistles of Clement' mentioned at the end of some list of canonical books, might suppose that the two letters with which alone he was acquainted were meant, and thus assign to them this quasi-canonical position in his MS.

Though the fact has been questioned, there can be no reasonable doubt that these two epistles were known to Epiphanius and accepted by him as genuine. Arguing against those heretics who received the Itinerary of Peter as a genuine writing of Clement (*Hær.* xxx. 15, p. 139), he urges that 'Clement himself refutes them on all points from the encyclical letters which he wrote and which are read in the holy churches (ἀφ᾽ ὧν ἔγραψεν ἐπιστολῶν ἐγκυκλίων τῶν ἐν ταῖς ἁγίαις ἐκκλησίαις ἀναγινωσκομένων); for his faith and discourse have a different stamp from the spurious matter fathered upon his name by these persons in the Itinerary. He himself teaches virginity, and they do not admit it; he himself praises Elias and David and Samson and all the prophets, whom these men abominate.' This is an exact description in all respects of the Epistles to Virgins; while on the other hand the letters to the Corinthians (not to mention that they could not properly be called 'encyclical') contain no special praise of virginity (for the passages § 38 ὁ ἁγνὸς κ.τ.λ. and § 48 ἤτω ἁγνὸς κ.τ.λ. are not exceptions) but speak of the duties of married life (§ 1, 21), and make no mention at all of Samson. Indeed it appears highly probable that Epiphanius had no acquaintance with the Epistles to the Corinthians. He once alludes to the genuine letter, but not as though he himself had seen it. 'Clement,' he writes (*Hær.* xxvii. 6, p. 107), 'in one of his epistles says, Ἀναχωρῶ, ἄπειμι, ἐνσταθήτω (l. εὐσταθείτω) ὁ λαὸς τοῦ Θεοῦ, giving this advice to certain persons: for I have found this noted down in certain memoranda (ηὕρομεν γὰρ ἔν τισιν ὑπομνηματισμοῖς τοῦτο ἐγκείμενον).' This is doubtless meant for a passage in the genuine epistle (§ 54). But the quotation is loose, and the reference vague. Moreover Epiphanius states that he got it at second hand: for I suppose that by ὑπομνηματισμοί he must mean some common place book which had fallen into his hands.

To Jerome also these epistles were known. He must be referring to them when he writes (*adv. Jovin.* i. 12, II. p. 257), 'Ad hos (i.e. eunuchos) et Clemens successor Apostoli Petri, cujus Paulus Apostolus meminit, scribit epistolas, *omnemque fere sermonem suum de virginitatis puritate contexit.*' On the other hand it is strange that in his Catalogue of Christian writers (§ 15) he mentions only the two

Epistles to the Corinthians. Here indeed, as in other parts of this treatise, he copies Eusebius implicitly; but as he proffers his own opinion ('quæ *mihi* videtur') of the resemblance between the First Epistle of Clement and the Epistle to the Hebrews (though even this opinion exactly coincides with the statement of Eusebius), and as moreover in several other passages he quotes from the genuine letter (*in Is.* lii. 13, IV. p. 612; *ad Ephes.* ii. 2, VII. p. 571; *ad Ephes.* iv. 1, VII. p. 606), it is most probable that he had himself read it. The quotations, if they had stood alone, he might possibly have borrowed from earlier commentators.

Epiphanius was intimately connected with Syria and Palestine, and Jerome spent some time there. Both these fathers therefore would have means of acquainting themselves with books circulated in these churches. As regards the latter, we must suppose that he first became acquainted with the Epistles to Virgins in the not very long interval between the publication of the Catalogue and of the work against Jovinianus; and, as this interval was spent at Bethlehem, the supposition is reasonable. The alternative is, that in writing against Jovinianus he for polemical purposes assumed the genuineness of these Clementine letters, which he had silently ignored a year or two before. Besides the references in Epiphanius and Jerome, the 'First Epistle on Virginity' is quoted also by Timotheus of Alexandria († A.D. 535) in his work against the Council of Chalcedon, of which parts are preserved in a Syriac translation (Cureton *Corp. Ign.* pp. 212, 244, 354). But it would appear that these epistles were not known or not commonly known westward of these regions. Even Eusebius betrays no knowledge of them. The fact which Epiphanius mentions, that they were read in the churches, is noteworthy, if true. In this case the reading would probably be confined to a few congregations in Syria and Palestine. But it is possible that he carelessly repeats a notice which he had read elsewhere and which in his original authority referred not to these, but to the two Epistles to the Corinthians. The existing Syriac text is doubtless a translation from a Greek original, as the phenomena of the letters themselves suggest (see Beelen p. lxiii), and as the references in these fathers seem to require. The writing or writings of Clement mentioned in Ebed-Jesu's Catalogue (Assemani *Bibl. Orient.* III. p. 13) may be these epistles, but the allusion is more probably to the Apostolic Constitutions.

5. *The Epistle to James the Lord's brother*, giving an account of S. Clement's appointment by S. Peter as his successor in the see of Rome, and containing also the Apostle's directions relating to the

functions of church-officers and the general administration of the Church. Whether this letter was originally prefixed to the Homilies or to the Recognitions or to some other work of the Petro-Clementine cycle different from either, is still a moot question. Under any circumstances its date can hardly be earlier than the middle of the second century or much later than the beginning of the third. In the original Greek it is now found prefixed to the Homilies in the MSS, and may be read conveniently in the editions of this work (e.g. Dressel or Lagarde). About the end of the fourth century it was translated into Latin by Rufinus. In the preface to the Recognitions, which he afterwards translated, he mentions this fact, and excuses himself from again reproducing it partly on this ground. Not unnaturally his translation of the one came to be attached to his translation of the other: and the letter is often found in the MSS prefixed or affixed to the larger work. In the earliest known MS of the Recognitions (*Vercell.* I. clviii), belonging to the sixth or seventh century, the letter follows the main work. Notwithstanding its questionable doctrine, this epistle is quoted as genuine by the synod of Vaison (Concilium Vasense; see Mansi *Conc.* VI. p. 454) held A.D. 442, and is cited occasionally by popes and synods from this time onward.

Besides many important questions relating to the early history of Christianity which are connected with this letter, it is interesting also as having been made the starting point of the most momentous and gigantic of mediæval forgeries, the Isidorian Decretals. In its first form, as left by Rufinus, the Latin ends 'sub eo titulo quem ipse (i.e. Petrus) præcepit affigi, id est Clementis Itinerarium Prædicationis Petri[1]; sed et nunc jam exponere quæ præcepit incipiam,' in accordance with the Greek. But when incorporated in the false Decretals, where it stands at the head of the pontifical letters, it is extended to more than twice its original length by some additional instructions of S. Peter for which the words 'exponere quæ præcepit incipiam' furnish the occasion, and ends 'regni ejus mereamur esse consortes.' In this longer form it may be read conveniently in Mansi *Concilia* I. p. 91 (Flor. 1759),

---

[1] As this title is sometimes read 'Clementis Itinerarium non Prædicationis Petri' (so Cotelier *Patr. Ap.* I. p. 620), and as arguments respecting the letter have been built upon this fact (*e.g.* Uhlhorn *Homil. u. Recogn.* p. 82, Hilgenfeld *Nov. Test. extr. Can. Rec.* IV. p. 53), I may say that of some 30 MSS which I have examined, only one (*Brussels* 5220, 10th cent.) has the negative; that it is absent in the oldest of all (*Vercelli* I. clviii); and that it must therefore be regarded as a mere interpolation, whether by accident or from design. In the Brussels MS the epistle occurs as one of the Decretal letters; but even in such copies I have not elsewhere found the negative.

or in Migne's *Patrol. Græc.* I. p. 463, where all the Decretal letters bearing the name of Clement are printed.

6. *A Second Epistle to James*, relating to the administration of the eucharist, to church furniture, etc. The date of this forgery is uncertain, but it is evidently much later than the former. It would form a very obvious sequel to the earlier letter which spoke of ecclesiastical officers, and was doubtless suggested by it. As no Greek original is known to exist, and it appears to have been written in Latin, its date must at all events be after Rufinus' translation of the First Letter to James, *i.e.* not before the beginning of the fifth century.

This letter is generally found in company with the preceding, and sometimes the two are attached to copies of the Recognitions, but this only occurs in comparatively late MSS. Like the First Epistle to James, this also was incorporated in the false Decretals, forming the second in the series of pontifical letters; and for this purpose it appears to have been interpolated and enlarged in a similar manner[1]. In its shorter form it begins 'Clemens Jacobo carissimo,' and ends 'damnationem accipiet (*or* acquiret)': in its longer form the opening generally runs 'Clemens Romanæ ecclesiæ præsul,' and the ending is 'reverentissime frater [Amen].' The two forms will be found in Mansi *Conc.* I. pp. 126, 158.

When attached to the Recognitions, the two letters to James have almost universally the shorter form, as might be expected. Among a large number of MSS of the Recognitions which I have examined, I have only found one exception, *Turin* D. III. 17 (cod. CC, Passini), where they are so attached in the longer form, though probably other examples exist.

The MSS of these two epistles, both separate from and attached to the Recognitions, are very numerous; and in the Latin Church after the age of S. Jerome, when the 'Two Epistles of Clement' are mentioned, we may generally assume that the reference is to these. Such, I can hardly doubt, is the case in the 'Liber Pontificalis,' where in the

---

[1] The sources of these false Decretals are investigated by Knust *de Fontibus et Consilio Pseudoisid. Coll.*, Göttingen 1832. For the literature of the subject generally see Migne's *Patrol. Lat.* CXXX. p. xxiv. Rosshirt *Zu den Kirchenr. Quellen* etc. p. 39. Rosshirt himself (p. 47) states that the *two* letters to James were translated from the Greek by Rufinus. This is a mistake. In some MSS indeed the 2nd Epistle is stated to have been translated by him, but then the same statement is likewise made of one or more of the remaining three included in the false Decretals. It must therefore be regarded either as a device of the forger aiming at verisimilitude, or as an error of some transcriber carrying on the statement from the 1st Epistle to those following. Internal probability and external evidence alike are unfavourable to the supposition that Rufinus translated the second letter.

notice of Clement it is said, 'Hic fecit duas epistolas quæ canonicæ (*al.* catholicæ) nominantur' (Migne *Patrol. Lat.* CXXVII. p. 1079, CXXVIII. p. 1405)[1]. Indeed the writer, or a later interpolator, shortly afterwards mentions Clement's letter to James relating to his appointment to the Roman see; and there is no reason for supposing that he intended to distinguish this from the two letters already mentioned (as Cotelier and others think). Moreover the letters to James are distinctly named in another similar and apparently not independent notice in the Lives of the Roman pontiffs ascribed to Luitprand (Migne *Patrol. Lat.* CXXIX. p. 1153), 'Hic scripsit duas epistolas Jacobo Hierosolymorum episcopo, quæ catholicæ nominantur.' Anastasius Bibliothecarius indeed (*c.* A.D. 872) refers to the genuine Epistle to the Corinthians, but he must not be taken as representing the Latin Church: for he does not speak from personal knowledge, but translates, or rather mistranslates, a passage of Georgius Syncellus. The words of Georgius are τούτου ἐπιστολὴ μία γνησία Κορινθίοις φέρεται ὡς ἀπὸ τῆς Ῥωμαίων ἐκκλησίας γραφεῖσα, στάσεως ἐν Κορίνθῳ συμβάσης τότε, ὡς μαρτυρεῖ Ἡγήσιππος, ἥτις καὶ ἐκκλησιάζεται (*Chronogr.* I. p. 651, ed. Dind.). Anastasius writes 'Hujus epistola fertur ad Corinthios missa, quam tota recipit, ut Egesippus testatur, ecclesia' (*Hist. Eccl.* p. 17, Paris 1649), where the testimony of Hegesippus is transferred to the wrong point. So little was known of the genuine epistle even by the ablest mediæval writers of the Latin Church, that in the thirteenth century S. Thomas Aquinas speaks of some Antenicene writers having attributed the Epistle to the Hebrews to Clement the pope, because 'ipse scripsit *Atheniensibus* quasi per omnia secundum stilum istum' (*prol. ad Hebr.*), and the error in the name is repeated by Nicolas of Lyra († 1340) *de Libr. Bibl. Can.* (see the passages in Credner's *Einl. in das N. T.* pp. 511, 512).

The false Decretals made their appearance in the east of France, and the date of the forgery may be fixed within narrow limits (A.D. 829 to A.D. 847)[2]. The writer enlarged the two existing Latin letters (5 and 6) in the manner already described, and raised the whole number to five by forging three additional letters.

---

[1] If the reading 'canonicæ' be correct (and it is much less likely to have been substituted for 'catholicæ' than the converse) this is decisive; for the two letters to James are strictly 'canonicæ' in the technical sense, *i.e.* they contain ecclesiastical canons and directions. But even 'catholicæ' is more appropriate to these than to the Epistles to the Corinthians, for they are addressed to the 'bishop of bishops' and are of Church-wide application, whereas the Corinthian letters deal with the internal feuds of a single community.

[2] Milman's *Latin Christianity*, II. p. 303 sq. The history of the appearance and reception of these false Decretals is given fully by Gfrörer *Gesch. der Ost- u. Westfränk. Carolinger*, I. p. 71 sq.

TO THE CORINTHIANS. 21

These three Clementine forgeries of the ninth century are:

7. A letter addressed 'omnibus coepiscopis presbyteris diaconis ac reliquis clericis et cunctis principibus majoribus minoribusve, etc.'

8. Another beginning 'Clemens Romanæ urbis episcopus carissimis fratribus Julio et Juliano ac reliquis consodalibus nostris gentibus que quæ circa vos sunt.'

9. A third 'Dilectissimis fratribus et condiscipulis Hierosolymis cum carissimo fratre Jacobo coepiscopo habitantibus Clemens episcopus.'

These three letters require no comment.

If the above account be correct, it follows that the 'two letters of Clement' would be differently understood in different branches of the Church. To the Greek they would suggest the two Epistles to the Corinthians; to the Latin the two addressed to James; and to the Syrian probably the two in praise of virginity. It is stated likewise by Abulbarcatus (as represented by Assemani, *Bibl. Orient.* III. p. 14), that the Coptic Church also received two epistles of Clement. These might have been either those to the Corinthians or those to Virgins. The great estimation in which the former were held at Alexandria, as appears from the extant MS and the quotations of the Alexandrian fathers, would promote their circulation among the native Egyptian Christians. On the other hand the high value which was attached to celibacy in Egypt would make the Epistles on Virginity very acceptable to this Church. It will be seen presently that both sets of epistles were known to and quoted by Timotheus the patriarch of Alexandria († 535).

But the above list of nine letters probably does not comprise all which at one time or other were circulated in the name of Clement. At the beginning of the seventh century Maximus the Confessor, who (as we have seen) quotes the genuine epistle, speaking of the omissions of Eusebius, complains that he has mentioned only two epistles of this apostolic father (*prol. ad Dionys. Areop.* οὔτε Πανταίνου τοὺς πόνους ἀνέγραψεν, οὔτε τοῦ Ῥωμαίου Κλήμεντος πλὴν δύο καὶ μόνων ἐπιστολῶν, i.e. no other works besides his epistles, and only two of these). And about the same time in the *Sacr. Rer. Lib. II* of Leontius and John (Mai, *Script. Vet. Nov. Coll.* VII. p. 84) the writers, after quoting a passage from the genuine First Epistle to the Corinthians, give another quotation headed 'From the *ninth* Epistle of Saint Clement' (τοῦ ἁγίου Κλήμεντος ἐκ τῆς θ' ἐπιστολῆς, where Hilgenfeld's conjecture of θείας for θ' is improbable). As not more than five of the extant epistles, including the two addressed to Virgins, can ever have existed in Greek, we must assume several lost Clementine letters. The difficulty however might be overcome in another way, by reading ε for θ (5th for 9th) and supposing the quotation to be taken from the lost end of our Second Epistle. Again Timotheus of Alexandria, who before has quoted 'the First Epistle on Virginity,' immediately afterwards cites the opening of our Second Epistle to the Corinthians as 'Of the same Clement from the beginning of the *Third* Epistle' (Cureton *Corp. Ign.* pp. 212, 244, 254). This shows that the Epistles were differently arranged in different collections. It is not improbable that some of the fragments, which are printed below after the text of the two Epistles to the Corinthians, belonged to these lost letters. Their homiletic tone, if not in harmony with a genuine letter, is quite in character with a forgery. The Epistle of Clement, to which Dionysius Barsalibi alludes as written against those who reject matrimony (so he is reported by Assemani, *Bibl. Orient.* II. p. 158), may have been one of these; but as the First Epistle to James urges very strongly the importance of early marriages (§ 7), I am disposed to think that he referred to this. This opinion is confirmed by the language of Epiphanius quoted above, p. 16.

5.

Of the Two Epistles to the Corinthians, the one genuine and the other spurious, only one MS exists or is known to have existed since the revival of learning. From this therefore all the printed texts are derived. In the Alexandrian MS (A) of the Greek Bible these two Epistles stand (fol. 159 a) at the close of the New Testament and immediately after the Apocalypse. The title of the First is mutilated, so that it begins ... C ΚΟΡΙΝΘΙΟΥC Α̅. It ends towards the bottom of fol. 168 a. col. 1; and below is written

ΚΛΗΜΕΝΤΟCΠΡΟCΚΟ

ΡΙΝΘΙΟΥCΕΠΙCΤΟΛΗ

A.

The Second commences fol. 168 a. col. 2, without any heading. As the end leaves of the MS are wanting, this Second Epistle is only a fragment and terminates abruptly in the middle of a sentence (fol. 169 b). Both epistles are included in the table of contents prefixed by the scribe to the MS (see Baber's *Codex Alexandrinus* I. tab. IV), where the list of books under the heading Η ΚΑΙΝΗ ΔΙΑΘΗΚΗ ends thus:

ἀποκαλυψι[ϲιωα]ννογ
κ[λη]μεντοϲ[επιϲτο]λη α̅
[κλημ]εντοϲε[πιϲτολη] β̅

[ομ]ογβιβλια[......]

ψαλμ[ο]ιϲολομ[ω]ντοϲ
ι̅η̅

As the edges of the leaves are worn in many places and the vellum is in other parts very fragile, words or parts of words have occasionally disappeared. Moreover the use of galls by the first editor, Patrick Young, has rendered some passages wholly or in part illegible. In addition to this, a leaf is wanting towards the close of the First Epistle, between fol. 167 and fol. 168 (i. e. between § 57 and § 58). The hiatus is detected by the numerals in ancient Arabic characters at the tops of the pages, where 132 (fol. 167) is followed immediately by 134 (fol. 168). My attention was first called to this fact respecting the Arabic numerals by Mr H. Bradshaw of the Cambridge University Library; and it has since been noticed by Tischendorf (p. xv). The first editor, Patrick Young, had said 'Desideratur hic in exemplari antiquo folium integrum.' Bp. Jacobson accounts for this statement by remarking 'Forte codicem conferre contigit priusquam a bibliopego Anglico praescissus fuerat et in corio compactus,' which was perhaps the case. It is strange however that the Arabic numerals, which set the question at rest, should have been so long overlooked. The lacuna accounts for the fact that a few quotations from Clement's Epistle to the Corinthians, which occur in ancient writers, are not found in the existing text.

The Alexandrian MS was presented to Charles I by Cyril Lucar, patriarch first of Alexandria and then of Constantinople, and brought to England in the year 1628. It was transferred from the King's Library and placed in the British Museum, where it now is, in 1753. The Epistles of Clement are written in the same hand with the rest of the MS, and the whole may be assigned to about the middle of the 5th century. More detailed accounts of the MS, as a whole, will be found in the well known introductions to the New Testament (e.g. Tregelles *Horne's Introduction to the N. T.* p. 152 sq., or Scrivener *Introduction to the Criticism of the N. T.* p. 79).

The Epistles of Clement are transcribed with tolerable but not strict accuracy, and the lacunae supplied for the most part with felicity, by the first editor, Patricius Junius (Patrick Young), A.D. 1633. But an *editio princeps* necessarily left much to be done. Collations were accordingly made by Mill and Grabe; and Wotton, in preparing his edition (A.D. 1718), not only employed these collations, but also examined the MS itself. Lastly, Dr Jacobson (1st ed. 1838) recollated it throughout and corrected many inaccuracies which had run through previous editions. Hitherto however, while facsimiles had been made of the text of the New Testament in this MS by Woide (1786) and subsequently of the Old by Baber (1816—1821), nothing of the kind had been done for the Epistles of Clement, though here the MS is unique. But in the year 1856 Sir F. Madden, the keeper of the MSS at the British Museum, owing to a memorial from the Divinity Professors and others of Oxford and Cambridge and by permission of the Trustees of the Museum, published a photograph of this portion of the MS. Hilgenfeld, the latest editor of these epistles (1866), seems to have been unaware of the existence of this photograph, though it had appeared ten years before; but in a foreigner this ignorance was very excusable. Where the MS has not been injured by time or by the application of galls, the photograph is all that could be desired; but passages which have suffered in this way may often be read accurately in the MS itself, though wholly illegible in the photograph. For this reason Tischendorf's reproduction of these epistles, published in his *Appendix Codicum Celeberrimorum Sinaitici, Vaticani, Alexandrini* (Lips. 1867), was not superfluous, but supplied fresh materials for a more accurate text. Before I was aware that Tischendorf was engaged upon this facsimile, I had with a view to this edition procured a new and thorough collation of the text of these epistles through the kindness of Mr A. A. Vansittart, who at my request undertook the work; and we found that notwithstanding the labours of previous editors the gleanings were still a sufficient reward for the trouble. On the appearance of Tischendorf's facsimile, I compared it with Mr Vansittart's collation, and found that they agreed in the great majority of instances where there was a divergence from previous editors (e.g. in the reading .τίς ἀρκετὸς ἐξειπεῖν § 49, where the printed texts have hitherto read τίς ἀρκεῖ ὡς δεῖ εἰπεῖν). In some readings however they differed: and in such cases I have myself inspected the MS (repeating the inspection at three different times, where the writing was much defaced), in order to get the result as accurate as possible. There still remain however a few passages where the MS is so injured that it is impossible to determine the reading with certainty. Tischendorf's text contains several errors, which however are for the most part corrected in the preface. A few still remain, of which the most important is διακονιαν (§ 35), where the MS has διανοιαν, as even the photograph shows.

On the whole the MS appears to give a good text. The shortcomings of the scribe are generally such that they can be easily corrected; for they arise from petty carelessness and ignorance, and not from perverse ingenuity. Thus there are errors of the ordinary type arising from repetition or omission, where the same letters recur, e. g. § 2, αμαμνησικακοι, § 11 ετερογνωμυσ[?], § 12 υποτοτοεγοσ, § 17 δομενου, § 19 ταπεινοφρονον, § 25 τελευτηκοτοσ, § 32 ημερασ, § 35 μον, αδελφουσσου, § 48 διακριακρισει, § 50 μακακαριοι, ii § 9 αιωνιον (for αινοναωνιον), ii § 11 ασουκ (for ασουσουκ): there is the usual substitution of wrong case-endings, arising mostly from confusion with the context, e. g. § 3 της, § 16 ελθοντοσ, § 19 αλλασ, § 32 του, § 43 κεκοσμημενω, § 44 μεμαρτυρημενοισ, ii § 1 εχοντεσ, ii § 6 αιχμαλωσια; there is now and then a transposition, e. g. § 4 ζηλοσ and διαζηλοσ, § 39 σητον[?]τροποσ for σητοστροπον; there are also several paltry blunders of omission or miswriting or substitution, which cannot be classed under any of these heads, e. g. § 2 εδεδετο, πεποιηθησεωσ, § 3 δοθη, απεγαλακτισεν, § 8 διελεχθωμεν, § 10 πιστισ, § 15 αναστησομεν, § 16 εψεται, § 20 κρυματα, § 21 εγκαυχωμενοιεν, § 23 εξαιχνησ, § 25 μονογενησ, § 29 αριθον, § 30 αγνουσ, εδεηθη, § 33 εγγοισ, § 34 λιτουργουν, § 35 καταλιλιασ, φιλοξενιαν, § 38 τμμελειτω, § 41 συνειδησιν, καταξιωθημεν, § 44 μετοξυ, μεταγαγετε, § 45 επιτασθαι, στυητοι, § 51 οι, § 56 ουκοψεται, § 59 ανεπεμψατε, ii § 7 θι, ii § 9 πουντες: there is lastly the common phenomenon of debased and ungrammatical forms, e. g. § 1 ασφαλην, § 14 ασεβην, § 15 κατηρουντο[?], § 18 πλυνιεισ, § 26 (comp. ii. § 8) σαρκαν, §§ 1, 29 επιεικην, § 40 υπερτατω, § 42 καθεστανον, § 59 επιποθητην, ii § 1 ελπιδαν, ii § 12 δηλοσ, with several others, though in some cases they may be attributed to the author rather than the scribe. In the instances which I have given the correct text is generally obvious. But one or two deeper corruptions remain, where emendation is more difficult; e. g. § 2 συνειδησεωσ, § 6 δαηαιδεσκαιδιρκαι, § 45 επαφροι.

This MS also exhibits the usual interchanges of like-sounding vowels and diphthongs; of ο and ω, as § 48 εξομολογησωμαι, § 54 τοπωσ, ii § 4 αυτων, and on the other hand, § 25 βασταζον, § 45 ειπομεν, ii § 6 οιομεθα; of η and ι, as § 1 αιφνηδιουσ, καθικουσαν, § 4 γυλησθησαν, § 8 προστηθεισ, § 39 μυκτιρηζουσιν, § 47 προσκλησεισ, ii § 10 ηληκην; of ε and αι, as § 14 αιπερομενον (for επαιρομενον), § 6 οσταιων, § 10 οραιων, §§ 21, 52 ναιουσ, ναιον, §§ 25, 26, ορναιον, ορναιουν, § 39 επεσεν (for έπαισεν), § 4 παιδιον, παιδιω, (for πεδίον, πεδίω), § 2, 9, 18, 22, ii § 3 ελαιοσ, ελαιουσ, etc. (for έλεος, ελέους, etc.); and lastly, of ι and ει, e. g. § 26 το μεγαλιον τησ επαγγελειασ, § 27 ποιησειν for ποιησιν, § 40 λειτουργειασ but §. 41 λιτουργιασ and § 44 λιτουργειασ, § 2 ειλεικρινεισ but § 32 ιλικριν[ωσ] and ii. § 9 ιλικρινουσ, § 14 στασισ for στασεισ but §§ 6, 44, ερεισ for ερωσ. In all such cases I have substituted the ordinary classical spelling: but when we call to mind that half a century later the heretic Marcus (Iren. *Hær.* I. 15. 1, Hippol. *Ref.* vi. 49) founds a theory on the fact that σιγή contains five letters (cεɪ̄γн) and Χριστός eight (χρειcτοc), and that about this very time the Roman biographer confuses Χριστός and Χρηστός (Suet. *Claud.* 25), we cannot feel at all sure that Clement might not in this respect have allowed himself the same latitude in spelling which we find in our scribe.

The contractions which I have noted in these epistles (besides the line over the previous letter as a substitute for the final *ν*) are the following; ᾱν̄ο̄c, ᾱν̄ο̄ȳ, etc., for ανθρωπος, ανθρωπου, etc.; ο̄ȳν̄ο̄c, ο̄ȳν̄ο̄ȳ, etc., for ουρανος, ουρανου; π̄η̄ρ̄, π̄ρ̄ο̄c, etc., for πατηρ, πατρος, etc.; μ̄η̄ρ̄ for μητηρ; θ̄c̄, θ̄ȳ, etc., κ̄c̄, κ̄ȳ, etc., χ̄c̄, χ̄ȳ, etc., ῑc̄, ῑȳ etc., for θεος, θεου, etc., κυριος, κυριου, etc., χριστος, χριστου, etc., ιησους, ιησου, etc. (but, where Joshua is meant § 12, it is written in full); π̄ν̄ᾱ,•π̄ν̄c̄, π̄ν̄ῑ, etc., for πνευμα, πνευματος, πνευματι, etc.; δᾱδ̄ for δανειδ; ιλη̄μ̄ for ιερουσαλημ; ιc̄λ̄ (§§ 4, 29, 43, 55) and ιη̄λ̄ (§ 8) for ισραηλ.

The difficulty of filling in the lacunæ, where the MS is worn or defaced, is not the least which an editor of these epistles encounters. In supplying the missing words and letters, I have in each case named the critic who (so far as I could discover) first suggested the reading which I have adopted as the best. Where no other name is mentioned, the first editor, Patrick Young, is to be understood. I think it will be allowed that Mr Vansittart has correctly divined the opening of § 58, of which editors had hitherto despaired.

In establishing the text we are occasionally assisted by the quotations in the fathers. The references to these will be given in their respective places. The citations of Clement of Alexandria are especially valuable, from their number, their length, and their early date: and we are more than once enabled by their means to correct errors in the MS. Whether other MSS may not yet be discovered, it is impossible to say. Tischendorf (p. xv) mentions an eager chase after a palimpsest reported to be at Ferrara, which turned out after all to be a copy of the legendary life of Clement. The unwary may be deceived by seeing 'Clementis Epistolæ duæ' entered in the catalogues of MSS in some of the great libraries of Europe. These are the two Latin Epistles to James.

It should be added in conclusion, that a record is preserved of a

TO THE CORINTHIANS. 27

MS of these epistles of a different character from our extant MS. In the copy which Photius used (*Bibl.* 126) the two Epistles of Clement were bound up in a small volume (βιβλιδάριον) with the Epistle of Polycarp to the Philippians.

6.

The *Literature* connected with the Epistle.

EDITIONS.
*1633 Oxon. *Clementis ad Corinthios Epistola Prior;* PATRICIUS JUNIUS (P. Young). The 'editio princeps'. After the 1st Epistle is added *Fragmentum Epistolæ Secundæ ex eodem MS*, but it is not named on the title page.
1637 Oxon. A second edition of the same.
1654 Helmest. *Clementis ad Corinthios Epistola Prior;* J. J. MADER: taken from Young's edition. Some introductory matter is prefixed, and the 2nd Epistle is added as in Young.
1669 Oxon. *S. Patris et Martyris Clementis ad Corinthios Epistola;* J. FELL (the name however is not given). The 2nd Epistle is wanting.
1677 Oxon. A 2nd edition of the same. *Clementis ad Corinthios Epistola II* is added, but not named on the title page. The name of the editor is still suppressed.
*1672 Paris. *SS. Patrum qui temporibus Apostolicis floruerunt etc. Opera etc.;* J. B. COTELERIUS (Cotelier).
1698 Antverp. The same: 'recensuit J. CLERICUS' (Leclerc).
1724 Amstelæd. Another edition of Cotelier by Leclerc. The notes of W. Burton and J. Davies are here printed with others, some of them for the first time.
1687 Londini. *S. Clementis Epistolæ duæ ad Corinthios* etc.; P. COLOMESIUS (Colomiès).
1695 Londini. The same; 'editio novissima, prioribus longe auctior'.
1699 Lipsiæ. *Bibliotheca Patrum Apostolicorum Græco-Latina;* L. T. ITTIGIUS.
*1718 Cantabr. *Sancti Clementis Romani ad Corinthios Epistolæ duæ;* H. WOTTON. See above, p. 24. This edition contains notes by J. Bois, Canon of Ely, not before edited.
1721 Paris. *Epistolæ Romanorum Pontificum* etc.; P. COUSTANT.
1796 Gotting. The same, re-edited by C. T. G. SCHOENEMANN.

1742   Basil. *Epistolæ Sanctorum Patrum Apostolicorum* etc.; J. L. FREY.
1746   Londini. *SS. Patrum Apostolicorum* etc. *Opera Genuina* etc.; R. RUSSEL.
1765   Venet. *Bibliotheca Veterum Patrum* etc. (I. p. 3 sq.); A. GALLANDIUS. The editor has availed himself of a treatise by A. Birr, *Animadversiones in B. Clementis Epistolas*, Basil. 1744.
1839   Tubing. *Patrum Apostolicorum Opera;* C. J. HEFELE. The 4th ed. appeared in 1855.
*1840 Oxon. *S. Clementis Romani, S. Ignatii, S. Polycarpi, Patrum Apostolicorum, quæ supersunt;* GUL. JACOBSON. See above, p. 24. The 4th edition appeared in 1863.
1857   Lipsiæ. *Patrum Apostolicorum Opera;* A. R. M. DRESSEL. The so called 2nd edition (1863) is a mere reissue, with the addition of a collation of the Sinaitic text of Barnabas and Hermas.
*1866 Lipsiæ. *Clementis Romani Epistulæ* etc.; A. HILGENFELD. It forms the first part of the *Novum Testamentum extra Canonem Receptum*.

To these editions should perhaps be added such translations as those by Wake (revised by Chevallier, Cambr. 1833) into English, and by Wocher (Tübing. 1830) into German.

The above list is not intended to be exhaustive; but I have not (except from ignorance) omitted any edition which has contributed in any degree to the criticism or exegesis of the epistle. Mere reproductions have been omitted. Viewed by this standard, the list will appear too large rather than too meagre. The most important works are those marked with an asterisk. Further details about editions and translations will be found in Fabricius *Bibl. Græc.* IV. p. 829 sq. (ed. Harles), and Jacobson's *Patres Apostolici* p. lxiv sq.

MONOGRAPHS, ARTICLES, ETC.

1848   *Clemens I Papst;* HEFELE in *Wetzer u. Welte's Kirchen-Lexicon* (II. p. 580 sq.).
1851   *Clément de Rome;* KAYSER in the *Revue de Théologie* etc. II. p. 85 sq. Strasbourg.
1854   *Disq. Crit. et Hist. de Clementis Romani Priore ad Corinthios Epistola;* E. EKKER. Traj. ad Rhen.

TO THE CORINTHIANS.   29

1854, 5, *Der Erste Brief des Clemens Romanus an die Corinther;*
E. GUNDERT.   In the *Zeitschrift f. lutherische Theologie u.
Kirche* (XIV. p. 638 sq., XV. p. 29 sq., p. 450 sq.).
1854   *Clemens von Rom;* G. UHLHORN.   In *Herzog's Real-Encyklo-
pädie* (II. p. 720 sq.).
1855   *De Clementis Romani Epistola ad Corinthios Priore Disquisitio;*
R. A. LIPSIUS.   Lipsiæ.
1856   *Ueber Clemens von Rom und die nächste Folgezeit;* G. VOLKMAR.
In the *Theologische Jahrbücher*, v. p. 287.   Tübing.
1863   *Zur Kritik des Clemens von Rom;* J. C. M. LAURENT.   In the
Zeitschrift f. lutherische Theologie u. Kirche (XXIV. p. 416).
1862   *Historische Analekten aus dem ersten Briefe des Clemens Rom.
an die Corinther;* KNÖDEL.   In *Theologische Studien u. Kri-
tiken* (1862, Hft. I. p. 764 sq.).

Of these the most important is the monograph of Lipsius. The work of A. Kestner, *Die Agape oder der geheime Weltbund der Christen von Klemens in Rom unter Domitians Regierung gestiftet* (Jena, 1819), has been justly described as a romance.

GENERAL WORKS, illustrating the epistle.

(i) *Apostolic Fathers:*
Die Apostolischen Väter; A. HILGENFELD (1853).
The Apostolical Fathers; J. DONALDSON. Being the first volume of *A Critical History of Christian Literature and Doctrine* (1864).
Other works are mentioned by Donaldson, p. 89.

(ii) *Patristic Literature:*
CAVE, DUPIN, FABRICIUS, GRABE, LUMPER, MÖHLER, TILLEMONT, and others.

(iii) *Church Histories:*
MOSHEIM, NEANDER, GIESELER, BAUR, SCHAFF, DE PRES-
SENSÉ, and others.

(iv) *Miscellaneous:*
Entwicklungsgeschichte der Lehre von der Person Christi;
J. A. DORNER.
Histoire de la Théologie Chrétienne au Siècle Apostolique;
E. REUSS (2nd ed. 1860).
The Credibility of the Gospel History; N. LARDNER.
Zur Geschichte des Kanons; K. A. CREDNER (1847).

A General Survey of the History of the Canon of the New Testament; B. F. WESTCOTT (2nd ed. 1866).
Geschichte des Neutestamentlichen Kanon; C. A. CREDNER. Edited by G. VOLKMAR.
Geschichte des Volkes Israel (Band VII); H. EWALD.
Die Anfänge der Christlichen Kirche etc.; R. ROTHE.
Die Clementinen etc.; A. SCHLIEMANN.
Das Nachapostolische Zeitalter etc.; A. SCHWEGLER.
Die Enstehung der Altkatholischen Kirche; A. RITSCHL (2nd ed. 1857).
Das Apostolische u. das Nachapostolische Zeitalter etc.; G. V. LECHLER (2nd ed. 1857).
Hippolytus and his Age; C. C. J. BUNSEN (2nd ed. 1854).

This last list might be considerably increased; but I have confined it to the works which are either most important in themselves or bear most directly on this epistle. To these should be added the more important editions of the other Clementine letters, and works relating to the pseudo-Clementine literature generally.

ΠΡΟΣ ΚΟΡΙΝΘΙΟΥΣ Α.

['Η 'ΕΚΚΛΗ]ϹΙΑ τοῦ Θεοῦ ἡ παροικοῦσα ['Ρώμην]
τῇ ἐκκλησίᾳ τοῦ Θεοῦ τῇ πα[ροικού]σῃ Κόρινθον, κλη-

Throughout this Epistle the brackets [ ] *mark the portions which have perished or are illegible in the MS and have been supplied by conjecture: see above, p. 26.*
ΠΡΟϹ ΚΟΡΙΝΘΙΟΥϹ Α. For the title of this epistle in the MS see above p. 22.

'THE CHURCH OF ROME to the CHURCH OF CORINTH, elect and consecrate: greeting in Christ Jesus.'

On the form of the address, as connected with the question of the authorship, see the introduction, p. 3. The writer's name is suppressed here, as it seems also to have been suppressed in another letter of the Church of Rome to the Church of Corinth written more than half a century later during the episcopate of Soter; see Dionys. Corinth. in Euseb. *H. E.* iv. 23.

1. παροικοῦσα] '*sojourning in.*' The distinction between πάροικος a *temporary* and κάτοικος a *permanent* resident appears from Philo *Sacr. Ab. et Cain.* § 10 (I. p. 170) ὁ γὰρ τοῖς ἐγκυκλίοις μόνοις ἐπανέχων παροικεῖ σοφίᾳ οὐ κατοικεῖ, *de Conf. ling.* § 17 (I. p. 416) κατῴκησαν ὡς ἐν πατρίδι, οὐχ ὡς ἐπὶ ξένης παρῴκησαν, Greg. Naz. *Orat.* xiv (I. p. 271) τίς τὴν κάτω σκηνὴν καὶ τὴν ἄνω πόλιν (διαιρήσει); τίς παροικίαν καὶ κατοικίαν; *Orat.* vii (I. p. 200) ἐκ τῆς παροικίας εἰς τὴν κατοικίαν μετασκευαζόμενοι: comp. Gen. xxxvi. 44 (xxxvii. 1) κατῴκει δὲ Ἰακὼβ ἐν τῇ γῇ οὗ παρῴκησεν ὁ πατὴρ αὐτοῦ ἐν γῇ Χαναάν, Heb. xi. 9, Luke xxiv. 18. Thus πάροικος, παροικεῖν, παροικία, are said of the captivities of Egypt (Acts vii. 6 from LXX, xiii. 17) and of Babylon (Theoph. *ad Aut.* iii. 25, 28). See especially the uses of παροικεῖν, κατοικεῖν, in reference to the migrations of Israel, in Judith v. 7—10. Of these captivities the present earthly condition of the Christian people is the antitype (Heb. iv. 1). Their fatherland is heaven, and they dwell in the world as aliens, ξένοι, παρεπίδημοι, πάροικοι, I Pet. i. 17, ii. 11: comp. Heb. xi. 13. So too *Clem. Rom.* ii. § 5 καταλείψαντες τὴν παροικίαν τοῦ κόσμου τούτου, *Ep. ad Diogn.* 5 πατρίδας οἰκοῦσιν ἰδίας ἀλλ' ὡς πάροικοι· μετέχουσι πάντων ὡς πολῖται καὶ πάνθ' ὑπομένουσιν ὡς ξένοι· πᾶσα ξένη πατρίς ἐστιν αὐτῶν καὶ πᾶσα πατρὶς ξένη, where the writer is describing the Christians. Compare also the parable in Hermas *Vis.* I. 1. In the prologue to Ecclesiasticus οἱ ἐν τῇ παροικίᾳ are the Jews of the dispersion, so that παροικία is al-

τοῖς, ἡγι[ασμέν]οις ἐν θελήματι Θεοῦ διὰ τοῦ [Κυρίου ἡμ]ῶν Ἰησοῦ Χριστοῦ. [χάρις ὑ]μῖν καὶ εἰρήνη ἀπὸ παντο[κράτο]ρος Θεοῦ διὰ Ἰησοῦ Χριστοῦ πληθυνθείη.
1. [Διὰ τὰς] αἰφνιδίους καὶ ἐπαλλήλους [γενομ]ένας

4 διὰ τὰς] Wotton. δι' Pearson (*Vind. Ign.* i. 3). αἰφνιδίους] αιφνηδιουσ A. γενομένας] Pearson (*l.c.*).

most equivalent to διασπορά; and, as the latter word is transferred to the Christian people, the spiritual Israel (1 Pet. i. 1 παρεπιδήμοις διασπορᾶς), so is the former. Hence the form of address here, which appears also Polyc. *Phil.* τῇ ἐκκλησίᾳ τοῦ Θεοῦ τῇ παροικούσῃ Φιλίππους, *Mart. Polyc.* ἡ παροικοῦσα Σμύρναν κ.τ.λ., Dionys. Corinth. in Euseb. *H.E.* iv. 23 τῇ παροικούσῃ Γορτύναν, *Epist. Gall.* in Euseb. *H.E.* v. 1 οἱ ἐν Βιέννῃ καὶ Λουγδούνῳ τῆς Γαλλίας παροικοῦντες δοῦλοι Χριστοῦ. From this the substantive παροικία came to be used in a concrete sense, 'the body of aliens,' for the Christian brotherhood in a town or district. The earliest instances which I have observed are *Mart. Polyc.* inscr. πάσαις ταῖς κατὰ πάντα τόπον τῆς ἁγίας καὶ καθολικῆς ἐκκλησίας παροικίαις, Dionys. Corinth. [?] in Euseb. *H.E.* iv. 23 ἅμα ταῖς λοιπαῖς κατὰ Κρήτην παροικίαις, Iren. in Euseb. *H.E.* v. 24 εἰρήνευον τοῖς ἀπὸ τῶν παροικιῶν ἐν αἷς ἐτηρεῖτο, Apollon. in Euseb. *H.E.* v. 18 ἡ ἰδία παροικία αὐτὸν ὅθεν ἦν οὐκ ἐδέξατο: whence *parochia, parish*. It seems not strictly correct to say that παροικία was equivalent to the later term διοίκησις; for παροικία, though it is sometimes a synonyme for διοίκησις (e.g. *Conc.Ancyr.* Can. 18), appears to have been used much more generally. The explanation often given of παροικία, as though it denoted the aggregate of Christian communities in the neighbourhood of a large town, receives no countenance from the earliest usage of πάροικος, etc.; for the preposition is not local but temporal, and denotes not *proximity* but *transitoriness*. For the accusative after παροικεῖν see the note on Polyc. *Phil.*inscr.

1. κλητοῖς κ.τ.λ.] taken from the salutation in 1 Cor. i. 1, 2, ἡγιασμένοις ἐν Χριστῷ Ἰησοῦ, κλητοῖς ἁγίοις. Clement not unnaturally echoes the language of S. Paul's Epistle to the Corinthians, even where he does not directly quote it. Similarly the Epistle of Ignatius to the Ephesians presents parallels to S. Paul's Epistle to the same church, especially in the opening salutation. The same relation again exists between Polycarp's Epistle to the Philippians and the corresponding letter of S. Paul. For the meaning of ἡγιασμένοις, 'consecrated to be God's people,' see the notes on τοῖς ἁγίοις Phil. i. 1.

2. χάρις κ.τ.λ.] χάρις ὑμῖν καὶ εἰρήνη is the common salutation in S. Paul, excepting the Pastoral Epistles. With the addition of πληθυνθείη however it occurs only in the two Epistles of S. Peter, from whom probably Clement derived the form, as the First Epistle is frequently quoted in this letter.

παντοκράτορος] The LXX rendering of צבאות in the expression 'the Lord of Hosts' (see Stanley, *Jewish Church* II. p. 87), apparently not a classical word. In the New Testament it occurs once only out of the Apocalypse, 2 Cor. vi. 18, where S. Paul is quoting from the LXX. Comp. §§ 2, 32, and Polyc.*Phil.*inscr. (with the note).

1. 'We should have written sooner,

ἡμῖν συμφορὰς καὶ [περὶ]πτώσεις, ἀδελφοί, βράδιον
[νομ]ίζομεν ἐπιστροφὴν πεποιη[κέν]αι περὶ τῶν ἐπιζη-
τουμένων [πα]ρ' ὑμῖν πραγμάτων, ἀγαπητοί, [τ]ῆς τε
ἀλλοτρίας καὶ ξένης τοῖς ἐκλεκτοῖς τοῦ Θεοῦ, μιαρᾶς

5 βράδιον] βραδειον A.   6 νομίζομεν] Young (notes, but δυσοίζομεν text).
              8 ξένης] Young (marg.).   ξενοισ A.

but our own troubles have hindered us. We are grieved to hear that one or two headstrong ring-leaders have fanned the flame of discord among you. This was not your wont in former days. Your firm faith, your sober piety, your large hospitality, your sound knowledge, were the admiration of all. Authority was duly respected by you. Your young men were modest ; your wives were quiet and orderly.'

4. Διὰ τὰς αἰφνιδίους κ.τ.λ.] This language accurately describes the persecution which the Roman Christians endured under Domitian. Their treatment by this emperor was capricious, and the attacks upon them were repeated. While the persecution of Nero was one fierce and wholesale onslaught in which the passions of the multitude were enlisted on the emperor's side, Domitian on the other hand made use of legal forms and arraigned the Christians from time to time on various paltry charges: see the accounts in Euseb. *H. E.* iii. 17 sq., *Chron.* an. 95 (with the authorities given by Eusebius), and comp. Dion Cass. lxvii. 14, Suet. *Domit.* 12, 15. So *Mart. Ign.* 1 speaks of οἱ πολλοὶ ἐπὶ Δομετιανοῦ διωγμοί (though this refers especially to Antioch). In one of these attacks the writer's namesake, Flavius Clemens, a kinsman of the emperor, fell a victim: see *Philippians*, p. 22. Thus the notice here accords with external testimony which places the Corinthian feuds to which this letter refers in the reign of Do-

mitian: see introduction p. 4. Volckmar (*Theol. Jahrb.* 1856, p. 286 sq.), who assigns a much later date to this epistle, is obliged to refer the notice here to the sufferings of the Christians under Trajan ; but there is no evidence that this persecution extended to Rome. (On this theory see again the note § 55.) Our epistle therefore was probably written towards the close of Domitian's reign or on the accession of Nerva (A.D. 96). Other notices of time in the body of the letter agree with this result: see esp. §§ 5, 44, 47.

ἐπαλλήλους] '*successive, repeated,*' a comparatively late but common word, *e.g.* Plut. *Pomp.* 25 κινδύνοις ἐπαλλήλοις καὶ πολέμοις: see Lobeck *Paral.* p. 471. It is restored indeed by Hermann in Soph. *Ant.* 57, but this restoration is very doubtful, and the word there must have the sense 'reciprocal.' For ἐπαλλήλους γενομένας comp. Alciphr. *Ep.* 1. 23 χιὼν πυκνὴ καὶ ἐπάλληλος φερομένη. Otherwise we might read ἐπαλλήλως, which occurs *Epist. Gall.* § 14 in Euseb. *H. E.* v. 1.

6. νομίζομεν] The whole passage will mean '*Owing to the sudden and repeated calamities and reverses which have befallen us, we consider we have been somewhat slow to pay attention to the questions of dispute among you.*' Other restorations proposed for νομίζομεν are δυσοίζομεν, οἰκτίζομεν, but these are less natural. It would appear that the Roman Christians had not been directly con-

καὶ ἀνοσίου στάσεως, ἣν ὀλίγα πρόσωπα προπετῆ καὶ
αὐθάδη ὑπάρχοντα εἰς τοσοῦτον ἀπονοίας ἐξέκαυσαν,
ὥστε τὸ σεμνὸν καὶ περιβόητον καὶ πᾶσιν ἀνθρώποις
ἀξιαγάπητον ὄνομα ὑμῶν μεγάλως βλασφημηθῆναι. τίς
γὰρ παρεπιδημήσας πρὸς ὑμᾶς τὴν πανάρετον καὶ βε- 5
βαίαν ὑμῶν πίστιν οὐκ ἐδοκίμασεν; τήν τε σώφρονα
καὶ ἐπιεικῆ ἐν Χριστῷ εὐσέβειαν οὐκ ἐθαύμασεν; καὶ
τὸ μεγαλοπρεπὲς τῆς φιλοξενίας ὑμῶν ἦθος οὐκ ἐκήρυξεν; καὶ τὴν τελείαν καὶ ἀσφαλῆ γνῶσιν οὐκ ἐμα-

6 ὑμῶν πίστιν] A. πίστιν ὑμῶν Clem. Al. 610.   7 ἐπιεικῆ ἐν] Clem. Al.
επιεικηην A.   9 ἀσφαλῆ] Clem. Al. ασφαλην A.   10 ἀπροσωπολήμπτως] A.
ἀπροσωπολήπτως Clem. Al. (edd.).   ἐποιεῖτε] Clem. Al. εποιειται A.

sulted by the Church of Corinth, but having heard of the feuds by common report (§ 47 αὕτη ἡ ἀκοή) wrote this letter unsolicited.

8. ξένης] doubtless the right reading: comp. *Clem. Hom.* vi. 14 ὡς ἀληθείας ἀλλοτρίαν οὖσαν καὶ ξένην. No sense can be made of ξένοις. The doubling of epithets (ἀλλοτρίας καὶ ξένης) is after Clement's manner, especially in this opening chapter, *e.g.* μιαρᾶς καὶ ἀνοσίου, προπετῆ καὶ αὐθάδη, πανάρετον καὶ βεβαίαν, etc.

1. πρόσωπα] not simply '*persons*' but '*ringleaders:*' comp. § 47, and see the note on *Ign. Magn.* 6. The authors of these feuds are again mentioned as few in number, § 47 δι' ἓν ἢ δύο πρόσωπα στασιάζειν πρὸς τοὺς πρεσβυτέρους.

2. εἰς τοσοῦτον κ.τ.λ.] '*have kindled to such a pitch of recklessness:*' comp. § 46 εἰς τοσαύτην ἀπόνοιαν ἐρχόμεθα. Editors have taken offence at the expression, but its awkwardness is no sufficient reason for altering the text; comp. § 45 εἰς τοσοῦτο ἐξήρισαν θυμοῦ. Otherwise ὑπὸ ἀπονοίας might be read. In ἀπόνοια *shamelessness* rather than *folly* is the prominent idea, so that the ἀπονενοημένος is de-

scribed by Theophrastus (*Char.* xiii) as one wholly devoid of self-respect.

3. τὸ σεμνὸν κ.τ.λ.] So § 47 τὸ σεμνὸν τῆς περιβοήτου φιλαδελφίας: comp. Ign. *Eph.* 8 ἐκκλησίας τῆς διαβοήτου τοῖς αἰῶσιν.

4. τίς γὰρ κ.τ.λ.] The whole passage as far as ἐπορεύεσθε is quoted by Clem. Alex. *Strom.* iv. 17 (p. 610) ναὶ μὴν ἐν τῇ πρὸς Κορινθίους ἐπιστολῇ ὁ ἀπόστολος Κλήμης καὶ αὐτὸς ἡμῖν τύπον τινὰ τοῦ γνωστικοῦ ὑπογράφων λέγει, Τίς γὰρ κ.τ.λ.

5. πανάρετον] not found either in LXX or New Testament, but a favourite word with Clement: see §§ 2, 45, 57, with the note on the last passage. He delights in such compounds, e.g. παμμεγεθής, πανάγιος, παμπληθής, παντεπόπτης.

7. ἐπιεικῆ] '*forbearing.*' This yielding temper, this deference to the feelings of others, was the quality especially needed at such a time: see § 54. For ἐπιείκεια comp. §§ 13, 56, and see *Philippians* iv. 5.

8. τὸ μεγαλοπρεπὲς κ.τ.λ.] For the reproof lurking under this allusion to their past hospitality, see the note on ἀφιλοξενίαν § 35.

11. τοῖς νομίμοις] '*by the ordinan-*

κάρισεν; ἀπροσωπολήμπτως γὰρ πάντα ἐποιεῖτε, καὶ τοῖς νομίμοις τοῦ Θεοῦ ἐπορεύεσθε, ὑποτασσόμενοι τοῖς ἡγουμένοις ὑμῶν καὶ τιμὴν τὴν καθήκουσαν ἀπονέμοντες τοῖς παρ' ὑμῖν πρεσβυτέροις· νέοις τε μέτρια καὶ σεμνὰ νοεῖν ἐπετρέπετε· γυναιξίν τε ἐν ἀμώμῳ καὶ σεμνῇ καὶ ἁγνῇ συνειδήσει πάντα ἐπιτελεῖν παρηγγέλλετε, στεργούσας καθηκόντως τοὺς ἄνδρας ἑαυτῶν· ἔν τε τῷ κανόνι τῆς ὑποταγῆς ὑπαρχούσας τὰ κατὰ τὸν οἶκον σεμνῶς οἰκουρεῖν ἐδιδάσκετε, πάνυ σωφρονούσας.

11 τοῖς νομίμοις] τοισνομοισ A. ἐν τοῖς νομίμοις Clem. Al., which is approved by Wotton and others. I have adopted νομίμοις from Clem. Al.; but ἐν is not wanted (see the explanatory note) and was probably his own insertion. ἐπορεύεσθε] Clem. Al. πορεύεσθαι A. 12 καθήκουσαν] καθικουσαν A. 13 οἰκουρεῖν] Bois. οἰκουργειν A.

ces': so § 3 ἐν τοῖς νομίμοις τῶν προσταγμάτων αὐτοῦ πορεύεσθαι, § 40 τοῖς νομίμοις τοῦ δεσπότου ἀκολουθοῦντες, Hermas *Vis.* i. 3 ἐὰν τηρήσωσιν τὰ νόμιμα τοῦ Θεοῦ. The phrase τοῖς νομίμοις πορεύεσθαι occurs LXX Lev. xviii. 3, xx. 23, and ἐν τοῖς νομίμοις πορεύεσθαι Jer. xxvi (xxxiii). 4, Ezek. v. 7, xx. 18. For the dative, denoting the rule or standard, see *Galatians* v. 16, 25, vi. 16.

12. τοῖς ἡγουμένοις] i.e. the officers of the Church, as § 21 τοὺς προηγουμένους ἡμῶν: comp. Heb. xiii. 7 μνημονεύετε τῶν ἡγουμένων ὑμῶν οἵτινες ἐλάλησαν ὑμῖν τὸν λόγον τοῦ Θεοῦ, and again xiii. 17, 24; Hermas *Vis.* ii. 2, iii. 9 οἱ προηγούμενοι τῆς ἐκκλησίας. Similarly οἱ προϊστάμενοι ὑμῶν 1 Thess. v. 12. The reference therefore is not to civil officers, as some take it; and the πρεσβυτέροις in the next clause refers to age, not to office, as the following νέοις shows. Similarly § 21, where, as here, προηγούμενοι, πρεσβύτεροι, νέοι, γυναῖκες, occur in succession.

14. ἐπετρέπετε] '*ye enjoined,*' as e.g. in Plat. *Legg.* p. 784 C, Xen. *Anab.* vi. 5. 11 (see Kühner's note).

γυναιξίν τε κ.τ.λ.] See Polyc. *Phil.* 4 ἔπειτα καὶ τὰς γυναῖκας κ.τ.λ., where Polycarp follows Clement's language here and in § 21.

16. στεργούσας] should probably be taken with the foregoing clause, and I have altered the punctuation accordingly. For the change from the dative (γυναιξίν) to the accusative (στεργούσας) comp. Mark vi. 39 ἐπέταξεν αὐτοῖς ἀνακλιθῆναι πάντας, Acts xv. 22 ἔδοξεν τοῖς ἀποστόλοις κ.τ.λ. ἐκλεξαμένους ἄνδρας ἐξ αὐτῶν πέμψαι, and see Jelf's *Gram.* §§ 675, 676.

ἔν τε τῷ κανόνι κ.τ.λ.] i.e. 'not overstepping the line, not transgressing the limits of obedience:' see § 41 μὴ παρεκβαίνων τὸν ὡρισμένον τῆς λειτουργίας αὐτοῦ κανόνα, and § 7. On the metaphor of κανών, '*a measuring line,*' see *Galatians* vi. 16.

18. οἰκουρεῖν] '*to mind the house,*' as Philo *de Spec. Leg.* 31 (II. p. 327) θηλείαις (ἐφαρμόζει) οἰκουρία, *de Execr.* 4 (II. p. 431) γυναῖκας σώφρονας οἰκούρους καὶ φιλάνδρους: comp. Tit. ii. 5 σώφρονας, ἁγνάς, οἰκουρούς, ἀγαθάς, ὑποτασσομένας τοῖς ἰδίοις ἀνδράσιν, and the illustrative passages in Wetstein. In the passage last quoted the best

II. Πάντες τε ἐταπεινοφρονεῖτε, μηδὲν ἀλαζονευόμενοι, ὑποτασσόμενοι μᾶλλον ἢ ὑποτάσ[σ]οντες, ἥδιον διδόντες ἢ λαμβά[ν]οντες, τοῖς ἐφοδίοις τοῦ Θεοῦ

MS authority is certainly in favour of οἰκουργούς, which A reads there, as here. But it is very doubtful whether such a word exists.

II. 'Submission and contentment were the rule of your lives. The teaching of God was in your breasts; the passion of Christ before your eyes. Peace and good-will reigned among you. Spiritual graces and incessant prayers distinguished you. You loved the brethren; you bore no malice to any; you loathed faction; you rejoiced in doing good. The ordinances of God were graven on your hearts.'

2. ὑποτασσόμενοι κ.τ.λ.] See Ephes. v. 21, Phil. ii. 3, Rom. xii. 10, 16, and 1 Pet. v. 5 (v. l.).

3. ἥδιον κ.τ.λ.] Doubtless a reference to our Lord's words recorded Acts xx. 35, μακάριόν ἐστιν μᾶλλον διδόναι ἢ λαμβάνειν; see below, § 13, where the context of the passage is echoed. It was no new commandment however, though instinct with a new meaning. Maxims similarly expressed had been uttered by the two opposite schools of philosophy, starting from different principles and speaking with different motives. For the Epicureans see Plut. *Mor.* p. 778 C 'Επίκουρος τοῦ εὖ πάσχειν τὸ εὖ ποιεῖν οὐ μόνον κάλλιον ἀλλὰ καὶ ἥδιον εἶναί φησι, and for the Stoics, Seneca *Epist.* lxxxi. § 17 'Errat si quis beneficium accipit libentius quam reddit' (both quoted by Wetstein on Acts l.c.).

τοῖς ἐφοδίοις κ.τ.λ.] i.e. 'the provision which God has supplied for the journey of life.' Similarly Seneca *Epist.* lxvii. § 3 'Quia quantumcumque haberem, tamen plus jam mihi superesset viatici quam viae,' Epictet. *Diss.* iii. 21. 9 ἔχοντάς τι ἐφόδιον τοιοῦτον εἰς τὸν βίον, Plut. *Mor.* p. 160 B ὡς μὴ μόνον τοῦ ζῆν ἀλλὰ καὶ τοῦ ἀποθνήσκειν τὴν τροφὴν ἐφόδιον οὖσαν; comp. Dionys. Corinth. in Euseb. *H. E.* iv. 23 ἐκκλησίαις πολλαῖς ταῖς κατὰ πᾶσαν πόλιν ἐφόδια πέμπειν. It is the same sentiment as 1 Tim. vi. 8, ἔχοντες διατροφὰς καὶ σκεπάσματα τούτοις ἀρκεσθησόμεθα. The idea of *spiritual* sustenance seems to be out of place here, though ἐφόδια not unfrequently has this sense. If this meaning were taken, it would be necessary to punctuate with some editors, τοῖς ἐφοδίοις τοῦ Θεοῦ ἀρκούμενοι καὶ προσέχοντες; but such a combination of words is awkward, nor indeed is ἀρκεῖσθαι τοῖς ἐφοδίοις τοῦ Θεοῦ itself natural with the meaning thus assigned to it. For this reason the words τοῖς ἐφ. τοῦ Θ. ἀρκ. must be connected with the preceding clauses, so that the new idea is introduced by καὶ προσέχοντες.

4. τοὺς λόγους] For the accusative after προσέχοντες compare e.g. Exod. xxxiv. 11 πρόσεχε σὺ πάντα ὅσα ἐγὼ ἐντέλλομαί σοι, Is. i. 10 προσέχετε νόμον Θεοῦ, Neh. ix. 34 οὐ προσέσχον τὰς ἐντολάς (v.l.) σου καὶ τὰ μαρτύριά σου.

5. ἐνεστερνισμένοι] 'ye took them to heart,' i.e. τοὺς λόγους, which is the accusative to ἐνεστερνισμένοι as well as to προσέχοντες; so § 12 εἰσδεξαμένη αὐτοὺς ἔκρυψεν. For ἐνστερνίζεσθαι compare the passages quoted by the previous editors, Clem. Alex. *Pæd.* 1. 6 (p. 123) τὸν σωτῆρα ἐνεστερνίσασθαι, Euseb. *Mart. Pal.* 8 μείζονα τοῦ σώματος τὸν λογισμὸν ἐνεστερνισμένη, *ib.* 11 μνήμας αὐτῶν (τῶν γραφῶν) ἐνεστέρ-

ἀρ[κ]ούμενοι· καὶ προσέχοντες τοὺς λόγους αὐτοῦ ἐπιμελῶς ἐνεστερνισμένοι ἦτε τοῖς σπλάγχνοις, καὶ τὰ παθήματα αὐτοῦ ἦν πρὸ ὀφθαλμῶν ὑμῶν. Οὕτως εἰ-

5 ἐνεστερνισμένοι] Bois. εστερνισμενοι A.

νιστο, *Apost. Const.* procem. ἐνεστερνισμένοι τὸν φόβον αὐτοῦ, *ib.* v. 14 ἐνστερνισάμενος αὐτόν. There seems to be no such word as στερνίζεσθαι, and therefore ἐνεστερνισμένοι must be read. If ἐστερνισμένοι could stand, Cotelier's explanation would probably be correct, 'Clementi ἐστερνισμένοι sunt, qui Latinis pectorosi, homines lati capacisque pectoris (2 Cor. vi. 11),' as the analogy of σπλαγχνίζεσθαι suggests; and later critics seem to be wrong in making it equivalent to ἐνεστερνισμένοι, which owes its transitive sense to the preposition.

τὰ παθήματα αὐτοῦ] i.e. τοῦ Θεοῦ, for there is no other word to which αὐτοῦ can be referred. Compare Gal. iii. 1 οἷς κατ' ὀφθαλμοὺς Ἰησοῦς Χριστὸς προεγράφη ἐσταυρωμένος, of which Clement's expression is perhaps a reminiscence. The early Christian writers occasionally used language so strong in expressing their belief of our Lord's divinity, as almost to verge on patripassianism; so Ign. *Ephes.* 1 ἀναζωπυρήσαντες ἐν αἵματι Θεοῦ, *Ign. Rom.* 6 ἐπιτρέψατέ μοι μιμητὴν εἶναι τοῦ πάθους τοῦ Θεοῦ μου, Melito (Routh *Rel. Sacr.* I. p. 122) ὁ Θεὸς πέπονθεν ὑπὸ δεξιᾶς Ἰσραηλίτιδος. The nearest parallel in the New Testament is Acts xx. 28, τὴν ἐκκλησίαν τοῦ Θεοῦ ἣν περιεποιήσατο διὰ τοῦ αἵματος τοῦ ἰδίου; but even if τοῦ Θεοῦ be the correct reading (as possibly it is), the form of expression is far less strong than in these patristic references. In this passage of Clement it has been proposed to read μαθήματα for παθήματα; and the confusion of μαθητής, παθητής, in *Ign.*

Polyc. 7, and μαθήματα, παθήματα, in *Ign. Smyrn.* 5, shows that the interchange would be easy. But (1) The parallels above quoted prove that no alteration is needed, since τὰ παθήματα αὐτοῦ would be a natural expression to a writer of this age; (2) The reading μαθήματα would destroy the propriety of the expressions in the parallel clauses as read in the MS, ἐνεστερνισμένοι referring to τοὺς λόγους and πρὸ ὀφθαλμῶν to τὰ παθήματα, 'the words in your *hearts*, the sufferings before your *eyes*'; (3) While τὰ παθήματα is a common expression in the New Testament, being used especially to denote the sufferings of Christ, the word μάθημα does not once occur either there or in the Apostolic fathers; and in the only passage in the LXX where it is found (Jer. xiii. 21), there is a v.l. μαθητὰς (for μαθήματα) which approaches more nearly to the original Hebrew; (4) Though τὰ μαθήματα τοῦ Θεοῦ might stand, still αἱ διδαχαὶ τοῦ Θεοῦ (or some similar expression) would be more natural. It is urged indeed that, as Photius (*Bibl.* 126) complains of Clement's language in this epistle ὅτι ἀρχιερέα καὶ προστάτην τὸν Κύριον ἡμῶν Ἰησοῦν Χριστὸν ἐξονομάζων· οὐδὲ τὰς θεοπρεπεῖς καὶ ὑψηλοτέρας ἀφῆκε περὶ αὐτοῦ φωνάς, he cannot have had τὰ παθήματα αὐτοῦ in his text. But, as the declaration of Christ's divinity lurks under the reference of the preposition αὐτοῦ, it might very easily have escaped the notice of Photius who in the course of this single embassy read as large a number of books as would have sufficed many a

ῥήνη βαθεῖα καὶ λιπαρὰ ἐδέδοτο πᾶσιν καὶ ἀκόρεστος
πόθος εἰς ἀγαθοποιΐαν, καὶ πλήρης πνεύματος ἁγίου
ἔκχυσις ἐπὶ πάντας ἐγίνετο· μεστοί τε ὁσίας βουλῆς
ἐν ἀγαθῇ προθυμίᾳ μετ' εὐσεβοῦς πεποιθήσεως ἐξετεί-
νατε τὰς χεῖρας ὑμῶν πρὸς τὸν παντοκράτορα Θεόν, 5
ἱκετεύοντες αὐτὸν †ἵλεως† γενέσθαι, εἴ τι ἄκοντες ἡμάρ-
τετε. ἀγὼν ἦν ὑμῖν ἡμέρας τε καὶ νυκτὸς ὑπὲρ πάσης

1 λιπαρὰ ἐδέδοτο] λειπαραεδεδετο A.   4 πεποιθήσεως] πεποιηθησεωσ A.
8 ἐλέους] ελαιουσ A.   9 εἰλικρινεῖς] ειλεικρινεισ A.   10 ἀκέραιοι] ακερεοι A.

man not ill-informed for a life-time. It must be remembered too that our MS is some centuries older than Photius, and therefore carries more authority. On the other hand Caius (or rather Hippolytus) early in the third century in the *Little Labyrinth* (Euseb. *H. E.* v. 28; see Routh *Rel. Sacr.* II. p. 129) mentions Clement with Justin, Miltiades, and Tatian, besides 'several others', among those ἐν οἷς θεολογεῖται ὁ Χριστός. Routh (p. 145) supposes Clement of Rome to be meant (as also does Bunsen, *Hippol.* I. p. 440), because the author of the *Little Labyrinth* refers distinctly to works written '*before* the time of Victor' who became bishop about A.D. 185 or 190, and indeed the whole argument turns on this point. To this it may be added that Hippolytus afterwards (p. 131) uses an expression resembling the language of the Roman Clement here, ὁ εὔσπλαγχνος Θεὸς καὶ Κύριος ἡμῶν Ἰησοῦς Χριστὸς οὐκ ἐβούλετο...ἀπόλεσθαι μάρτυρα τῶν ἰδίων παθῶν, and that Clement of Alexandria (who is the alternative) can only have died a very few years (ten or at most twenty) before the passage was written. On the other side it may be urged that the order of the names, Ἰουστίνου καὶ Μιλτιάδου καὶ Τατιανοῦ καὶ Κλήμεντος καὶ ἑτέρων πλειόνων, points to the Alexandrian Clement; but this is not conclusive, since in the very next sentence the chronological order of Melito and Irenæus, is inverted, τὰ γὰρ Εἰρηναίου τε καὶ Μελίτωνος καὶ τῶν λοιπῶν τίς ἀγνοεῖ βιβλία; The question therefore must remain undecided; though the reasons in favour of the Roman Clement seem to preponderate. As it is very improbable that so early a writer as Hippolytus should have recognised as genuine any other writings ascribed to Clement of Rome, his judgment must have been founded upon this epistle.

2. ἀγαθοποιΐαν] '*beneficence*;' again just below and §§ 33, 34: comp. 1 Pet. iv. 19, *Test. xii. Patr.* Jos. 18. The allied words occur several times in S. Peter: ἀγαθοποιεῖν 1 Pet. ii. 15, 20, iii. 6, 17; ἀγαθοποιός, 1 Pet. ii. 14. While καλοποιΐα regards the abstract character of the action, ἀγαθοποιΐα looks to its results and more especially to its effect on others.

6. †ἵλεως† γενέσθαι] The adverb ἱλέως is recognised by Hesychius, but no instances are given in the lexicons. As it appears only to occur in the expression ἵλεως γίνεσθαι (as a v.l. in 2 Macc. ii. 22, vii. 37, x. 26), it is probably a grammatical mistake of the later language, the true construction being forgotten and the word

τῆς ἀδελφότητος, εἰς τὸ σώζεσθαι μετ' ἐλέους καὶ
†συνειδήσεως† τὸν ἀριθμὸν τῶν ἐκλεκτῶν αὐτοῦ· εἰλικρινεῖς καὶ ἀκέραιοι ἦτε καὶ ἀμνησίκακοι εἰς ἀλλήλους·
πᾶσα στάσις καὶ πᾶν σχίσμα βδελυκτὸν ὑμῖν· ἐπὶ τοῖς
παραπτώμασιν τοῖς πλησίον ἐπενθεῖτε· τὰ ὑστερήματα
αὐτῶν ἴδια ἐκρίνετε· ἀμεταμέλητοι ἦτε ἐπὶ πάσῃ ἀγα-
θοποιΐᾳ, ἕτοιμοι εἰc πᾶν ἔργον ἀγαθόν· τῇ παναρέτῳ

10 ἀμνησίκακοι] αμαμνησικακοι A. So I read the MS with Tisch., but previous editors give it αναμνησικακοι.   14 ἕτοιμοι] αιτοιμοι A.

being erroneously treated as an adverb (ἴλεως instead of ἴλεως). In this passage it may be due to the transcriber and not to Clement himself. At all events our MS (A) in the three passages of 2 Maccabees has ἴλεως, where B has a proper grammatical construction ἴλεω γενομένου, ἴλεω γενέσθαι, ἴλεω γενόμενον.

7. ἀγὼν ἦν κ.τ.λ.] Comp. Col. ii. 1.

ἡμέρας τε καὶ νυκτός] Hilgenfeld calls attention to the fact that the writer elsewhere has the same order 'day and night' §§ 20, 24, and argues thence 'scriptorem non e Judæis, qui noctem anteponunt, sed e gentilibus, Romanis quidem, ortum esse.' This argument is more specious than sound. Thus in the Apocalypse the order is always 'day and night,' iv. 8, vii. 15, xii. 10, xiv. 11, xx. 10; in S. Paul always 'night and day,' 1 Thess. ii. 9, iii. 10, 2 Thess. iii. 8, 1 Tim. v. 5, 2 Tim. i. 3; while by S. Luke either order is used indifferently in both the Gospel (ii. 37, xviii. 7) and the Acts (ix. 24, xx. 31, xxvi. 7).

8. ἀδελφότητος] a word peculiar to S. Peter in the New Testament; 1 Pet. ii. 17, v. 9.

9. †συνειδήσεως†] If the reading be correct, it must mean 'with the consent of God,' but this is hardly possible. I hazard the conjecture εὐδοκήσεως (ΕΥΔΟΚΗCΕΩC for CΥΝΕΙΔΗ-CΕΩC), which is less violent than συναινέσεως and other emendations. This conjecture struck me before I was aware that Davis had suggested συνευδοκήσεως, of which word I cannot find any instance. The clause would then mean 'Of His mercy and good pleasure:' comp. § 9 ἱκέται γενόμενοι τοῦ ἐλέους καὶ τῆς χρηστότητος αὐτοῦ. The Lexicons supply a few instances of the form εὐδόκησις (e.g. Diod. xv. 6, Dion. Hal. iii. 13), which also occurs below § 40 (see the note). In the N. T. the allied word εὐδοκία is generally said of God; Matt. xi. 26 (Luke x. 21), Eph. i. 5, 9, Phil. ii. 13.

τὸν ἀριθμὸν κ.τ.λ.] Comp. *Apost. Const.* viii. 22 τὸν ἀριθμὸν τῶν ἐκλεκτῶν σου διαφυλάττων. So too in our Burial Service, 'Shortly to accomplish the number of thine elect.'

εἰλικρινεῖς καὶ ἀκέραιοι] For εἰλικρινεῖς, see *Philippians* i. 10; for ἀκέραιοι *Philippians* ii. 15.

10. ἀμνησίκακοι] *Test. xii Patr.* Zab. 8 ἀμνησίκακοι γίνεσθε, Clem. Alex. *Strom.* vii. 14 (p. 883) ἀμνησίκακον εἶναι διδάσκει, Hermas *Mand.* ix. αὐτὸς ἀμνησίκακός ἐστι: comp. *Strom.* ii. 18 (p. 398) δι' ἀμνησικακίας.

12. τοῖς πλησίον] a brachylogy for τοῖς τῶν πλησίον. Jacobson quotes Eur. *Hec.* 996 μηδ' ἔρα τῶν πλησίον.

13. ἀμεταμέλητοι κ.τ.λ.] i.e. 'When you had done good, you did not wish

καὶ σεβασμίῳ πολιτείᾳ κεκοσμημένοι πάντα ἐν τῷ φόβῳ αὐτοῦ ἐπετελεῖτε· τὰ προστάγματα καὶ τὰ δικαιώματα τοῦ Κυρίου ἐπὶ τὰ πλάτη τῆς καρδίας ὑμῶν ἐγέγραπτο.

III. Πᾶσα δόξα καὶ πλατυσμὸς ἐδόθη ὑμῖν, καὶ ἐπετελέσθη τὸ γεγραμμένον· ἔφαγεν καὶ ἔπιεν καὶ 5 ἐπλατύνθη καὶ ἐπαχύνθη καὶ ἀπελάκτισεν ὁ ἠγαπημένος. Ἐκ τούτου ζῆλος καὶ φθόνος καὶ ἔρις καὶ στάσις, διωγμὸς καὶ ἀκαταστασία, πόλεμος καὶ αἰχμαλωσία.

2 ἐπετελεῖτε] επετελειται Α.   4 ἐδόθη] δοθη Α.
6 ἀπελάκτισεν] Deut. xxxii. 15.   απεγαλακτισεν Α.

it undone: when there was an opportunity of doing good, you seized it.' The latter clause ἕτοιμοι κ.τ.λ. is from Titus iii. 1 πρὸς πᾶν ἔργον ἀγαθὸν ἑτοίμους εἶναι: comp. 2 Cor. ix. 8, and see below § 34 with the note.

1. πολιτείᾳ] 'the graces of your heavenly citizenship:' see Phil. i. 27, Ephes. ii. 12, 19. For πολιτεία, πολιτεύεσθαι, see §§ 3, 6, 21, 44, 51, 54.

2. αὐτοῦ] i.e. τοῦ Θεοῦ, understood from τῇ παναρέτῳ καὶ σεβασμίῳ πολιτείᾳ; comp. § 54 τὴν ἀμεταμέλητον πολιτείαν τοῦ Θεοῦ.

τὰ προστάγματα] The two words occur together frequently in the LXX: see esp. Mal. iv. 4, and comp. 1 Sam. xxx. 25, Ezek. xi. 20, xviii. 9, xx. 11, etc.

3. ἐπὶ τὰ πλάτη κ.τ.λ.] taken from the LXX of Prov. vii. 3, ἐπίγραψον δὲ ἐπὶ τὸ πλάτος τῆς καρδίας σου, where πλάτος corresponds to the Hebrew לוּחַ 'a tablet.' The phrase is repeated in the LXX Prov. xxii. 20, and in some copies also in Prov. iii. 3; but as there is nothing corresponding in the Hebrew of either passage, these are probably interpolations from Prov. vii. 3. Wotton's statement that πλάτος occurs in this sense 'passim' in the LXX is erroneous. From this LXX reading the expression τὸ πλάτος τῆς καρδίας is not uncommon in the Christian fathers (e.g. Iren. I. praef. 3, and other passages quoted by Wotton), and τὰ πλάτη was doubtless written by Clement here. But it seems not improbable that the expression arose from a very early corruption of the LXX text (a confusion of πλάτος and πλακός), since πλάξ is the natural equivalent of לוּחַ and is frequently used elsewhere in the LXX to translate it. S. Paul's metaphor in 2 Cor. iii. 3 is derived from the original of Prov. vii. 3.

III. 'But, like Jeshurun of old, you waxed wanton with plenty. Hence strife and faction and open war. Hence the ignoble, the young, the foolish, have risen against the highly-esteemed, the old, the wise. Peace and righteousness are banished. The law of God, the life after Christ, are disregarded. You have fostered jealousy, whereby death entered into the world.'

4. πλατυσμός] 'enlargement, room to move in,' i.e. freedom and plenty, opposed to θλίψις, στενοχωρία, ἀνάγκη; as 2 Sam. xxii. 20 προέφθασάν με ἡμέραι θλίψεώς μου καὶ ἐγένετο Κύριος ἐπιστήριγμά μου καὶ ἐξήγαγέ με εἰς πλατυσμὸν καὶ ἐξείλετό με, Ps. cxvii. 5 ἐκ θλίψεως ἐπεκαλεσάμην τὸν

III] TO THE CORINTHIANS. 41

οὕτως ἐπηγέρθησαν οἱ ἄτιμοι ἐπὶ τοὺς ἐντίμους, οἱ ἄδοξοι
10 ἐπὶ τοὺς ἐνδόξους, οἱ ἄφρονες ἐπὶ τοὺς φρονίμους, οἱ
νέοι ἐπὶ τοὺς πρεσβυτέρους. διὰ τοῦτο πόρρω ἄπεστιν
ἡ δικαιοσύνη καὶ εἰρήνη, ἐν τῷ ἀπολείπειν ἕκαστον τὸν
φόβον τοῦ Θεοῦ καὶ ἐν τῇ πίστει αὐτοῦ ἀμβλυωπῆσαι
μηδὲ ἐν τοῖς νομίμοις τῶν προσταγμάτων αὐτοῦ πορεύ-
15 εσθαι μηδὲ πολιτεύεσθαι κατὰ τὸ καθῆκον τῷ Χριστῷ,
ἀλλὰ ἕκαστον βαδίζειν κατὰ τὰς ἐπιθυμίας αὐτοῦ τὰς

12 ἀπολείπειν] απολειπῖ A.   13 πίστει] πιστι A.
16 τὰς πονηρὰς] τησπονηρασ A.

Κύριον καὶ ἐπήκουσέ μου εἰς πλατυσ-
μόν: comp. Ps. xvii. 20, cxviii. 45,
Ecclus. xlvii. 12. See also the opposition of ἐν εὐρυχώρῳ and στενοχω-
ρεῖσθαι, Hermas *Mand.* v. 1.
5. ἔφαγεν κ.τ.λ.] A very free quotation from the LXX of Deut. xxxii. 14,
15, καὶ αἷμα σταφυλῆς ἔπιεν (v. l. ἔπιον)
οἶνον· καὶ ἔφαγεν Ἰακὼβ καὶ ἐνεπλήσθη
καὶ ἀπελάκτισεν ὁ ἠγαπημένος, ἐλιπάνθη,
ἐπαχύνθη, ἐπλατύνθη. It diverges still
more from the original Hebrew.
Justin *Dial.* 20 (p. 237 B) quotes the
same passage, but his quotation has
no special resemblances to that of
Clement.
7. ζῆλος κ.τ.λ.] The words occur in
an ascending scale: *first* the inward
sentiment of division (ζῆλος developing into φθόνος); *next*, the outward
demonstration of this (ἔρις developing into στάσις); *lastly*, the direct
conflict and its results (διωγμός, ἀκαταστασία, πόλεμος, αἰχμαλωσία).
ζῆλος καὶ φθόνος] These words occur together also below, §§ 4, 5:
comp. Gal. v. 20, 21, *Test. xii. Patr.*
Sym. 4 ἀπὸ παντὸς ζήλου καὶ φθόνου.
For the distinction between them see
Trench *N. T. Syn.* ser. 1 § xxvi, and
Galatians l. c. Ζῆλος is 'rivalry, am-
bition,' the desire of equalling or
excelling another. It does not necessarily involve the wish to deprive
him of his advantages, which is implied in φθόνος; but, if unduly cherished, it will lead to this; § 4 διὰ
ζῆλος Δαυεὶδ φθόνον ἔσχεν, Plat. *Me-
nex.* p. 242 A πρῶτον μὲν ζῆλος ἀπὸ
ζήλου δὲ φθόνος, Æsch. *Agam.* 939
ὁ δ' ἀφθόνητός γ' οὐκ ἐπίζηλος πέλει,
Arist. *Rhet.* ii. 4 ὑφ' ὧν ζηλοῦσθαι
βούλονται καὶ μὴ φθονεῖσθαι.
8. ἀκαταστασία] '*tumult*'; Comp.
Luke xxi. 9 πολέμους καὶ ἀκαταστασίας,
2 Cor. xii. 20 ἔρις, ζῆλος...ἀκαταστα-
σίαι, James iii. 16 ὅπου γὰρ ζῆλος καὶ
ἐρίθεια, ἐκεῖ ἀκαταστασία κ.τ.λ.
9. οἱ ἄτιμοι κ.τ.λ.] Is. iii. 5 προσ-
κόψει τὸ παιδίον πρὸς τὸν πρεσβύτην,
ὁ ἄτιμος πρὸς τὸν ἔντιμον.
11. πόρρω ἄπεστιν κ.τ.λ.] Is. lix. 14
καὶ ἡ δικαιοσύνη μακρὰν ἀφέστηκεν.
13. ἀμβλυωπῆσαι] '*grown dim-
sighted*'. The Atticists condemned
ἀμβλυωπεῖν and preferred ἀμβλυώττειν; Thom. Mag. p. 39. The word
and the form ἀμβλυωπεῖν are as old
as Hippocrates, *Progn.* 1. p. 38 (ed.
Foes.). In the LXX it occurs 1 Kings
xiv. 4 (displaced and found between
xii. 24 and xii. 25 in B). But in most
places where it occurs there is a v. l.
ἀμβλυώττειν. Comp. a Gnostic writer
in Hippol. *Ref.* v. 16 (p. 133 ad fin.).
15. τὸ καθῆκον τῷ Χριστῷ] The ex-

πονηράς, ζῆλον ἄδικον καὶ ἀσεβῆ ἀνειληφότας, δι' οὗ καὶ θάνατος εἰσῆλθεν εἰς τὸν κόσμον.

IV. Γέγραπται γὰρ οὕτως· καὶ ἐγένετο μεθ' ἡμέρας, ἤνεγκεν Κάϊν ἀπὸ τῶν καρπῶν τῆς γῆς θυσίαν τῷ Θεῷ, καὶ Ἄβελ ἤνεγκεν καὶ αὐτὸς ἀπὸ τῶν πρωτοτόκων τῶν προ- 5 βάτων καὶ ἀπὸ τῶν στεάτων αὐτῶν. καὶ ἐπεῖδεν ὁ Θεὸς ἐπὶ Ἄβελ καὶ ἐπὶ τοῖς δώροις αὐτοῦ, ἐπὶ δὲ Κάϊν καὶ ἐπὶ ταῖς θυσίαις αὐτοῦ οὐ προςέσχεν. καὶ ἐλυπήθη Κάϊν λίαν

6 ἐπεῖδεν] επιδε A.

pression has a close parallel in Phil. i. 27 ἀξίως τοῦ εὐαγγελίου τοῦ Χριστοῦ πολιτεύεσθε, from which perhaps it is taken. The emendations suggested (Χριστιανῷ or ἐν Χριστῷ for Χριστῷ) are therefore unnecessary.

1. ζῆλον κ.τ.λ.] Comp. § 45 ἄδικον ζῆλον ἀνειληφότων.

2. καὶ θάνατος κ.τ.λ.] From Wisd. ii. 24 φθόνῳ δὲ διαβόλου θάνατος εἰσῆλθεν εἰς τὸν κόσμον; comp. Rom. v. 12. The following passage of Theophilus connects the quotation from the book of Wisdom with Clement's application of it: *ad Autol.* ii. 29 (p. 39) ὁ Σατανᾶς ... ἐφ' ᾧ οὐκ ἴσχυσεν θανατῶσαι αὐτοὺς φθόνῳ φερόμενος, ἡνίκα ἑώρα τὸν Ἄβελ εὐαρεστοῦντα τῷ Θεῷ, ἐνεργήσας εἰς τὸν ἀδελφὸν αὐτοῦ τὸν καλούμενον Κάϊν ἐποίησεν ἀποκτεῖναι τὸν ἀδελφὸν αὐτοῦ τὸν Ἄβελ, καὶ οὕτως ἀρχὴ θανάτου ἐγένετο εἰς τόνδε τὸν κόσμον κ.τ.λ.

IV. 'Said I not truly that death came into the world through jealousy? It was jealousy which prompted the first murder and slew a brother by a brother's hand; jealousy which drove Jacob into exile, which sold Joseph as a bondslave, which compelled Moses to flee before his fellow-countryman and before Pharaoh, which excluded Aaron and Miriam from the camp, which swallowed up Dathan and Abiram alive, which exposed David to the malice not only of foreigners but even of the Israelite king.'

The idea of jealousy bringing death into the world had a prominent place in the teaching of the Ophites as reported by Iren. i. 30. 9, 'Ita ut et dum fratrem suum Abel occideret, primus *zelum et mortem* ostenderet': and Irenæus himself also speaks of the ζῆλος of Cain, iii. 23. 4, iv. 18. 3 (see the last passage especially). Mill supposes that the idea was borrowed from Clement. As regards the Ophites however it is more probable that they derived it from a current interpretation of the name Κάϊν: comp. *Clem. Hom.* iii. 42 τὸν μὲν πρῶτον καλέσας Κάϊν, ὃ ἑρμηνεύεται ζῆλος, ὃς καὶ ζηλώσας ἀνεῖλεν τὸν ἀδελφὸν αὐτοῦ Ἄβελ. In a previous passage (iii. 25) this Pseudo-Clement calls Cain ἀμφοτερίζον ὄνομα, because διχῆ ἔχει τῆς ἑρμηνείας τὴν ἐκδοχήν, ἑρμηνεύεται γὰρ καὶ κτῆσις (קנה) καὶ ζῆλος (קנא) κ.τ.λ. The interpretation κτῆσις is adopted by Philo *de Cherub.* 15 (I. p. 148), *de Sacr. Ab. et Ca.* 1 (I. p. 163), *quod Det. pot. ins.* 10 (I. p. 197), etc., and by Josephus *Ant.* I. 2. 1.

3. καὶ ἐγένετο κ.τ.λ.] Gen. iv. 3—8, quoted almost word for word from the LXX. The divergences from the

IV] TO THE CORINTHIANS. 43

καὶ ϲυνέπεϲεν τῷ προϲώπῳ αὐτοῦ. καὶ εἶπεν ὁ Θεὸϲ πρὸϲ
10 Κάϊν, ἵνα τί περίλυποϲ ἐγένου; καὶ ἵνα τί ϲυνέπεϲεν τὸ
πρόϲωπόν ϲου; οὐκ ἐὰν ὀρθῶϲ προϲενέγκηϲ ὀρθῶϲ δὲ μὴ
διέλῃϲ, ἥμαρτεϲ; ἡϲύχαϲον· πρόϲ ϲε ἡ ἀποϲτροφὴ αὐτοῦ,
καὶ ϲὺ ἄρξειϲ αὐτοῦ. καὶ εἶπεν Κάϊν πρὸϲ Ἄβελ τὸν ἀδελφὸν αὐτοῦ· διέλθωμεν εἰϲ τὸ πεδίον. καὶ ἐγένετο ἐν τῷ
15 εἶναι αὐτοὺϲ ἐν τῷ πεδίῳ ἀνέϲτη Κάϊν ἐπὶ Ἄβελ τὸν ἀδελφὸν αὐτοῦ καὶ ἀπέκτεινεν αὐτόν. *Ὁρᾶτε, ἀδελφοί, ζῆλος*

14 πεδίον] παιδιον Λ.   15 πεδίῳ] παιδιω Α.

Hebrew text are very considerable.

9. τῷ προσώπῳ] The case is difficult to account for, except as a very early transcriber's error; for the form of the Hebrew is the same here as in the following verse, where it is translated συνέπεσεν τὸ πρόσωπον, and the dative though intelligible is awkward.

11. οὐκ ἐὰν ὀρθῶς κ.τ.λ.] The meaning of the original is obscure, but the LXX translation which Clement here follows must be wrong. The words ὀρθῶς διέλῃς stand for לפתח תיטיב ('doest good, at the door'), which the translators appear to have understood 'doest right to open'; unless indeed they read פתה for פתח, as seems more probable (for in the older characters the resemblance of ב and ם is very close). At all events it would seem that they intended διέλῃς to refer to apportioning the offerings (comp. Lev. i. 12, where it represents נתח and is used of dividing the victim): and they might have understood the offence of Cain to consist in reserving to himself the best and giving God the worst: see Philo *Quæst. in Gen.* I. § 62—64 (I. p. 43 sq. Aucher), *de Agric.* 29 (I. p. 319), and *de Sacr. Ab. et Ca.* 13, 20 sq., (I. p. 171 sq., 176 sq.), in illustration of this sense. The Christian fathers however frequently give it a directly moral bearing, explaining ὀρθῶς μὴ διέλῃς to refer either to the obliquity of Cain's moral sense or to his unfairness in his relations with his brother, e.g. Iren. iii. 23. 4 'Quod non recte divisisset eam quae erga fratrem erat communionem,' iv. 18. 3 'Quoniam cum zelo et malitia quæ erat adversus fratrem divisionem habebat in corde, etc.', Origen *Sel. in Gen.* (II. p. 30) οὐ διεῖλεν ὀρθῶς· τῆς θείας νομοθεσίας κατεφρόνησεν κ.τ.λ.

12. ἡσύχασον] corresponds to the Hebrew רבץ 'lying,' which the LXX have treated as an imperative 'lie still'; comp. Job xi. 19. Much stress is laid on ἡσύχασον by Philo *de Sobr.* 10 (I. p. 400), and by early Christian expositors, e.g. *Clem. Hom.* iii. 25, Iren. ll. cc.

14. διέλθωμεν εἰς τὸ πεδίον] wanting in the Hebrew and Targum of Onkelos, but found in the LXX, the Samaritan and Syriac versions, and the later Targums. Origen's comment is interesting: *Sel. in Genes.* (II. p. 39) ἐν τῷ Ἑβραϊκῷ τὸ λεχθὲν ὑπὸ τοῦ Κάϊν πρὸς τὸν Ἄβελ οὐ γέγραπται καὶ οἱ περὶ Ἀκύλαν ἔδειξαν ὅτι ἐν τῷ ἀποκρύφῳ φασὶν οἱ Ἑβραῖοι κεῖσθαι τοῦτο ἐνταῦθα κατὰ τὴν τῶν ἑβδομήκοντα ἐκδοχήν. These or similar words are plainly wanted for the sense, and can

καὶ φθόνος ἀδελφοκτονίαν κατειργάσατο. διὰ ζῆλος ὁ πατὴρ ἡμῶν Ἰακὼβ ἀπέδρα ἀπὸ προσώπου Ἠσαῦ τοῦ ἀδελφοῦ αὐτοῦ. ζῆλος ἐποίησεν Ἰωσὴφ μέχρι θανάτου διωχθῆναι καὶ μέχρι δουλείας εἰσελθεῖν. ζῆλος φυγεῖν ἠνάγκασεν Μωϋσῆν ἀπὸ προσώπου Φαραὼ βασι- 5 λέως Αἰγύπτου ἐν τῷ ἀκοῦσαι αὐτὸν ἀπὸ τοῦ ὁμοφύλου τίc ce κατέcτηcεν κριτὴν ἢ δικαcτὴν ἐφ' ἡμῶν; μὴ ἀνελεῖν με cὺ θέλεις, ὃν τρόπον ἀνεῖλες ἐχθὲς τὸν Αἰγύπτιον; διὰ ζῆλος Ἀαρὼν καὶ Μαριὰμ ἔξω τῆς παρεμβολῆς ηὐλίσθησαν. ζῆλος Δαθὰν καὶ Ἀβειρὼν ζῶντας κατή- 10

9 διὰ ζῆλος] ζηλοσ (without δια) A. ζῆλος] διαζηλοσ (add. δια) A. 10 ηὐλίσθησαν] ηυλησθησαν A. 12 Δαυείδ] δᾱδ A. I have followed the best MSS of the N. T. for the orthography of the word. 15 ὑποδειγμάτων] υποδιγματων A. 17 γενναῖα] γεννεα A. 18 οἱ κάλλιστοι] or οἱ κράτιστοι. So only have been omitted accidentally. The Masoretes reckon this one of the twenty-eight passages where there is a lacuna in the text: see Fabric. *Cod. Apocr. V. T.* I. p. 104 sq. Philo enlarges on the allegorical meaning of τὸ πεδίον.

1. διὰ ζῆλος] On the two declensions of ζῆλος see Winer § ix. p. 78, A. Buttmann p. 20. Clement (or his transcriber) uses the masculine and the neuter forms indifferently.

2. ὁ πατὴρ ἡμῶν] So § 31 ὁ πατὴρ ἡμῶν Ἀβραάμ. From these passages it has been inferred that the writer was a Jewish Christian. The inference however is not safe; since Clement, like S. Paul (Gal. iii. 7, 9, 29, Rom. iv. 11, 18, ix. 6—8) or Justin (*Dial.* 134), might refer to spiritual rather than actual parentage; comp. 1 Pet. iii. 6 Σάρρα... ἧς ἐγενήθητε τέκνα. So too Theophilus of Antioch (quoted by Jacobson), though himself a Gentile, speaks of Abraham (*ad Autol.* iii. 28, comp. iii. 24) and David (iii. 25) as 'our forefather.'

To these references add *ib.* iii. 20 οἱ Ἑβραῖοι, οἱ καὶ προπάτορες ἡμῶν, ἀφ' ὧν καὶ τὰς ἱερὰς βίβλους ἔχομεν κ.τ.λ.

7. τίς σε κ.τ.λ.] From the LXX of Exod. ii. 14, which follows the Hebrew closely, inserting however χθές (or ἐχθές). Clement has κριτὴν ἢ for ἄρχοντα καί, perhaps from confusion with Luke xii. 14. The LXX is quoted more exactly in Acts vii. 27. The life of Moses supplies Clement with a twofold illustration of his point; for he incurred not only the envy of the king (ἀπὸ προσώπου Φαραώ), but also of his fellow-countrymen (ἐν τῷ ἀκοῦσαι αὐτὸν κ.τ.λ.), as in the parallel case of David below.

9. Ἀαρὼν κ.τ.λ.] The Mosaic record mentions only the exclusion of Miriam from the camp, Num. xii. 14, 15. In this instance and in the next (Dathan and Abiram) the jealous persons are themselves the sufferers.

11. τὸν θεράποντα κ.τ.λ.] The expression is used of Moses several times, e. g. Exod. iv. 10, xiv. 31, Num.

IV] TO THE CORINTHIANS. 45

γαγεν εἰς ᾅδου, διὰ τὸ στασιάσαι αὐτοὺς πρὸς τὸν
θεράποντα τοῦ Θεοῦ Μωϋσῆν. διὰ ζῆλος Δαυεὶδ φθόνον ἔσχεν οὐ μόνον ὑπὸ τῶν ἀλλοφύλων, ἀλλὰ καὶ
ὑπὸ Σαοὺλ βασιλέως Ἰσραὴλ ἐδιώχθη.
15 V. Ἀλλ' ἵνα τῶν ἀρχαίων ὑποδειγμάτων παυσώ-
μεθα, ἔλθωμεν ἐπὶ τοὺς ἔγγιστα γενομένους ἀθλητάς·
λάβωμεν τῆς γενεᾶς ἡμῶν τὰ γενναῖα ὑποδείγματα.
Διὰ ζῆλον καὶ φθόνο[ν οἱ κάλλι]στοὶ καὶ δικαιότατοι
στύλ[οι ἐδιώ]χθησαν καὶ ἕως θανάτο[υ ἦλθον]. Λάβω-
20 μεν πρὸ ὀφθαλμῶ[ν ἡμῶν] τοὺς ἀγαθοὺς ἀποστόλου[ς.

I would supply the lacuna on account of the space. Birr had suggested ἄριστοι or
μέγιστοι or κράτιστοι, and recent editors generally read οἱ μέγιστοι. All these seem
insufficient for the space, while on the other hand Young's reading ἐκκλησίας πίστοι
takes up too much room.   19 ἦλθον] Wotton (notes).

xii. 7, 8, Josh. viii. 31, 33: comp. below §§ 43, 51, 53, Barnab. § 14, Just. Mart. *Dial.* 56 (p. 274 D), Theoph. *ad Autol.* iii. 9, 18, etc. Ὁ θεράπων τοῦ Θεοῦ was a recognised title of Moses, as ὁ φίλος τοῦ Θεοῦ was of Abraham.

13. ὑπὸ τῶν ἀλλοφύλων] The Philistines, 1 Sam. xxi. 11, xxix. 4 sq.

14. ὑπὸ Σαούλ] 1 Sam. xviii. 9 'And Saul eyed (ὑποβλεπόμενος LXX, A) David from that day and forward.'

V. 'Again, take examples from our own generation. Look at the lives of the chief Apostles. See how Peter and Paul suffered from jealousy; how through many wanderings, through diverse and incessant persecutions, they bore testimony to Christ; how at last they sealed their testimony with their blood, and departed to their rest and to their glory.'

16. ἔγγιστα] '*very near*,' as compared with the examples already quoted. The expression must be qualified and explained by the mention of ἡ γενεὰ ἡμῶν just below. It has been shown that the close of Domitian's reign is pointed out both by tradition and by internal evidence as the date of this epistle (see the introd. p. 2 with the references there given to the notes). The language here coincides with this result. It could hardly be used to describe events which had happened within the last year or two, as must have been the case if the letter were written at the end of Nero's reign. And on the other hand ἡ γενεὰ ἡμῶν would be wholly out of place, if it dated from the time of Hadrian, some 50 years after the death of the two Apostles.

ἀθληταί] See the note on Ign. *Polyc.* 1.

19. στύλοι] See the note on *Galatians* ii. 9, where it is used of S. Peter and other Apostles.

20. ἀγαθούς] Editors and critics have indulged in much licence of conjecture, suggesting ἁγίους, πρώτους, θείους, etc., in place of ἀγαθούς. This

46   THE EPISTLE OF CLEMENT   [v

Ὁ Πέτρ]ος διὰ ζῆλον ἄδικον οὐχ ἕ[να οὐ]δὲ δύο ἀλλὰ

1 Ὁ Πέτρος] Jacobson. Πέτρες Young; but this is hardly sufficient for the space.   2 ὑπήνεγκεν] Young read ὑπέμεινεν; but Mill and others professed to see the H, and Wotton accordingly says 'Proculdubio legendum est

has led to the statement made in Volkmar's edition of Credner's *Gesch. des N. T. Kanon*, p. 51 that the MS reads ἃ οὖς (a supposed contraction for πρώτους). Nothing can be farther from the truth. The word ἀγαθοὺς is distinctly legible in full in the MS and must be retained. Such an epithet may be most naturally explained on the supposition that Clement is speaking in affectionate remembrance of those whom he had known personally. Otherwise the epithet seems to be somewhat out of place.

1. Πέτρος] It will be noticed that the name is supplied by conjecture, only the last two letters being legible. Of its correctness however no doubt is or can well be entertained. Indeed a passage in Peter of Alexandria (*de Pœnit.* 9, see Routh's *Rel. Sacr.* IV. p. 34), where the two Apostles are mentioned in conjunction, was probably founded on Clement's account here, for it closely resembles his language. This juxtaposition of S. Peter and S. Paul, where the Roman Church is concerned, occurs not unfrequently. The language of Ignatius, *Rom.* 4, seems to imply that they had both preached in Rome; and half a century later Dionysius of Corinth (Euseb. *H. E.* ii. 25) states explicitly that they went to Italy and suffered martyrdom there κατὰ τὸν αὐτὸν καιρόν. This is affirmed also a generation later by Tertullian who mentions the different manners of their deaths (*Scorp.* 15, *de Præscr.* 36); and soon after Caius (Hippolytus?), himself a Roman Christian, mentions the sites of their graves in the immediate neighbourhood of Rome (Euseb. *H.E.*

ii. 25); see also Lactant. *de Mort. Pers.* 2, Euseb. *Dem. Ev.* iii. 3, p. 116. The existing *Acta Petri et Pauli* (*Act. Apost. Apocr.* p. 1, ed. Tischendorf) are occupied with the preaching and death of the two Apostles at Rome; and this appears to have been the subject also of a very early work bearing the same name, on which see Hilgenfeld *Nov. Test. extr. Can. Rec.* IV. p. 68.

But not only was this juxtaposition of the two Apostles appropriate as coming from the Roman Church; it would also appeal powerfully to the Corinthians. The latter community, no less than the former, traced its spiritual pedigree to the combined teaching of both Apostles; and accordingly Dionysius (l. c.), writing from Corinth to the Romans, dwells with emphasis on this bond of union between the two Churches: comp. 1 Cor. i. 12, iii. 22.

2. μαρτυρήσας] '*having borne his testimony*.' The word μάρτυς was very early applied especially, though not solely, to one who sealed his testimony with his blood. It is so applied in the Acts (xxii. 20) to S. Stephen, and in the Revelation (ii. 13) to Antipas. Our Lord himself is styled the faithful and true μάρτυς (Rev. i. 5, iii. 14), and His μαρτυρία before Pontius Pilate is especially emphasized (1 Tim. vi. 13). Ignatius speaks of his desire to attain to the rank of a disciple διὰ τοῦ μαρτυρίου (*Ephes.* 1), where martyrdom is plainly meant. Doubtless the Neronian persecution had done much to promote this sense, aided perhaps by its frequent occurrence in the Revela-

πλείονας ὑπ[ήνεγκεν] πόνους, καὶ οὕτω μάρτυ[ρήσας]

ὑπήνεγκεν'. According to Jacobson 'Hodie nihil nisi γπ restat'. On the other hand Tischendorf sees part of an H. I could discern traces of a letter, but these might belong equally well to an ε or an H.

tion. After the middle of the second century at all events μάρτυς, μαρτυρεῖν, were used absolutely to signify martyrdom; *Martyr. Polyc.* 19 sq., Melito in Euseb. *H. E.* iv. 26, Dionys. Corinth. *ib.* ii. 25, Hegesippus *ib.* ii. 23, iv. 22, Epist. Gall. *ib.* v. 1, 2, Anon. adv. Cataphr. *ib.* v. 16, Iren. *Hær.* 1. 28. 1, iii. 3. 3, 4, iii. 12. 10, iii. 18. 5, etc. Still even at this late date they continued to be used simultaneously of other testimony borne to the Gospel, short of death: e. g. by Hegesippus, Euseb. *H.E.* iii. 2c, 32, by Apollonius *ib.* v.'18 (several times), and in a document quoted by Serapion *ib.* v. 19. A passage in the Epistle of the Churches of Gaul (A.D. 177) illustrates the usage, as yet not definitely fixed but tending to fixity, at this epoch: οὐχ ἅπαξ οὐδὲ δὶς ἀλλὰ πολλάκις μαρτυρήσαντες καὶ ἐκ θηρίων αὖθις ἀναληφθέντες...οὔτ' αὐτοὶ μάρτυρας ἑαυτοὺς ἀνεκήρυττον οὔτε μὴν ἡμῖν ἐπέτρεπον τούτῳ τῷ ὀνόματι προσαγορεύειν αὐτούς· ἀλλ' εἴποτέ τις ἡμῶν δι' ἐπιστολῆς ἢ διὰ λόγου μάρτυρας αὐτοὺς προσεῖπεν, ἐπέπλησσον πικρῶς· ἡδέως γὰρ παρεχώρουν τὴν τῆς μαρτυρίας προσηγορίαν τῷ Χριστῷ τῷ πιστῷ καὶ ἀληθινῷ μάρτυρι...καὶ ἐπεμιμνήσκοντο τῶν ἐξεληλυθότων ἤδη μαρτύρων καὶ ἔλεγον· ἐκεῖνοι ἤδη μάρτυρές εἰσιν οὓς ἐν τῇ ὁμολογίᾳ Χριστὸς ἠξίωσεν ἀναληφθῆναι, ἐπισφραγισάμενος αὐτῶν διὰ τῆς ἐξόδου τὴν μαρτυρίαν· ἡμεῖς δὲ ὁμόλογοι μέτριοι καὶ ταπεινοί (Euseb. *H.E.* v. 2). The distinction between μάρτυς and ὁμόλογος, which the humility of these sufferers suggested, became afterwards the settled usage of the Church; but that it was not so at the close of the second century appears from the Alexandrian Clement's comments on Heracleon's account of ὁμολογία in *Strom.* iv. 9, p. 596; and even half a century later the two titles are not kept apart in Cyprian's language. The Decian persecution however would seem to have been instrumental in fixing this distinction.

Thus the mere use of μαρτυρεῖν in this early age does not in itself necessarily imply the martyrdoms of the two Apostles; but on the other hand we need not hesitate (with Merivale, *Hist. of the Romans* vi. p. 282, note 2) to accept the passage of Clement as testimony to this fact. For (1) Clement evidently selects extreme cases of men who ἕως θανάτου ἦλθον; (2) The emphatic position of μαρτυρήσας points to the more definite meaning; (3) The expression is the same as that in which Hegesippus describes the final testimony, the *martyrdom*, of James (Euseb. *H.E.* ii. 23 καὶ οὕτως ἐμαρτύρησεν) and of Symeon (Euseb. *H.E.* iii. 32 καὶ οὕτω μαρτυρεῖ); (4) Dionysius of Corinth couples the two Apostles together, as they are coupled here, saying ἐμαρτύρησαν κατὰ τὸν αὐτὸν καιρόν (Euseb. *H. E.* ii. 25), where martyrdom is plainly meant and where probably he was writing with Clement's language in his mind. The early patristic allusions to the martyrdoms of the two Apostles have been already quoted (p. 46). It should be added that S. Peter's martyrdom is clearly implied in John xxi. 18, and that S. Paul's is the almost inevitable consequence of his position as described by himself in 2 Tim. iv. 6 sq.

ἐπορεύθη εἰς τὸν ὀφειλ[όμενον] τόπον τῆς δόξης. Διὰ ζῆλον [καὶ ὁ] Παῦλος ὑπομονῆς βραβεῖον [ὑπέδει]ξεν, ἑπτάκις δεσμὰ φορέσας, [φυγα]δευθείς, λιθασθείς, κῆρυξ

2 καὶ ὁ] Jacobson. It was previously read ὁ, but more is wanted to fill the space. βραβεῖον] βραβιον A. ὑπέδειξεν] So I would restore the reading for reasons given in the note below. Young printed ἀπεσχεν, but Mill formerly and Jacobson recently read the MS γ....εΝ. Accordingly Wotton and most later editors have written ὑπεσχεν. As regards the γ my own observation entirely agrees with Tischendorf's, who says 'post βραβιον membrana abscissa neque litteræ quæ sequebatur vestigium superest'. Indeed (if I am right) there can hardly have been any such trace since the MS was bound, so that Jacobson was certainly mistaken and Mill probably so; but I have so far regarded this statement, as to offer a conjecture which respects the γ. On the other hand the ξ at the beginning of the next line is clearly legible even in the photograph, though it has not been discerned by previous editors.

1. τὸν ὀφειλόμενον τόπον] The expression is copied by Polycarp (*Phil.* 9), where speaking of S. Paul and the other Apostles he says, εἰς τὸν ὀφειλόμενον αὐτοῖς τόπον εἰσὶ παρὰ τῷ Κυρίῳ. So Acts i. 25 τὸν τόπον τὸν ἴδιον (comp. *Ign. Magn.* 5), Barnab. 19 τὸν ὡρισμένον τόπον, and below § 44 τοῦ ἰδρυμένου αὐτοῖς τόπου. An elder in Irenæus (probably Papias) discourses at length on the *different* abodes prepared for the faithful according to their deserving, *Hær.* v. 36. 1 sq.

2. βραβεῖον] S. Paul's own word, 1 Cor. ix. 24, Phil. iii. 14. See also *Mart. Polyc.* 17 βραβεῖον ἀναντίρρητον ἀπενηνεγμένον, Tatian *ad Græc.* 33 ἀκρασίας βραβεῖον ἀπηνέγκατο: and comp. *Orac. Sib.* ii. 45, 149.

ὑπέδειξεν] '*pointed out the way to*, taught by his example'; comp. § 6 ὑπόδειγμα κάλλιστον ἐγένοντο ἐν ἡμῖν. The idea of ὑπέδειξεν is carried out by ὑπογραμμός below; for the two words occur naturally together, as in Lucian *Rhet. præc.* 9 ὑποδεικνὺς τὰ Δημοσθένους ἴχνη...παραδείγματα παρατιθεὶς τῶν λόγων οὐ ῥᾴδια μιμεῖσθαι... καὶ τὸν χρόνον πάμπολυν ὑπογράψει τῆς ὁδοιπορίας: so ὑποδεικνύειν ἐλπίδας and ὑπογράφειν ἐλπίδας are converti-

ble phrases, *Polyb.* ii. 70. 7, v. 36. 1. The only possible alternative reading which occurs to me (retaining the ξ which is legible in the MS) is ἐκήρυξεν, but the following κῆρυξ γενόμενος seems to exclude this.

3. ἑπτάκις] In 2 Cor. xi. 23 S. Paul speaks of himself as ἐν φυλακαῖς περισσοτέρως; but the imprisonment at Philippi is the only one recorded in the Acts before the date of the Second Epistle to the Corinthians. Clement therefore must have derived his more precise information from some other source. Zeller (*Theol. Jahrb.* 1848, p. 530) suggests that the writer of this letter added the captivities at Cæsarea and at Rome to the *five* punishments which S. Paul mentions in 2 Cor. xi. 24. But the πεντάκις there has no reference to imprisonments, which are mentioned separately in the words already quoted. I should not have thought it necessary to call attention to this very obvious inadvertence, if the statement had not been copied with approval or without disapproval by several other writers.

φυγαδευθείς] We read of S. Paul's flight from Damascus (Acts ix. 25, 2 Cor. xi. 33), from Jerusalem (Acts

v] TO THE CORINTHIANS. 49

γ[ενό]μενος ἕν τε τῇ ἀνατολῇ καὶ ἐ[ν τῇ] δύσει, τὸ γεν-
5 ναῖον τῆς πίστεως αὐτοῦ κλέος ἔλαβεν, δικαιοσύνην διδάξας ὅλον τὸν κόσμον καὶ ἐπὶ τὸ τέρμα τῆς δύσεως

Tisch. says '⁊ quum paullo minus appareat, possit erasum credi'. The letter is
certainly faint, but I see no traces of erasure.

3 φυγαδευθείς] Young reads παιδευθείς, Cotelier ῥαβδευθείς. Wotton says, 'Neuter
ad fidem MSti codicis qui exhibet φ cum majore parte τοῦ γ spatioque duarum lite-
rarum, δευθείς. Restituo igitur φυγαδευθείς'. Jacobson's statement is 'Cod. MS usque
adhuc φ exhibet', but he apparently does not see any part of the γ. Tisch. can read
nothing after φορεσασ, and this was my own case. The photograph, if I mistake not,
shows that there is no room for any letter on the existing parchment after the final
σ of φορεσασ. Probably however φυγαδευθείς is the right reading; see below.

5 πίστεως] τιϲταιωϲ A. 6 ἐπί] The word is distinctly legible in the
MS, and therefore the conjecture ὑπό (see below) is inadmissible.

ix. 30), from Antioch of Pisidia (xiii.
50), from Iconium (xiv. 6), from Thes-
salonica (xvii. 10), from Berœa (xvii.
14), and perhaps from Corinth (xx. 3).
Some of these incidents would be described by φυγαδευθείς, but it is perhaps too strong a word to apply to
all. On φυγαδεύειν, which though
found even in Attic writers was regarded by purists as questionable,
see Lobeck *Phryn.* p. 385. The alternative reading ῥαβδευθείς (comp. 2
Cor. xi. 25) is objectionable, because
the form ῥαβδίζειν alone is used in
the LXX and O. T. (and perhaps elsewhere, in this sense).

3. λιθασθείς] At Lystra (Acts xiv. 19).
An attempt was made also to stone
him at Iconium, but he escaped in
time (xiv. 5). Hence he says (2 Cor.
xi. 25) ἅπαξ ἐλιθάσθην. See Paley
Hor. Paul. iv. § 9.

κῆρυξ] S. Paul so styles himself
2 Tim. i. 11. Epictetus too calls his
ideal philosopher κῆρυξ τῶν θεῶν, *Diss.*
i ii. 21. 13, iii. 22. 69.

4. τὸ γενναῖον κ.τ.λ.] 'the noble renown which he had won by his faith;'
i.e. his faith in his divine mission to
preach to the Gentiles: see Credner's
Gesch. des N. T. Kanon (1860) p. 52.

6. ὅλον τὸν κόσμον κ.τ.λ.] In the spurious letter of Clement to James prefixed to the *Homilies* it is said of S.
Peter ὁ τῆς δύσεως τὸ σκοτεινότερον τοῦ κόσμου μέρος ὡς πάντων
ἱκανώτερος φωτίσαι κελευσθείς...τὸν
ἐσόμενον ἀγαθὸν ὅλῳ τῷ κόσμῳ μη-
νύσας βασιλέα, μέχρις ἐνταῦθα τῆς Ῥώμης γενόμενος...αὐτὸς τοῦ νῦν βίου βιαί-
ως τὸ ζῆν μετήλλαξεν (§ 1, p. 6 Lagarde).
This passage is, I think, plainly
founded on the true Clement's account
of S. Paul here; and thus it accords
with the whole plan of this Judaic
writer in *transferring* the achievements of S. Paul to S. Peter whom
he makes the Apostle of the Gentiles:
see *Galatians* p. 315.

τὸ τέρμα τῆς δύσεως] '*the extreme
west.*' In the Epistle to the Romans
(xv. 24) S. Paul had stated his intention of visiting Spain. From the
language of Clement here it appears that this intention was fulfilled.
Two generations later (*c.* A.D. 170) an
anonymous writer mentions his having gone thither; 'Sed et profec-
tionem Pauli ab urbe ad Spaniam
proficiscentis, *Fragm. Murat.* (pp.
19, 40, ed. Tregelles, Oxon. 1867; or
Westcott *Hist. of Canon*, p. 479).

CLEM. 4

ἐλθών· καὶ μαρτυρήσας ἐπὶ τῶν ἡγουμένων, οὕτως ἀπηλ-
λάγη τοῦ κόσμου καὶ εἰς τὸν ἅγιον τόπον ἐπορεύθη,
ὑπομονῆς γενόμενος μέγιστος ὑπογραμμός.
VI. Τούτοις τοῖς ἀνδράσιν ὁσίως πολιτευσαμένοις

7 διωχθεῖσαι] διωχθισαι A.   8 νεάνιδες παιδίσκαι] Wordsworth (see below).
δαη | αιδεσκαιδιρκαι A. The MS is creased here and the letters blurred in consequence;

For the expression τὸ τέρμα τῆς δύσεως pointing to the western extremity
of Spain, the pillars of Hercules,
comp. Strab. ii. 1 (p. 67) πέρατα δὲ αὐτῆς (τῆς οἰκουμένης) τίθησι πρὸς δύσει
μὲν τὰς Ἡρακλείους στήλας, ii. 4 (p.
106) μέχρι τῶν ἄκρων τῆς Ἰβηρίας ἅπερ
δυσμικώτερά ἐστι, iii. 1 (p. 137) τοῦτό
(τὸ ἱερὸν ἀκρωτήριον) ἐστι τὸ δυτικώτα-
τον οὐ τῆς Εὐρώπης μόνον ἀλλὰ καὶ τῆς
οἰκουμένης ἁπάσης σημεῖον· περατοῦται
γὰρ ὑπὸ τῶν δυεῖν ἠπείρων ἡ οἰκουμένη
πρὸς δύσιν, τοῖς τε τῆς Εὐρώπης ἄκροις
καὶ τοῖς πρώτοις τῆς Λιβύης, iii. 5 (p.
169) ἐπειδὴ κατὰ τὸν πορθμὸν ἐγένοντο
τὸν κατὰ τὴν Κάλπην, νομίσαντας τέρ-
μονας εἶναι τῆς οἰκουμένης...τὰ ἄκρα,
ib. (p. 170) ζητεῖν ἐπὶ τῶν κυρίως λε-
γομένων στηλῶν τοὺς τῆς οἰκουμένης
ὅρους (these references are corrected
from Credner's *Kanon* p. 53), and
see Strabo's whole account of the
western boundaries of the world and
of this coast of Spain. Similarly
Vell. Paterc. I. 2 'In ultimo Hispa-
niæ tractu, in extremo nostri orbis
termino.' It is not improbable also
that this western journey of S. Paul
included a visit to Gaul (2 Tim. iv.
10: see *Galatians* p. 31). But for the
patriotic belief of some English writers (see Ussher *Brit. Eccl. Ant.* c.
1, Stillingfleet *Orig. Brit.* c. 1), who
have included Britain in the Apostle's travels, there is neither evidence
nor probability; comp. Haddan and
Stubbs *Counc. and Eccles. Doc.* I.
p. 22 sq. This journey westward
supposes that S. Paul was liberated

after the Roman captivity related
in the Acts, as indeed (independently of the phenomena in the Pastoral Epistles) his own expectations
expressed elsewhere (Phil. ii. 24,
Philem. 22) would suggest. Those
who maintain that this first Roman
captivity ended in his martyrdom
are obliged to explain τὸ τέρμα τῆς
δύσεως of Rome itself. But it is in-
credible that a writer living in the
metropolis and centre of power and
civilization could speak of it as 'the
extreme west,' and this at a time
when many eminent Latin authors
and statesmen were or had been
natives of Spain, and when the commercial and passenger traffic with
Gades was intimate and constant.
(For this last point see Friedländer
Sittengesch. Roms II. p. 43, with his
references). On the other hand Philostratus says that, when Nero banished philosophers from Rome, Apollonius of Tyana τρέπεται ἐπὶ τὰ ἑσπέ-
ρια τῆς γῆς (iv. 47), and the region
which he visited is described immediately afterwards (v. 4) τὰ Γάδειρα
κεῖται κατὰ τὸ τῆς Εὐρώπης τέρμα
(quoted by Pearson *Minor Theol.
Works* I. p. 362). This is the natural
mode of speaking. It is instructive
to note down various interpretations
of ἐπὶ τὸ τέρμα τῆς δύσεως which have
been proposed: (1) 'to his extreme
limit towards the west' (Baur, Schen-
kel); (2) 'to the sunset of his labours'
(Reuss); (3) 'to the boundary between the east and west' (Schrader,

VI] TO THE CORINTHIANS. 51

5 συνηθροίσθη πολὺ πλῆθος ἐκλεκτῶν, οἵτινες πολλαῖς
αἰκίαις καὶ βασάνοις, διὰ ζῆλος παθόντες, ὑπόδειγμα
κάλλιστον ἐγένοντο ἐν ἡμῖν. Διὰ ζῆλος διωχθεῖσαι
γυναῖκες, νεάνιδες, παιδίσκαι, αἰκίσματα δεινὰ καὶ ἀνόσια

but the 3rd letter seems certainly to be H, and not N as all previous editors (and even Tischendorf) represent it. The second Δ begins a new line, and another letter may possibly have stood after the H, as the page is worn; but this is not probable.

Hilgenfeld); (4) 'to the goal or centre of the west' (Matthies); (5) 'before (ὑπὸ for ἐπί) the supreme power of the west' (Wieseler, Schaff). Such attempts are a strong testimony to the plain inference which follows from the passage simply interpreted.

1. ἐπὶ τῶν ἡγουμένων] 'before rulers': comp. § 37 τοῖς ἡγουμένοις ἡμῶν...τοῦ βασιλέως καὶ τῶν ἡγουμένων, § 51 οἱ ἡγούμενοι Αἰγύπτου, § 55 πολλοὶ βασιλεῖς καὶ ἡγούμενοι. The names of Nero and Helius (Dion Cass. lxiii. 12), of Tigellinus and Sabinus (the prætorian prefects A. D. 67), etc., have been suggested. In the absence of information it is waste of time to speculate. Clement's language does not imply that the Apostle's μαρτυρία ἐπὶ τῶν ἡγουμένων took place in the extreme west (as Hilgenfeld argues), for there is nothing to show that ἐπὶ τὸ τέρμα κ.τ.λ. and μαρτυρήσας ἐπὶ τῶν ἡγουμένων are intended to be synchronous. Indeed the clause καὶ ἐπὶ τὸ τέρμα τῆς δύσεως ἐλθών seems to be explanatory of the preceding δικαιοσύνην διδάξας ὅλον τὸν κόσμον, and the passage should be punctuated accordingly.

3. ὑπογραμμός] 'a copy, an example,' as for instance a pencil-drawing to be traced over in ink or an outline to be filled in and coloured. The word occurs again §§ 16, 33; comp. 2 Macc. ii. 28, 29, 1 Pet. ii. 21, Polyc. *Phil.* 8, *Clem. Hom.* iv. 16. The classical word is ὑπογραφή. For an explanation of the metaphor see Aristot. *Gen. An.* ii. 6 (I. p. 743) καὶ γὰρ οἱ γραφεῖς

ὑπογράψαντες ταῖς γραμμαῖς οὕτως ἐναλείφουσι τοῖς χρώμασι τὸ ζῶον. The sister art of sculpture supplies a similar metaphor in ὑποτύπωσις, the first rough model, 1 Tim. i. 16, 2 Tim. i. 13.

VI. 'But besides these signal instances, many less distinguished saints have fallen victims to jealousy and set us a like example of forbearance. Even feeble women have borne extreme tortures without flinching. Jealousy has separated husbands and wives: it has overthrown cities, and uprooted nations.'

5. πολὺ πλῆθος] The reference must be chiefly, though not solely, to the sufferers in the Neronian persecution, since they are represented as contemporaries of the two Apostles. Thus ἐν ἡμῖν will mean 'among us Roman Christians', and the αἰκίαι καὶ βάσανοι are the tortures described by Tacitus *Ann.* xv. 44. The Roman historian's expression 'multitudo ingens' is the exact counterpart to Clement's πολὺ πλῆθος.

πολλαῖς αἰκίαις κ.τ.λ.] 'by or amid many sufferings.' Previous editors have substituted the accusative, πολλὰς αἰκίας; but, as the dative is frequently used to denote the means, and even the accessories, the circumstances (see Madvig *Gr. Synt.* § 39 sq.), I have not felt justified in altering the reading. In this case διὰ ζῆλος παθόντες will be used absolutely, and πολλαῖς αἰκίαις κ.τ.λ. will explain ὑπόδειγμα ἐγένοντο.

8. νεάνιδες, παιδίσκαι] The first word

4—2

παθοῦσαι, ἐπὶ τὸν τῆς πίστεως βέβαιον δρόμον κατήντη-
[σαν] καὶ ἔλαβον γέρας γενναῖον αἱ ἀσθενεῖς τῷ σώματι.
ζῆλος ἀπηλλοτρίωσεν γαμετὰς ἀνδρῶν καὶ ἠλλοίωσεν
τὸ ῥηθὲν ὑπὸ τοῦ πατρὸς ἡμῶν Ἀδάμ, τοῦτ[ο] νῦν
ὀστοῦν ἐκ τῶν ὀστέων μ[ου] καὶ ϲὰρξ ἐκ τῆϲ ϲαρκόϲ μου. 5
ζῆλος καὶ ἔρις πόλεις μεγάλας κατέστρεψεν καὶ ἔθνη
μεγάλα ἐξερίζωσεν.

5 ὀστέων] οσταιων A.   6 ἔρις] ερεισ A.   12 εὐκλεῆ] ευκλαιη A.

in the MS is ΔΑΗΑΙΔΕϹ, not ΔΑΝΑΙΔΕϹ as represented by all previous collators (including Tischendorf). This indicates some carelessness in the scribe at this point, and is an additional reason for discrediting the reading Δαναΐδες καὶ Δίρκαι, which yields no tolerable meaning. I have therefore adopted the acute emendation of Wordsworth (on Theocritus xxvi. 1) γυναῖκες, νεάνιδες, παιδίσκαι, as highly probable and giving an excellent sense; 'Women, tender maidens, even slave-girls': comp. August. *Serm.* cxliii (v. p. 692 sq.) 'Non solum viri sed etiam *mulieres* et pueri et *puellæ* martyres vicerunt,' Leo *Serm.* lxxiv (1. p. 294) 'Non solum viri sed etiam *fœminæ* nec tantum impubes pueri sed etiam *teneræ virgines* usque ad effusionem sui sanguinis decertarunt'; quoted by Wordsworth (l.c.). For the meaning of παιδίσκη in Hellenistic Greek see the notes *Galatians* iv. 22. Under any circumstances the reading of the MS can hardly be retained. Besides the awkwardness of expression, the Danaids and Dirce would be no parallel to the Christian martyrs. Clement of Alexandria indeed (*Strom.* iv. 19, p. 618) mentions the daughters of Danaus with several other examples of womanly bravery among the heathens, and in the earlier part of the same chapter he has quoted the passage of his Roman namesake (§ 55) relating to Esther and Judith; but this does not meet the difficulty. It has been suggested again, that these may have been actual names of Christian women martyred at Rome: but the names are perhaps improbable in themselves, and the plurals cannot well be explained. It has been thought again that female martyrs were made to personate these mythical characters, as a scenic spectacle, and punished in this guise; but, though the legend of Dirce was not ill adapted to such a purpose, the story of the Danaids would be unmanageable; and even were it otherwise, there is no evidence of such a practice; while moreover the expression in itself is harsh and unnatural.

1. κατήντησαν κ.τ.λ.] The verb καταντᾶν signifies to arrive at a *destination*, and the corresponding substantive κατάντημα is 'a destination, a goal,' Ps. xix. 6: comp. Schol. on Arist. *Ran.* 1026 (993) ἐλαῖαι στιχηδὸν ἵστανται, οὖσαι κατάντημα τοῦ δρόμου. Here ὁ βέβαιος δρόμος 'the sure course,' i.e. the point in the stadium where the victory is secured, is almost equivalent to 'the goal.' For καταντᾶν ἐπί comp. 2 Sam. iii. 29, Polyb. x. 37. 3, xiv 1. 9.

4. τοῦτο νῦν κ.τ.λ.] From the LXX

VII. Ταῦτα, ἀγαπητοί, οὐ μόνον ὑμᾶς νουθετοῦν-
τες ἐπιστέλλομεν, ἀλλὰ καὶ ἑαυτούς †ὑπομνήσκον[τες]†·
10 ἐν γὰρ τῷ αὐτῷ ἐσμὲν σκάμμα[τι], καὶ ὁ αὐτὸς ἡμῖν
ἀγὼν ἐπίκει[ται]. Διὸ ἀπολείπωμεν τὰς κενὰς κ[αὶ]
ματαίας φροντίδας, καὶ ἔλθω[μεν] ἐπὶ τὸν εὐκλεῆ καὶ

of Gen. ii. 23, which corresponds with the Hebrew.
6. ζῆλος καὶ ἔρις] The two words occur together, Rom. xiii. 13, 2 Cor. xii. 20, Gal. v. 20: see above, § 3. πόλεις μεγάλας κ.τ.λ.] See Ecclus. xxviii. 14 πόλεις ὀχυρὰς καθεῖλε καὶ οἰκίας μεγιστάνων κατέστρεψε.
7. ἐξερίζωσεν] For the form see Tischendorf *Nov. Test.* I. p. lvi (ed. 7), A. Buttmann *Gramm.* p. 28 sq. Most editors needlessly alter the MS reading to ἐξερρίζωσεν. Compare μεγαλορρήμονα § 15, φυλλοροεῖ § 23 and ii. § 11.
VII. 'While instructing you, we would remind ourselves also. We are all entered in the same lists; we must all run on the straight path; obeying the will of God and respecting the blood of Christ. Examples of penitence in all ages are before our eyes. Noah preached repentance to his generation: Jonah to the men of Nineveh. All whosoever listened to them were saved.'
9. ὑπομνήσκοντες] Comp. *Orph. Hymn.* lxxvii. 6 (p. 345, Herm.) φιλάγρυπνος ὑπομνήσκουσά τε πάντα (a reference given by Hefele). So also μνήσκομαι in Anacr. ap. Athen. xi. p. 463 A μνήσκεται εὐφροσύνης (which editors perhaps unnecessarily alter into μήσεται or μνήσεται). But as our scribe blunders elsewhere in adding and omitting letters under similar circumstances (see above p. 25), we cannot feel sure about the reading.
10. σκάμματι] '*lists.*' The σκάμμα is the ground marked out by digging a trench or (as Krause supposes) by lowering the level for the arena of a contest: see Boeckh *Corp. Inscr.* no 2758, with the references in Krause *Hellen.* I p. 105 sq., and for its metaphorical use Polyb. xl. 5. 5 οὐδὲ ἐπὶ τοῦ σκάμματος ὢν τὸ δὴ λεγόμενον, Epict. *Diss.* iv. 8. 26 εἰς τοσοῦτο σκάμμα προεκαλεῖτο πάντα ὁντιναοῦν. A large number of examples of this metaphor in Christian writers is given by Suicer *s. v.* This word and many others referring to the games, as agonotheta, epistates, brabium, etc., are adopted by the Latins (see esp. the long metaphor in Tertull. *ad Mart.* § 3), just as conversely military terms are naturalised from Latin into Greek: see Ign. *Polyc.* 6 with the notes. In the phrase ὑπὲρ τὰ ἐσκαμμένα πηδᾶν, ἅλλεσθαι (e.g. Plat. *Crat.* p. 413 A, Lucian *Gall.* 6; see below on κανών), 'to do more than is required or expected,' τὰ ἐσκαμμένα is the trench cut at the end of the leap beyond the point which it is supposed the greatest athlete will reach (Pind. *Nem.* v. 36 μακρὰ δὴ αὐτόθεν ἅλμαθ' ὑποσκάπτοι τις· ἔχω γονάτων ἐλαφρὸν ὁρμάν). Krause indeed (*Hellen.* I. p. 393) interprets τὰ ἐσκαμμένα of the line marking the leap of the preceding combatant, but this explanation does not account for the metaphorical use.
11. ἐπίκειται] '*awaits*'; as Ign. *Rom.* 6 ὁ τοκετός μοι ἐπίκειται: comp. Heb. xii. 1 τὸν προκείμενον ἡμῖν ἀγῶνα, Clem. *Rom.* ii. § 7 ἐν χερσὶν ὁ ἀγών.
κενὰς καὶ ματαίας] '*empty and futile*,' the former epithet pointing to the quality, the latter to the aim or ef-

σεμνὸν τ[ῆς τελειώ]σεως ἡμῶν κανόνα. [γινώσκω]μεν τί
καλὸν καὶ τί τερπνὸν [καὶ εὐπρό]σδεκτὸν ἐνώπιον τοῦ
ποι[ήσαντ]ος ἡμᾶς. [ἀτενίσ]ωμεν εἰς τὸ αἷμα τοῦ
Χριστοῦ [καὶ ἴδ]ωμεν ὡς ἔστιν τίμιον τῷ Θεῷ [καὶ

1 τῆς τελειώσεως] So Tischendorf, prolegom. p. xviii. τελειώσεως Mill. See below.
γινώσκωμεν] So I would supply the lacuna; βλέπωμεν is read by previous editors, but would hardly fill the space. 2 καὶ εὐπροσδεκτόν] See below. καὶ τί προσδεκτόν Tisch. 5 καὶ πατρί] See below. πατρί Bleek (in Dressel). An upright

fect of the action. The combination is not uncommon; e.g. LXX Is. xxx. 7, Hos. xii. 1, Job xx. 18; comp. Theoph. *ad Aut.* iii. 3, Plut. *Vit. Artax.* 15, *Mor.* p. 1117 A.

1. κανόνα] This is probably a continuation of the metaphor in σκάμμα: comp. Pollux iii. 151 τὸ δὲ μέτρον τοῦ πηδήματος κανών, ὁ δὲ ὅρος τὰ ἐσκαμμένα· ὅθεν ἐπὶ τῶν τὸν ὅρον ὑπερπηδώντων οἱ παροιμιαζόμενοι λέγουσι πηδᾶν ὑπὲρ τὰ ἐσκαμμένα. See § 41 (with the note). Thus κανών will be the measure of the leap or the race assigned to the athlete. For this reason I had conjectured ἀθλήσεως to fill up the lacuna, before Hilgenfeld's edition appeared; and was glad to find that the same word had occurred independently to him. He refers to *Martyr. Ign.* 5 τοῦ στεφάνου τῆς ἀθλήσεως (comp. *ib.* § 4). This would add another to Clement's many coincidences with the diction of the Epistle to the Hebrews; see x. 32 πολλὴν ἄθλησιν ὑπεμείνατε παθημάτων. But I have been obliged reluctantly to fall back upon τῆς τελειώσεως as better fitted to the space: comp. § 6 τὸν τῆς πίστεως βέβαιον δρόμον. The other conjectures τ[ῆς ἁγίας κλή]σεως, τ[ῆς κλήσ]εως, are respectively too long and too short for the room.

τί καλὸν κ.τ.λ.] From Ps. cxxxii. 1 ἰδοὺ δὴ τί καλὸν ἢ τί τερπνόν κ.τ.λ.

2. εὐπρόσδεκτον ἐνώπιον] So ἀπόδεκτον ἐνώπιον. 1 Tim. ii. 3 τοῦτο καλὸν καὶ ἀπόδεκτον ἐνώπιον τοῦ σωτῆρος ἡμῶν Θεοῦ, of which Clement's language here seems to be a reminiscence: comp. 1 Tim. v. 4, where καλὸν καὶ is interpolated in the common texts from the earlier passage. The choice of reading here lies between τί πρόσδεκτον and εὐπρόσδεκτον. If τί πρόσδεκτον is slightly better fitted to the space, on the other hand εὐπρόσδεκτος is a much more common word in the N.T. and occurs three times besides in Clement, § 35 and twice in § 40. The simple πρόσδεκτος however appears in the LXX, Prov. xi. 20, xvi. 15, Wisd. ix. 12; comp. *Mart. Polyc.* 14.

4. τίμιον τῷ Θεῷ] Compare 1 Pet. i. 19 τιμίῳ αἵματι ὡς ἀμνοῦ ἀμώμου καὶ ἀσπίλου Χριστοῦ.

καὶ πατρί] I have read καὶ πατρὶ rather than πατρὶ alone for two reasons; (1) If πατρὶ were contracted πρι, as is most usual in the MS, the letters would not be sufficient to fill the space; (2) We find ὁ Θεὸς καὶ πατήρ frequently in the Apostolic writings followed by τοῦ Κυρίου, etc. (e.g. Rom. xv. 6, 2 Cor. i. 3, etc., 1 Pet. i. 3, Rev. i. 6), whereas ὁ Θεὸς πατήρ is never so found. In fact with any genitive following, the alternative seems to be ὁ Θεὸς καὶ πατήρ or Θεὸς πατήρ. On the other hand ὁ Θεὸς πατήρ occurs once only in the N.T. (Col. iii. 17, with a v.l.), and

VII]   TO THE CORINTHIANS.   55

5 πατρ]ὶ αὐτοῦ, ὅτι διὰ τὴν ἡμετέραν [σωτ]ηρίαν ἐκχυθὲν
παντὶ τῷ κό[σμ]ῳ μετανοίας χάριν ὑπήνεγκεν. [ἀνέλθ]-
ωμεν εἰς τὰς γενεὰς πάσας [καὶ] καταμάθωμεν ὅτι ἐν
γενεᾷ [κα]ὶ γενεᾷ μετανοίας τόπον ἔδω[κ]εν ὁ δεσπότης
τοῖς βουλομένοις ἐπιστραφῆναι ἐπ' αὐτόν. Νῶε ἐκήρυ-

stroke (probably ι) and a portion of the preceding letter (which might be ρ) are visible in the MS. Thus Young's reading (αἷμα), which is followed by most editors, cannot stand.   6 ἀνέλθωμεν Wotton.

there it is used absolutely.
6. ὑπήνεγκεν] '*offered*.' So it is generally taken, but this sense is unsupported; for Xen. *Hell.* iv. 7. 2, Soph. *El.* 834, are not parallels. Perhaps '*won* (*rescued*) *for the whole world*.'
8. γενεᾷ καὶ γενεᾷ] '*each successive generation*.' A Hebraism preserved in the LXX, Esth. ix. 27, Ps. xlviii. 11, lxxxix. 1, xc. 1, etc. : comp. Luke i. 50 γενεὰς καὶ γενεάς (vv. ll.).
τόπον] The same expression διδόναι τόπον μετανοίας occurs also in Wisd. xii. 10; comp. Heb. xii. 17 μετανοίας τόπον οὐχ εὗρεν, Tatian. *ad Græc.* 15 οὐκ ἔχει μετανοίας τόπον. The emendation τύπον therefore is not needed.
δεσπότης] Very rarely applied to the Father in the New Testament (Luke ii. 29, Acts iv. 24, Rev. vi. 10, and one or two doubtful passages), but occurring in this one epistle nearly twenty times. The idea of *subjection*, to God is thus very prominent in Clement, while the idea of *sonship*, on which the Apostolic writers dwell so emphatically, is kept in the background: see Lipsius p. 69. This fact is perhaps due in part to the subject of the epistle, which required Clement to emphasize the duty of *submission;* but it must be ascribed in some degree to the spirit of the writer himself.
9. Νῶε ἐκήρυξεν κ.τ.λ.] The Mosaic narrative says nothing about Noah as a preacher of repentance.

The nearest approach to this conception in the Canonical Scriptures is 2 Pet. ii. 5, where he is called δικαιοσύνης κῆρυξ. The preaching of Noah however is one of the more prominent ideas in the Sibylline Oracles; see especially i. 128 sq. Νῶε δέμας θάρσυνον ἐὸν λαοῖσί τε πᾶσι κήρυξον μετάνοιαν κ.τ.λ. This passage, though forming part of a comparatively late poem, was doubtless founded on the earliest (pre-Christian) Sibylline (iii. 97—828 of the existing collection) which is mutilated at the beginning and takes up the narrative of the world's history at a later point than the deluge. Indeed this earliest Sibyl (if the closing passage of the book still belongs to the same poem) connects herself with the deluge by claiming to be a daughter-in-law of Noah (iii. 826). As these Oracles were known to and quoted by Clement in another part of this epistle (see the note after § 57), it seems probable that he, perhaps unconsciously, derived this conception of Noah from them. To this same source may probably be traced the curious identification in Theophilus *ad Autol.* iii. 19 Νῶε καταγγέλλων τοῖς τότε ἀνθρώποις μέλλειν κατακλυσμὸν ἔσεσθαι προεφήτευσεν αὐτοῖς λέγων· Δεῦτε καλεῖ ὑμᾶς ὁ Θεὸς εἰς μετάνοιαν· διὸ οἰκείως Δευκαλίων ἐκλήθη; for Theophilus has elsewhere preserved a long fragment from the

ξεν μετάνοιαν, καὶ οἱ ὑπακούσαντες ἐσώθησαν. Ἰωνᾶς Νινευίταις καταστροφὴν ἐκήρυξεν, οἱ δὲ μετανοήσαντες ἐπὶ τοῖς ἁμαρτήμασιν αὐτῶν ἐξιλάσαντο τὸν Θεὸν ἱκετεύσαντες καὶ ἔλαβον σωτηρίαν, καίπερ ἀλλότριοι τοῦ Θεοῦ ὄντες.   5

VIII. Οἱ λειτουργοὶ τῆς χάριτος τοῦ Θεοῦ διὰ

6 λειτουργοί] λιτουργοι A.

lost opening of the earliest Sibylline (*ad Autol.* ii. 36), and this very passage incorporates several fragments of hexameters, e.g. Δεῦτε καλεῖ...Θεὸς εἰς μετάνοιαν. As Josephus also quotes the Sibyllines, he too in his account of Noah (*Ant.* I. 3. 1 ἔπειθεν ἐπὶ τὸ κρεῖττον αὐτοὺς τὴν διάνοιαν καὶ τὰς πράξεις μεταφέρειν, quoted by Hilgenfeld here) may have been influenced by them. For the Mohammedan legends of Noah, as a preacher of repentance, see Fabricius *Cod. Pseud. Vet. Test.* I. p. 262. To the passages there collected from apocryphal and other sources respecting Noah's preaching add this from the *Apocalypse of Paul* § 50 (quoted also by Hilgenfeld) ἐγὼ εἰμὶ Νῶε...καὶ οὐκ ἐπαυσάμην τοῖς ἀνθρώποις κηρύσσειν· Μετανοεῖτε, ἰδοὺ γὰρ κατακλυσμὸς ἔρχεται (p. 68, ed. Tisch.). A passage cited by Georg. Syncell. (*Chron.* p. 47 ed. Dind.) from Enoch, but not found in the extant book, seems to have formed part of Noah's preaching of repentance: see Dillmann's *Henoch* pp. xxxviii, lxi. See also below § 9, with the note on παλιγγενεσία.

2. καταστροφήν] '*overthrow, ruin*,' comp. Jonah iii. 4 καὶ Νινευὴ καταστραφήσεται.

4. ἀλλότριοι τ. Θ.] '*aliens from God*' i.e. 'Gentiles': comp. Ephes. ii. 12 ἀπηλλοτριωμένοι τῆς πολιτείας τοῦ Ἰσραήλ...καὶ ἄθεοι ἐν τῷ κόσμῳ. Both ἀλλότριοι and ἀλλόφυλοι are

thus used, as opposed to the covenant-people.

VIII. 'God's ministers through the Spirit preached repentance. The Almighty Himself invites all men to repent. Again and again in the Scriptures He bids us wash away our sins and be clean; He proclaims repentance and promises forgiveness.'

6. οἱ λειτουργοί] i.e. the prophets; though they are not so called in the LXX or New Testament.

9. ζῶ γὰρ ἐγώ κ.τ.λ.] Loosely quoted from Ezek. xxxiii. 11 ζῶ ἐγώ, τάδε λέγει Κύριος, οὐ βούλομαι τὸν θάνατον τοῦ ἀσεβοῦς ὡς ἀποστρέψαι τὸν ἀσεβῆ ἀπὸ τῆς ὁδοῦ αὐτοῦ καὶ ζῆν αὐτόν. ἀποστροφῇ ἀποστρέψατε ἀπὸ τῆς ὁδοῦ ὑμῶν· καὶ ἵνα τί ἀποθνήσκετε, οἶκος Ἰσραήλ; κ.τ.λ.

11. μετανοήσατε κ.τ.λ.] It is usual to treat these words as a loose quotation from Ezek. xviii. 30 sq. οἶκος Ἰσραήλ, λέγει Κύριος, ἐπιστράφητε καὶ ἀποστρέψατε ἐκ πασῶν τῶν ἀσεβειῶν ὑμῶν...καὶ ἵνα τί ἀποθνήσκετε, οἶκος Ἰσραήλ; διότι οὐ θέλω τὸν θάνατον τοῦ ἀποθνήσκοντος. If taken from the Canonical Book of Ezekiel, the words are probably a confusion of this passage with the context of the other (Ezek. xxxiii. 11), as given in the preceding note. See however what follows.

12. ἐὰν ὦσιν κ.τ.λ.] This passage is generally considered to be made up

VIII] TO THE CORINTHIANS. 57

πνεύματος ἁγίου περὶ μετανοίας ἐλάλησαν, καὶ αὐτὸς
δὲ ὁ δεσπότης τῶν ἁπάντων περὶ μετανοίας ἐλάλησεν
μετὰ ὅρκου· Ζῶ Γὰρ ἐγώ, λέΓει Κýριος, ογ βούλομαι τὸν
10 θάνατον τοῦ ἁμαρτωλοῦ, ὡς τὴν μετάνοιαν· προστιθεὶς
καὶ γνώμην ἀγαθήν· Μετανοήσατε, οἶκος Ἰσραήλ, ἀπὸ τῆς
ἀνομίας ὑμῶν· εἴπον τοῖς γίοῖς τοῦ λαοῦ μογ· Ἐὰν ὦςιν

10 προστιθείς] προστηθεισ A.

of Ps. ciii. 10, 11 οὐ κατὰ τὰς ἁμαρτίας ἡμῶν ἐποίησεν ἡμῖν οὐδὲ κατὰ τὰς ἀνομίας ἡμῶν ἀνταπέδωκεν ἡμῖν· ὅτι κατὰ τὸ ὕψος τοῦ οὐρανοῦ ἀπὸ τῆς γῆς ἐκραταίωσε Κύριος τὸ ἔλεος αὐτοῦ, and Jer. iii. 19, 22 καὶ εἶπα, Πατέρα καλέσετέ με καὶ ἀπ' ἐμοῦ οὐκ ἀποστραφήσεσθε... ἐπιστράφητε υἱοὶ ἐπιστρέφοντες καὶ ἰάσομαι τὰ συντρίμματα ὑμῶν, together with Is. i. 18 ἐὰν ὦσιν αἱ ἁμαρτίαι κ.τ.λ. Such fusions are not uncommon in early Christian writers and occur many times in Clement himself. But several objections lie against this solution here; (1) No satisfactory account is thus rendered of the words ἐὰν ὦσιν πυρρότεραι κόκκου καὶ μελανώτεραι σάκκου κ.τ.λ.; for the passage of Isaiah, from which they are supposed to be loosely quoted, is given as an *independent* quotation immediately afterwards. (2) The expression προστιθεὶς καὶ γνώμην ἀγαθὴν seems to imply that, even if not a continuation of the same passage, they were at all events taken from the same prophet as the words quoted just before. (3) This inference is borne out by the language used just below in introducing the passage from Isaiah, καὶ ἐν ἑτέρῳ τόπῳ, implying that the previous words might be regarded as a single quotation. (4) A great portion of the quotation is found in two different passages of Clement of Alexandria, and in one of these the words are attributed to Ezekiel: *Quis div.*

salv. 39 (p. 957) οὐ βούλομαι τὸν θάνατον τοῦ ἁμαρτωλοῦ ἀλλὰ τὴν μετάνοιαν· κἂν ὦσιν αἱ ἁμαρτίαι[ὑμῶν ὡς φοινικοῦν ἔριον, ὡς χιόνα λευκανῶ, κἂν μελάντερον τοῦ σκότους, ὡς ἔριον λευκὸν ἐκνίψας ποιήσω, and *Pædag.* i. 10 (p. 151) φησὶ γὰρ διὰ Ἰεζεκιήλ· Ἐὰν ἐπιστραφῆτε ἐξ ὅλης τῆς καρδίας καὶ εἴπητε, Πάτερ, ἀκούσομαι ὑμῶν ὡς λαοῦ ἁγίου. Thus it seems to follow either (1) That in the recension of the Canonical Ezekiel used by the two Clements the passage xxxiii. 11 was followed by a long interpolation containing substantially the words here quoted by Clement of Rome; or (2) That he is here citing some apocryphal writing ascribed to Ezekiel, which was a patchwork of passages borrowed from the Canonical prophets. The latter supposition is favoured by the language of Josephus (*Ant.* x. 5. 1), οὐ μόνον οὗτος (Ἰερεμίας) προυεθέσπισε ταῦτα τοῖς ὄχλοις ἀλλὰ καὶ ὁ προφήτης Ἰεζεκίηλος πρῶτος περὶ τούτων δύο βιβλία γράψας κατέλιπεν. This statement however may be explained by a bipartite division of the Canonical Ezekiel, such as some modern critics have made; and as Josephus in his account of the Canon (*c. Apion.* i. 8) and elsewhere appears not to recognise this second Ezekiel, this solution is perhaps more probable. Or again his text may be corrupt, β'(= δύο) having been merely a repetition of the first letter of βι-

αἱ ἁμαρτίαι ὑμῶν ἀπὸ τῆς γῆς ἕως τοῦ οὐρανοῦ, καὶ ἐὰν
ὦσιν πυρρότεραι κόκκου καὶ μελανώτεραι σάκκου, καὶ ἐπιστραφῆτε πρός με ἐξ ὅλης τῆς καρδίας καὶ εἴπητε, Πάτερ,
ἐπακούσομαι ὑμῶν ὡς λαοῦ ἁγίου. καὶ ἐν ἑτέρῳ τόπῳ
λέγει οὕτως· Λούσασθε καὶ καθαροὶ γένεσθε· ἀφέλεσθε τὰς 5
πονηρίας ἀπὸ τῶν ψυχῶν ὑμῶν ἀπέναντι τῶν ὀφθαλμῶν
μου· παύσασθε ἀπὸ τῶν πονηριῶν ὑμῶν, μάθετε καλὸν
ποιεῖν, ἐκζητήσατε κρίσιν, ῥύσασθε ἀδικούμενον, κρίνατε
ὀρφανῷ καὶ δικαιώσατε χήρᾳ, καὶ δεῦτε καὶ [δ]ιελεγχθῶμεν,
λέγει· καὶ ἐὰν ὦσιν [αἱ] ἁμαρτίαι ὑμῶν ὡς φοινικοῦν, [ὡς] 10
χιόνα λευκανῶ· ἐὰν δὲ ὦσιν ὡς κόκκινον, ὡς ἔριον λευ-

4 λαοῦ ἁγίου] Clem. Al. 152. λαωαγιω Α.   5 λούσασθε] λουσασθαι Α.
γενέσθε] γενεσθαι Α.   ἀφέλεσθε] αφελεσθαι Α.   7 παύσασθε] παυσασθαι Α.

βλία. See also the remarks of Ewald *Gesch. des V. Isr.* IV. p. 19. Apocryphal writings of Ezekiel are mentioned in the Stichometry of Nicephorus (see Westcott *Canon*, p. 504), and from the connexion (Βαρούχ, Ἀββακούμ, Ἐζεκιήλ, καὶ Δανιήλ, ψευδεπίγραφα) it may be conjectured that they were interpolations of or additions to the genuine Ezekiel, like the Greek portions of Daniel. This hypothesis will explain the form of the quotations here. At all events it appears that some apocryphal writ-ings attributed to Ezekiel existed, for Tertullian (*de Carn. Christ.* 23: comp. Clem. Alex. *Strom.* vii. 16, p. 890) and others quote as from Ezekiel words not found in the Canonical book: see the passages collected in Fabric. *Cod. Pseud. Vet. Test.* p. 1117. Hilgenfeld points out that one of these, 'In quacunque hora ingemuirit peccator salvus erit', is closely allied to Clement's quotation here. This apocryphal or interpolated Ezekiel must have been known to Justin Martyr also, for he quotes a sentence, ἐν οἷς ἂν ὑμᾶς καταλάβω, ἐν τούτοις καὶ κρινῶ (*Dial.* 47, p. 267), which we know from other sources to have belonged to this false Ezekiel (see Fabric. *l.c.* p. 1118); though Justin himself from lapse of memory ascribes it to our Lord, perhaps confusing it in his mind with Joh. v. 30. (On the other hand see Westcott *Introd. to Gosp.* p. 426). So too apocryphal passages of other prophets, as Jeremiah (Justin. *Dial.* 72, p. 298) and Zephaniah (Clem. Alex. *Strom.* v. 11, p. 692), are quoted by the early fathers. The passage of Jeremiah quoted by Justin must have been an interpolation, such as I suppose was the case with Clement's citation from Ezekiel; for he writes αὕτη ἡ περικοπὴ ἡ ἐκ τῶν λόγων τοῦ Ἰερεμίου ἔτι ἐστὶν ἐγγεγραμμένη ἔν τισιν ἀντιγράφοις τῶν ἐν συναγωγαῖς Ἰουδαίων, πρὸ γὰρ ὀλίγου χρόνου ταῦτα ἐξέκοψαν κ.τ.λ. On the apocryphal quotations in Clement see below §§ 13, 17, 23, 29, 46, (notes).

2. μελανώτεραι] The comparative μελανώτερος occurs Strabo xvi. 4 § 12

κανῶ. καὶ ἐὰν θέλητε καὶ εἰσακούσητέ μου, τὰ ἀγαθὰ τῆς
γῆς φάγεσθε· ἐὰν δὲ μὴ θέλητε μηδὲ εἰσακούσητέ μου,
μάχαιρα ὑμᾶς κατέδεται· τὸ γὰρ στόμα Κυρίου ἐλάλησεν
15 ταῦτα. Πάντας οὖν τοὺς ἀγαπητοὺς αὐτοῦ βουλόμενος
μετανοίας μετασχεῖν, ἐστήριξεν τῷ παντοκρατορικῷ
βουλήματι αὐτοῦ.

IX. Διὸ ὑπακούσωμεν τῇ μεγαλοπρεπεῖ καὶ ἐνδόξῳ
βουλήσει αὐτοῦ, καὶ ἱκέται γενόμενοι τοῦ ἐλέους καὶ τῆς
20 χρηστότητος αὐτοῦ προσπέσωμεν καὶ ἐπιστρέψωμεν ἐπὶ
τοὺς οἰκτιρμοὺς αὐτοῦ, ἀπολιπόντες τὴν ματαιοπονίαν
τήν τε ἔριν καὶ τὸ εἰς θάνατον ἄγον ζῆλος. Ἀτενίσωμεν

8 ῥύσασθε] ρυσασθαι A.   9 διελεγχθῶμεν] .ιελεχθωμεν A.   13 φάγεσθε] φαγε-
σθαι A.   θέλητε] θεληται A.   19 ἐλέους] ελαιους A.   21 οἰκτιρμούς] οικτειρμους A.

(p. 772), but I cannot verify Jacobson's further statement 'hanc formam habes saepius in LXX'. It is derived from the late form μελανός=μέλας, on which see Lobeck *Paral.* p. 139. Another late form of the superlative is μελαινότατος.

σάκκου] Comp. Rev. vi. 12 καὶ ὁ ἥλιος ἐγένετο μέλας ὡς σάκκος τρίχινος, Is. l. 3 ἐνδύσω τὸν οὐρανὸν σκότος καὶ ὡς σάκκον θήσω τὸ περιβόλαιον αὐτοῦ. It was a black haircloth. Thus Hilgenfeld's emendation λάκκου is superfluous, besides being out of place, for the comparison is between garment and garment. The σκότους of the existing text of Clem. Alex. may at once be rejected.

4. ἐν ἑτέρῳ τόπῳ] Is. i. 16—20. The quotation is almost word for word from the LXX.

9. δικαιώσατε χήρᾳ] 'give redress to the widow,' preserving the same construction as in κρίνατε ὀρφανῷ. The LXX however has the accusative χήραν in the second clause.

10. λέγει] sc. ὁ Κύριος, which words occur in the LXX of Isaiah in accordance with the Hebrew.

16. παντοκρατορικῷ] Apparently the earliest instance of this word.

IX. 'Let us therefore obey His gracious summons. Let us contemplate the bright examples of obedience in past ages: Enoch who was translated and saw not death: Noah through whom a remnant was saved in the ark.'

21. ματαιοπονίαν] The word occurs in Classical writers, e.g. Plut. *Mor.* 119 E, Lucian *Dial. Mort.* x. 8 (I. p. 369); comp. Theoph. *ad Autol.* ii. 7, 12, iii. 1. Polycarp, *Phil.* 2, apparently remembering this passage has ἀπολιπόντες τὴν κένην ματαιολογίαν καὶ τὴν τῶν πολλῶν πλάνην. But this does not justify a change of reading here; for ματαιοπονίαν is more appropriate, and a transcriber's error is more likely in the MSS of Polycarp (all derived from one very late source) than in our copy of Clement: nor is it impossible that Polycarp's memory deceived him. Ματαιολογία occurs 1 Tim. i. 6.

22. ἀτενίσωμεν κ.τ.λ.] Clement of

εἰς τοὺς τελείως λειτουργήσαντας τῇ μεγαλοπρεπεῖ δόξῃ αὐτοῦ. λάβωμεν Ἐνώχ, ὃς ἐν ὑπακοῇ δίκαιος εὑρεθεὶς μετετέθη, καὶ οὐχ εὑρέθη αὐτοῦ θάνατος. Νῶε πιστὸς εὑρεθεὶς διὰ τῆς λειτουργίας αὐτοῦ παλιγγενεσίαν κόσμῳ ἐκήρυξεν, καὶ διέσωσεν δι' αὐτοῦ ὁ δεσπότης τὰ εἰσελ- 5 θόντα ἐν ὁμονοίᾳ ζῶα εἰς τὴν κιβωτόν.

X. Ἀβραάμ, ὁ φίλος προσαγορευθείς, πιστὸς εὑ-

1 λειτουργήσαντας] λιτουργησαντασ A.   4 λειτουργίας] λιτουργιασ A.
7 πιστός] πιστις A.

Alexandria *Strom* iv. 16 (p. 610) after giving an earlier passage from this epistle (see above § 1) adds εἶτ' ἐμφανέστερον Ἀτενίσωμεν κ.τ.λ. down to 'Ραὰβ ἡ πόρνη (§ 12), but contents himself with a brief abridgement, and does not quote in full, so that he gives but little aid in determining the text.

1. τῇ μεγαλοπρεπεῖ δόξῃ] The same expression occurs in 2 Pet. i. 17. The word μεγαλοπρεπής is frequent in Clement, §§ 1, 19, 45, 58, and just above. It is only found this once in the N. T.

2. Ἐνώχ] Clement is here copying Heb. xi. 5 Ἐνὼχ μετετέθη τοῦ μὴ ἰδεῖν θάνατον καὶ οὐχ ηὑρίσκετο (comp. Gen. v. 24); though the words are displaced, as often happens when the memory is trusted. In the sequence of his first three instances also, Enoch, Noah, Abraham—he follows the writer of that Epistle. See also the language in Ecclus. xliv. 16, 17, to which Clement's expressions bear some resemblance.

δίκαιος] The book of Enoch is quoted as Ἐνὼχ ὁ δίκαιος in *Test. xii Patr.* Levi 10, Juda 18, Dan 5, Benj. 9. Thus it seems to have been a recognised epithet of this patriarch, and perhaps formed part of the title of the apocryphal book bearing his name. It was probably the epithet applied to him also in the opening of the extant book, i. 2, in the original.

4. αὐτοῦ] i.e. Noah himself. For this reflexive use of αὐτοῦ see A. Buttmann p. 98 sq. Comp. also §§ 12, 14, 30.

παλιγγενεσίαν] i.e. 'a second birth, a renewal,' of the world after the flood; as *Orac. Sib.* i. 195 (comp. vii. 11) καὶ δεύτερος ἔσσεται αἰών, words put into the mouth of Noah himself. See Philo *Vit. Moys.* ii. 12 (ii. p. 144) παλιγγενεσίας ἐγένοντο ἡγεμόνες καὶ δευτέρας ἀρχηγέται περιόδου, where also it is used of the world renovated after the flood. Somewhat similar is the use in Matt. xix. 28; where it describes the 'new heaven and new earth.' The Stoics also employed this term to designate the renewed universe after their great periodic conflagrations; see Philo *de Mund. incorr.* 14 (II. p. 501) οἱ τὰς ἐκπυρώσεις καὶ τὰς παλιγγενεσίας εἰσηγούμενοι τοῦ κόσμου, Marc. Anton. xi. 1 τὴν περιοδικὴν παλιγγενεσίαν τῶν ὅλων (with Gataker's note). For Christian uses see Suicer s.v. Any direct reference to the baptismal water (λουτρὸν παλιγγενεσίας, Tit. iii. 5), as typified by the flood (comp. 1 Pet. iii. 21), seems out of place here; but παλιγγενεσία appears to allude indirectly to the renewal of the Corinthian Church by repentance. See the next note.

6. ἐν ὁμονοίᾳ] An indirect reference

x]   TO THE CORINTHIANS.   61

ρέθη ἐν τῷ αὐτὸν ὑπήκοον γενέσθαι τοῖς ῥήμασιν τοῦ
Θεοῦ. οὗτος δι' ὑπακοῆς ἐξῆλθεν ἐκ τῆς γῆς αὐτοῦ καὶ
10 ἐκ τῆς συγγενείας αὐτοῦ καὶ ἐκ τοῦ οἴκου τοῦ πατρὸς
αὐτοῦ, ὅπως γῆν ὀλίγην καὶ συγγένειαν ἀσθενῆ καὶ οἶκον
μικρὸν καταλιπὼν κληρονομήσῃ τὰς ἐπαγγελίας τοῦ
Θεοῦ. λέγει γὰρ αὐτῷ· Ἄπελθε ἐκ τῆς γῆς coy κὰι ἐκ
τῆς cυγγενείας coy κὰι ἐκ τοῦ οἴκου τοῦ πατρός coy εἰς τὴν

10 συγγενείας] συγγενιασ A.   12 ἐπαγγελίας] επαγγελειασ A.

to the feuds at Corinth. Even the dumb animals set an example of concord: see below § 20 τὰ ἐλάχιστα τῶν ζώων τὰς συνελεύσεις αὐτῶν ἐν ὁμονοίᾳ καὶ εἰρήνῃ ποιοῦνται. The word ὁμόνοια is of frequent occurrence in Clement.

X. 'Abraham by obedience left his home and kindred, that he might inherit the promises of God. Not once or twice only was a blessing pronounced upon him for his faith. He was promised a race countless as the stars or the sand in multitude, and in his old age a son was granted to him.'

7. ὁ φίλος] From Is. xli. 8 'Abraham my friend' (LXX ὃν ἠγάπησα): comp. 2 Chron. xx. 7. See also James ii. 23 καὶ φίλος Θεοῦ ἐκλήθη, and below § 17 φίλος προσηγορεύθη τοῦ Θεοῦ. In the short paraphrase of the Alexandrian Clement this chapter relating to Abraham is abridged thus, 'Ἀβραὰμ ὃς διὰ πίστιν καὶ φιλοξενίαν φίλος Θεοῦ πατὴρ δὲ τοῦ Ἰσαὰκ προσηγορεύθη; and it has therefore been suggested to read ΘΥ ΦΙΛΟC for Ο ΦΙΛΟC. But no alteration is needed. Abraham is here called 'the friend' absolutely, as among the Arabs at the present day he is often styled 'El-Khalil' simply: see d'Herbelot s. v. *Abraham*, and Stanley's *Jewish Church* I. p. 13. So too *Clem. Hom.*

xviii. 13 οὕτως δύναται...οὐδὲ Ἐνὼχ ὁ εὐαρεστήσας μὴ εἰδέναι οὔτε Νῶε ὁ δίκαιος μὴ ἐπίστασθαι οὔτε Ἀβραὰμ ὁ φίλος μὴ συνιέναι, which has other resemblances with this passage of the genuine Clement; *Clem. Recogn.* i. 32 'Abraham pro amicitiis quibus erat ei familiaritas cum Deo.' It is an indication how familiar this title of Abraham had become in the Apostolic age, that Philo once inadvertently quotes Gen. xviii. 17 Ἀβραὰμ τοῦ φίλου μου for τοῦ παιδός μου and argues from the expression, *de Sobr.* 11 (I. p. 401), though elsewhere he gives the same text correctly *de Leg. All.* iii. 8 (I. p. 93), *Quæst. in Gen.* iv. 21 (p. 261 Aucher). At a much earlier date one Molon (Joseph. *c. Ap.* ii. 14, 33) who wrote against the Jews and is quoted by Alexander Polyhistor (Euseb.*Præp.Ev.*ix. 19, p.420)interpreted the name Abraham as πατρὸς φίλον, apparently reading אברהם as if it were אבהרם. And in the Book of Jubilees c. 19 (Dillmann in *Ewald's Jahrb.* III. p. 15) it is said of this patriarch that 'he was written down on the heavenly tablets as a friend of the Lord.' Later Rabbinical illustrations of this title will be found in Wetstein on James ii. 23, and especially in Beer *Leben Abraham's*, notes 427, 431, 950.

13. ἄπελθε κ.τ.λ.] From LXX Gen.

ΓΗΝ ἩΝ ἂΝ COI ΔΕΊΞΩ, ΚΑΊ ΠΟΙΉCΩ CE ΕἸC ἔΘΝΟC ΜΈΓΑ ΚΑῚ ΕΥ̓-
ΛΟΓΉCΩ CE ΚΑῚ ΜΕΓΑΛΥΝῶ ΤΟ ὄΝΟΜΆ COY, ΚΑῚ ἔCῌ ΕΥ̓ΛΟΓΗΜΈ-
ΝΟC· ΚΑῚ ΕΥ̓ΛΟΓΉCΩ ΤΟῪC ΕΥ̓ΛΟΓΟΥ̂ΝΤΆC CE ΚΑῚ ΚΑΤΑΡΆCΟΜΑΙ
ΤΟῪC ΚΑΤΑΡΩΜΈΝΟΥC CE, ΚΑῚ ΕΥ̓ΛΟΓΗΘΉCΟΝΤΑΙ ἐΝ COI ΠΑ̂CΑΙ ΑἹ
ΦΥΛΑῚ ΤΗ̂C ΓΗ̂C. καὶ πάλιν ἐν τῷ διαχωρισθῆναι αὐτὸν 5
ἀπὸ Λὼτ εἶπεν αὐτῷ ὁ Θεός· ἈΝΑΒΛΈΨΑC ΤΟΙ̂C ὀΦΘΑΛ-
ΜΟΙ̂C COY, ἴΔΕ ἀΠΟ ΤΟΥ̂ ΤΌΠΟΥ, ΟΥ̓̂ ΝΥ̂Ν CῪ ΕΙ̂, ΠΡῸC ΒΟΡΡΑ̂Ν ΚΑῚ ΛΊΒΑ
ΚΑῚ ἈΝΑΤΟΛᾺC ΚΑῚ ΘΆΛΑCCΑΝ· ὅΤΙ ΠΑ̂CΑΝ ΤῊΝ ΓΗ̂Ν, ἩΝ CῪ ὁΡᾳ̂C,
COῚ ΔΏCΩ ΑΥ̓ΤῊΝ ΚΑῚ Τῷ CΠΈΡΜΑΤΊ COY ἕΩC ΑἸῶΝΟC· ΚΑῚ
ΠΟΙΉCΩ ΤῸ CΠΈΡΜΑ COY ὣC ΤῊΝ ἄΜΜΟΝ ΤΗ̂C ΓΗ̂C· ΕἸ ΔΎΝΑΤΑΊ 10
ΤΙC ἐΞΑΡΙΘΜΗ̂CΑΙ ΤῊΝ ἄΜΜΟΝ ΤΗ̂C ΓΗ̂C, ΚΑῚ ΤῸ CΠΈΡΜΑ COY ἐΞΑ-
ΡΙΘΜΗΘΉCΕΤΑΙ. καὶ πάλιν λέγει· ἘΞΉΓΑΓΕΝ ὁ Θεὸς τὸν Ἀβρα-
ὰμ καὶ εἶπεν αὐτῷ· ἈΝΆΒΛΕΨΟΝ ΕἸC ΤῸΝ ΟΥ̓ΡΑΝῸΝ ΚΑῚ ἀΡΙ-
ΘΜΗCΟΝ ΤΟῪC ἈCΤΈΡΑC, ΕἸ ΔΥΝΉCῌ ἐΞΑΡΙΘΜΗ̂CΑΙ ΑΥ̓ΤΟΎC· ΟΥ̓̂ΤΩC

18 ὀρέων] οραιων A. 21 κριθείσης] A, as I read it; but Tisch. and Jacobs. give it κριθησησ. 22 θείου] θιου A.

xii. 1—3 with slight but unimportant variations. In omitting καὶ δεῦρο after τοῦ πατρός σου Clement agrees with A and the Hebrew against B which inserts the words. He also reads εὐλογηθήσονται with A against B (ἐνευλογηθήσονται) but εὐλογημένος with B against A (εὐλογητός).

5. ἐν τῷ διαχωρισθῆναι] The expression is taken from Gen. xiii. 14 μετὰ τὸ διαχωρισθῆναι τὸν Λὼτ ἀπ' αὐτοῦ.

6. ἀναβλέψας κ.τ.λ.] From LXX Gen. xiii. 14—16, almost word for word.

12. ἐξήγαγεν] From LXX Gen. xv. 5, 6, with unimportant variations.

16. φιλοξενίαν] i.e. his entertaining the angels: comp. Heb. xiii. 2. Similarly of Lot just below, § 11, and of Rahab, § 12. The stress laid on this virtue seems to point to a failing in the Corinthian Church. See also the note on ἀφιλοξενίαν below, § 35.

18. πρὸς ἕν κ.τ.λ.] Gen. xxii. 2 ἐφ' ἓν τῶν ὀρέων ὧν ἄν σοι εἴπω.

XI. 'Lot's faith and good deeds saved him from the destruction of Sodom and Gomorrah; while his own wife perished and remains a monument to all ages of the punishment with which God visits the disobedient and wavering.'

21. κριθείσης διὰ πυρός] Comp. Is. lxvi. 16 ἐν τῷ πυρὶ Κυρίου κριθήσεται πᾶσα ἡ γῆ. The emendation κανθείσης for κριθείσης is unnecessary as well as weak.

22. ποιήσας] A nominative absolute; see Winer § xxviii. p. 194, A. Buttmann p. 251 sq.

23. ἑτεροκλινεῖς] 'swerving aside', especially in a bad sense; Epictet. Diss. iii. 12. 7 ἑτεροκλινῶς ἔχω πρὸς ἡδονήν. See below, § 47 τοὺς ἑτεροκλινεῖς ὑπάρχοντας ἀφ' ἡμῶν. So ἑτερο-

TO THE CORINTHIANS.

ἔσται τὸ σπέρμα σου· ἐπίστευσεν δὲ Ἀβραὰμ τῷ Θεῷ, καὶ
ἐλογίσθη αὐτῷ εἰς δικαιοσύνην. Διὰ πίστιν καὶ φιλοξενίαν ἐδόθη αὐτῷ υἱὸς ἐν γήρᾳ, καὶ δι' ὑπακοῆς προσήνεγκεν αὐτὸν θυσίαν τῷ Θεῷ πρὸς ἓν τῶν ὀρέων ὧν
ἔδειξεν αὐτῷ.

XI. Διὰ φιλοξενίαν καὶ εὐσέβειαν Λὼτ ἐσώθη ἐκ
Σοδόμων, τῆς περιχώρου πάσης κριθείσης διὰ πυρὸς καὶ
θείου· πρόδηλον ποιήσας ὁ δεσπότης, ὅτι τοὺς ἐλπίζοντας ἐπ' αὐτὸν οὐκ ἐγκαταλείπει, τοὺς δὲ ἑτεροκλινεῖς
ὑπάρχοντας εἰς κόλασιν καὶ αἰκισμὸν τίθησιν· συνεξελ-
θούσης γὰρ αὐτῷ τῆς γυναικός, ἑτερογνώμονος ὑπαρχού-
σης καὶ οὐκ ἐν ὁμονοίᾳ, εἰς τοῦτο σημεῖον ἐτέθη ὥστε
γενέσθαι αὐτὴν στήλην ἁλὸς ἕως τῆς ἡμέρας ταύτης, εἰς
τὸ γνωστὸν εἶναι πᾶσιν ὅτι οἱ δίψυχοι καὶ οἱ διστάζον-

25 ἑτερογνώμονος] A is read ετερογνωμοσ by Tisch. and Jacobs., ετερογνωμιου by Vansittart. The last letter appeared to me like c with possibly γ superposed.

κλινία Clem. Hom. Ep. ad Jac. 15, said of the ship of the Church heeling over, when not properly trimmed.

25. ἑτερογνώμονος] The word has two senses, either (1) 'dissentient, otherwise-minded', Cyril. Alex. in Es. xlviii (II. p. 642), lii (II. p. 736) ὀλοτρόπως ἑτερογνώμονας παρ' ἐκείνους; or (2) 'wavering, double-minded', Cyril. Alex. Cord. Cat. in Ps. I. p. 225 διψύχον τε καὶ ἑτερογνώμονος. As it seems to be defined here by οὐκ ἐν ὁμονοίᾳ, the first meaning must be adopted; though Lot's wife was also ἑτερογνώμων in the other sense, and as such is classed among οἱ δίψυχοι καὶ διστάζοντες below. In ἐν ὁμονοίᾳ there is again an allusion to the feuds at Corinth; see above § 9.

26. εἰς τοῦτο κ.τ.λ.] Here ὥστε is dependent not on εἰς τοῦτο, but on σημεῖον ἐτέθη; and εἰς τοῦτο 'to this end' stands independently, being afterwards explained by εἰς τὸ γνωστὸν εἶναι κ.τ.λ.

27. ἕως τῆς ἡμ. ταύτης] A pillar of salt identified with Lot's wife is mentioned as standing in Wisdom x. 7, ἀπιστούσης ψυχῆς μνημεῖον ἑστηκυῖα στήλη ἁλός, and in Joseph. Ant. i. 11. 4 who says that he himself had seen it. So too Irenæus (Hær. iv. 31. 3) speaks of it as 'statua salis semper manens', which he makes a type of the Church. Cyril of Jerusalem also, Catech. xix. 8 (p. 309), describes Lot's wife as ἐστηλιτευμένη δι' αἰῶνος. The region abounds in such pillars of salt (see Robinson's Biblical Researches, etc. II. p. 108 sq.). Mediæval and even modern travellers have delighted to identify one or other of these with Lot's wife.

28. οἱ δίψυχοι] The word occurs only twice, James i. 8, iv. 8, in the New Testament. Both the word and the

τες περὶ τῆς τοῦ Θεοῦ δυνάμεως εἰς κρίμα καὶ εἰς σημείωσιν πάσαις ταῖς γενεαῖς γίνονται.

XII. Διὰ πίστιν καὶ φιλοξενίαν ἐσώθη Ῥαὰβ ἡ πόρνη· ἐκπεμφθέντων γὰρ ὑπὸ Ἰησοῦ τοῦ τοῦ Ναυὴ κατασκοπῶν εἰς τὴν Ἱεριχώ, ἔγνω ὁ βασιλεὺς τῆς γῆς ὅτι ἥκασιν κατασκοπεῦσαι τὴν χώραν αὐτῶν, καὶ ἐξέπεμψεν ἄνδρας τοὺς συλλημψομένους αὐτούς, ὅπως συλλημφθέντες θανατωθῶσιν. ἡ οὖν φιλόξενος Ῥαὰβ εἰσδεξαμένη αὐτοὺς ἔκρυψεν εἰς τὸ ὑπερῷον ὑπὸ τὴν λινοκαλάμην. ἐπισταθέντων δὲ τῶν παρὰ τοῦ βασιλέως καὶ λεγόντων· [ἰδού, εἰcĤλ]θον οἱ κατάσκοποι τῆς

1 σημείωσιν] σημιωσιν A.   4 ἐκπεμφθέντων] εκπεφθεντων A.   7 συλλημψομένους] συλληψομενουσ A, though just below it has συλλημφθεντεσ. For the omission of μ compare εκπεφθεντων above.   11 ἰδού, εἰσῆλθον] See below.   12 γῆς, σὺ οὖν] See below.   ἐναντίαν] See below. Tisch. prints εκ... as though the 2nd letter

warning are very frequent in Clement's younger contemporary Hermas, *Vis.* ii. 2, iii. 2, 3, 4, 7, 10, 11, iv. 1, 2, *Sim.* viii. 7, etc., but especially *Mand.* ix, x. See below § 23 with the note (comp. *Clem. Rom.* ii. § 11).

XII. 'Rahab also was saved by her faith and her hospitality. She believed in the might of the Lord God, and she rescued the spies; therefore she and her family were spared. She was gifted too with a prophetic spirit, for the scarlet thread typified the saving power of Christ's blood'.

3. Ῥαάβ] This account is taken from the book of Joshua; but Clement gives it in his own words, even when recording the conversational parts. The instance of Rahab was doubtless suggested by Heb. xi. 31, James ii. 25; for both these epistles were known to S. Clement and are quoted elsewhere. His expression διὰ πίστιν καὶ φιλοξενίαν connects the two aspects, to which the two Apostolic writers severally direct attention, the πίστις of the one, the ἔργα of the other; comp. §§ 31, 33, 34, 49, (notes). See also the note on the φιλοξενία of Abraham § 10.

4. τοῦ τοῦ Ναυή] In the LXX Num. xxxii. 12, Deut. xxxii. 44, Josh. vi. 6, etc., he is called Ἰησοῦς ὁ τοῦ Ναυή, and the same expression is adopted here, though in the genitive it sounds somewhat awkwardly.

6. αὐτῶν] not αὑτῶν, as most editors print it; comp. § 9 and see the note on *Philippians* iii. 21.

7. τοὺς συλλημψομένους] i.e. οἱ συλλήμψονται. For this construction see Winer § xviii. p. 121 and the notes *Galatians* i. 7.

10. λινοκαλάμην] 'flax-stalks' laid on the flat roof of the house to dry; see Josh. ii. 6. So Joseph. (*Ant.* v. 1. 2) explains it, λίνου γὰρ ἀγκαλίδας ἐπὶ τοῦ τέγους ἔψυχε. The word ὑπερῷον does not occur in the original narrative, which describes the men's lurking

[ΓΗC· CY OYN] ἐξάγαγε ἀγτούς, ὁ ΓᾺΡ Βα[ϲιλεγϲ ΟΥ̓]τως
κελεγει ἡ δὲ ἀπεκρίθη· Εἰϲῆλθον [οἱ δγο ἀν]Δρεϲ, ογϲ
ΖΗΤΕΙΤΕ, πρόϲ με, [ἀλλὰ ταχε]ωϲ ἀπῆλθον καὶ πορεγον[ται·
ὁδὸν] ὑποδεικνύουσα αὐτοῖς ἐ[ναντίαν]. Καὶ εἶπεν πρὸς
τοὺς ἄνδρας· Γ[ινώ]ϲκογϲα Γινώϲκω ἐρὼ ὅτι [Κύριος ὁ
Θεός] ΫΜῶΝ παραδίδωϲιν ΫΜῖΝ [τὴν πό]λιν ταὐτην, ὁ Γὰρ
φόβοϲ καὶ ὁ [τρό]μοϲ ΫΜῶΝ ἐπέπεϲεν τοῖϲ κα[τοι]κοῦϲιν
αὐτήν. ὡϲ ἐὰν οΫ̓ν Γέν[ηται] λαβεῖν αὐτὴν Ϋμᾶϲ, διαϲώ-
ϲατέ με καὶ τὸν οἶκον τογ̓ πατρόϲ μου. καὶ εἶπαν αὐτῇ·
Ἔσται οΫ̓τωϲ ὡϲ ἐλάληϲαϲ ἡμῖν. ὡϲ ἐὰν οΫ̓ν Γνῷϲ παραγι-
νομένουϲ ἡμᾶϲ, ϲγνάξειϲ πάνταϲ τοὺϲ ϲούϲ ὑπὸ τὸ τέΓοϲ

were legible; but nothing more than ει can be discerned, and the ι might as well be the upright stroke of ν as of κ.   18 καὶ ὁ] The article can be read in the MS, though omitted by editors.   22 τὸ τέγος] τοτοεγοσ A. See below. For the next word A reads σου, not ου as sometimes stated.

place as on the house-top (ἐπὶ τοῦ δώματος). But Clement would not necessarily be familiar with Eastern customs and might easily substitute a wrong expression.

11. ἰδοὺ κ.τ.λ.] The lacunae are generally supplied [ἄνδρες πρός σε ἦλ]θον οἱ κατάσκοποι τῆς [γῆς ἡμῶν]· ἐξάγαγε αὐτούς, after Young; but ἄνδρες οἱ κατάσκοποι can hardly stand, and the whole sentence reads awkwardly. I have therefore suggested another mode of filling in the missing portions.

15. ὁδὸν κ.τ.λ.] If this mode of supplying the lacuna be adopted (after Young), Clement must have made a slip of memory, as he has done already in ὑπερῷον; for in the original narrative Rahab shows the opposite route not to the king's messengers but to the spies. His accuracy is saved by reading [οὐκ] ὑποδεικνύουσα αὐτοῖς ἐ[κείνους] with Cotelier; but this is so much more awkward than Young's reading, that

I have preferred not to adopt it.

18. ὁ φόβος κ.τ.λ.] does not occur in the LXX here, but is common elsewhere; e.g. Gen. ix. 2, Deut. ii. 25, xi. 25. These passages illustrate not only the combination of φόβος and τρόμος, but the repetition of the article before the latter. Cotelier observes that Clement seems to have had in his copy of the LXX (Josh. ii. 9) the words καὶ κατέπτησσον πάντες οἱ κατοικοῦντες τὴν γῆν ἀφ' ὑμῶν which are wanting in all the best MSS, though supplied in the Complutensian edition and represented in the original Hebrew. The existing text of the LXX has only ἐπιπέπτωκε γὰρ ὁ φόβος ὑμῶν ἐφ' ἡμᾶς.

22. τέγος] The text of the MS here makes it difficult to decide whether we should read στεγος or τεγος. The former occurs in the LXX only once, Epist. Jer. 8; the latter not at all in the LXX, but in Aquila Num. xxv. 8. In these passages they are used for 'lupanar'; and τέγος especially has

CLEM.   5

cου, καὶ διαcωθήcονται· ὅcοι γὰρ ἐὰν εὑρεθῶcιν ἔξω τῆc οἰκίαc, ἀπολοῦνται. καὶ προσέθεντο αὐτῇ δοῦναι σημεῖον, ὅπως κρεμάσῃ ἐκ τοῦ οἴκου αὐτῆς κόκκινον, πρόδηλον ποιοῦντες ὅτι διὰ τοῦ αἵματος τοῦ Κυρίου λύτρωσις ἔσται πᾶσιν τοῖς πιστεύουσιν καὶ ἐλπίζουσιν ἐπὶ τὸν 5 Θεόν. Ὁρᾶτε, ἀγαπητοί, οὐ μόνον πίστις ἀλλὰ προφητεία ἐν τῇ γυναικὶ γέγονεν.

XIII. Ταπεινοφρονήσωμεν οὖν, ἀδελφοί, ἀποθέμενοι πᾶσαν ἀλαζονείαν καὶ τῦφος καὶ ἀφροσύνην καὶ

9 ἀλαζονείαν] αλαζονιαν A.

frequently this bad sense elsewhere (e.g. *Orac. Sibyll.* iii. 186, v. 387). But the word is perhaps not intended to bear the meaning here.

2. προσέθεντο κ.τ.λ.] '*They went on to give her a sign*'. The word is used in imitation of the LXX diction, where it very frequently renders יָסַף and thus reproduces the Hebraism 'to add to do'.

3. πρόδηλον κ.τ.λ.] So Justin *Dial.* 111 (p. 338) τὸ σύμβολον τοῦ κοκκίνου σπαρτίου... τὸ σύμβολον τοῦ αἵματος τοῦ Χριστοῦ ἐδήλου, δι' οὗ οἱ πάλαι πόρνοι καὶ ἄδικοι ἐκ πάντων τῶν ἐθνῶν σώζονται κ.τ.λ., perhaps getting the idea from this passage. Irenæus (iv. 20. 12) copies Justin, 'Raab fornicaria conservata est cum universa domo sua, fide signi coccini etc.' See also Origen *In Jes. Hom.* iii § 5 (II. p. 405), vi § 4 (II. p. 411), *In Matth. Comm. Ser.* 125 (III. p. 919). From this time forward it becomes a common type with the fathers. Barnabas (§ 7) similarly explains the scarlet wool of the scapegoat (see the note there). Compare also Heb. ix. 19, which may have suggested this application to Clement.

6. ἀλλὰ προφητεία] So Origen *in Jes. Hom.* iii. § 4 (II. p. 403) 'Sed et ista meretrix quæ eos suscepit ex meretrice efficitur jam propheta etc.'

XIII. 'Let us therefore be humble, and lay aside anger and pride. The Holy Spirit condemns all self-exaltation. Let us call to mind the words in which the Lord Jesus commends a gentle and forgiving spirit. The promise of grace is held out to patient forbearance'.

8. ἀποθέμενοι κ.τ.λ.] Comp. Heb. xii. 1 ὄγκον ἀποθέμενοι πάντα, James i. 21, 1 Pet. ii. 1.

9. τῦφος] A neuter form like ἔλεος, ζῆλος, πλοῦτος, etc., for which see Winer § ix. p. 78 and Jacobson's note on ζῆλος above § 4. For an example of τῦφος Jacobson here quotes *Conc. Ephes.* Can. 8 (Routh *Script. Eccl. Opusc.* p. 395). As the υ is long in the older writers but short in the more recent (e.g. Greg. Naz. pp. 490 v. 44, 880 v. 45, ed. Caillau), I have accentuated it according to this later usage; see L. Dindorf in *Steph. Thes.* s.v. and compare the analogy of στῦλος, στύλος, *Galatians* ii. 9.

11. μὴ καυχάσθω κ.τ.λ.] This passage is taken from 1 Sam. ii. 10, or from Jer. ix. 23, 24, or from both combined. The editors have overlooked the first of these passages, quoting only the second, though in several points Cle-

ὀργάς, καὶ ποιήσωμεν τὸ γεγραμμένον· λέγει γὰρ τὸ πνεῦμα τὸ ἅγιον· Μὴ καγχάσθω ὁ σοφὸς ἐν τῇ σοφίᾳ αὐτοῦ, μηδὲ ὁ ἰσχυρὸς ἐν τῇ ἰσχύϊ αὐτο[ῦ], μηδὲ ὁ πλούσιος ἐν τῷ πλούτῳ αὐτοῦ, ἀλλ' ἢ ὁ καυχώμενος ἐν Κυρίῳ καυχάσθω, τοῦ ἐκζητεῖν αὐτὸν καὶ ποιεῖν κρίμα καὶ δικαιοσύν[ην]· μάλιστα μεμνημένοι τῶν λόγων τοῦ Κυρίου Ἰησοῦ, οὓς ἐλάλησεν διδάσκω[ν] ἐπιείκειαν καὶ μακροθυμίαν· [οὕ]τως γὰρ εἶπεν· Ἐλεᾶτε ἵνα ἐλεηθ[ῆ]τε, ἀφίετε ἵνα ἀφεθῇ ὑμῖν· ὡ[ς] ποιεῖτε, οὕτω ποιηθήσεται ὑμ[ῖν]· ὡς δίδοτε, οὕτως δοθήσεται

16 ἐπιείκειαν] επιεικιαν A.

ment's language more closely resembles the first. The latter part in 1 Sam. ii. 10 runs ἀλλ' (ἀλλ' ἢ A) ἐν τούτῳ καυχάσθω ὁ καυχώμενος συνιεῖν καὶ γινώσκειν τὸν Κύριον καὶ ποιεῖν κρίμα καὶ δικαιοσύνην ἐν μέσῳ τῆς γῆς; while the corresponding passage in Jeremiah diverges still more from Clement's quotation. On the other hand S. Paul quotes twice (1 Cor. i. 31 καθὼς γέγραπται, 2 Cor. x. 17) ὁ καυχώμενος ἐν Κυρίῳ καυχάσθω. The resemblance of Clement's language to S. Paul may be explained in two ways; either (1) S. Paul does not quote literally but gives the sense of one or other passage (1 Sam. ii. 10 or Jer. ix. 23 sq.); and Clement, writing afterwards, unconsciously combines and confuses S. Paul's quotation with the original text; or (2) A recension of the text of Jeremiah (or Samuel) was in circulation in the first century which contained the exact words ὁ καυχώμενος ἐν Κυρίῳ καυχάσθω. The former is the more probable hypothesis. Iren. iv. 17. 3 quotes Jer. ix. 24 as it stands in our texts. In neither passage does the Hebrew aid in solving the difficulty. In 1 Sam. ii. 10 it is much shorter than and quite different from the LXX. Lucifer *pro*

Athan. ii. 2 (Galland. *Bibl. Vet. Patr.* VI. p. 180), as Cotelier remarks, seems to have read ἐκζητεῖν with Clement, for he has 'inquirere,' but the coincidence may be accidental. On the other hand Antioch. Palæst. *Hom*. xliii (*Bibl. Vet. Patr.* p. 1097, Paris 1624) quotes directly from 1 Sam. ii. 10, and betrays no connexion with Clement's language (see above p. 11).

15. μεμνημένοι κ.τ.λ.] Comp. Acts xx. 35 μνημονεύειν τῶν λόγων τοῦ Κυρίου Ἰησοῦ, ὅτι εἶπεν κ.τ.λ. See above § 2 ἥδιον λαμβάνοντες κ.τ.λ. (with the note), where Clement's language reflects the context of this quotation.

17. ἐλεᾶτε κ.τ.λ.] The same saying which is recorded in Matt. vii. 1, 2, Luke vi. 36—38, to which should be added Matt. v. 7 μακάριοι οἱ ἐλεήμονες ὅτι αὐτοὶ ἐλεηθήσονται, vi. 14 ἐὰν γὰρ ἀφῆτε τοῖς ἀνθρώποις κ.τ.λ., Luke vi. 31 καθὼς θέλετε ἵνα ποιῶσιν κ.τ.λ. As Clement's quotations are often very loose, we need not go beyond the Canonical Gospels for the source of this passage. The resemblance to the original is much closer here, than it is for instance in his account of Rahab above § 12. The hypothesis therefore that Clement derived the saying from oral tradition or from

5—2

[ὑμῖν]· ὡς κρίνετε, οὕτως κριθήσε[ται ὑμῖν· ὡς χρ]ηστεύεσθε, οὕτως χρη[στευθή]σεται ὑμῖν· ᾧ μέτρῳ με[τρεῖτε], ἐν αὐτῷ μετρηθήσεται ὑμῖν. [Ταύτῃ τ]ῇ ἐντολῇ καὶ τοῖς παραγ- γέλ[μασιν] τούτοις στηρίξωμεν ἑαυ[τοὺς εἰ]ς τὸ πορεύεσ- θαι ὑπηκόους [ἡμᾶ]ς τοῖς ἁγιοπρεπέσι λόγοις αὐ[τοῦ, τ]α- 5 πεινοφρονοῦντες. [φησ]ὶν γὰρ ὁ ἅγιος λόγος· Ἐπὶ τίνα [ἐπι]βλέψω, ἀλλ' ἢ ἐπὶ τὸν πραῢν καὶ [ἡσ]ύχιον καὶ τρέμοντά μου τὰ λόγια;

XIV. [Δί]καιον οὖν καὶ ὅσιον, ἄνδρες· ἀδελφοί, ὑπη- κόους ἡμᾶς μᾶλλον γενέσθαι τῷ Θεῷ ἢ τοῖς ἐν ἀλαζονείᾳ 10

1 κρίνετε] κρίνεται Λ.   χρηστεύεσθε] χρηστεύεσθαι Λ.   2 αὐτῷ] αυτη A.
4 ἑαυτοὺς εἰς] So Tisch. and Vansittart. This is better adapted to the space than some lost Gospel, is not needed. Polycarp indeed (*Phil.* 2) in much the same words quotes our Lord as saying ἀφίετε καὶ ἀφεθήσεται ὑμῖν, ἐλεεῖτε ἵνα ἐλεηθῆτε, but it can hardly be doubted from his manner of introducing the quotation (μνημονεύοντες ὧν εἶπεν ὁ Κύριος διδάσκων) that he had this passage of Clement in his mind and does not quote independently. On the form ἐλεᾶν (for ἐλεεῖν) see Winer § xv p. 97 sq., A. Buttmann p. 50: comp. *Clem. Hom.* xviii. 6. Previous editors needlessly read ἐ- λεεῖτε here.

1. ὡς χρηστεύεσθε] The corresponding words in S. Luke (vi. 36) are γίνεσθε οἰκτίρμονες. In Justin *Dial.* 96 and *Apol.* i. 15 they are quoted γίνεσθε δὲ χρηστοὶ καὶ οἰκτίρμονες, and in *Clem. Hom.* iii. 57 γίνεσθε ἀγαθοὶ καὶ οἰκτίρμονες. The verb χρηστεύεσθαι occurs 1 Cor. xiii. 4.

2. ᾧ μέτρῳ κ.τ.λ.] Quoted also indirectly *Clem. Hom.* xviii. 16 ᾧ μέτρῳ ἐμέτρησαν, μετρηθῇ αὐτοῖς τῷ ἴσῳ. See Mark iv. 24 besides the passages already quoted from the other Evangelists.

5. ἁγιοπρεπέσι] Compare Polyc.

Phil. 1. This is apparently the earliest passage in which the word occurs. Suicer gives it a place 'quia a lexicographis omissa', but does not quote either of these passages in the Apostolic fathers.

6. ἐπὶ τίνα κ.τ.λ.] A quotation from the LXX of Is. lxvi. 2 with slight and unimportant variations. For a distinction between πραῢς and ἡσύχιος see Bengel on 1 Pet. iii. 4 (where both words occur).

XIV. 'We ought to obey God rather than man. If we follow men, we shall plunge ourselves into strife and peril; if we follow God, we shall be gentle and loving. The Scriptures teach us, that the guileless and meek shall inherit the earth; but that the proud and insolent shall be blotted out'.

9. Δίκαιον κ.τ.λ.] This passage as far as καλῶς ἔχοντος is quoted in Nicon the Monk, in an extract given by Cotelier from the Paris MSS *Reg.* 2418, 2423, 2424. He strings together with this passage quotations from §§ 15, 46, of this epistle, and § 3 of the second. See the several references.

11. μυσεροῦ] The form μυσερὸς

XIV] TO THE CORINTHIANS. 69

καὶ ἀκαταστασίᾳ μυσεροῦ ζήλους ἀρχηγοῖς ἐξακολου-
θεῖν. βλάβην γὰρ οὐ τὴν τυχοῦσαν, μᾶλλον δὲ κίνδυνον ὑποίσομεν μέγαν, ἐὰν ῥιψοκινδύνως ἐπιδῶμεν ἑαυτοὺς τοῖς θελήμασιν τῶν ἀνθρώπων, οἵτινες ἐξακοντί-
5 ζουσιν εἰς ἔριν καὶ στάσεις εἰς τὸ ἀπαλλοτριῶσαι ἡμᾶς
τοῦ καλῶς ἔχοντος. χρηστευσώμεθα αὐτοῖς κατὰ τὴν
εὐσπλαγχνίαν καὶ γλυκύτητα τοῦ ποιήσαντος ἡμᾶς.
γέγραπται γάρ· Χρηϲτοὶ ἔϲονται οἰκήτορεϲ ϲῆϲ, ἄκακοι
δὲ ὑπολειφθήϲονται ἐπ' ἀὐτῆϲ· οἱ δὲ παρανομοῦντεϲ ἐξο-
10 λεθρευθήϲονται ἀπ' ἀὐτῆϲ· καὶ πάλιν λέγει· Εἶδον ἀϲεβῆ

ἑαυτοὺς πρός (Jacobs.). 10 ἀλαζονείᾳ] ἀλαζονια Α. 15 ἔριν] A. αἱρέσεις Nicon.
στάσεις] στασισ A. εἰς τό] A. τοῦ Nicon. 20 εἶδον ἀσεβῆ] ιδονασεβην A.

occurs again below § 30; and in both places the editors have altered it to μυσαρός. This is not necessary: see Lobeck *Pathol.* p. 276. In Lev. xviii. 23 it is so written in A; and similarly in Mark i. 42 ἐκαθερίσθη is read in the best MSS: see Tischendorf on Acts x. 15 and prol. p. l (ed. 7), Winer § v. p. 56.

ἀρχηγοῖς] Comp. § 51 ἀρχηγοὶ τῆς στάσεως.

13. ῥιψοκινδύνως] '*in a foolhardy spirit*': Appian *Civ.* i. 103. It does not occur in the LXX or New Testament.

14. ἐξακοντίζουσιν] here appears to mean, 'launch out'. Generally, when it occurs metaphorically, λόγους or γλώσσας would be understood, if not expressed.

16. αὐτοῖς] '*towards them*', the leaders of the schism; comp. 2 Thess. iii. 15 μὴ ὡς ἐχθρὸν ἡγεῖσθε κ.τ.λ. This must be done 'in imitation of the compassion of the Creator himself' (κατὰ τὴν εὐσπλαγχνίαν κ.τ.λ.); comp. Matt. v. 45. Others substitute αὐτοῖς = ἀλλήλοις, but this is not so good. Moreover, as the contracted form αὐτοῦ etc., for ἑαυτοῦ etc., seems never to

occur in the New Testament, it is a question whether Clement would have used it: see the note on αὐτῶν § 12.

18. χρηστοὶ κ.τ.λ.] From Prov. ii. 21, 22. The first part of the quotation χρηστοί...ἐν αὐτῇ is found in A with a very slight variation (and partially in א), but B omits the words; the second runs in all the best MSS of the LXX, ὁδοὶ [δὲ] ἀσεβῶν ἐκ γῆς ὀλοῦνται, οἱ δὲ παράνομοι ἐξωσθήσονται ἀπ' αὐτῆς. In quoting the latter part Clement seems to be confusing it with Ps. xxxvii. 39 οἱ δὲ παράνομοι ἐξολοθρευθήσονται ἐπὶ τὸ αὐτό, which occurs in the context of his next quotation.

19. ἐξολεθρευθήσονται] On the varying forms ὀλεθρεύειν and ὀλοθρεύειν see Tischendorf *Nov. Test.* p. xlix. Our MS for the most part writes the word with an ε.

20. εἶδον ἀσεβῆ κ.τ.λ.] From the LXX of Ps. xxxvii. 36—38 with unimportant variations. The LXX has καὶ ἐζήτησα αὐτὸν καὶ οὐχ εὑρέθη ὁ τόπος αὐτοῦ. In the Hebrew there is nothing corresponding to ὁ τόπος αὐτοῦ. Without hinting that he is quoting from a previous writer, Cle-

ὑπερυψούμενον καὶ ἐπαιρόμενον ὡς τὰς κέδρους τοῦ Λιβάνου, καὶ παρῆλθον καὶ ἰδοὺ οὐκ ἦν, καὶ ἐξεζήτησα τὸν τόπον αὐτοῦ καὶ οὐχ εὗρον. Φύλασσε ἀκακίαν καὶ ἴδε εὐθύτητα, ὅτι ἐστὶν ἐνκατάλειμμα ἀνθρώπῳ εἰρηνικῷ.

XV. Τοίνυν κολληθῶμεν τοῖς μετ' εὐσεβείας εἰρηνεύουσιν, καὶ μὴ τοῖς μεθ' ὑποκρίσεως βουλομένοις εἰρήνην. λέγει γάρ που· Οὗτος ὁ λαὸς τοῖς χείλεσίν με τιμᾷ, ἡ δὲ καρδία αὐτῶν πόρρω ἄπεστιν ἀπ' ἐμοῦ. καὶ πάλιν· Τῷ στόματι αὐτῶν εὐλογοῦσαν, τῇ δὲ καρδίᾳ αὐτῶν κατηρῶντο. [κ]αὶ πάλιν λέγει· Ἠγάπησαν αὐτὸν τῷ στόματι αὐτῶν

1 ἐπαιρόμενον] αιπερομενον A.   4 ἐνκατάλειμμα] ενκαταλιμμα A.
5 κολληθῶμεν] A.   ἀκολουθήσωμεν Nicon.   8 ἄπεστιν] A. ἀπέχει Nicon. See
below.   9 κατηρῶντο] Tisch. says of the MS reading 'κατηρουντο certum est,'

ment of Alexandria, *Strom.* iv. 6 (p. 577), strings together these same six quotations, beginning with Ps. xxxvii. 36 sq. and ending with Ps. xii. 4 sq. (παρρησιάσομαι ἐν αὐτῷ). In comparing the two, we observe of the Alexandrian Clement, that (1) In his first passage he restores the text of the LXX, and quotes καὶ ἐζήτησα αὐτὸν κ.τ.λ.; (2) For the most part he follows Clement of Rome, e.g. in the remarkable omission noted below (on ἄλαλα γενηθήτω κ.τ.λ.); (3) He inserts between the quotations an explanatory word or sentence of his own; (4) He ends this string of quotations with the very words of the Roman Clement, ταπεινοφρονούντων γάρ... τὸ ποίμνιον αὐτοῦ, without any indication that he is citing from another.

4. ἐνκατάλειμμα] '*a remnant*,' i.e. a family or a memorial of some kind, as in ver. 39 τὰ ἐγκαταλείμματα τῶν ἀσεβῶν ἐξολοθρεύσεται: comp. Ps. xxxiv. 16 τοῦ ἐξολοθρεῦσαι ἐκ γῆς τὸ μνημόσυνον αὐτῶν, quoted by Clement below § 22.

XV. 'Let us then attach ourselves to the guileless and peaceful; but avoid hypocrites who make a show of peace. Against such the denunciations of Scripture are frequent and severe; against the idle profession of God's service—against the deceitful and proud lips.'

7. Οὗτος ὁ λαός] From Is. xxix. 13, which is quoted also Matt. xv. 8, Mark vii. 6. Clement follows the Evangelists rather than the original text. For the opening words of the original, ἐγγίζει μοι ὁ λαὸς οὗτος ἐν τῷ στόματι αὐτοῦ καὶ ἐν τοῖς χείλεσιν αὐτῶν τιμῶσίν με, they give the sentence in a compressed form οὗτος ὁ λαός (ὁ λαὸς οὗτος Matt.) τοῖς χείλεσίν με τιμᾷ as here. Both Evangelists have ἀπέχει with the LXX, where Clement has ἄπεστιν. Clem. Alex. follows our Clement, modifying the form however to suit his context. In *Clem. Rom.* ii. § 3 it is quoted exactly as here, except that ὁ λαὸς οὗτος stands for οὗτος ὁ λαός. Justin quotes the LXX, *Dial.* 78 (p. 305).

8. τῷ στόματι κ.τ.λ.] From LXX Ps. lxii. 4, with unimportant variations.

9. εὐλογοῦσαν] for εὐλόγουν. See Sturz *Dial. Mac.* p. 58, and the refe-

TO THE CORINTHIANS.

καὶ τῇ γλώσσῃ αὑ[τ]ῶν ἐψεύσαντο αὐτόν, ἡ δὲ καρδία αὐτῶν
οὐκ εὐθεῖα μετ' αὐτοῦ, οὐδὲ ἐπιστώθησαν ἐν τῇ διαθήκῃ
αὐτοῦ. Ἄλαλα γενηθήτω τὰ χείλη τὰ δόλια. Ἐξολεθρεύσαι
Κύριος πάντα τὰ χείλη τὰ δόλια, γλῶσσαν μεγαλορήμονα,
τοὺς εἰπόντας, Τὴν γλῶσσαν ἡμῶν μεγαλύνωμεν, τὰ χείλη
ἡμῶν παρ' ἡμῖν ἐστιν· τίς ἡμῶν κύριός ἐστιν; ἀπὸ τῆς
ταλαιπωρίας τῶν πτωχῶν καὶ ἀπὸ τοῦ στεναγμοῦ τῶν πενή-
των νῦν ἀναστήσομαι, λέγει Κύριος· θήσομαι ἐν σωτηρίᾳ
παρρησιάσομαι ἐν αὐτῷ.

but I looked several times and could not distinguish it. On such forms as κατηρουντο see Tisch. *Nov. Test.* prol. p. lvii (ed. 7). τὰ χείλη τὰ δόλια] om. A. See below.

13 ἐξολεθρεύσαι Κύριος πάντα 18 ἀναστήσομαι] αναστησομεν A.

rences in Winer § xiii. p. 89. In the LXX here אB have εὐλογοῦσαν. Clem. Alex. (edd.) quotes εὐλογοῦσι.

10. *ἠγάπησαν κ.τ.λ.*] From Ps. lxxviii. 36, 37, almost word for word. Ἐπιστώθησαν is here a translation of נאמנו, 'were stedfast.' Though ἠγάπησαν is read by the principal MSS (אB) of the LXX, the original reading was probably ἠπάτησαν, as this corresponds with the Hebrew.

13. *ἄλαλα κ.τ.λ.*] The words ἄλαλα γενηθήτω τὰ χείλη τὰ δόλια are taken from the LXX, Ps. xxxi. 19. Those which follow are from the LXX Ps. xii. 3—6 ἐξολοθρεύσαι Κύριος πάντα τὰ χείλη τὰ δόλια [καὶ] γλῶσσαν μεγαλορήμονα τοὺς εἰπόντας κ.τ.λ. Since in the quotation of Clement, as it stands in the MS, γλῶσσαν μεγαλορήμονα has no government, it seems clear that the transcriber's eye has passed from one τὰ χείλη τὰ δόλια to the other and omitted the introductory words of the second quotation. I have therefore inserted the words ἐξολεθρεύσαι Κύριος πάντα τὰ χείλη τὰ δόλια. Wotton and others detected the omission but made the insertion in the form [καὶ Ἐξ. Κ. π. τ. χ. τὰ δόλια καὶ]. This does not explain the scribe's error. The καὶ before γλῶσσαν μεγαλορήμονα, though found in AB, is marked as to be erased in א and is omitted in many MSS in Holmes and Parsons; and in our Clement's text of the LXX it must have been wanting. The Hebrew omits the conjunction in the corresponding place. The existing omission in the text of the Roman Clement seems to be as old as the end of the second century, for his Alexandrian namesake (see the note on εἶδον ἀσεβῆ κ.τ.λ. above) gives the passage, ἄλαλα γενηθήτω πάντα τὰ χείλη τὰ δόλια καὶ γλῶσσαν μεγαλορήμονα κ.τ.λ., inserting a καὶ before γλῶσσαν, though quoting it in the main as it is quoted here. Or we have the alternative of supposing that a transcriber of the Alexandrian Clement has independently made a similar omission to the transcriber of the Roman. For the form μεγαλορήμονα see the note on ἐξερίζωσεν § 6.

16. *παρ' ἡμῖν*] '*in our power, our own.*' It represents the Hebrew אתנו. The dative is correctly read also by Clem. Alex. and some MSS of the LXX: but אAB have παρ' ἡμῶν.

18. *ἀναστήσομαι*] The reading of the MS αναστησομεν has arisen from αναστησομε (see p. 25), whence ανα-

XVI. Ταπεινοφρονούντων γάρ έστιν ὁ Χριστός, οὐκ ἐπαιρομένων ἐπὶ τὸ ποίμνιον αὐτοῦ. τὸ σκῆπτρον τῆς μεγαλωσύνης τοῦ Θεοῦ, ὁ Κύριος ἡμῶν Χριστὸς Ἰησοῦς, οὐκ ἦλθεν ἐν κόμπῳ ἀλαζονείας οὐδὲ ὑπερηφανίας, καίπερ δυνάμενος, ἀλλὰ ταπεινοφρονῶν, καθὼς τὸ 5 πνεῦμα τὸ ἅγιον περὶ αὐτοῦ ἐλάλησεν· φησὶν γάρ· Κγριε, τίc ἐπίcτεγcεn τῇ ἀκοῇ ἡμῶn; καὶ ὁ βραχίωn Κγρίογ τίνι ἀπεκαλγφθη; ἀνηγγείλαμεν ἐναντίον αγτογ, ὡc παιδίον, ὡc ῥίζα ἐν γῇ διψώcῃ· ογκ ἔcτιν εἶδοc αγτῷ, ογδὲ δόξα·

4 ἀλαζονείας] αλαζονιασ A.   8 ἀνηγγείλαμεν] ανηγγιλαμεν A.

στησομε̄ : comp. αἰχμαλωσιᾶ (αἰχμαλωσία for αἰχμαλωσια (αἰχμαλωσίᾳ) in ii § 6. So too § 41 συνειδησιν (συνειδησῖ) for συνειδησι = συνειδήσει. θήσομαι κ.τ.λ.] '*I will place him in safety, I will deal boldly by him.*' The Hebrew of the last clause is wholly different from the LXX. For σωτηρίᾳ Clem. Alex. and the LXX have σωτηρίῳ.
XVI. 'Christ is the friend of the lowly: He Himself is our great pattern of humility. This is the leading feature in the portrait which the evangelic prophet has drawn of the lamb led to the slaughter. This too is declared by the lips of the Psalmist. If then He our Lord was so lowly, what ought we His servants to be?'
2. οὐκ ἐπαιρομένων κ.τ.λ.] Comp. 1 Pet. v. 3, Acts xx. 29. The word ποίμνιον occurs again §§ 44, 54, 57.
τὸ σκῆπτρον κ.τ.λ.] The expression is apparently suggested by Heb. i. 8, where Ps. xlv. 6 ῥάβδος εὐθύτητος ἡ ῥάβδος τῆς βασιλείας σου is applied to our Lord. Fell refers to the application of the same text made by Justin *Dial.* 63 (pp. 286 sq.) to show ὅτι καὶ προσκυνητός ἐστι καὶ Θεὸς καὶ Χριστός. Jerome *in Isai.* lii. 13 (IV. p. 612) quotes this passage of Clement, 'Sceptrum Dei, Dominus Jesus Christus, non venit in jactantia superbiae, quum possit omnia, sed in humilitate.' This application of our Lord's example bears a resemblance to Phil. ii. 6 sq. and may be an echo of it.
4. ἀλαζονείας κ.τ.λ.] The adjectives ἀλαζὼν and ὑπερήφανος occur together, Rom. i. 30, 2 Tim. iii. 2. The one refers to the expression, the other to the thought: see the distinction in Trench *N. T. Syn.* § xxix. 1st ser.
7. Κύριε κ.τ.λ.] A Messianic application is made of this 53rd chapter of Isaiah by S. Matthew viii. 17 (ver. 4), by S. Mark xv. 28 (ver. 12), by S. Luke xxii. 37 (ver. 12), by S. John i. 29 (ver. 4, 7), xii. 38 (ver. 1), by S. Paul Rom. x. 16 (ver. 1), and by S. Peter 1 Pet. ii. 23 sq. (ver. 5, 9). Barnabas also (§ 5) applies ver. 5, 7, to our Lord; and Justin both in the *Apology* and in the *Dialogue* interprets this chapter so frequently: see esp. *Apol.* I. 50, 51 (p. 85 sq.), *Dial.* 13 (p. 230 sq.), in both which passages it is quoted in full. For early Jewish Messianic interpretations of this chapter see Hengstenberg *Christol.* II p. 310 sq. (Eng. trans.), Schöttgen *Hor. Hebr.* II. p. 138 sq.

10 καὶ εἴδομεν αὐτόν, καὶ οὐκ εἶχεν εἶδος οὐδὲ κάλλος, ἀλλὰ
τὸ εἶδος αὐτοῦ ἄτιμον, ἐκλεῖπον παρὰ τὸ εἶδος τῶν ἀνθρώ-
πων· ἄνθρωπος ἐν πληγῇ ὢν καὶ πόνῳ καὶ εἰδὼς φέρειν
μαλακίαν, ὅτι ἀπέστραπται τὸ πρόσωπον αὐτοῦ, ἠτιμάσθη
καὶ οὐκ ἐλογίσθη. οὗτος τὰς ἁμαρτίας ἡμῶν φέρει καὶ περὶ
15 ἡμῶν ὀδυνᾶται, καὶ ἡμεῖς ἐλογισάμεθα αὐτὸν εἶναι ἐν πόνῳ
καὶ ἐν πληγῇ καὶ ἐν κακώσει. αὐτὸς δὲ ἐτραυματίσθη διὰ
τὰς ἁμαρτίας ἡμῶν καὶ μεμαλάκισται διὰ τὰς ἀνομίας ἡμῶν.
παιδεία εἰρήνης ἡμῶν ἐπ' αὐτόν· τῷ μώλωπι αὐτοῦ ἡμεῖς

11 ἐκλεῖπον] εκλιπον A.   18 παιδεία] παιδια A.

Clement's quotation for the most part follows the LXX tolerably closely. The more important divergences from the LXX are noticed below. The LXX itself differs considerably from the Hebrew in many points.

8. ἀνηγγείλαμεν κ.τ.λ.] The LXX reading here is devoid of sense and must be corrupt, though the MSS and early quotations all present ἀνηγγείλαμεν. As this word corresponds to the Hebrew ויעל (Aq. Theod. ἀναβήσεται, Symm. ἀνέβη), Is. Voss proposed ἀνετείλαμεν (see Grabe *Diss. de Variis Vitiis LXX*, p. 38); but even this alteration is not enough, and we should require ἀνέτειλεν. The following meaning however seems generally to have been attached to the words; 'We—the preachers—announced Him before the Lord; as a child is He, as a root etc.' (see Eusebius and Jerome on the passage); but Justin *Dial.* 42 (p. 261) strangely explains ὡς παιδίον of the child-like submission of the Church to Christ. The interpretation of Origen *ad Rom.* viii. § 6 (IV. p. 627) is not quite clear. The fathers of the fourth and fifth centuries generally interpret ὡς ῥίζα ἐν γῇ διψώσῃ as referring to the miraculous con-

ception. In the order ἐν. αὐτ. ὡς παιδ. Clement agrees with אA Justin p. 230 (p. 85, 260 sq., ἐνώπιον αὐτοῦ); and so the old Latin, e.g. Tertull. *adv. Marc.* iii. 17 (and elsewhere) 'Annuntiavimus coram ipso velut puerulus etc.': but B has ὡς παιδ. ἐν. αὐτ., the order of the Hebrew.

11. παρὰ τὸ εἶδ. τ. ἀνθρ.] The LXX א, Clem. Alex. p. 440, παρὰ πάντας (א corr. from παν) τοὺς υἱοὺς τῶν ἀνθρώπων; B, Justin p. 230, Tertull. *adv. Marc.* iii. 7, *adv. Jud.* 14, παρὰ τοὺς υἱοὺς τῶν ἀνθρώπων; A, Tertull. *adv. Marc.* iii. 17, παρὰ πάντας ἀνθρώπους; Justin p. 85, Clem. Alex. p. 252, παρὰ τοὺς ἀνθρώπους.

12. καὶ πόνῳ] Wanting in the LXX. The words must have crept in from below, ἐν πόνῳ καὶ ἐν πληγῇ, either by a lapse of memory on Clement's part or by an error in his copy of the LXX or in the transcription of Clement's own text.

13. ἀπέστραπται] The original is במסתר פנים ממנו, '*as hiding the face from him*' or '*from us*'. The LXX seem to adopted the latter sense, though they have omitted ממנו; '*His face is turned away*', i.e. as one ashamed or loathed; comp. Lev. xiii. 45.

17. ἁμαρτίας, ἀνομίας] So B, Justin p.

ἰάθημεν. πάντες ὡς πρόβατα ἐπλανήθημεν, ἄνθρωπος τῇ ὁδῷ αὐτοῦ ἐπλανήθη· καὶ Κύριος παρέδωκεν αὐτὸν ὑπὲρ τῶν ἁμαρτιῶν ἡμῶν. καὶ αὐτὸς διὰ τὸ κεκακῶσθαι οὐκ ἀνοίγει τὸ στόμα· ὡς πρόβατον ἐπὶ σφαγὴν ἤχθη, καὶ ὡς ἀμνὸς ἐναντίον τοῦ κείραντος ἄφωνος, οὕτως οὐκ ἀνοίγει 5 τὸ στόμα αὐτοῦ. ἐν τῇ ταπεινώσει ἡ κρίσις αὐτοῦ ἤρθη· τὴν γενεὰν αὐτοῦ τίς διηγήσεται; ὅτι αἴρεται ἀπὸ τῆς γῆς ἡ ζωὴ αὐτοῦ· ἀπὸ τῶν ἀνομιῶν τοῦ λαοῦ μου ἥκει εἰς θάνατον. καὶ δώσω τοὺς πονηροὺς ἀντὶ τῆς ταφῆς αὐτοῦ καὶ

6 κρίσις] κρισεισ A.

230; but אA, Barnab. § 5, Justin p. 85, transpose the words, reading ἀνομίας in the first clause and ἁμαρτίας in the second.

1. ἄνθρωπος] 'each man', distributive; a Hebraism not uncommon in the LXX; and the use is somewhat similar in John ii. 25, 1 Cor. xi. 28.

2. ὑπὲρ τῶν ἁμαρτιῶν] The LXX has ταῖς ἁμαρτίαις, and so Justin pp. 86, 230, Clem. Alex. p. 138; but Tertull. adv. Prax. 30 ' pro delictis nostris'.

6. ἐν τῇ ταπεινώσει κ.τ.λ.] This passage is also quoted from the LXX in Acts viii. 33 ἐν τῇ ταπεινώσει [αὐτοῦ] ἡ κρίσις αὐτοῦ ἤρθη, where the first αὐτοῦ should be omitted with the best MSS, so that S. Luke's quotation accords exactly with the LXX. For the probable meaning of the LXX here see the commentators on Acts l.c.; and for patristic interpretations of γενεά, Suicer I. p. 744, s.v. The Hebrew is different.

8. ἥκει] ἤχθη LXX and Tertull. adv. Jud. 10; but ἥκει is read by Justin pp. 86, 230, though elsewhere he has ἤχθη p. 261 (MSS ἤχθην), comp. p. 317 ὅτι ἀπὸ τῶν ἀνομιῶν τοῦ λαοῦ ἀχθήσεται εἰς θάνατον. As ἤχθη may easily have been introduced from ver. 7, ἥκει was perhaps the original reading of the LXX; and so it stands in some MSS in Holmes and Parsons.

9. καὶ δώσω κ.τ.λ.] The LXX clearly means that the wicked and the wealthy should die in requital for His death: as Justin Dial. 32 (p. 249) ἀντὶ τοῦ θανάτου αὐτοῦ τοὺς πλουσίους θανατωθήσεσθαι. Thus the reference to the crucifixion of the thieves and the entombment in Joseph's grave, which the original has suggested to later Christian writers, is rendered impossible in the LXX. This application however is not made in the Gospels, where only ver. 12 ἐν τοῖς ἀνόμοις ἐλογίσθη is quoted in this connexion, nor (I believe) in any father of the second century nor even in Tertullian or Origen.

11. οὐδὲ εὑρέθη δόλος] So A in the LXX, but אB (corrected however in א by later hands) have simply οὐδὲ δόλον, following the Hebrew more closely. In 1 Pet. ii. 22 are the words ὃς ἁμαρτίαν οὐκ ἐποίησεν οὐδὲ εὑρέθη δόλος ἐν τῷ στόματι αὐτοῦ, though this is not given as a direct quotation and may have been intended merely as a paraphrase, like much of the context. But it is quoted by Justin also καὶ οὐχ εὑρέθη δόλος p. 230, and οὐδὲ εὑρέθη δόλος p. 86, though in a third passage he has οὐδὲ δόλον p. 330.

10 τοὺς πλουσίους ἀντὶ τοῦ θανάτου αὐτοῦ· ὅτι ἀνομίαν οὐκ
ἐποίησεν, οὐδὲ εὑρέθη δόλος ἐν τῷ στόματι αὐτοῦ. καὶ
Κύριος βούλεται καθαρίσαι αὐτὸν τῆς πληγῆς· ἐὰν δῶτε περὶ
ἁμαρτίας, ἡ ψυχὴ ὑμῶν ὄψεται σπέρμα μακρόβιον. καὶ Κύριος
βούλεται ἀφελεῖν ἀπὸ τοῦ πόνου τῆς ψυχῆς αὐτοῦ, δεῖξαι
15 αὐτῷ φῶς καὶ πλάσαι τῇ συνέσει, δικαιῶσαι δίκαιον εὖ δου-
λεύοντα πολλοῖς· καὶ τὰς ἁμαρτίας αὐτῶν αὐτὸς ἀνοίσει. διὰ
τοῦτο αὐτὸς κληρονομήσει πολλοὺς καὶ τῶν ἰσχυρῶν μεριεῖ
σκῦλα· ἀνθ᾽ ὧν παρεδόθη εἰς θάνατον ἡ ψυχὴ αὐτοῦ καὶ τοῖς

13 ὄψεται] εψεται A.

And so likewise Tertull. *adv. Jud.* 10 'nec dolus in ore ejus inventus est,' Origen I. p. 91 C, II. pp. 250 D, 287 C, and Hippol. *in Psalm.* 7 (p. 191 Lagarde). The passage of S. Peter might have influenced the form of quotation and even the reading of the MSS in some cases: but the passages where οὐδὲ εὑρέθη δόλος appears are so numerous, that we must suppose it to have been so read in some copies of the LXX at least as early as the first century. This reading is found in several MSS in Holmes and Parsons.

12. τῆς πληγῆς] So אB Justin pp. 86, 230; but A (LXX) has ἀπὸ τῆς πληγῆς. For καθαρίζειν or καθαίρειν τινος comp. Herod. i. 44. So the intransitive verb καθαρεύειν (Plato *Epist.* viii. p. 356 E) and the adjective καθαρός (Herod. ii. 38) may take a genitive.

δῶτε] So also LXX (אAB) and Justin pp. 86, 230 (MSS, but many edd. δῶσαι). Eusebius comments on this as the LXX reading, and Jerome distinctly states it to be so. Accordingly it was interpreted, 'If ye make an offering' (or, translated into its Christian equivalent, 'If ye be truly contrite and pray for pardon'). With δοῦναι περὶ comp. Heb. v. 3 περὶ ἑαυ-

τοῦ προσφέρειν περὶ ἁμαρτιῶν. The meaning of the original is doubtful, but δῶτε seems to be a rendering of תשים taken as a second person, '*thou shalt give*'. The reading δῶται '*give himself*', which some editors here would adopt, is quite late and can hardly stand.

13. Κύριος βούλεται κ.τ.λ.] The LXX departs very widely from the Hebrew, but its meaning is fairly clear. For ἀφελεῖν ἀπό, '*to diminish from*', comp. Rev. xxii. 19, Exod. v. 11, and so frequently. Tertullian however reads τὴν ψυχήν, 'eximere a morte animam ejus', *adv. Jud.* 10. Πλάσαι (sc. αὐτόν) stands in the present text of the LXX (אAB), and in Justin pp. 86, 230, nor is there any indication of a different reading: but, as ישבע stands in the corresponding place in the Hebrew, the original reading of the LXX was probaby πλῆσαι, as Grabe suggested (*Diss. de Vit. Var. LXX*, p. 39). Compare the vv. ll. ῥάσσει and ῥήσσει in Mark ix. 18.

18. τοῖς ἀνόμοις] ἐν τοῖς ἀνόμοις LXX (אAB), Justin pp. 86, 231, (though in the immediate neighbourhood of the first passage he has μετὰ τῶν ἀνόμων, p. 85): μετὰ ἀνόμων, Luke xxii. 37, († Mark xv. 28†).

76 THE EPISTLE OF CLEMENT [XVI

ἀνόμοιc ἐλοΓίcθH· καὶ αὐτὸc ἁμαρτίαc πολλῶν ἀνήνεΓκεν καὶ
διὰ τὰc ἁμαρτίαc αὐτῶν παρεδόθH. Καὶ πάλιν αὐτός φησιν·
᾿Εγὼ δέ εἰμι cκώληξ καὶ οὐκ ἄνθρωπος, ὄνειδος ἀνθρώπων
καὶ ἐξουθένHμα λαοῦ. πάντες οἱ θεωροῦντές με ἐξεμυκτHρι-
cαν με, ἐλάλHcαν ἐν χείλεcιν, ἐκίνHcαν κεφαλήν, ῎Hλπιcεν 5
ἐπὶ Κύριον, ῥυcάcθω αὐτόν, cωcάτω αὐτόν, ὅτι θέλει αὐτόν.
῾Ορᾶτε, ἄνδρες ἀγαπητοί, τίς ὁ ὑπογραμμὸς ὁ δεδομέ-
νος ἡμῖν· εἰ γὰρ ὁ Κύριος οὕτως ἐταπεινοφρόνησεν, τί
ποιήσωμεν ἡμεῖς οἱ ὑπὸ τὸν ζυγὸν τῆς χάριτος αὐτοῦ
δι' αὐτοῦ ἐλθόντες; 10
XVII. Μιμηταὶ γενώμεθα κἀκείνων, οἵτινες ἐν δέρ-

5 ἐκίνηςαν] εκεινησαν A.   10 ἐλθόντες] ελθοντοσ A.   17 ταπεινοφρονῶν]

2. αὐτός] Christ Himself, in whose person the Psalmist is speaking. Comp. § 22, where αὐτὸς προσκαλεῖται has a similar reference. The words are an exact quotation from the LXX Ps. xxii. 6—8. The application to our Lord is favoured by Matt. xxvii. 43.

7. ὁ ὑπογραμμός] See the note above on § 5.

9. τὸν ζυγὸν τῆς χάριτος] a verbal paradox, explained by the 'easy yoke' of Matt. xi. 29, 30. The following δι' αὐτοῦ is 'through His humiliation and condescension'.

XVII. 'We should also copy the humility of the prophets who went about in sheepskins and goatskins; of Abraham the friend of God, who confessed that he was mere dust and ashes; of Job the blameless, who condemned himself and all men as impure in the sight of God; of Moses the trusty servant, who declared his nothingness before the Lord'.

The whole of this chapter and part of the next are quoted by Clem. Alex. Strom. iv. 16 (p. 610) in continuation of § 9 sq. (see the note there): but he cites so freely, abridging and enlarging at pleasure, and interspersing his own commentary (e.g. τὴν οὐχ ὑποπίπτουσαν νόμῳ αἰνιττόμενος ἁμαρτίαν γνωστικῶς μετριοπαθῶν), that he cannot generally be taken as an authority for the text, and (except in special cases) I have not thought it worth while to record his variations.

11. ἐν δέρμασιν κ.τ.λ.] From Heb. xi. 37. For the prophets' dress comp. Zach. xiii. 4 'The prophets shall be ashamed...neither shall they wear a garment of hair' (where the LXX omits the negative and destroys the sense, καὶ ἐνδύσονται δέρριν τριχίνην); see also Bleek Hebr. l.c., Stanley's Sinai and Palestine p. 305. The word μηλωτή is used in the LXX to translate אַדֶּרֶת, paludamentum, 'a mantle'; e.g. of Elijah and Elisha, 1 Kings xix. 13, 19, 2 Kings ii. 8, 13, 14. Though not a strict equivalent, it was doubtless adopted as describing the recognised dress of the prophet. Ezekiel is fitly classed with the older prophets, as representing a stern and ascetic type. His dress is nowhere mentioned in the O.T., but might

μασιν αἰγείοις καὶ μηλωταῖς περιεπάτησαν κηρύσσοντες τὴν ἔλευσιν τοῦ Χριστοῦ· λέγομεν δὲ Ἡλίαν καὶ
Ἐλισαιὲ ἔτι δὲ καὶ Ἰεζεκιήλ, τοὺς προφήτας· πρὸς τού-
15 τοις καὶ τοὺς μεμαρτυρημένους. ἐμαρτυρήθη μεγάλως
Ἀβραὰμ καὶ φίλος προσηγορεύθη τοῦ Θεοῦ, καὶ λέγει
ἀτενίζων εἰς τὴν δόξαν τοῦ Θεοῦ, ταπεινοφρονῶν· Ἐγὼ
Δέ ειμι Γῆ καὶ cποΔός. ἔτι δὲ καὶ περὶ Ἰὼβ οὕτως γέ-
γραπται· Ἰὼβ ἦν Δίκαιος καὶ ἄμεμπτος, ἀληθινός, θεοce-
20 βής, ἀπεχόμενος ἀπὸ παντὸς κακοῦ· ἀλλ' αὐτὸς ἑαυτοῦ
κατηγ[ορεῖ λέγων], Οὐδεὶς καθαρὸς ἀπὸ ῥύπ[ου, οὐδ' εἰ]

ταπεινοφρωνων Α.   19 ἀληθινός] αληθεινοσ Α. ἀληθινὸς καὶ Clem. Alex. 611.
21 κατηγορεῖ λέγων] See below.   οὐδ' εἰ] See below.

be taken for granted as the ordinary garb of his office. Clem. Alex. after μηλωταῖς adds καὶ τριχῶν καμηλείων πλέγμασιν, as after Ἰεζεκιὴλ he adds καὶ Ἰωάννην, the former interpolation preparing the way for the latter.

14. Ἐλισαιέ] A frequent form in the best MSS of the LXX (with a single or a double σ), e.g. 2 Kings ii. 1 sq. The editors have quite needlessly changed it into Ἐλισσαῖον, which is the form in Clem. Alex.

τοὺς προφήτας] Epiphanius has been thought to refer to this passage in *Hær.* xxx. 15, αὐτὸς (Κλήμης) ἐγκωμιάζει Ἡλίαν καὶ Δαβὶδ καὶ Σαμψὼν καὶ πάντας τοὺς προφήτας κ.τ.λ.; but the reference must be to the spurious *Epistles on Virginity*, where Samson, as well as the others, is mentioned by name (see above p. 15).

15. τοὺς μεμαρτυρημένους] *'borne witness to, approved'*, whether by God or by men; see below §§ 18, 19, 44, 47, Acts vi. 3, Heb. xi. 2, 4, 5, 39, 3 Joh. 12, etc. Here the testimony of God's voice in Scripture seems to be intended, as appears from the examples following.

16. φίλος προσηγορεύθη] Comp. James ii. 23, and see above § 10 with the note.

17. τὴν δόξαν] i.e. the outward manifestation, the visible light and glory which betokened His presence; as e.g. Exod. xvi. 7, 10, xxiv. 16, 17, xxxiii. 19, 22, xl. 28, 29, Luke ii. 9, 1 Cor. xv. 40 sq., 2 Cor. iii. 7 sq., etc.

ταπεινοφρονῶν] A favourite word with Clement; see § 2, 13 (twice), 16 (three times), 19, 30, 38, 48. In like manner ταπεινοφροσύνη and ταπείνωσις occur several times. The transcriber reads ταπεινοφρων ων here, as he reads ταπεινοφρον ον § 19. In both cases his reading must be corrected. This verb occurs only once in the LXX (Ps. cxxxi. 2), and not once in the New Testament.

ἐγὼ δέ κ.τ.λ.] quoted exactly from the LXX Gen. xviii. 27.

19. Ἰὼβ ἦν κ.τ.λ.] A loose quotation from Job i. 1, where אB have ἀληθινὸς ἄμεμπτος δίκαιος θεοσεβής, and A ἄμεμπτος δίκαιος ἀληθινὸς θεοσεβής.

21. κατηγορεῖ λέγων] I prefer this to κατηγορῶν λέγει or κατηγορῶν εἶπεν. Wotton is certainly wrong in saying

μιᾶς ἡμέρας ἡ ζωὴ αὐτο[ῦ]. Μωϋσῆς πιστὸς ἐν ὅλῳ [τῷ οἴκῳ] αὐτοῦ ἐκλήθη, καὶ διὰ τῆς [ὑπηρε]σίας αὐτοῦ ἔκρινεν ὁ Θεὸς Α[ἴγυπτον] διὰ τῶν μαστίγων καὶ τῶν [αἰκι]σμάτων αὐτῶν. ἀλλὰ κἀκε[ῖνος] δοξασθεὶς μεγάλως οὐκ ἐμ[εγα]λορημόνησεν, ἀλλ' εἶπεν, ἐ[κ τῆς] βάτου 5 χρηματισμοῦ αὐτῷ διδο[μέ]νου, Τίς εἰμι ἐγώ, ὅτι με

2 ὑπηρεσίας] Wotton.   3 Αἴγυπτον] Wotton. See below.

that he could read εἶπεν in the MS. There is no trace of the word and cannot have been any. He must have made some confusion with the εἶπεν below, which is blurred.
οὐδεὶς κ.τ.λ.] A loose quotation from the LXX Job xiv. 4, 5.
οὐδ' εἰ] All the best MSS of the LXX agree in reading ἐὰν καὶ, which many editors have preferred here. On the other hand Clem. Alex. *Strom.* iv. 16 (p. 610) has οὐδ' εἰ, and, as in the rest of this quotation he follows his namesake pretty closely where he departs from the LXX, he probably did so in this instance. Origen, who frequently quotes the text, generally has οὐδ' ἂν (e.g. II. p. 829) or οὐδ' εἰ (III. pp. 160, 685), but sometimes omits the negative. The passage is one of very few outside of the Pentateuch quoted by Philo, *de Mut. Nom.* 6 (I. p. 585), who reads τίς γὰρ...καὶ ἂν...
1. πιστὸς κ.τ.λ.] He is so called Num. xii. 7; comp. Heb. iii. 2.
2. ὑπηρεσίας] Comp. Wisd. xiii. 11, xv. 7. Other suggestions for filling the lacuna, such as προστασίας and θεραπευσίας, are not so good.
3. Αἴγυπτον] So Wotton correctly supplied the lacuna. Compare § 11 κριθείσης διὰ πυρός. Moses was the instrument in fulfilling the prophecy uttered before, Gen. xv. 14 (comp. Acts vii. 7) τὸ δὲ ἔθνος ᾧ ἐὰν δουλεύσωσι

κρινῶ ἐγώ. Others have supplied λαὸν αὐτοῦ Ἰσραήλ, τοὺς υἱοὺς Ἰσραήλ, or similar words; but the context seems to require the triumph of Moses over an enemy, and indeed the A of Αἴγυπτον is partly visible in the MS.
5. ἐμεγαλορημόνησεν] See the note on ἐξερίζωσεν, § 6.
6. τίς εἰμι ἐγώ] From Exod. iii. 11 τίς εἰμι ἐγώ, ὅτι πορεύσομαι κ.τ.λ.
7. ἐγὼ δὲ κ.τ.λ.] From Exod. iv. 10 ἰσχνόφωνος καὶ βραδύγλωσσος ἐγώ εἰμι.
8. ἐγὼ δέ εἰμι ἀτμὶς κ.τ.λ.] This quotation is not found in the Old Testament or in any apocryphal book extant whole or in part. The nearest parallel is James iv. 14, ποία γὰρ ἡ ζωὴ ὑμῶν; ἀτμὶς [γάρ] ἐστε ἡ πρὸς ὀλίγον φαινομένη κ.τ.λ. Compare also Hosea xiii. 3 'As smoke from the chimney' (or 'the window'), where the LXX seems to have translated originally ἀτμὶς ἀπὸ ἀκρίδων (see Simson's *Hosea* p. 44), corrupted into ἀπὸ δακρύων in B and corrected into ἐκ καπνοδόχης from Theodotion in A; and Ps. cxix. 83 'I am become like a bottle in the smoke', where again the LXX mistranslates ὡσεὶ ἀσκὸς ἐν πάχνῃ. In none of these passages however are the words very close, nor are they spoken by Moses. Perhaps therefore this should be reckoned among S. Clement's quotations

πέμπ[εις;] ἐγὼ δέ εἰμι ἰcχνόφωνοc καὶ βρ[α]δύγλωccoc. καὶ
πάλιν λέγει, Ἐγὼ δέ εἰμι ἀτμὶc ἀπὸ κύθραc.
XVIII. Τί δὲ εἴπωμεν ἐπὶ τῷ μεμαρτυρημένῳ
10 Δαυείδ; πρὸc ὃν εἶπεν ὁ Θεός, Εὗρον ἄνδρα κατὰ τὴν
καρδίαν μου, Δαυεὶδ τὸν τοῦ Ἰεccαί, ἐν ἐλέει αἰωνίῳ ἔχριcα
αὐτόν. ἀλλὰ καὶ αὐτὸς λέγει πρὸς τὸν Θεόν· Ἐλέηcον

10, 11 Δαυείδ] δᾱδ A. See above, § 4.   11 ἐλέει] ελαιει A. See below.

from apocryphal books on which Photius (*Bibl.* 126 ῥητά τινα ὡς ἀπὸ τῆς θείας γραφῆς ξενίζοντα παρεισάγει) remarks: see also §§ 8, 13, 23, 30, 46 (notes). Hilgenfeld is sure that the words were taken from the *Assumption of Moses*. This is not impossible; but the independent reason which he gives for the belief that Clement was acquainted with that apocryphal work is unsatisfactory; see the note on the phoenix below, § 25. I have pointed out elsewhere (§ 23) another apocryphal work, from which they might well have been taken. The metaphor is common with the Stoics: see Seneca *Troad.* 392 sq. 'Ut calidis fumus ab ignibus Vanescit...Sic hic quo regimur spiritus effluit', M. Anton. x. 31 καπνὸν καὶ τὸ μηδέν, xii. 33 νεκρὰ καὶ καπνός; so also Empedocles (in Plut. *Op. Mor.* p. 360 C, quoted by Gataker on x. 31) had said, ὠκύμοροι καπνοῖο δίκην ἀρθέντες ἀπέπταν.

κύθρας] Another form of χύτρας, just as κιθών and χιτών are interchanged. The proper Ionic genitive would be κύθρης, which is used by Herodes in Stob. *Floril.* lxxviii. 6 (quoted in Hase and Dindorf's *Steph. Thes.*). · Clem. Alex. *Paed.* ii. 1 (p. 165) has κυθριδίοις; and for instances of κυθρῖνος (for χυτρῖνος) see Lobeck *Pathol.* p. 209. In the text of Clem. Alex. here χύτρας is read.

XVIII. 'Again take David as an example of humility. He is declared to be the man after God's own heart. Yet he speaks of himself as overwhelmed with sin, as steeped in impurity, and prays that he may be cleansed by God's Spirit'.

10. πρὸς ὅν] Comp. Rom. x. 21, Heb. i. 7, and see Winer § xlix. p. 424.
εὗρον κ.τ.λ.] A combination of Ps. lxxxix. 21 εὗρον Δαυεὶδ τὸν δοῦλόν μου, ἐν ἐλαίῳ ἁγίῳ μου ἔχρισα αὐτόν, with 1 Sam. xiii. 14 ἄνθρωπον κατὰ τὴν καρδίαν αὐτοῦ, or rather with Acts xiii. 22 εὗρον Δαυεὶδ τὸν τοῦ Ἰεσσαί, ἄνδρα κατὰ τὴν καρδίαν μου (itself a loose quotation from 1 Sam. xiii. 14): In the first passage ἐλαίῳ the reading of אA is doubtless correct, the corresponding Hebrew being שמן; though ἐλέει is read by B. But our MS here has ελαιει (i.e. ἐλέει), and so Clement appears to have read. Similarly in § 56, when quoting Ps. cxli. 5, he reads ελαιοσ (i.e. ἔλεος) ἁμαρτωλῶν for ἔλαιον ἁμαρτωλῶν. On the interchange of αι and ε in this word see above, p. 25. On the other hand Clem. Alex. *Strom.* iv. 17 (p. 611), quoting this passage of his namesake, restores the correct word ἐλαίῳ, as he would do naturally, if accustomed to this reading in the Psalms.

12. ἐλέησόν κ.τ.λ.] The 51st Psalm quoted from the LXX almost word for word. The variations are very slight and unimportant.

με, ὁ Θεός, κατὰ τὸ μέγα ἔλεός σου, καὶ κατὰ τὸ πλῆθος
τῶν οἰκτιρμῶν σου ἐξάλειψον τὸ ἀνόμημά μου. ἐπὶ πλεῖον
πλῦνόν με ἀπὸ τῆς ἀνομίας μου, καὶ ἀπὸ τῆς ἁμαρτίας μου
καθάρισόν με· ὅτι τὴν ἀνομίαν μου ἐγὼ γινώσκω, καὶ ἡ
ἁμαρτία μου ἐνώπιόν μού ἐστιν διὰ παντός. σοὶ μόνῳ ἥμαρ- 5
τον, καὶ τὸ πονηρὸν ἐνώπιόν σου ἐποίησα· ὅπως ἂν δικαιωθῇς ἐν τοῖς λόγοις σου, καὶ νικήσῃς ἐν τῷ κρίνεσθαί σε.
ἰδοὺ γὰρ ἐν ἀνομίαις συνελήμφθην, καὶ ἐν ἁμαρτίαις ἐκίσ-
σησέν με ἡ μήτηρ μου. ἰδοὺ γὰρ ἀλήθειαν ἠγάπησας· τὰ
ἄδηλα καὶ τὰ κρύφια τῆς σοφίας σου ἐδήλωσάς μοι. ῥαν- 10
τιεῖς με ὑσσώπῳ, καὶ καθαρισθήσομαι· πλυνεῖς με, καὶ ὑπὲρ
χιόνα λευκανθήσομαι· ἀκουτιεῖς με ἀγαλλίασιν καὶ εὐφροσύ-
νην· ἀγαλλιάσονται ὀστᾶ τεταπεινωμένα. ἀπόστρεψον τὸ
πρόσωπόν σου ἀπὸ τῶν ἁμαρτιῶν μου, καὶ πάσας τὰς ἀνομίας μου ἐξάλειψ[ον]. καρδίαν καθαρὰν κτίσον ἐν ἐμο[ὶ], ὁ 15

ἔλεος] ελαιοσ A.   2 οἰκτιρμῶν] οικτειρμων A.   πλεῖον] πλιον A.
7 νικήσῃς] νικησεισ A.   11 πλυνεῖς] πλυνιεισ A.

2. *ἐπὶ πλεῖον κ.τ.λ.*] i.e. 'wash me again and again'. The Hebrew is 'multiply (and) wash me'.

6. *ὅπως κ.τ.λ.*] This verse is quoted also Rom. iii. 4. The middle κρίνεσθαι, 'to have a cause adjudged, to plead', is said of one of the parties to a suit. The 'pleading' of God is a common image in the Old Testament; e.g. Is. i. 18, v. 3. In this passage however the natural rendering of the Hebrew would be κρίνειν, not κρίνεσθαι.

7. *νικήσῃς*] The future νικήσεις is improbable (see Winer § xli. p. 304), especially with a preceding δικαιωθῇς; and the MS is of no authority where it is a question between H and EI. The LXX text (אB) has νικήσῃς.

8. *ἐκίσσησεν*] 'conceived', not found elsewhere in the LXX. The sense and construction which the word has here seem to be unique. Elsewhere it denotes the fastidious appetite of women at such a time and takes a genitive of the object desired; comp. Arist. *Pax* 497.

9. *τὰ ἄδηλα κ.τ.λ.*] The LXX translators have missed the sense of the original here.

11. *ὑσσώπῳ*] As one defiled by leprosy or some other taint was purged according to the law; see Lev. xiv. 4 sq., Num. xix. 6, 18, and Perowne *On the Psalms*, ad loc.

12. *ἀκουτιεῖς*] For the word ἀκουτίζειν see Sturz *de Dial. Mac.* p. 144. It was perhaps invented to translate the Hiphil of ישמע.

16. *εὐθές*] A common form of the neuter in the LXX, e.g. Judges xvii. 6, xxi. 25, 2 Sam. xix. 6, 18, etc. The masculine εὐθής also occurs, e.g. Ps. xcii. 14.

Θεός, καὶ πνεῦμα εὐθὲς ἐγκαίνισον ἐν τοῖς ἐγκάτοις μου.
μὴ ἀπο[ρί]ψῃς με ἀπὸ τοῦ προςώπου ςου, [καὶ τὸ π]νεῦμα τὸ
ἅγιόν ςου μὴ ἀντανέ[λῃς ἀπ' ἐ]μοῦ. ἀπόδος μοι τὴν ἀγαλ-
[λίασιν τ]οῦ σωτηρίου ςου, καὶ πνεύματι [ἡγεμο]νικῷ ςτή-
20 ρισόν με. Διδά[ξω ἀνό]μους τὰς ὁδούς ςου, καὶ ἀ[ςεβεῖ]ς
ἐπιςτρέψουςιν ἐπί ςε. [ῥῦςαί] με ἐξ αἱμάτων, ὁ Θεος, ὁ Θεὸς
τῆς [ςωτ]ηρίας μου. [ἀγαλ]λιάςεται ἡ γλῶσσά μου τὴν
[δικ]αιοςύνην ςου. Κύριε, τὸ ςτόμα μου [ἀν]οίξεις, καὶ τὰ
χείλη μου ἀναγ[γ]ελεῖ τὴν αἴνεςίν ςου· ὅτι εἰ ἠ[θ]έληςας
25 θυςίαν, ἔδωκα ἄν· ὁλοκαυτώματα οὐκ εὐδοκήςεις. θυςία
τῷ Θεῷ πνεῦμα ςυντετριμμένον· καρδίαν ςυντετριμμένην
καὶ τεταπεινωμένην ὁ Θεὸς οὐκ ἐξουθενώςει.

XIX. Τῶν τοσούτων οὖν καὶ τοιούτων οὕτως μεμαρτυρημένων τὸ ταπεινοφρονοῦν καὶ τὸ ὑποδεὲς διὰ
30 τῆς ὑπακοῆς οὐ μόνον ἡμᾶς ἀλλὰ καὶ τὰς πρὸ ἡμῶν

16 ἐγκάτοις] ενκατοισ A. 29 ταπεινοφρονοῦν] ταπεινοφρονον A.
30 ἀλλά] αλλασ A.

19. ἡγεμονικῷ] In the Hebrew נְדִיבָה, 'willing, ready'. The LXX have adopted a secondary meaning 'liberal', and so 'noble, princely'. The adjective ἡγεμονικὸς does not occur elsewhere in the LXX. Comp. παντοκρατορικός, § 8.

στήρισον] So ℵ reads in the LXX, but B στήριξον. On these double forms see Buttmann *Ausf. Gr. Spr.* § 92 (I. p. 372); and on the use of στήρισον, etc., in the New Testament, Winer § xv. p. 101. Clement, or his transcriber, is inconsistent; for he has ἐστήριξεν § 8, στηρίξωμεν § 13, but ἐστήρισεν § 33, and στήρισον here.

21. αἱμάτων] The plural denotes especially '*bloodshed*', as in Plat. *Legg.* ix. p. 872 E, and the instances collected in Blomfield's Gloss. to Æsch. *Choeph.* 60: see also *Test. xii Patr.*

Sym. 4 εἰς αἵματα παροξύνει, Anon. in Hipp. *Hær.* v. 16 αἵμασι χαίρει ὁ τοῦδε τοῦ κόσμου δεσπότης, Tatian. *ad Græc.* 8. The same is the force also of the Hebrew plural דָּמִים, of which αἵματα here and elsewhere is a rendering: comp. Exod. xxii. 1, where, as here, 'bloodshed' is equivalent to 'blood-guiltiness'.

XIX. 'These bright examples of humility we have before our eyes. But let us look to the fountain-head of all truth; let us contemplate the mind of the universal Father and Creator, as manifested in His works, and see how patience and order and beneficence prevail throughout creation'.

28. τῶν τοσούτων κ.τ.λ.] An imitation of Heb. xii. 1.

29. ταπεινοφρονοῦν] See the note on ταπεινοφρονῶν above, § 17.

γενεὰς βελτίους ἐποίησεν, τούς τε καταδεξαμένους τὰ λόγια αὐτοῦ ἐν φόβῳ καὶ ἀληθείᾳ. Πολλῶν οὖν καὶ μεγάλων καὶ ἐνδόξων μετειληφότες πράξεων, ἐπαναδράμωμεν ἐπὶ τὸν ἐξ ἀρχῆς παραδεδομένον ἡμῖν τῆς εἰρήνης σκοπόν, καὶ ἀτενίσωμεν εἰς τὸν πατέρα καὶ κτιστὴν τοῦ 5 σύμπαντος κόσμου, καὶ ταῖς μεγαλοπρεπέσι καὶ ὑπερβαλλούσαις αὐτοῦ δωρεαῖς τῆς εἰρήνης εὐεργεσίαις τε κολληθῶμεν· ἴδωμεν αὐτὸν κατὰ διάνοιαν καὶ ἐμβλέψωμεν τοῖς ὄμμασιν τῆς ψυχῆς εἰς τὸ μακρόθυμον αὐτοῦ βούλημα· νοήσωμεν πῶς ἀόργητος ὑπάρχει πρὸς πᾶσαν 10 τὴν κτίσιν αὐτοῦ.

3 πράξεων] πραξαιων A.

1. καταδεξαμένους] Davies proposes καταδεξομένους. The emendation would have been more probable if the preposition were different, διαδεξομένους and not καταδεξομένους.

3. μετειληφότες] '*participated in*',· i.e. profited by as examples. The achievements of the saints of old are the heritage of the later Church.

4. εἰρήνης σκοπόν] '*the mark, the goal, of peace*'. God Himself is the great exemplar of peaceful working, and so the final goal of all imitation.

10. ἀόργητος] '*calm*'; Ign. *Philad.* 1, Polyc. *Phil.* 12 (note). Aristotle attaches a bad sense to the word, as implying a want of sensibility, *Eth. Nic.* ii. 7. Others however distinguished ἀοργησία from ἀναισθησία (see Aul. Gell. i. 27); and with the Stoics it was naturally a favourite word, e.g. Epict. *Diss.* iii. 20. 9 τὸ ἀνεκτικόν, τὸ ἀόργητον, τὸ πρᾶον, iii. 18. 6 εὐσταθῶς, αἰδημόνως, ἀοργήτως, M. Anton. I. I τὸ καλόηθες καὶ ἀόργητον. The word does not occur in the LXX or New Testament.

XX. 'All creation moves on in peace and harmony. Night and day succeed each other. The heavenly bodies roll in their proper orbits. The earth brings forth in due season. The ocean keeps within its appointed bounds. The seasons, the winds, the fountains, accomplish their work peacefully and minister to our wants. Even the dumb animals observe the same law. Thus God has by this universal reign of order manifested His beneficence to all, but especially to us who have sought His mercy through Christ Jesus'.

12. σαλευόμενοι] If the reading be correct, this word must refer to the motion of the heavenly bodies, apparently uneven but yet recurrent and orderly; and this reference seems to be justified by ἐξελίσσουσιν below. Σαλεύεσθαι is indeed frequently used in the Old Testament to express terror and confusion, in speaking of the earth, the hills, etc.; but never of the heavens. So too in the Sibylline Oracles, iii. 675, 714, 751. On the other hand Young would read μὴ σαλευόμενοι; and Davies, improving upon this correction, suggests οὐ σαλευόμενοι, repeating the last letters of αὐτοῦ. But such passages in the New Testament as Matt. xxiv. 29,

TO THE CORINTHIANS.

XX. Οἱ οὐρανοὶ τῇ διοικήσει αὐτοῦ σαλευόμενοι ἐν εἰρήνῃ ὑποτάσσονται αὐτῷ· ἡμέρα τε καὶ νὺξ τὸν τεταγμένον ὑπ' αὐτοῦ δρόμον διανύουσιν, μηδὲν ἀλλήλοις 5 ἐμποδί[ζ]οντα. ἥλιός τε καὶ σελήνη ἀστέ[ρ]ων τε χοροὶ κατὰ τὴν διαταγὴν [α]ὐτοῦ ἐν ὁμονοίᾳ δίχα πάσης [π]αρεκβάσεως ἐξελίσσουσιν [το]ὺς ἐπιτεταγμένους αὐτοῖς ὁρισμούς. γῆ κυοφοροῦσα κατὰ τὸ θέλημα αὐτοῦ τοῖς ἰδίοις καιροῖς τὴν πανπληθῆ ἀνθρώποις τε καὶ θηρσὶν 0 καὶ πᾶσιν τοῖς οὖσιν ἐπ' αὐτὴν ζώοις ἀνατέλλει τροφήν, μὴ διχοστατοῦσα μηδὲ ἀλλοιοῦσά τι τῶν δεδογματισμένων ὑπ' αὐτοῦ. ἀβύσσων τε ἀνεξιχνίαστα καὶ νερτέρων ἀνεκδιήγητα †κρίματα† τοῖς αὐτοῖς συνέχεται προσ-

Heb. xii. 26, 27, are not sufficient to justify the alteration; for some expression of *motion* is wanted. Not 'fixity, rest,' but 'regulated change' is the idea of this and the following sentences. For this reason I have retained σαλευόμενοι. In the passage of Chrysostom quoted by Young in defence of his reading, *in Psalm.* cxlviii. § 2 (v. p. 491) οὐδὲν συνεχύθη τῶν ὄντων· οὐ θάλαττα τὴν γῆν ἐπέκλυσεν, οὐχ ἥλιος τόδε τὸ ὁρώμενον κατέκαυσεν, οὐκ οὐρανὸς παρεσαλεύθη κ.τ.λ., this father would seem purposely to have chosen the compound παρασαλεύεσθαι to denote *disorderly* motion.

17. ἐξελίσσουσιν] Comp. Plut. *Mor.* p. 368 A τοσαύταις ἡμέραις τὸν αὐτῆς κύκλον ἐξελίσσει (of the moon), Heliod. *Æth.* v. 14 οἱ δὲ περὶ τὸν νομέα κύκλους ἀγερώχους ἐξελίττοντες (both passages given in Hase and Dindorf's *Steph. Thes.*). Thus the word continues the metaphor of χοροί, describing the tangled mazes of the dance, as e. g. Eur. *Troad.* 3. The ὁρισμοί therefore are their defined orbits.

20. ἐπ' αὐτήν] For the accusative so used see Winer § xlix. p. 426.

ἀνατέλλει] Here transitive, as e. g. Gen. iii. 18, Is. xlv. 8, Matt. v. 45; comp. Epiphanes in Clem. Alex. *Strom.* iii. 2, p. 512, ἥλιος κοινὰς τροφὰς ζώοις ἅπασιν ἀνατέλλει (MSS ἀνατέλλειν), which closely resembles our Clement's language here.

23. †κρίματα†] '*statutes, ordinances,*' i. e. the laws by which they are governed, as e.g. 2 Chron. xxx. 16 ἔστησαν ἐπὶ τὴν στάσιν αὐτῶν κατὰ τὸ κρίμα αὐτῶν ('as they were appointed'), 2 Chron. iv. 7 τὰς λυχνίας κατὰ τὸ κρίμα αὐτῶν (comp. ver. 20). But κρίματα is most awkward, and several emendations have been suggested, of which κλίματα is the best. We may either adopt this, or (as I would suggest in preference) strike out the word altogether. In either case we may fall back upon the conjecture of Lipsius (p. 155, note) that κρίματα was written down by some thoughtless scribe from Rom. xi. 33 ἀνεξερεύνητα τὰ κρίματα αὐτοῦ καὶ ἀνεξιχνίαστοι αἱ ὁδοὶ αὐτοῦ (he gives the reference ix. 33, which is repeated by Jacobson, and still further corrupted ix. 23 by Hilgenfeld). Indeed the

τάγμασιν. τὸ κύτος τῆς ἀπείρου θαλάσσης κατὰ τὴν δημιουργίαν αὐτοῦ συσταθὲν εἰς τὰς ϲυΝΑΓωΓὰϲ οὐ παρεκβαίνει τὰ περιτεθειμένα αὐτῇ κλεῖθρα, ἀλλὰ καθὼς διέταξεν αὐτῇ, οὕτως ποιεῖ. εἶπεν γάρ· Ἕωϲ ὧΔε ἥξεις, καὶ τὰ κύματά ϲου ἐν ϲοὶ ϲυΝΤριβήϲεται. ὠκεανὸς 5

2 δημιουργίαν] δημιουργειαν Α.   5 κύματα] κρυματα Α.

same word seems still to be running in the scribe's head when below he writes κρυματα for κυματα. The νέρτερα are the 'subterranean regions' regarded physically.

1. τὸ κύτος] 'the hollow, the basin', as Ps. lxiv. 7 ὁ συνταράσσων τὸ κύτος τῆς θαλάσσης. In Dan. iv. 8 τὸ κύτος is opposed to τὸ ὕψος.

2. εἰς τὰς συναγωγάς] From LXX Gen. i. 9 καὶ συνήχθη τὸ ὕδωρ τὸ ὑποκάτω τοῦ οὐρανοῦ εἰς τὰς συναγωγὰς αὐτῶν, wanting in the Hebrew. It refers to the great bodies of water, the Mediterranean, the Caspian, the Red Sea, etc.

3. παρεκβαίνει κ.τ.λ.] From Job xxxviii. 10, 11 ἐθέμην δὲ αὐτῇ ὅρια περιθεὶς κλεῖθρα καὶ πύλας, εἶπα δὲ αὐτῇ Μέχρι τούτου ἐλεύσῃ καὶ οὐχ ὑπερβήσῃ, ἀλλ' ἐν σεαυτῇ συντριβήσεταί σου τὰ κύματα: comp. also Ps. civ. 9, Jer. v. 22.

5. ὠκεανὸς κ.τ.λ.] This passage is directly quoted by Clem. Alex. *Strom.* v. 12 (p. 693), by Origen *de Princ.* ii. 6 (I. p. 82, 83), *Select. in Ezech.* viii. 3 (III. p. 422), by Jerome *ad Ephes.* ii. 2 (VII. p. 571). It must also have suggested the words of Irenæus *Hær.* ii. 28. 2 'Quid autem possumus exponere de oceani accessu et recessu, quum constet esse certam causam? quidve de his quæ ultra eum sunt enuntiare, qualia sint?' On the other hand the expression ὁ πολὺς καὶ ἀπέραντος ἀνθρώποις ὠκεανὸς used by Dionys. Alex. in Euseb. *H. E.* vii. 21 may be derived indirectly through Clement or Origen. On Photius see below, p. 97.

6. ἀπέρατος] '*impassable*,' as the context shows, and as it is rendered in the translation of Origen *de Princ.* ii. 3 ('intransmeabilis'). The common form in this sense is ἀπέρατος; though ἀπέραντος is read here not only in our MS, but by Clem. Alex. p. 693 and Dionys. Alex. in Euseb. *H. E.* vii. 21, or their transcribers, and may possibly be correct. Yet as I could not find any better instances of this use than Eur. *Med.* 212, Æsch. *Prom.* 159 (where Blomf. suggests ἀπέρατος), and in both passages the meaning may be questioned, I have preferred reading ἀπέρατος as quoted by Origen *Select. in Ezech.* viii. 3.

οἱ μετ' αὐτὸν κόσμοι κ.τ.λ.] Clement may possibly be referring to some known but hardly accessible land, lying without the pillars of Hercules and in foreign seas: as Ceylon (Plin. *N. H.* vi. 22 'Taprobanen alterum orbem terrarum esse diu existimatum est, Antichthonum appellatione'), or Britain (Joseph. *B. J.* ii. 16. 4 ὑπὲρ ὠκεανὸν ἑτέραν ἐζήτησαν οἰκουμένην καὶ μέχρι τῶν ἀνιστορήτων πρότερον Βρεττανῶν διήνεγκαν τὰ ὅπλα). But more probably he contemplated some unknown land in the far west beyond the ocean, like the fabled Atlantis of Plato or the real America of modern discovery. From Aristotle onwards (*de Cælo* ii. 14, p. 298, *Meteor.* ii. 5, p. 362), and even earlier, theories had

xx] TO THE CORINTHIANS. 85

ἀνθρώποις ἀπέρατος καὶ οἱ μετ' αὐτὸν κόσμοι ταῖς αὐταῖς
ταγαῖς τοῦ δεσπότου διευθύνονται. καιροὶ ἐαρινοὶ καὶ
θερινοὶ καὶ μετοπωρινοὶ καὶ χειμερινοὶ ἐν εἰρήνῃ μετα-
παραδιδόασιν ἀλλήλοις. ἀνέμων σταθμοὶ κατὰ τὸν

6 ἀπέρατος] Origen. απεραντος A, Clem. Alex., Dionys. Alex. See below.
7 ταγαῖς] A. διαταγαῖς Origen. See below. 8 μετοπωρινοί] μεθοπωρινοι A.

from time to time been broached, which contemplated the possibility of reaching the Indies by crossing the western ocean, or maintained the existence of islands or continents towards the setting sun. The Carthaginians had even brought back a report of such a desert island in the Atlantic, which they had visited, [Aristot.] *Mirab. Ausc.* § 84 p. 836, § 136 p. 844, Diod. v. 19, 20; see Humboldt *Exam. Crit.* I. p. 130. In the generations before and after the time of Clement such speculations were not uncommon. Of these the prophecy in Seneca's *Medea* ii. 375 'Venient annis sæcula seris Quibus Oceanus vincula rerum Laxet et ingens pateat tellus etc.,' is the most famous, because so much stress was laid on it by Columbus and his fellow discoverers: but the statements in Strabo i. 4 (p. 65), Plut. *Mor.* p. 941, are much more remarkable. The opinions of ancient writers on this subject are collected and examined in the 1st volume of A. von Humboldt's *Exam. Crit. de la Géogr. du Nouveau Continent:* see also other works mentioned in Prescott's *Ferdinand and Isabella* II. p. 102. This interpretation is quite consistent with the fact that Clement below (§ 33) speaks of the ocean, as τὸ περιέχον τὴν γῆν ὕδωρ.

At all events this passage was seemingly so taken by Irenæus and Clement of Alexandria, and it is distinctly explained thus by Origen (*Sel.*

in Ezech. viii. 3 sq., *de Princ.* ii. 6) who discusses it at great length. All these fathers acquiesce in the existence of these 'other worlds.' At a later date however this opinion came to be regarded with suspicion by Christian theologians. Tertullian, *de Pall.* 2, *Hermog.* 25, was the first to condemn it. The idea of the Antipodes is scouted by Lactantius *Div. Inst.* ii. 24, with other fathers of the fourth century and later (comp. August. *de Civ. Dei* xvi. 9); and in the reign of Justinian (c. A.D. 535) the speculations of Cosmas Indicopleustes (Montfaucon *Coll. Nov. Patr.* II. p. 113 sq.), who describes the earth as a plain surface and a parallelogram in form (see Humboldt *l. c.* I. p. 41 sq.), stereotyped for many centuries the belief of Christian writers on this subject.

7. ταγαῖς] '*directions*,' as Hermes in Stob. *Ecl.* i. 52. 40 ἐποπτὴρ τοίνυν ταγῆς ἔσται τῶν ὅλων ὀξυδερκὴς θεὸς Ἀδράστεια, with other passages quoted by Hase in *Steph. Thes.* s. v. Origen *Sel. in Ezech.* l. c., and apparently also *de Princ.* l.c. (for the Latin is *dispositionibus*), has διαταγαῖς, which some editors adopt; but he would naturally substitute a common for an unusual word, and his quotation throughout is somewhat loose.

8. μεταπαραδιδόασιν] '*give way in succession*'; again a rare word, of which a few instances are collected in Hase and Dindorf's *Steph. Thes.*

9. ἀνέμων σταθμοί] From Job

ἴδιον καιρὸν τὴν λειτουργίαν αὐτῶν ἀπροσκόπως ἐπιτελοῦσιν· ἀέναοί τε πηγαὶ πρὸς ἀπόλαυσιν καὶ ὑγείαν δημιουργηθεῖσαι δίχα ἐλλείψεως παρέχονται τοὺς πρὸς ζωῆς ἀνθρώποις μαζούς. τά τε ἐλάχιστα τῶν ζώων τὰς συνελεύσεις αὐτῶν ἐν ὁμονοίᾳ καὶ εἰρήνῃ ποιοῦνται. 5 Ταῦτα πάντα ὁ μέγας δημιουργὸς καὶ δεσπότης τῶν ἁπάντων ἐν εἰρήνῃ καὶ ὁμονοίᾳ προσέταξεν εἶναι, εὐεργετῶν τὰ πάντα, ὑπερεκπερισσῶς δὲ ἡμᾶς τοὺς προσπεφευγότας τοῖς οἰκτιρμοῖς αὐτοῦ διὰ τοῦ Κυρίου ἡμῶν

1 λειτουργίαν] λειτουργειαν A.   9 οἰκτιρμοῖς] οικτειρμοισ A.

xxviii. 25 ἐποίησεν δὲ ἀνέμων σταθμὸν καὶ ὑδάτων μέτρα, where it means 'weight', as the original shows. Clement however may have misunderstood the meaning; for he seems to use the word in a different sense, 'the fixed order' or 'the fixed stations,' as the context requires. The common Greek expression in this sense is στάσεις, e. g. Polyb. i. 75. 8 κατά τινας ἀνέμων στάσεις, ix. 5. 23 ἐπιχώριοι τὰς τῶν ἀνέμων στάσεις κάλλιστα γινώσκουσι: see Schweighäuser on Polyb. i. 48. 2. A good illustration of Clement's meaning is the noble passage in Lucretius v. 737 sq.

2. ὑγείαν] A common form in late writers: see Lobeck Paral. p. 28 (with the references), Phryn. p. 493, Pathol. p: 234. It is so written in several inscriptions, and so scanned in Orph. Hymn. lxxxiv. 8 (p. 350, Herm.) ὄλβον ἐπιπνείουσα καὶ ἠπιόχειρον ὑγείαν (unnecessarily altered by Porson, Eur. Orest. 229, into ἠπιόχειρ᾽ ὑγίειαν), and elsewhere. Editors therefore should not have substituted ὑγίειαν. Compare ταμεῖα § 50.

3. τοὺς πρὸς ζωῆς μαζούς] The metaphor was perhaps suggested by Jer. xviii. 14 (LXX) μὴ ἐκλείψουσιν ἀπὸ πέτρας μαστοί, which however departs from the existing reading of the Hebrew. For πρὸς ζωῆς, 'on the side of life', 'conducive to life,' comp. Acts xxvii. 34 πρὸς τῆς ὑμετέρας σωτηρίας, Clem. Hom. viii. 14 πρὸς κόσμου καὶ τέρψεως, and see Winer § xlvii. p. 391. This sense of πρὸς is more common in classical Greek.

5. συνελεύσεις] Comp. Jer. viii. 7 'The stork in the heaven knoweth his appointed times; and the turtle and the crane and the swallow observe the time of their coming', etc. Or it may refer to their pairing at the proper season of the year. Comp. Ptolem. Geogr. i. 9 (quoted in Steph. Thes.).

6. δημιουργός] Only once in the New Testament, Heb. xi. 10: in the LXX again only in 2 Macc. iv. 1 (and there not of the Creator). On the Christian use of this Platonic phrase see Jahn's Methodius II. pp. 11, 39, 91.

8. προσφεύγειν] Altogether a late and somewhat rare word: see 1 Sam. xxix. 3 (Sym.). It does not occur in the LXX or New Testament.

10. ἡ δόξα καὶ ἡ μεγ.] So again § 58. In the doxology Jude 25 also the two words occur together; comp. Ecclus. xliv. 2.

XXI. 'His blessings will turn to

10 Ἰησοῦ Χριστοῦ, ᾧ ἡ δόξα καὶ ἡ μεγαλωσύνη εἰς τοὺς αἰῶνας τῶν αἰώνων. ἀμήν.

XXI. Ὁρᾶτε, ἀγαπητοί, μὴ αἱ εὐεργεσίαι αὐτοῦ αἱ πολλαὶ γένωνται εἰς κρίμα πᾶσιν ἡμῖν, ἐὰν μὴ ἀξίως αὐτοῦ πολιτευόμενοι τὰ καλὰ καὶ εὐάρεστα ἐνώπιον αὐ-
15 τοῦ ποιῶμεν μεθ' ὁμονοίας. λέγει γάρ που· Πνεῦμα Κυρίου λύχνος ἐρευνῶν τὰ ταμιεῖα τῆς γαστρός. Ἴδωμεν πῶς ἐγγύς ἐστιν, καὶ ὅτι οὐδὲν λέληθεν αὐτὸν τῶν ἐννοιῶν ἡμῶν οὐδὲ τῶν διαλογισμῶν ὧν ποιούμεθα. δί-

16 λύχνος] Clem. Alex. 611. λυχνον Α.   ταμεῖα] A. ταμεῖα Clem. Alex.

our curse unless we seek peace and strive to please Him. He sees all our most secret thoughts. Let us therefore offend foolish and arrogant men rather than God. Let us honour Christ; let us respect our rulers, and revere old age; let us instruct our wives in purity and gentleness, and our children in humility and the fear of God. His breath is in us, and His pleasure can withdraw it in a moment'.

13. ἀξίως πολιτευόμενοι] The expression occurs in Phil. i. 27. Clement's language here is echoed by Polycarp *Phil.* 5.

14. εὐάρεστα ἐνώπιον] Heb. xiii. 21; comp. Ps. cxiv. 9.

15. λέγει γάρ κ.τ.λ.] Clem. Alex. *Strom.* iv. 17 (p. 611 sq.) cites the remainder of this section and the whole of the next, continuously after §§ 17, 18 (see the note § 17). For the most part he quotes in the same loose way, abridging and interpolating as before; but here and there, as in the long passage τὰς γυναῖκας ἡμῶν...ἀνελεῖ αὐτήν, he keeps fairly close to the words of his original and may be used as an authority for the readings.

πνεῦμα Κυρίου κ.τ.λ.] From Prov. xx. 27, which runs in the LXX φῶς Κυρίου πνοὴ ἀνθρώπων ὃς ἐρευνᾷ (ἐραυνᾷ) ταμεῖα (ταμιεῖα) κοιλίας. A adds ἡ λύχνος after ἀνθρώπων, but this must originally have been a gloss suggesting an alternative reading for φῶς, as λύχνος is actually read by Aq. Sym. Theod.; see a similar instance of correction in this MS noted above on § 17. Comp. also Prov. vi. 23 λύχνος ἐντολὴ Κυρίου καὶ φῶς from which passage perhaps λύχνος came to be interpolated here. Hilgenfeld prints λέγει γάρ που πνεῦμα Κυρίου Λύχνος ἐρευνῶν κ.τ.λ. and finds fault with Clem. Alex. for making the words πνεῦμα Κυρίου part of the quotation (λέγει γάρ που ἡ γραφή Πνεῦμα Κυρίου κ.τ.λ.); but they seem to be wanted to complete the sentence. Our Clement in fact quotes loosely, transposing words so as to give a somewhat different sense. See below, Is. lx. 17 quoted in § 42. For the exact words λέγει γάρ που see §§ 15, 26, and for other instances of λέγει (or φησί) with no nominative expressed, §§ 8, 10, 16, 29, 30, 46. On the spelling of ταμιεῖα (ταμεῖα) Clement (or his transcriber) is capricious: see § 50 (note).

17. ἐγγύς ἐστιν] As below § 27; comp. Ps. xxxiv. 18, cxix. 151, cxlv. 18, *Ign. Ephes.* 15 τὰ κρυπτὰ ἡμῶν ἐγγὺς αὐτῷ ἐστιν (with the note), Herm. *Vis.* ii. 3. There is no allusion here to the nearness of the advent, as in

καιον οὖν ἐστιν μὴ λιποτακτεῖν ἡμᾶς ἀπὸ τοῦ θελήματος αὐτοῦ· μᾶλλον ἀνθρώποις ἄφροσι καὶ ἀνοήτοις καὶ ἐπαιρομένοις καὶ ἐγκαυχωμένοις ἐν ἀλαζονείᾳ τοῦ λόγου αὐτῶν προσκόψωμεν ἢ τῷ Θεῷ. τὸν Κύριον Ἰησοῦν Χριστόν, οὗ τὸ αἷμα ὑπὲρ ἡμῶν ἐδόθη, ἐντρα- 5 πῶμεν· τοὺς προηγουμένους ἡμῶν αἰδεσθῶμεν, τοὺς πρεσβυτέρους ἡμῶν τιμήσωμεν, τοὺς νέους παιδεύσωμεν τὴν παιδείαν τοῦ φόβου τοῦ Θεοῦ, τὰς γυναῖκας ἡμῶν ἐπὶ τὸ ἀγαθὸν διορθωσώμεθα· τὸ ἀξιαγάπητον τῆς ἁγνείας ἦθος ἐνδειξάσθωσαν, τὸ ἀκέραιον τῆς πραΰτητος 10 αὐτῶν βούλημα ἀποδειξάτωσαν, τὸ ἐπιεικὲς τῆς γλώσσης αὐτῶν διὰ τῆς σιγῆς φανερὸν ποιησάτωσαν· τὴν ἀγάπην αὐτῶν, μὴ κατὰ προσκλίσεις, ἀλλὰ πᾶσιν τοῖς

3 ἐγκαυχωμένοις] ἐγκαυχωμενοι A. ἀλαζονείᾳ] αλαζονια A. 7 νέους] ναιουσ A. 8 παιδείαν] παιδιαν A. 10 ἁγνείας] αγνιασ A. Clem. Alex. 612 has ἦθος τῆς ἁγνείας. 12 σιγῆς] Clem. Alex. φωνησ A. 15 ἡμῶν] Clem. Alex. υμων A. μεταλαμβανέτωσαν] A. μεταλαβέτωσαν Clem. Alex.

Phil. iv. 5 (see the note there).
οὐδὲν λέληθεν κ.τ.λ.] This passage is copied by Polycarp *Phil.* 4 καὶ λέληθεν αὐτὸν οὐδὲν οὔτε λογισμῶν οὔτε ἐννοιῶν. On διαλογισμοί, '*inward questionings*,' see the note on Phil. ii. 14.

1. λιποτακτεῖν] So αὐτομολεῖν below § 28. Ignatius has the same metaphor but uses the Latin word, *Polyc.* 6 μήτις ὑμῶν δεσέρτωρ εὑρεθῇ: see the note there.

2. ἄφρ. καὶ ἀνόητ.] LXX Jer. x. 8 ἅμα ἄφρονες καὶ ἀνόητοί εἰσι, found in some copies, but not in the principal MSS. The former word points to defective reason, the latter to defective perception. Comp. § 39.

4. τὸν Κύριον κ.τ.λ.] Clem. Alex. (p. 611 sq.), as commonly punctuated, quotes the passage τὸν Κύριον Ἰησοῦν λέγω...οὗ τὸ αἷμα ὑπὲρ ἡμῶν ἡγιάσθη·

ἐντραπῶμεν οὖν τοὺς προηγουμένους ἡμῶν, καὶ αἰδεσθῶμεν τοὺς πρεσβυτέρους· τιμήσωμεν τοὺς νέους, παιδεύσωμεν τὴν παιδείαν τοῦ Θεοῦ. A different punctuation καὶ αἰδεσθῶμεν· τοὺς πρεσβυτέρους τιμήσωμεν· τοὺς νέους παιδεύσωμεν κ.τ.λ., would bring the quotation somewhat nearer to the original.

6. τοὺς προηγουμένους] i.e. the officers of the Church: see the note on τοῖς ἡγουμένοις § 1. The following τοὺς πρεσβυτέρους must therefore refer to age, not to office.

7. τοὺς νέους κ.τ.λ.] copied by Polycarp *Phil.* 4 τὰ τέκνα παιδεύειν τὴν παιδείαν τοῦ φόβου τοῦ Θεοῦ. Comp. Prov. xvi. 4 (xv. 33) φόβος Κυρίου παιδεία, and Ecclus. i. 27 where the same words are repeated.

12. σιγῆς] They must be eloquent by their silence, for γυναιξὶ κόσμον ἡ σιγὴ φέρει. This meaning is so obvi-

TO THE CORINTHIANS. 89

φοβουμένοις τὸν Θεὸν ὁσίως ἴσην παρεχέτωσαν· τὰ
15 τέκνα ἡμῶν τῆς ἐν Χριστῷ παιδείας μεταλαμβανέτωσαν·
μαθέτωσαν, τί ταπεινοφροσύνη παρὰ Θεῷ ἰσχύει, τί
ἀγάπη ἁγνὴ παρὰ τῷ Θεῷ δύναται, πῶς ὁ φόβος αὐτοῦ
καλὸς καὶ μέγας καὶ σώζων πάντας τοὺς ἐν αὐτῷ ὁσίως
ἀναστρεφομένους ἐν καθαρᾷ διανοίᾳ· ἐρευνητὴς γάρ ἐστιν
20 ἐννοιῶν καὶ ἐνθυμήσεων· οὗ ἡ πνοὴ αὐτοῦ ἐν ἡμῖν ἐστιν,
καὶ ὅταν θέλῃ ἀνελεῖ αὐτήν.

XXII. Ταῦτα δὲ πάντα βεβαιοῖ ἡ ἐν Χριστῷ πίσ-
τις· καὶ γὰρ αὐτὸς διὰ τοῦ πνεύματος τοῦ ἁγίου οὕτως
προσκαλεῖται ἡμᾶς· Δεῦτε τέκνα, ἀκούσατέ μου, φόβον
25 Κυρίου διδάξω ὑμᾶς. τίς ἐστιν ἄνθρωπος ὁ θέλων ζωήν,
ἀγαπῶν ἡμέρας ἰδεῖν ἀγαθάς; παῦσον τὴν γλῶσσάν σου ἀπὸ

16 ἰσχύει] ἰσχυι A. 17 τῷ] A. om. Clem. Alex. αὐτοῦ] A. τοῦ
Κυρίου Clem. Alex. 18 καὶ σωζων] A. om. καὶ Clem. Alex. 19 διανοίᾳ] A.
καρδίᾳ Clem. Alex. ἐστιν] om. Clem. Alex. 20 ἐνθυμήσεων] ἐνθυμησαιων A.
ἐνθυμημάτων Clem. Alex.

ously required, that we cannot hesitate to adopt σιγῆς from Clem. Alex.
in place of the senseless φωνῆς of the
MS. Hilgenfeld refers to 1 Cor. xiv.
34 sq., 1 Tim. ii. 11.
 τὴν ἀγάπην κ.τ.λ.] So too Polyc.
Phil. 4 ἀγαπώσας πάντας ἐξ ἴσου ἐν
πάσῃ ἐγκρατείᾳ. The numerous close
coincidences with this chapter in
Polycarp show plainly that he had
our epistle before him.
 13. κατὰ προσκλίσεις] From 1 Tim.
v. 21 μηδὲν ποιῶν κατὰ πρόσκλισιν.
The word πρόσκλισις occurs again
§§ 47, 50.
 14. ὁσίως] is best taken with παρε-
χέτωσαν, for it would be an unmeaning addition to τοῖς φοβουμένοις τὸν
Θεόν.
 19. ἐρευνητὴς κ.τ.λ.] As Heb. iv. 12
κριτικὸς ἐνθυμήσεων καὶ ἐννοιῶν καρδίας.
 20. οὗ...αὐτοῦ] A Hebraism, for

which see Winer § xxii. p. 161.
 21. ἀνελεῖ] On the rare future ἑλῶ
of αἱρέω see Winer § xv. p. 94 with
his references: comp. Exod. xv. 9,
2 Thess. ii. 6.
 XXII. 'All these things are as-
sured by faith in Christ. He himself
speaks to us by the lips of David,
promising all blessings to the peaceful and God-loving, but threatening
utter destruction to the sinful and
disobedient'.
 22. ταῦτα δὲ πάντα κ.τ.λ.] i.e. Faith
in Christ secures all these good results; for it is He Himself who thus
appeals to us, not indeed in the flesh,
but through the Spirit, where David
says 'Come etc.' For αὐτὸς προσκαλεῖται see above § 16 αὐτός φησιν, with
the note.
 24. δεῦτε κ.τ.λ.] From LXX Ps. xxxiv.
11 sq. almost word for word. The
differences are unimportant.

κακοῦ, καὶ χείλη τοῦ μὴ λαλῆσαι Δόλον· ἔκκλινον ἀπὸ κακοῦ καὶ ποίησον ἀγαθόν· ζήτησον εἰρήνην καὶ Δίωξον αὐτήν. ὀφθαλμοὶ Κυρίου ἐπὶ Δικαίους, καὶ ὦτα αὐτοῦ πρὸς Δέησιν αὐτῶν· πρ[όσωπον Δὲ] Κυρίου ἐπὶ ποιοῦντας κακὰ [τοῦ ἐξολε]θρεῦσαι ἐκ γῆς τὸ μνημ[όσυνον] αὐτῶν. ἐκέκραξεν 5 ὁ Δ[ίκαιος], καὶ ὁ Κύριος εἰσήκουσεν αὐτ[οῦ καὶ ἐκ] πασῶν τῶν θλίψεων α[ὐτοῦ ἐρύ]σατο αὐτόν. πολλαὶ αἱ μάς[τιγες]

1 χείλη] add. σου Clem. Alex.   3 πρός] A.   εἰς Clem. Alex.   5 ἐκέκραξεν
κ.τ.λ.] See below.   7 θλίψεων] θλιψαιων A.   αὐτοῦ] om. Clem. Alex.
αἱ] A.   μὲν γὰρ Clem. Alex.

5. τὸ μνημόσυνον] See the note on ἐνκατάλειμμα above § 14.
ἐκέκραξεν] In the existing text of Clem. Alex. this is read ἐκέκραξεν δὲ ὁ Κύριος καὶ εἰσήκουσε, obviously a corruption.
7. πολλαὶ κ.τ.λ.] An exact quotation from Ps. xxxii. 10 (LXX), except that τοὺς ἐλπίζοντας is substituted for τὸν ἐλπίζοντα.
XXIII. 'God is merciful to all that fear Him. Let us not spurn His gracious gifts. Far be from us the threats which the Scriptures hurl against the double-minded, the impatient, the sceptical. The Lord will certainly come, and come quickly'.
14. ἰνδαλλέσθω] '*indulge in caprices and humours*'. The word is generally passive, 'to be formed as an image', 'to appear', and with a dative 'to resemble'; see Ruhnken *Timaeus* s v. Here however it is a middle signifying 'to form images, to conjure up spectres', and so 'to indulge in idle fancies', like the later use of φαντάζεσθαι. The Lexicons do not recognise this use, but see Dion Chrys. *Orat.* xii. 53 (p. 209 M) πρότερον μὲν γὰρ ἅτε οὐδὲν σαφὲς εἰδότες ἄλλην ἄλλος ἀνεπλάττομεν ἰδέαν, πᾶν τὸ θνητὸν κατὰ τὴν ἑαυτοῦ δύναμιν καὶ φύσιν ἰνδαλλόμενοι καὶ ὀνειρώττοντες,

Sext. Emp. *adv. Math.* vii. 249 ἔνιαι (φαντασίαι) πάλιν ἀπὸ ὑπάρχοντος μέν εἰσιν, οὐκ αὐτὸ δὲ τὸ ὑπάρχον ἰνδάλλονται κ.τ.λ., xi. 122 ὁ τὸν πλοῦτον μέγιστον ἀγαθὸν ἰνδαλλόμενος, Clem. Alex. *Protr.* 10 (p. 81) χρυσὸν ἢ λίθον ἢ δένδρον ἢ πρᾶξιν ἢ πάθος ἢ νόσον ἢ φόβον ἰνδάλλεσθαι ὡς θεόν, Method, *Symp.* viii. 2 ἔτι ἐνδημοῦσαι τοῖς σώμασιν ἰνδάλλονται τὰ θεῖα. (The last two passages I owe to Jahn's *Method.* II. p. 51; the others I had collected before I saw his note). So ἴνδαλμα most frequently suggests the idea of an unreal, spectral, appearance, as Wisd. xvii. 3 ἰνδάλμασιν ἐκταρασσόμενοι, *Clem. Hom.* iv. 4 φαντάσματά τε γὰρ καὶ ἰνδάλματα ἐν μέσῃ τῇ ἀγορᾷ φαίνεσθαι ποιῶν δι' ἡμέρας πᾶσαν ἐκπλήττει τὴν πόλιν, Athenag. *Suppl.* 27 αἱ οὖν ἄλογοι αὗται καὶ ἰνδαλματώδεις τῆς ψυχῆς κινήσεις εἰδωλομανεῖς ἀποτίκτουσι φαντασίας, where he is speaking of false objects of worship.
16. ταλαίπωροι κ.τ.λ.] The same passage is quoted also in the 2nd Epistle ascribed to Clement (§ 11), being there introduced by the words λέγει γὰρ καὶ ὁ προφητικὸς λόγος. Though the quotation there is essentially the same, yet the variations which it presents show that it cannot have been de-

· τοŷ ἁμαρτωλοŷ, τοyc δὲ ἐλ[πίζον]τας ἐπὶ Κýριον ἔλεος κy-
κλώcε[ι].

10   XXIII. Ὁ οἰκτίρμων κατὰ πάντα κ[αὶ εὐερ]γετικὸς
πατὴρ ἔχει σπλάγχνα ἐ[πὶ] φοβουμένους αὐτόν, ἠπίως
[τε] καὶ προσηνῶς τὰς χάριτας αὐτ[οῦ] ἀποδιδοῖ τοῖς
προσερχομένοι[ς] αὐτῷ ἁπλῇ διανοίᾳ. διὸ μὴ διψυχῶμεν, μηδὲ ἰνδαλλέσθω ἡ ψυχὴ ἡμῶν ἐπὶ ταῖς ὑπερβαλ-
15 λούσαις καὶ ἐνδόξοις δωρεαῖς αὐτοῦ. πόρρω γενέσθω ἀφ'
ἡμῶν ἡ γραφὴ αὕτη, ὅπου λέγει· Ταλαίπωροί εἰcιν οἱ

8 τοῦ ἁμαρτωλοῦ] A.   τῶν ἁμαρτωλῶν Clem. Alex.   ἔλεοs] Clem. Alex.
ελαιοσ A.   10 οἰκτίρμων] οικτειρμων A.

rived directly or solely from the first Epistle. Moreover it is there continued, οὕτως καὶ ὁ λαός μου ἀκαταστασίας καὶ θλίψεις ἔσχεν, ἔπειτα ἀπολήψεται τὰ ἀγαθά. As this passage does not occur in the Old Testament, it must have been taken from some lost apocryphal writing. Some writers indeed have supposed that Clement here, as he certainly does elsewhere (e.g. §§ 18, 26, 29, 32, 35, 39, 46, 50, 52, 53, and just below ταχὺ ἥξει κ.τ.λ.), is fusing several passages of the Canonical Scriptures, such as James i. 8, 2 Pet. iii. 4, Mark iv. 26, Matt. xxiv. 32 sq. (Mark xiii. 28 sq., Luke xxi. 29 sq.); but the resemblances though striking are not sufficient; and this explanation does not account for the facts already mentioned. The description ὁ προφητικὸς λόγος and the form of the quotation ὁ λαός μου κ.τ.λ., as given in the 2nd Epistle, show that it must have been taken from some spurious prophetic book formed on the model of the Canonical prophecies. I would conjecture that it was *Eldad and Modad*, which was certainly known in the early Roman Church; see Herm. *Vis.* ii. 3 ἐγγὺς Κύριος τοῖς ἐπιστρεφομένοις, ὡς γέγραπται ἐν τῷ Ἐλδὰδ καὶ Μωδὰδ τοῖς προφητεύσασιν ἐν τῇ ἐρήμῳ τῷ λαῷ, a passage alleged by Hermas for the same purpose as our quotation, to refute one who is sceptical about the approaching afflictions of the last times. On this apocryphal book see Fabricius *Cod. Pseud. V.T.* I. p. 801. It may have been forged by some Christian to sustain the courage of the brethren under persecution by the promise of the Lord's advent; and, if so, the resemblances to the New Testament writings in this quotation are explained. Hilgenfeld suggests the *Assumption of Moses* (see the notes § 17, 25) as the source of this quotation, but does not assign any reason for this view except his own theory that Clement was acquainted with that work.

οἱ δίψυχοι κ.τ.λ.] Comp. James i. 8 ἀνὴρ δίψυχος ἀκατάστατος ἐν πάσαις ταῖς ὁδοῖς αὐτοῦ. For the parallels in Hermas see the note on § 11. The conjecture in the last note is confirmed by the fact that Hermas gives repeated warnings against διψυχία and even speaks thereupon in the context of the passage referring to 'Eldad and Modad.' For close re-

Δίψυχοι, οἱ διστάζοντες τὴν ψυχήν, οἱ λέγοντες, Ταῦτα ἠκού-
ϲαμεν καὶ ἐπὶ τῶν πατέρων ἡμῶν, καὶ ἰδοὺ γεγηράκαμεν
καὶ οὐδὲν ἡμῖν τούτων ϲυνβέβηκεν. ὦ ἀνόητοι, ϲυμβάλετε
ἑαυτοὺϲ ξύλῳ· λάβετε ἄμπελον· πρῶτον μὲν φυλλοροεῖ,
εἶτα βλαϲτὸϲ γίνεται, εἶτα φύλλον, εἶτα ἄνθος, καὶ μετὰ 5
ταῦτα ὄμφαξ, εἶτα ϲταφυλὴ παρεϲτηκυῖα. Ὁρᾶτε, ὅτι ἐν
καιρῷ ὀλίγῳ εἰς πέπειρον καταντᾷ ὁ καρπὸς τοῦ ξύλου.
ἐπ' ἀληθείας ταχὺ καὶ ἐξαίφνης τελειωθήσεται τὸ βούλημα αὐτοῦ, συνεπιμαρτυρούσης καὶ τῆς γραφῆς ὅτι
ταχὺ ἥξει καὶ οὐ χρονιεῖ, καὶ ἐξαίφνηϲ ἥξει ὁ Κύριος εἰς 10

7 πέπειρον] πεπιρον A.   8 ἐξαίφνης] εξεφνησ A.   10 ἐξαίφνης]
εξαιχνησ A.   13 ἐπιδείκνυται] επιδικνυται A.   16 καιρούς] See below.
18 ἀνίσταται ἡμέρα] After the H Tisch. thinks he sees part of a second H and would

semblances to this quotation see *Vis.*
iii. 4 διὰ τοὺς διψύχους τοὺς διαλογι-
ζομένους ἐν ταῖς καρδίαις αὐτῶν εἰ ἄρα
ἔσται ταῦτα ἢ οὐκ ἔσται, *Mand.* ix οἱ
γὰρ διστάζοντες εἰς τὸν Θεὸν οὗτοί εἰσιν
οἱ δίψυχοι κ.τ.λ.
1. οἱ λέγοντες κ.τ.λ.] 2 Pet. iii. 4
καὶ λέγοντες ποῦ ἐστιν ἡ ἐπαγγελία τῆς
παρουσίας αὐτοῦ; ἀφ' ἧς γὰρ οἱ πατέρες
ἐκοιμήθησαν, πάντα οὕτως διαμένει ἀπ'
ἀρχῆς κτίσεως.
2. καὶ ἐπὶ] '*also in the time of.*'
Either the speakers use the first
person ἠκούσαμεν as identifying themselves with the Israelite people of past
generations, or (as seems more probable) ἐπὶ τῶν πατέρων must mean
'when our fathers were still alive',
i.e. 'in our childhood and youth.'
It will be remembered that this apocryphal prophecy is supposed to be
delivered to the Israelites in the
wilderness. At all events we cannot
arbitrarily change ἐπὶ into ἀπὸ with
Young and most subsequent editors
(Jacobson and Hilgenfeld are exceptions), for ἐπὶ is read in the MS both
here and in ii § 11.
4. λάβετε ἄμπελον κ.τ.λ.] The
words strongly resemble Mark iv. 26

sq. (comp. Matt. xxiv. 32 sq., Mark xiii.
28 sq. Luke xxi. 29 sq.). See also
Epict. *Diss.* iii. 24. 86 ὡς σῦκον, ὡς
σταφυλή, τῇ τεταγμένῃ ὥρᾳ τοῦ ἔτους,
iii. 24. 91 τὸ φυλλοροεῖν καὶ τὸ ἰσχάδα
γίνεσθαι ἀντὶ σύκου καὶ ἀσταφίδας ἐκ
τῆς σταφυλῆς κ.τ.λ., M. Anton. xi. 35
ὄμφαξ, σταφυλή, σταφίς, πάντα μετα-
βολαὶ οὐκ εἰς τὸ μὴ ὂν ἀλλ' εἰς τὸ νῦν
μὴ ὄν.

φυλλοροεῖ] For the orthography
see the note on ἐξερίζωσεν § 6.
6. παρεστηκυῖα] '*ripe*'; Exod. ix.
31 ἡ γὰρ κριθὴ παρεστηκυῖα. So Theophrastus *Caus. Plant.* vi. 7. 5 παριστά-
μενος καὶ ἐξιστάμενος, of wine ripening
and going off (see Schneider's note).
Similarly παραγίνεσθαι is used, e.g.
Herod. i. 193 παραγίνεται ὁ σῖτος.
The words ὄμφαξ, σταφυλή, σταφίς
(ἀσταφίς), denote the sour, ripe, and
dried grape respectively; see the
passages in the previous note, and add
Anthol. III p. 3, IV p. 131 (ed. Jacobs).
Ὁρᾶτε κ.τ.λ.] This sentence is
generally treated by the editors as
part of the quotation, but I think
this wrong for two reasons; (1) In the
2nd Epistle, where also the passage
is cited, after σταφυλὴ παρεστηκυῖα fol-

τὸν ναὸν αὐτοῦ, καὶ ὁ ἅγιος ὃν ὑμεῖς προςδοκᾶτε.

XXIV. Κατανοήσωμεν, ἀγαπητοί, πῶς ὁ δεσπότης ἐπιδείκνυται διηνεκῶς ἡμῖν τὴν μέλλουσαν ἀνάστασιν ἔσεσθαι, ἧς τὴν ἀπαρχὴ[ν] ἐποιήσατο τὸν Κύριον Ἰησοῦν
15 Χριστὸν ἐκ νεκ[ρῶν] ἀναστήσας. ἴδωμεν, ἀγαπητοί, τὴν κατὰ και[ροὺς] γινομένην ἀνάστασιν. ἡμέρ[α καὶ] νὺξ ἀνάστασιν ἡμῖν δηλοῦσ[ιν]· κοιμᾶται ἡ νύξ, ἀνίσταται ἡ[μέρα] ἡ ἡμέρα ἄπεισιν, νὺξ ἐπέρ[χεται. βλέπωμ]εν τοὺς καρπούς· ὁ σπόρος [τῆς γῆς] τίνα τρόπον γίνεται;
20 ἐξῆλ[θεν ὁ c]πείρων καὶ ἔβαλεν εἰς τὴν γῆν· [καὶ βλη-

therefore read ἡ ἡμέρα. I could only discern a stroke which might as well belong to a M as to an H; and the parallelism of the clauses suggests the omission of the article. 19 τῆς γῆς] See below.

lows immediately the sentence οὕτως καὶ ὁ λαός μου κ.τ.λ.; the words ὁρᾶτε κ.τ.λ. not only not being quoted but being hardly compatible with the form of the context as there given; (2) ὁρᾶτε is an expression by which Clement himself elsewhere, after adducing a quotation or an example, enforces its lesson; as § 4, 12, 16, 41, 50.

7. εἰς πέπειρον] 'to maturity'. The construction καταντᾶν εἰς is common in the LXX and N. T.; see also above § 5.

10. ταχὺ ἥξει κ.τ.λ.] A combination of Is. xiii. 22 ταχὺ ἔρχεται καὶ οὐ χρονιεῖ (comp. Hab. ii. 3, Heb. x. 37), and Mal. iii. 1 καὶ ἐξαίφνης ἥξει εἰς τὸν ναὸν αὐτοῦ Κύριος ὃν ὑμεῖς ζητεῖτε καὶ ὁ ἄγγελος τῆς διαθήκης ὃν ὑμεῖς θέλετε.

XXIV. 'All the works of the Creator bear witness to the resurrection. The day arises from the grave of the night. The young and fruitful plant springs up from the decayed seed'.

The eloquent passage in Tertullian *de Resurr. Carn.* 12, 13, where the same analogies are adduced, is certainly founded on this passage of Clement (see above, p. 9). Compare also Theoph. *ad Aut.* i. 13, Tertull. *Apol.* 34, Minuc. Fel. 48.

14. τὴν ἀπαρχήν] 1 Cor. xv. 20 Χριστὸς ἐγήγερται ἐκ νεκρῶν ἀπαρχὴ τῶν κεκοιμημένων; comp. ver. 23. It is evident from what follows that Clement has this 15th chapter in his mind.

16. κατὰ καιρούς] 'at each recurring season'; as Theoph. *ad Aut.* i. 13 κατὰ καιροὺς προφέρουσιν τοὺς καρπούς. I have preferred κατὰ καιροὺς to κατὰ καιρόν (which is read by all previous editors) not only because the plural stands in the parallel passage of Theophilus, but because κατὰ καιρὸν commonly has the sense 'opportunely' (e.g. Rom. v. 6), which is out of place here.

19. τῆς γῆς] Or perhaps supply ἴδωμεν or κατ' ἔτος. Young reads πᾶσι δῆλον. At all events the κόκκου of Wotton and subsequent editors is objectionable, as needlessly violating the common rule respecting the article, which requires either ὁ σπόρος τοῦ κόκκου or σπόρος κόκκου.

20. ἐξῆλθεν κ.τ.λ.] The expression is borrowed from the Gospel narra-

θέ]ντων σπερμάτων, ἅτινα πέ[πτωκεν] εἰς τὴν γῆν ξηρὰ
καὶ γυμνά, δι[αλύεται]. εἶτ' ἐκ τῆς διαλύσεως ἡ μεγα-
[λειότ]ης τῆς προνοίας τοῦ δεσπότου [ἀνίσ]τησιν αὐτά,
καὶ ἐκ τοῦ ἑνὸς πλεί[ονα] αὔξει καὶ ἐκφέρει καρπόν.

tive; Matt. xiii. 3, Mark iv. 3, Luke viii. 5.

2. γυμνή] See I Cor. xv. 36 sq., from which this epithet is derived. It denotes the absence of germination: see the rabbinical passages quoted by Wetstein on 1 Cor. l. c., and Methodius in Epiphan. *Hær.* lxiv. 44 (p. 570) κατάμαθε γὰρ τὰ σπέρματα πῶς γυμνὰ καὶ ἄσαρκα βάλλεται εἰς τὴν γῆν κ.τ.λ.

διαλύεται] '*rots*'. Comp. Theoph. *ad Aut.* i. 13 πρῶτον ἀποθνήσκει καὶ λύεται. This analogy is derived from 1 Cor. xv. 36; comp. John xii. 24.

4. αὔξει] intransitive, as in Ephes. ii. 21, Col. ii. 19.

XXV. 'The phœnix is a still more marvellous symbol of the resurrection. After living five hundred years he dies. From his corpse the young bird arises. When he is fledged and strong, he carries his father's bones and lays them on the altar of the sun at Heliopolis. This is done in broad daylight before the eyes of all: and the priests, keeping count of the time, find that just five hundred years have gone by'.

7. ὄρνεον κ.τ.λ.] The earliest mention of the phœnix is in Hesiod (*Fragm.* 50 ed. Gaisf.), who however speaks merely of its longevity. It is from Herodotus (ii. 73) that we first hear the marvellous story of the burial of the parent bird by the offspring, as it was told him by the Egyptian priests, but he adds cautiously ἐμοὶ μὲν οὐ πιστὰ λέγοντες. It is mentioned again by Antiphanes (Athen. xiv. p. 655 B) ἐν Ἡλίου μέν φασι γίγ-νεσθαι πόλει φοίνικας. From the Greeks the story passed to the Romans. In B.C. 97 a learned senator Manilius (Plin. *N. H.* x. 2) discoursed at length on the phœnix, stating that the year in which he wrote was the 215th since its last appearance. He was the first Roman who took up the subject. At the close of the reign of Tiberius—A.D. 36 according to Pliny (following Cornelius Valerianus) and Dion Cassius (lviii. 27), but A.D. 34 as Tacitus reports the date—the marvellous bird was said to have reappeared in Egypt. The truth of the statement however was questioned by some, as less than 250 years had elapsed since the reign of the third Ptolemy when it was seen last (Tac. *Ann.* vi. 28). But the report called forth many learned disquisitions from savants in Egypt both native and Greek. A few years later (A.D. 47) the bird was actually exhibited in Rome ('in comitio propositus, *quod actis testatum est*,' are Pliny's words) and may have been seen by Clement, but no one doubted that this was an imposture. The story of the phœnix of course has a place in Ovid's *Metamorphoses* (xv. 392 'Una est quæ reparet seque ipsa reseminet ales' etc.), and allusions to it in Latin poets are naturally not unfrequent. Claudian devotes a whole poem to it. Another ascribed to Lactantius (*Corp. Poet. Lat.* p. 1416 ed. Weber) also takes this same subject. The references to the phœnix in classical and other writers are collected by Henrichsen *de Phœnicis fabula* Havn. 1825.

5 XXV. [Ἴδω]μεν τὸ παράδοξον σημεῖον, τὸ [γιν]ό-
μενον ἐν τοῖς ἀνατολικοῖς [τό]ποις, τουτέστιν τοῖς περὶ
τὴν Ἀραβίαν. ὄρνεον γάρ ἐστιν ὃ προσονομάζεται

7 ὄρνεον] ορναιον A.

The main features of the account seem to have been very generally believed by the Romans. Thus Mela (iii. 8), who seems to have flourished in the reign of Claudius, repeats the marvellous story without any expression of misgiving. Pliny indeed declines to pronounce whether it is true or not ('haud scio an fabulose'); but Tacitus says no doubt is entertained of the existence of such a bird, though the account is in some points uncertain or exaggerated. Again Ælian (*Hist. An.* vi. 58), who lived in Hadrian's reign, alleges the phœnix as an instance of the superiority of brute instinct over human reason, when a bird can thus reckon the time and discover the place without any guidance; and somewhere about the same time or later Celsus (Origen *c. Cels.* iv. 98, I. p. 576), arguing against the Christians, brings it forward to show the greater piety of the lower animals as compared with man. Still later Philostratus (*Vit. Apoll.* iii. 49) mentions the account without recording any protest. I do not lay any stress on such passing allusions as Seneca's (*Ep. Mor.* 42 'Ille alter fortasse tamquam phœnix semel anno quingentesimo nascitur'), or on descriptions in romance writers like Achilles Tatius (iii. 25), because no argument can be founded on them.

It thus appears that Clement is not more credulous than the most learned and intelligent heathen writers of the preceding and following generations. Indeed he may have thought that he had higher sanction than the testimony of profane authors. Tertullian (*de Resurr. Carn.* 10) took Ps. xcii. 12 δίκαιος ὡς φοῖνιξ ἀνθήσει to refer to this prodigy of nature, and Clement may possibly have done the same. Even Job xxix. 18 is translated by several recent critics, 'With my nest shall I die and like the phœnix lengthen my days' (comp. Lucian *Hermot.* § 53 ἦν μὴ φοίνικος ἔτη βιώσῃ), therein following some rabbinical authorities: but even if this be the correct rendering, the LXX version, through which alone it would be known to Clement, gives a different sense to the words, ἡ ἡλικία μου γηράσει ὥσπερ στέλεχος φοίνικος, πολὺν χρόνον βιώσω.

At all events, even before the Christian era the story had been adopted by Jewish writers. In a poem on the Exodus written by one Ezekiel, probably an Alexandrian Jew in the 2nd or 3rd century B.C. (see Ewald *Gesch.* IV. p. 297), the phœnix, the sacred bird of Egypt, is represented as appearing to the Israelite host (see the passage quoted by Alexander Polyhistor in Euseb. *Præp. Evang.* ix. 29, p. 446). Though the name is not mentioned, there can be no doubt that the phœnix is intended; for the description accords with those of Herodotus, Manilius (in Pliny), and Mela, and was doubtless taken from some Egyptian painting such as Herodotus saw and such as may be seen on the monuments to the present day (see Wilkinson's *Anc. Egypt.* 2nd ser. I. p. 304, Rawlinson's *Herod.* II. p. 122). In the *Assumption of Moses*

φοῖνιξ· τοῦτο μονογενὲς ὑπάρχον ζῇ ἔτη πεντακόσια·

1 μονογενές] μονογενησ A.

too, if the reading be correct (see Hilgenfeld *Nov. Test. extra Can. Rec.* I. p. 99), the 'profectio phœnicis' is mentioned in connexion with the exodus, and it seems probable that the writer borrowed the incident from Ezekiel's poem and used it in a similar way. The appearance of the phœnix would serve a double purpose; (1) It would mark the epoch; (2) It would betoken the homage paid by heathen religion to the true God and to the chosen people: for Alexandrian Jews sought to give expression to this last idea in diverse ways, through Sibylline oracles, Orphic poems, and the like; and the attendance of the sacred phœnix on the departing host would not be the least eloquent form of symbolizing this homage in the case of Egypt. But this Ezekiel, though he coloured the incident and applied it to his own purpose, appears not to have invented it. According to Egyptian chronology the departure of the Israelites was coincident or nearly coincident with an appearance of a phœnix (i.e. with the beginning of a phœnix-period). Tacitus (*Ann.* vi. 28) says that a phœnix had appeared in the reign of *Amasis*. If this were the earlier *Amosis* of the 17th or 18th dynasty, and not the later *Amosis* of the 26th dynasty (the *Amasis* of Herod. ii. 172), the time would coincide; for the Israelites were considered by some authorities (whether rightly or wrongly, it is unnecessary here to enquire) to have left Egypt in the reign of this sovereign; e.g. by Ptolemy the priest of Mendes (Apion in Tatian *ad Græc.* 38 and Clem. Alex. *Strom.* i. 21, p. 378) and by Julius Africanus (Routh's *Rel. Sacr.* (II. p. 256). For rabbinical references

to the phœnix, which seem to be numerous, see Buxtorf *Lex. Rab.* s.v. חול; comp. Henrichsen l.c. II. p. 19. The reference in a later Sibylline too (*Orac. Sib.* viii. 139 ὅταν φοίνικος ἐπέλθῃ πενταχρόνοιο) was probably derived from an earlier Jewish poem.

Thus the mere fact that the phœnix is mentioned in the *Assumption of Moses* affords no presumption (as Hilgenfeld supposes) that Clement was acquainted with that work; for the story was well known to Jewish writers. In the manner and purpose of its mention (as I interpret it) the *Assumption* presents no coincidence with Clement's Epistle.

Of subsequent Christian fathers, Tertullian, as we saw, accepted the story without misgiving. As Theophilus of Antioch (*ad Aut.* i. 13) follows Clement's analogies for the resurrection up to a certain point, but omits all mention of the phœnix, I infer that his knowledge of Egyptian antiquities (see ii. 6, iii. 20 sq.) saved him from the error. For the same reason, as we may conjecture, Origen also considers the fact to be very questionable (*c. Cels.* iv. 98, 1. p. 576). But for the most part it was believed by Christian writers. S. Cyril of Jerusalem (*Cat.* xviii. 8), S. Ambrose (see the reff. above, p. 10), Rufinus (*Symb. Apost.* 11, p. 73), and others, argue from the story of the phœnix without a shadow of misgiving. In *Apost. Const.* v. 7 it is urged against the heathen, as a fact which they themselves attest; and Epiphanius (*Ancor.* 84) says εἰς ἀκοὴν ἀφίκται πολλῶν πιστῶν τε καὶ ἀπίστων. On the other hand Euseb. (*Vit. Const.* iv. 72) gives it merely as a report, Greg. Naz. (*Orat.* xxxi § 10, 1. p.

γενόμενόν τε ἤδη πρὸς ἀπόλυσιν τοῦ ἀποθανεῖν αὐτό,

562 D) says cautiously εἰ τῷ πιστὸς ὁ λόγος, and Augustine *de Anim.* iv. 33 (20) (X. p. 404) uses similar language, 'Si tamen ut creditur'; while Photius (*Bibl.* 126) places side by side the resurrection of the phœnix and the existence of lands beyond the Atlantic (§ 20) as statements in Clement to which exception may be taken. Other less important patristic references will be found in Suicer's *Thes.* s. v. φοῖνιξ.

It is now known that the story owes its origin to the symbolic and pictorial representations of astronomy. The appearance of the phœnix is the recurrence of a period marked by the heliacal rising of some prominent star or constellation. Even Manilius (Plin. *N. H.* x. 2) had half seen the truth; for he stated 'cum hujus alitis vita magni conversionem anni fieri iterumque significationes tempestatum et siderum easdem reverti'. For the speculations of Egyptologers and others on the phœnix period see Lepsius *Chronol. d. Ægypt.* p. 180 sq., Uhlemann *Handb. d. Ægypt. Alterthumsk.* III. p. 39 sq., 79 sq., IV. p. 226 sq., Poole *Horæ Ægyptiacæ* p. 39 sq., Ideler *Handb. der Chron.* I. p. 183 sq., Creuzer *Symb. u. Mythol.* II. p. 163 sq.

Thus the phœnix was a symbol from the very beginning. Horapollo says that in the hieroglyphics this bird represented a soul, or an inundation, or a stranger paying a visit after long absence, or a restoration after a long period (ἀποκατάστασιν πολυχρόνιον), *Hierogl.* i. 34, 35, ii. 57. The way was thus prepared for the application of Clement. This Apostolic father however confines the symbolism to the resurrection of man. But later patristic writers diversified the application and took the phœnix also as a type of the Person of our Lord. The marvellous birth and the unique existence of this bird, as represented in the myth, were admirably adapted to such a symbolism: and accordingly it is so taken in Epiphan. (l. c.), Rufinus (l.c.), and others; see especially an unknown but apparently very ancient author in *Spicil. Solesm.* III. p. 345. Some of these writers press the parallel so far as to state that the phœnix arises after three days. The fact that a reputed appearance of the phœnix was nearly coincident with the year of the Passion and Resurrection (see above, p. 94) may have assisted this application. At a later date the Monophysites alleged the phœnix as an argument in favour of their peculiar doctrines (see Piper *Mythol. u. Symbol. der Christl. Kunst* I. 1, p. 454).

For the representations of the phœnix in early Christian art see Piper *l.c.* p. 456 sq. Before it appears as a Christian symbol, it is found on coins and medals of the Roman Emperors (for instances see Piper p. 449) to denote immortality or renovation, with the legend SAEC. AVR., or AETERNITAS, or ΑΙΩΝ. It is significant that this use begins in the time of Hadrian, the great patron and imitator of Egyptian art.

μονογενές] '*alone of its kind, unique*'. This epithet is applied to the phœnix also in Origen, Cyril, and Apost. Const., and doubtless assisted the symbolism mentioned in the last note. So also in Latin it is 'unica', 'semper unica', Mela iii. 9, Ovid *Am.* ii. 6. 54, Lactant. *Phœn.* 31, Claudian *Laud. Stil.* ii. 417. Thus Milton speaks of the 'self-begotten bird... that no second knows nor third.'

ἔτη πεντακόσια] The longevity of

CLEM. 7

σηκὸν ἑαυτῷ ποιεῖ ἐκ λιβάνου καὶ σμύρνης καὶ τῶν λοιπῶν ἀρωμάτων, εἰς ὃν πληρωθέντος τοῦ χρόνου εἰσέρχεται καὶ τελευτᾷ. σηπομένης δὲ τῆς σαρκὸς σκώληξ τις γεννᾶται, ὃς ἐκ τῆς ἰκμάδος τοῦ τετελευτηκότος ζώου ἀνατρεφόμενος πτεροφυεῖ· εἶτα γενναῖος γενόμενος αἴρει τὸν σηκὸν ἐκεῖνον ὅπου τὰ ὀστᾶ τοῦ προγεγονότος ἐστίν, καὶ ταῦτα βαστάζων διανύει ἀπὸ τῆς Ἀραβικῆς χώρας ἕως τῆς Αἰγύπτου εἰς τὴν λεγομένην Ἡλιούπολιν· καὶ ἡμέρας, βλεπόντων πάντων, ἐπιπτὰς ἐπὶ τὸν τοῦ ἡλίου βωμὸν τίθησιν αὐτά, καὶ οὕτως εἰς τοὐπίσω ἀφορμᾷ. οἱ οὖν ἱερεῖς ἐπισκέπτονται τὰς ἀναγραφὰς τῶν χρόνων καὶ εὑρίσ-

4 τετελευτηκότος] τελευτηκοτοσ Α.   7 βαστάζων] βασταζον Α.

the phœnix is differently stated. Hesiod gives it (9×4×3×9=) 972 generations of men; Manilius (Plin. *N. H.* x. 2) 509 years; Solinus (*Polyh.* 36) 540 years; authorities mentioned in Tacitus 1461 years, which is the length of the Sothic period; Martial (v. 7), Claudian, Lactantius, and others, 1000 years; Chæremon (in Tzetzes *Chil.* v. 6. 395) 7006 years. But, says Tacitus, 'maxime vulgatum quingentorum spatium'; and this is adopted by almost all the Christian fathers together with most heathen writers; of the latter see a list in Lepsius *Chron.* p. 180.

τοῦ ἀποθανεῖν αὐτό] '*so that it should die*,' explaining the preceding γενόμενον πρὸς ἀπόλυσιν ' at the eve of its dissolution'.

4. σκώληξ τις γεννᾶται] This mode of reproduction is not mentioned by Herodotus (ii. 73); but it formed part of the story as related by Manilius to the Romans and is frequently mentioned by subsequent writers. To this account is sometimes added the incident that the parent bird lights its own pyre and that the worm is found in the smouldering ashes; e.g. Artemid. *Oneirocr.* iv. 47 αὐτὸς ἑαυτῷ ποιησάμενος ἐκ κασίας τε καὶ σμύρνης πυρὰν ἀποθνήσκει· καυθείσης δὲ τῆς πυρᾶς μετὰ χρόνον ἐκ τῆς σποδοῦ σκώληκα γεννᾶσθαι λέγουσιν κ.τ.λ. (comp. Martial v. 7). It is interesting to observe the different stages in the growth of the story, as follows; (1) The longevity alone (Hesiod); (2) The entombment and burial of the parent by the offspring (Herodotus); (3) The miraculous birth of the offspring from the remains of the parent (Manilius); (4) The three days' interval between the death of the parent and resuscitation of the offspring (Epiphanius).

5. γενναῖος] '*strong, lusty*,' as e.g. Dion Chrys. vii. p. 228 R ἰσχυροὶ ἔτι νέοι καὶ γενναῖοι τὰ σώματα. It corresponds to Ovid's ' Quum dedit huic ætas vires'.

8. διανύει] '*makes its way*', frequently used absolutely, e.g. Polyb. iii. 56. 1 (ἀπό), iv. 70. 5 (ἐκ), ii. 54. 6

κουσιν αὐτὸν πεντακοσιοστοῦ ἔτους πεπληρωμένου ἐληλυθέναι.

5 XXVI. Μέγα καὶ θαυμαστὸν οὖν νομίζομεν εἶναι, εἰ ὁ δημιουργὸς τῶν ἁπάντων ἀνάστασιν ποιήσεται τῶν ὁσίως αὐτῷ δουλευσάντων ἐν πεποιθήσει πίστεως ἀγαθῆς, ὅπου καὶ δι' ὀρνέου δείκνυσιν ἡμῖν τὸ μεγαλεῖον τῆς ἐπαγγελίας αὐτοῦ; ·[λ]έγει γάρ που· Καὶ ο ἐzαναcτήcειc με καὶ ἐzομολογήcομαί coι· [κ]αὶ ἐκοιμήθην καὶ ὕπνωcα, ἐzη[γ]έρθην, ὅτι cὺ μετ' ἐμοῦ εἶ. [κα]ὶ πάλιν Ἰὼβ λέγει· Καὶ ἀναcτήcειc [τὴ]ν cάρκα μου ταύτην τὴν ἀναντλήcαcαν ταῦτα πάντα.

8 διανύει] Leclerc.   διανεύει Α. See below.   18 ὀρνέου δείκνυσιν] ορναιου δικνυσιν Α.   μεγαλεῖον] μεγαλιον Α.   19 ἐπαγγελίας] επαγγελειασ Α.   22 σάρκα] σαρκαν Α.

(πρός). The word occurs above, § 20. The reading of the MS, διανεύει, is out of place, for it could only mean 'turns aside', i.e. for the purpose of avoiding. Several instances of the confusion of διανύειν and διανεύειν by transcribers are given by Jahn *Methodius* II. p. 110.

12. τὰς ἀναγραφάς] 'the public records'; comp. Tatian *ad Graec.* 38 Αἰγυπτίων δέ εἰσιν αἱ ἐπ' ἀκριβὲς χρόνων ἀναγραφαί. For the Egyptian ἀναγραφαὶ see also Diod. Sic. i. 44, xvi. 51, Joseph. *c. Ap.* i. 6 sq. The recently discovered register of the epiphanies of the bulls Apis is a parallel instance of such chronological records; see Bunsen's *Egypt* I. p. 62 (2nd ed.).

XXVI. 'Is it then strange that God should raise all men, when He has given us this marvellous sign? To such a resurrection we have the testimony of the Scriptures'.

16. ὁ δημιουργὸς κ.τ.λ.] See above § 20. On this Platonic phrase compare Jahn *Methodius* II. pp. 39, 91.

17. ἐν πεποιθήσει κ.τ.λ.] '*in the confidence which comes of honest faith*': comp. Ephes. iii. 12 ἐν πεποιθήσει διὰ τῆς πίστεως αὐτοῦ, and below § 35 πίστις ἐν πεποιθήσει. The phrase πίστις ἀγαθὴ occurs Tit. ii. 10, where however πίστις seems to mean 'fidelity.'

18. τὸ μεγαλεῖον] '*the greatness*'; comp. §§ 32, 49. It occurs Acts ii. 11, Luke i. 49 (v. l.), and several times in the LXX.

19. λέγει γάρ που] taken apparently from Ps. xxviii. 7 καὶ ἀνέθαλεν ἡ σάρξ μου καὶ ἐκ θελήματός μου ἐξομολογήσομαι αὐτῷ (comp. Ps. lxxxviii. 11).

20. ἐκοιμήθην κ.τ.λ.] A confusion of Ps. iii. 6 ἐγὼ ἐκοιμήθην καὶ ὕπνωσα, ἐξηγέρθην ὅτι Κύριος ἀντιλήψεταί μου, and Ps. xxiii. 4 οὐ φοβηθήσομαι κακὰ ὅτι σὺ μετ' ἐμοῦ εἶ.

22. Ἰὼβ λέγει] From LXX Job xix. 26 ἀναστήσει δέ μου τὸ σῶμα τὸ ἀναντλοῦν ταῦτα as read in A, but אB have ἀναστῆσαι τὸ δέρμα μου τὸ ἀναντλοῦν (or ἀντλοῦν) ταῦτα. The Hebrew original is different from either.

XXVII. Ταύτῃ οὖν τῇ ἐλπίδι προσδεδέσθωσαν αἱ ψυχαὶ ἡμῶν τῷ πιστῷ ἐν ταῖς ἐπαγγελίαις καὶ τῷ δικαίῳ ἐν τοῖς κρίμασιν. ὁ παραγγείλας μὴ ψεύδεσθαι πολλῷ μᾶλλον αὐτὸς οὐ ψεύσεται· οὐδὲν γὰρ ἀδύνατον παρὰ τῷ Θεῷ, εἰ μὴ τὸ ψεύσασθαι. ἀναζωπυρη- 5
ῇ σάτω οὖν ἡ πίστις αὐτοῦ ἐν ἡμῖν, καὶ νοήσωμεν ὅτι πάντα ἐγγὺς αὐτῷ ἐστιν. ἐν λόγῳ τῆς μεγαλωσύνης αὐτοῦ συνεστήσατο τὰ πάντα, καὶ ἐν λόγῳ δύναται αὐτὰ καταστρέψαι. Τίς ἐρεῖ ἀγτῷ· τί ἐποίηcac; Ἤ τίc ἀντιcτήcεται τῷ κράτει τῆc ἰcχγοc ἀγτοῦ; ὅτε θέλει καὶ 10
ὡc θέλει ποιήcει πάντα, καὶ οὐδὲν μὴ παρέλθῃ τῶν δεδογματιcμένων ὑπ' αὐτοῦ. πάντα ἐνώπιον αὐτοῦ

XXVII. 'Let us therefore cling fast to God. He has promised, and He cannot lie. Whatsoever He wills, He is able to perform. To His power no bounds are set. To His eye and His mind all things are open. The heavens declare His glorious works'.

2. τῷ πιστῷ κ.τ.λ.] Comp. Heb. x. 23 πιστὸς γὰρ ὁ ἐπαγγειλάμενος, and xi. 11.

4. οὐδὲν γὰρ ἀδύνατον κ.τ.λ.] Compare Heb. vi. 18 ἐν οἷς ἀδύνατον ψεύσασθαι [τὸν] Θεόν, with Matt. xix. 26 (Mark x. 27); see also Tit. i. 2.

5. ἀναζωπυρησάτω] intransitive; see the note on Ign. *Ephes.* 1. The context seems to suggest that ἡ πίστις αὐτοῦ should be rendered 'His faithfulness', as in Rom. iii. 3; see *Galatians* p. 155.

7. ἐγγὺς αὐτῷ] So Ign. *Ephes.* 15 οὐδὲν λανθάνει τὸν Κύριον, ἀλλὰ καὶ τὰ κρυπτὰ ἡμῶν ἐγγὺς αὐτῷ ἐστιν, which is perhaps a reminiscence of this passage: compare § 21 above.

ἐν λόγῳ κ.τ.λ.] See Heb. i. 3 φέρων τὰ πάντα τῷ ῥήματι τῆς δυνάμεως αὐτοῦ: comp. Wisd. ix. 1.

9. τίς ἐρεῖ αὐτῷ κ.τ.λ.] From Wisd.

xii. 12 τίς γὰρ ἐρεῖ Τί ἐποίησας ἢ τίς ἀντιστήσεται τῷ κρίματί σου; comp. Wisd. xi. 22 κράτει βραχίονός σου τίς ἀντιστήσεται; The expression τὸ κράτος τῆς ἰσχύος αὐτοῦ occurs in Ephes. i. 19, vi. 10. The κράτος is the ἰσχὺς exerted on some object.

11. οὐδὲν μὴ παρέλθῃ κ.τ.λ.] Comp. Matt. v. 18.

13. εἰ Οἱ οὐρανοὶ κ.τ.λ.] '*seeing that* "*The heavens* etc."' The εἰ is no part of the quotation. So treated the passage presents no difficulty; and the corrections proposed (e.g. the omission of εἰ, or the reading καὶ οἱ οὐρανοί) are unnecessary. Perhaps also the καὶ before οὐκ εἰσὶν should be excluded from the quotation in the same way. The quotation is then word for word (except the interchange of λόγοι and λαλιαί) from the LXX Ps. xix. 1—3.

17. ὧν...αὐτῶν] See above the note on § 20.

XXVIII. 'Therefore, since He sees and hears all things, let us forsake our vile deeds and take refuge in His mercy. We cannot escape His powerful arm; neither in the

TO THE CORINTHIANS.

εἰσιν, καὶ οὐδὲν λέληθεν τὴν βουλὴν αὐτοῦ, εἰ Οἱ ογ-
ρανοὶ Διηγοῦνται Δόζαν Θεοῦ, ποίησιν Δὲ χειρῶν αγτοῦ
15 ἀναγγέλλει τὸ στερέωμα· Ἡ Ἡμέρα τῇ Ἡμέρᾳ ἐρεγγεται ῥῆμα,
καὶ νγὲ νγκτὶ ἀναγγέλλει γνῶσιν· καὶ ογκ εἰσὶν λόγοι ογδὲ
λαλιαί, ὧν ογχὶ ἀκογονται αἱ φωναὶ αγτῶν.

XXVIII. Πάντων οὖν βλεπομένων καὶ ἀκουομέ-
νων, φοβηθῶμεν αὐτὸν καὶ ἀπολείπωμεν φαύλων ἔργων
20 μιαρὰς ἐπιθυμίας, ἵνα τῷ ἐλέει αὐτοῦ σκεπασθῶμεν
ἀπὸ τῶν μελλόντων κριμάτων. ποῦ γάρ τις ἡμῶν
δύναται φυγεῖν ἀπὸ τῆς κραταιᾶς χειρὸς αὐτοῦ; ποῖος
δὲ κόσμος δέξεταί τινα τῶν αὐτομολούντων ἀπ' αὐτοῦ;
λέγει γάρ που τὸ γραφεῖον· Ποῦ ἀφήζω καὶ ποῦ κργ-

14 ποίησιν] ποιήσειν A.

height of heaven nor the abyss of ocean nor in the farthest parts of the earth'.

23. αὐτομολούντων] See above, ὑποτακτεῖν § 21, and the note on δεσίρτωρ Ign. *Polyc.* 6.

24. τὸ γραφεῖον] '*the writing*'. S. Clement here seems to adopt the threefold division of the Old Testament books which appears in Ecclus. (prol.), in S. Luke (xxiv. 44), in Philo (*de Vit. cont.* 3, II. p. 475), in Josephus (*c. Ap.* i. 8), and generally. The third division is called τὰ ἄλλα βιβλία and τὰ λοιπὰ τῶν βιβλίων in Ecclus., ψαλμοί in S. Luke, ὕμνοι in Philo and Josephus. Its more general name in Hebrew was כתובים, 'the writings', translated sometimes by γραφεῖα, sometimes by ἀγιόγραφα : comp. Epiphan. *Hær.* xxix. 7 (I. p. 122) οὐ γὰρ ἀπηγόρευται παρ' αὐτοῖς νομοθεσία καὶ προφῆται καὶ γραφεῖα τὰ παρὰ Ἰουδαίοις καλούμενα, and again παρ' αὐτοῖς γὰρ πᾶς ὁ νόμος καὶ οἱ προφῆται καὶ τὰ γραφεῖα λεγόμενα κ.τ.λ., *Mens. et pond.* 4 (II. p. 162) τὰ καλούμενα γραφεῖα παρά τισι δὲ ἀγιόγραφα λεγόμενα. In

the first of these passages however Epiphanius includes the historical books among the γραφεῖα, and in the second he confines the term to them, placing the Psalms, Job, Proverbs, etc., in a separate section which he calls οἱ στιχηρεῖς. This does not truly represent the Jewish tradition, in which 1, 2 Chronicles alone belonged to the כתובים, while the historical books generally were ranged with the Prophets; see Fürst *Der Kanon des Alten Testaments* p. 10 sq., p. 55 sq. Elsewhere he uses γραφεῖα more widely, *Hær.* xxvi. 12 (p. 94) ἄλλα μυρία παρ' αὐτοῖς πεπλασμένα γραφεῖα; comp. Deut. x. 4 (Aq.). John Damascene likewise (*de Fid. Orthod.* iv. 17. I. p. 284), following Epiphanius, describes the historical books from Joshua to 2 Chronicles, as τὰ καλούμενα γραφεῖα παρά τισι δὲ ἀγιόγραφα. In the Classical language (as also LXX Job xix. 24, Hex. Jer. xvii. 1) γραφεῖον is not 'a writing' but 'a pen.'

ποῦ ἀφήξω] A very loose quotation from Ps. cxxxix. 7—10, where

ΒΗϹΟΜΑΙ ἀπὸ τοῦ προϲώπογ ϹΟΥ; ἐὰν ἀναβῶ εἰϲ τὸν ογρα-
νόν, ϲγ εἶ ἐκεῖ· ἐὰν ἀπέλθω εἰϲ τὰ ἔϲχατα τῆϲ γῆϲ, ἐκεῖ ἡ
Δεξιά ϲογ· ἐὰν καταϲτρώϲω εἰϲ τὰϲ ἀβύϲϲογϲ, ἐκεῖ τὸ πνεῦμά
ϲογ. ποῖ οὖν τις ἀπέλθῃ ἢ ποῦ ἀποδράσῃ ἀπὸ τοῦ
τὰ πάντα ἐμπεριέχοντος;

the slight variations of the principal MSS of the LXX do not affect the wide divergences in Clement's quotation. Compare also the parallel passage in Amos ix. 2, 3, to which Clement's quotation presents some faint resemblances. It is important to observe that in using καταστρώσω, 'make my couch,' Clement conforms to the original אציעה, where the LXX has καταβῶ. This is the more remarkable, as he elsewhere shows no knowledge of the Hebrew and in the Psalms generally quotes pretty accurately from the LXX. Whence then did he get this word? We may conjecture that he was acquainted with one of the versions afterwards included by Origen in his Hexapla. The 5th version (ε in Origen) has στρώσω (see Field's *Hexapl.* ad loc.), and as this seems to have been the one found in an old cask either at Jericho or Nicopolis (Euseb. *H. E.* vi. 16, Epiphan. *Mens. et pond.* 18, p. 174; see Hody *de Bibl. Text. Orig.* etc. p. 587 sq.), it may very well have been an ancient Jewish translation prior to the age of Clement. Clem. Alex. *Strom.* iv. 22 (p. 625) quotes the passage nearly in the form which it has here (though substituting the LXX καταβῶ for καταστρώσω), and doubtless derived it through the medium of the Roman Clement, so that he is not an independent authority.

.. ἀφήξω] The verb ἀφήκειν is not found in the LXX or N. T., and is altogether a rare word; comp. Plato *Resp.* vii. p. 530 E, Antiphon in Bekker *Anecd.* p. 470 *s.v.* ἀφήκοντος.

XXIX. 'Therefore let us approach Him in prayer with pure hearts and undefiled hands. We are God's special portion and inheritance, of which the Scriptures speak once and again'.

7. ἀγνὰς κ.τ.λ.] 1 Tim. ii. 8 ἐπαίροντας ὁσίους χεῖρας, Athenag. *Suppl.* 13 ἐπαίρωμεν ὁσίους χεῖρας αὐτῷ; see also Heliodorus the tragedian in Galen. *de Antid.* ii. 7 (XIV p. 145 ed. Kuhn) ἀλλ' ὁσίας μὲν χεῖρας ἐς ἠέρα λαμπρὸν ἀείρας (quoted by Wetstein on 1 Tim. ii. 8). The expression describes the attitude of the ancients (as of Orientals at the present day) when engaged in prayer, with extended arms and uplifted palms.

9. ἐκλογῆς μέρος κ.τ.λ.] '*has made us His special portion,*' or rather '*has set apart for Himself a special portion*'. In either case the ἐκλογῆς μέρος is the Christian people, the spiritual Israel, who under the new covenant have taken the place of the chosen people under the old; as 1 Pet. ii. 9 ὑμεῖς δὲ γένος ἐκλεκτόν, βασίλειον ἱεράτευμα, ἔθνος ἅγιον, λαὸς εἰς περιποίησιν κ.τ.λ. See the notes on παροικοῦντες and ἡγιασμένοις (§ 1). Thus μέρος ἐκλογῆς here is coextensive with οἱ ἐκλελεγμένοι ὑπὸ τοῦ Θεοῦ διὰ Ἰησοῦ Χριστοῦ § 50 (comp. § 58). The words μέρος ἐκλογῆς are not to be translated 'a portion of his elect' but 'a portion set apart by election,' ἐκλογῆς being a genitive of the same kind as in Acts ix. 15 σκεῦος ἐκλογῆς, Iren. i. 6. 4 σπέρματα ἐκλογῆς. The expression therefore has no bearing on the question whether Clement was a Jewish or Gentile Christian. See the note on λαὸς below.

XXIX. Προσέλθωμεν οὖν αὐτῷ ἐν ὁσιότητι ψυχῆς, ἁγνὰς καὶ ἀμιάντους χεῖρας αἴροντες πρὸς αὐτόν, ἀγαπῶντες τὸν ἐπιεικῆ καὶ εὔσπλαγχνον πατέρα ἡμῶν ὃς ἐκλογῆς μέρος ἐποίησεν ἑαυτῷ. Οὕτω γὰρ γέγραπται· Ὅτε διεμέριζεν ὁ ὕψιστος ἔθνη, ὡς διέσπειρεν υἱοὺς Ἀδάμ, ἔστησεν ὅρια ἐθνῶν κατὰ ἀριθμὸν ἀγγέλων

8 ἐπιεικῆ] επιεικην A.   11 ἀριθμόν] αριθον A.

10. Ὅτε διεμέριζεν κ.τ.λ.] From the LXX Deut. xxxii. 8, 9, almost word for word.

11. κατὰ ἀριθμόν κ.τ.λ.] The idea conveyed by the LXX which Clement quotes is that, while the Gentile nations were committed to His inferior ministers, God retained the people of Israel under His own special guardianship: comp. Dan. x. 13 sq., xii. 1, but esp. Ecclus. xvii. 17 ἑκάστῳ ἔθνει κατέστησεν ἡγούμενον καὶ μερὶς Κυρίου Ἰσραήλ ἐστιν, and *Jubilees* § 15 (Ewald *Jahrb.* III. p. 10) ' Many are the nations and numerous the people, and all are His, and over all hath He set spirits as lords...but over Israel did He set no one to be Lord, neither angel nor spirit, but He alone is their ruler etc.', with the context. See also *Clem. Hom.* xviii. 4, *Clem. Recogn.* ii. 42 (references which I should have overlooked but for Hilgenfeld *Apost. Vät.* p. 65). Clem. Alex. *Strom.* vii. 2 (p. 832) uses the text to support his favourite idea that heathen philosophy is the handmaid of revelation; οὗτός ἐστιν ὁ διδοὺς καὶ τοῖς Ἕλλησι τὴν φιλοσοφίαν διὰ τῶν ὑποδεεστέρων ἀγγέλων· εἰσὶ γὰρ συνδιανενεμημένοι προστάξει θείᾳ τε καὶ ἀρχαίᾳ ἄγγελοι κατὰ ἔθνη, ἀλλ' ἡ μερὶς Κυρίου ἡ δόξα τῶν πιστευόντων. On the other hand the present text of the Hebrew runs ' He set the boundaries of the nations according to the number of the sons of Israel (לְמִסְפַּר בְּנֵי יִשְׂרָאֵל); for

(or 'while', כִּי) the portion of Jehovah is His people, Jacob is the rod of His inheritance'. So too the Peshito and Targum of Onkelos. But it is difficult to get any good sense out of this reading, and the parallelism of the verses is thus shattered. I can hardly doubt therefore that the LXX is right, and the error can be easily explained. The ends of the lines have got out of gear; יִשְׂרָאֵל, which in the present text occupies the end of ver. 8, has been displaced from its proper position at the end of ver. 9, and thrust out the original word הָאֱלֹהִים, which has thus disappeared. The 'sons of God' are mentioned Job i. 6, ii. 1, xxxviii. 7, and in all places are translated (as it appears, correctly) by ἄγγελοι in the LXX; see Gesen. *Thes.* p. 215. This conjecture is confirmed by the fact that the Samar. Pent. reads 'Israel' at the end of both verses, thus presenting an intermediate reading between the LXX and the present Hebrew text. Justin Martyr *Dial.* § 131 (p. 360 B) refers to the difference between the Hebrew and LXX texts; see also Origen *In Num. Hom.* xxviii. § 4 (II p. 385), *In Ezech. Hom.* xiii (III. p. 401). The reading of the Hebrew text is naturally adopted in *Clem. Hom.* xviii. 4, as it is by Justin's Jewish opponents. The writer lived late enough to have got it from one of the Judaizing versions. On the other hand the LXX is quoted by

θεοῦ. ἐγενήθη μερὶς Κυρίου λαὸς αὐτοῦ Ἰακώβ, σχοίνισμα κληρονομίας αὐτοῦ Ἰσραήλ. καὶ ἐν ἑτέρῳ τόπῳ λέγει· Ἰδοὺ Κύριος λαμβάνει ἑαυτῷ ἔθνος ἐκ μέσου ἐθνῶν, ὥσπερ λαμβάνει ἄνθρωπος τὴν ἀπαρχὴν αὐτοῦ τῆς ἅλω, καὶ ἐξελεύσεται ἐκ τοῦ ἔθνους ἐκείνου ἅγια ἁγίων. 5

XXX. Ἁγίου οὖν μερὶς ὑπάρχοντες ποιήσωμεν τὰ τοῦ ἁγιασμοῦ πάντα, φεύγοντες καταλαλιάς, μιαράς

6 Ἁγίου οὖν] ΑΓΙΟΥΝ (the ΟΥ above the line being written *prima manu*) A.

Philo *de Post. Ca.* 25 (I. p. 241), *de Plant.* 14 (I. p. 338).

2. λαός] We have here the common antithesis of λαός 'the chosen people', and ἔθνη 'the Gentiles'; as e.g. Luke ii. 32, Acts iv. 27, xxvi. 17, 23, Rom. xv. 10, 11, etc. By becoming the λαός however the Israelites do not cease to be called an ἔθνος (see esp. Joh. xi. 50), but are rather ἔθνος ἅγιον (as Exod. xix. 6, 1 Pet. ii. 9) or ἔθνος ἐκ μέσου ἐθνῶν (as below): so Justin *Dial.* 24 (p. 242) ἵνα γένηται ἔθνος δίκαιον, λαὸς φυλάσσων πίστιν (from Is. xxvi. 2). All such titles, referring primarily to the Israel after the flesh, are transferred by Clement, following the Apostolic writers, to the Israel after the spirit; see above the notes on § 1, and comp. below § 58 εἰς λαὸν περιούσιον, and especially Justin *Dial.* 119 (p. 347). I call attention to this, because Hilgenfeld (*Zeitschr. f. Wissensch. Theol.* 1858, p. 585, and here) distinguishes the λαός of the first passage and the ἔθνος of the second, as though they referred to the Jewish and Gentile Christians respectively. Of such a distinction the context gives no indication; and this interpretation moreover supposes that Clement departs from the obvious meaning of the passages incorporated in the second quotation, where the original reference of ἔθνος is plainly to the Israelites. See the note on ἐκλογῆς μέρος above. Hilgenfeld moreover (in order to support this interpretation) reads Ἁγίων μερὶς for Ἁγίου οὖν μερὶς at the beginning of § 30, but this is certainly not the MS reading.

σχοίνισμα] 'a portion measured out by a line' (see the note on κανών, § 7), a common word in the LXX exactly representing the Hebrew חבל.

3. ἰδοὺ Κύριος κ.τ.λ.] A combination of several passages; Deut. iv. 34 εἰ ἐπείρασεν ὁ Θεὸς εἰσελθὼν λαβεῖν ἑαυτῷ ἔθνος ἐκ μέσου ἔθνους ἐν πειρασμῷ κ.τ.λ., Deut. xiv. 2 καὶ σὲ ἐξελέξατο Κύριος ὁ Θεός σου γενέσθαι σε λαὸν αὐτῷ περιούσιον ἀπὸ πάντων τῶν ἐθνῶν κ.τ.λ. (comp. vii. 6).

ὥσπερ λαμβάνει κ.τ.λ.] The passages most nearly resembling this are, Num. xviii. 27 λογισθήσεται ὑμῖν τὰ ἀφαιρέματα ὑμῶν ὡς σῖτος ἀπὸ ἅλω καὶ ἀφαίρεμα ἀπὸ ληνοῦ, 2 Chron. xxxi. 14 δοῦναι τὰς ἀπαρχὰς Κυρίου καὶ τὰ ἅγια τῶν ἁγίων, Ezek. xlviii. 12 ἔσται αὐτοῖς ἡ ἀπαρχὴ δεδομένη ἐκ τῶν ἀπαρχῶν τῆς γῆς, ἅγιον ἁγίων ἀπὸ τῶν ὁρίων κ.τ.λ. with the context; but in all these passages the reference of the 'firstfruits' is different. As Clement's quotations elsewhere are so free (e.g. §§ 18, 26, 32, 35, 39, etc.), he may only have combined these passages and applied them from memory; but

τε καὶ λάγνους συμπλοκάς, μέθας τε καὶ νεωτερισμοὺς
καὶ βδελυκτὰς ἐπιθυμίας, μυσερὰν μοιχείαν, βδελυκτὴν
10 ὑπερηφανίαν. Θεὸς Γάρ, φησιν, ὑπερηφάνοις ἀντιτάσσε-
ται, ταπεινοῖς Δὲ Δίδωσιν χάριν. Κολληθῶμεν οὖν ἐκείνοις οἷς ἡ χάρις ἀπὸ τοῦ Θεοῦ δέδοται. ἐνδυσώμεθα
τὴν ὁμόνοιαν, ταπεινοφρονοῦντες, ἐγκρατευόμενοι, ἀπὸ
παντὸς ψιθυρισμοῦ καὶ καταλαλιᾶς πόρρω ἑαυτοὺς
15 ποιοῦντες, ἔργοις δικαιούμενοι καὶ μὴ λόγοις. λέγει

8 λάγνους] Colomiés. αγνουσ A.   9 μοιχείαν] μοιχιαν A.

the alternative remains that he is quoting from some apocryphal writing, such as the spurious or interpolated Ezekiel quoted above (see the notes §§ 8, 13, 17, 23, 46). The ἅγια ἁγίων are the specially consecrated things, the offerings or first-fruits, as in the passages just quoted; see also Lev. xxi. 22, Ezek. xlii. 13. The expression is applied here either to the people of God themselves, or to their spiritual oblations (see below, §§ 40, 44).

XXX. 'Therefore, as the portion of the Holy One, let us be holy ourselves; let us lay aside all sins which defile; let us shun pride and ensue peace; let us be on our guard against slander and backbiting; let us seek not our own praise, but the praise of God. Self-will is accursed in His sight; but His blessing rests on the gentle and lowly-minded'.

6. Ἁγίου οὖν μερίς] i.e. 'As the special portion of a Holy God': comp. 1 Pet. i. 15 sq; κατὰ τὸν καλέσαντα ὑμᾶς ἅγιον καὶ αὐτοὶ ἅγιοι ἐν πάσῃ ἀναστροφῇ γενήθητε, διότι γέγραπται (Lev. xi. 44) Ἅγιοι ἔσεσθε ὅτι ἐγὼ ἅγιος.

7. φεύγ. καταλ.] 1 Pet. ii. 1 ἀποθέμενοι...πάσας καταλαλιάς.

8. λάγνους] Comp. Athenag. *Suppl.* 19 τοῖς ἀκολάστοις καὶ λάγνοις, 21 λαγ-

νείας ἢ βίας ἢ πλεονεξίας, Clem. Recogn. ix. 17 (the Greek is preserved in Cæsarius) μεθύσους, λάγνους, δαιμονῶντας, *Acta Petri* in Isid. Pelus. *Ep.* ii. 99 (see Hilgenfeld's *Nov. Test. extr. Can. Rec.* IV. p. 7c) ὁ γὰρ φιλοχρήματος οὐκ ἐχώρησε τὸν τῆς ἀκτημοσύνης λόγον οὐδὲ ὁ λάγνος τὸν περὶ σωφροσύνης κ.τ.λ., Clem. Alex. *Pæd.* ii. 10 (p. 222—225). I have preferred λάγνους to ἀνάγνους, because the former was more liable to be misread or misunderstood by a scribe than the latter; and the passages quoted show that it was likely to be used by an early Christian writer. It also accords better with the strong epithets in the context. Neither word occurs in the LXX or New Testament. The common form was λάγνος, the Attic λάγνης; see Lobeck *Phryn.* p. 184.

9. μυσεράν] For this form see the note on § 14.

10. Θεὸς γάρ κ.τ.λ.] From Prov. iii. 34 Κύριος ὑπερηφάνοις κ.τ.λ. In 1 Pet. v. 5, James iv. 6, it is quoted ὁ Θεὸς ὑπερηφάνοις κ.τ.λ. The Hebrew has simply הוא 'he'.

14. ψιθ. καὶ καταλ.] See below § 35. The words occur together also 2 Cor. xii. 20; comp. Rom. i. 30 ψιθυριστάς, καταλάλους.

15. ἔργοις δικαιούμενοι] See the note at the beginning of § 33.

γάρ· Ὁ τὰ πολλὰ λέγων καὶ ἀντακούσεται· ἢ ὁ εὔλαλος οἴεται εἶναι δίκαιος; εὐλογημένος γεννητὸς γυναικὸς ὀλιγόβιος· μὴ πολὺς ἐν ῥήμασιν γίνου. Ὁ ἔπαινος ἡμῶν ἔστω ἐν Θεῷ καὶ μὴ ἐξ αὐτῶν, αὐτεπαινετοὺς γὰρ μισεῖ ὁ Θεός. ἡ μαρτυρία τῆς ἀγαθῆς πράξεως ἡμῶν διδόσθω ὑπ' ἄλλων, καθὼς ἐδόθη τοῖς πατράσιν ἡμῶν τοῖς δικαίοις. θράσος καὶ αὐθάδεια καὶ τόλμα τοῖς κατηραμένοις ὑπὸ τοῦ Θεοῦ· ἐπιείκεια καὶ ταπεινοφροσύνη καὶ πραΰτης παρὰ τοῖς ηὐλογημένοις ὑπὸ τοῦ Θεοῦ.

XXXI. Κολληθῶμεν οὖν τῇ εὐλογίᾳ αὐτοῦ, καὶ

6 ἐδόθη] εδεηθη A. 8 ἐπιείκεια] επιεικια A. 17 αὐτοῦ δι' ἀδελφον] Jacobson.
20 'Εάν] See below.   εἰλικρινῶς] ιλικριν... A.   22 δωρεῶν] δωραιων A.

1. ὁ τὰ πολλὰ κ.τ.λ.] From the LXX of Job xi. 2, 3, almost word for word. It diverges widely from the Hebrew, and the sentiment εὐλογημένος κ.τ.λ. has no connexion with the context. It may be conjectured that the words γεννητὸς γυναικὸς ὀλιγόβιος crept in from xiv. 1 βροτὸς γὰρ γεννητὸς γυναικὸς ὀλιγόβιος, which may have stood next to this passage in a parallel column, and the εὐλογημένος will have come from the first word of the next verse, ברוך misread ברון.

2. γεννητός] See the note on Ign. Ephes. 7.

3. ὁ ἔπαινος κ.τ.λ] See Rom. ii. 29 οὗ ὁ ἔπαινος οὐκ ἐξ ἀνθρώπων ἀλλ' ἐκ τοῦ Θεοῦ, 2 Cor. x. 18 οὐ γὰρ ὁ ἑαυτὸν συνιστάνων κ.τ.λ.; comp. 1 Cor. iv. 5.

4. αὐτῶν] So read for αὑτῶν. On the forms αὑτοῦ, αὑτῷ, etc., as inadmissible here, see §§ 9, 12, 14, 32 (notes).

αὐτεπαινετούς] No other instance of the word is given in the Lexicons.

6. ὑπ' ἄλλων] See Prov. xxvii. 2.

9. πραΰτης] is distinguished from ταπεινοφροσύνη, Trench N. T. Syn. 1st ser. § xliv, and from ἐπιείκεια ib. § xliii.

XXXI. 'Let us therefore cling to His blessing: let us study the records of the past, and see how it was won by our fathers, by Abraham and Isaac and Jacob'.

12. ἀνατυλίξωμεν] 'unroll' and so 'pore over'; comp. Lucian Nigr. 7 τοὺς λόγους οὓς τότε ἤκουσα συναγείρων καὶ ἀνατυλίττων.

13. ὁ πατὴρ ἡμῶν] See the note on § 4.

14. οὐχὶ δικαιοσύνην κ.τ.λ.] Combining the statement of S. Paul (Rom. iv. 1 sq., Gal. iii. 6 sq.) with that of S. James (ii. 21 sq.). See the note at the beginning of § 33.

16. ἡδέως κ.τ.λ.] There is nothing in the original narrative which suggests that Isaac was a willing sacrifice; Gen. xxii. 7, 8. According to Josephus however, Ant. i. 14. 4, on hearing his father's purpose he δέχεται πρὸς ἡδονὴν τοὺς λόγους and ὥρμησεν ἐπὶ τὸν βωμὸν καὶ τὴν σφαγήν. See also Beer's Leben Abrahami's p. 65 sq.

ἴδωμεν τίνες αἱ ὁδοὶ τῆς εὐλογίας. ἀνατυλίξωμεν τὰ
ἀπ' ἀρχῆς γενόμενα. τίνος χάριν ηὐλογήθη ὁ πατὴρ
ἡμῶν Ἀβραάμ; οὐχὶ δικαιοσύνην καὶ ἀλήθειαν διὰ πίσ-
15 τεως ποιήσας; Ἰσαὰκ μετὰ πεποιθήσ[εως γινώ]σκων
τὸ μέλλον ἡδέ[ως ἐγένε]το θυσία. Ἰακὼβ μετὰ ταπει-
νοφρ[οσύνης] ἐξεχώρησεν τῆς γῆς αὑ[τοῦ δι' ἀδελ]φὸν
καὶ ἐπορεύθη πρὸς [Λαβὰν] καὶ ἐδούλευσεν, καὶ ἐδόθ[η
αὐτῷ] τὸ δωδεκάσκηπτρον τοῦ [Ἰσραήλ].
20 XXXII. [Ἐάν] τις καθ' ἓν ἕκαστον εἰλικριν[ῶς] κα-
τανοήσῃ, ἐπιγνώσεται [τὰ με]γαλεῖα τῶν ὑπ' αὐτοῦ
δεδομέ[νων] δωρεῶν. ἐξ αὐτοῦ γὰρ ἱερεῖ[ς τε] καὶ λευῖ-

αὐτοῦ] αντων A. ἱερεῖς τε καί] Tisch. ἱερεῖς previous edd., but τε is required for the space.

with the notes 709 sq., where ample rabbinical authorities are collected for this addition to the narrative. The idea is brought out strongly by Melito (Routh's *Rel. Sacr.* I. p. 123) ὁ δὲ Ἰσαὰκ σιγᾷ πεπεδημένος ὡς κριός, οὐκ ἀνοίγων τὸ στόμα οὐδὲ φθεγγόμενος φωνῇ· τὸ γὰρ ξίφος οὐ φοβηθεὶς οὐδὲ τὸ πῦρ πτοηθεὶς οὐδὲ τὸ παθεῖν λυπηθεὶς ἐβάστασεν τὸν τύπον τοῦ Κυρίου κ.τ.λ. Philo *de Abr.* 32 (II. p. 26) is seemingly ignorant of this turn given to the incident.

19. τὸ δωδεκάσκηπτρον] equivalent to τὸ δωδεκάφυλον, which occurs below § 55 and Acts xxvi. 7; for σκῆπτρον (שֵׁבֶט), 'a branch or rod', is a synonyme for 'a tribe'; e.g. 1 Kings xi. 31, 32 καὶ δώσω σοι δέκα σκῆπτρα καὶ δύο σκῆπτρα ἔσται αὐτῷ, and again ver. 35, 36 (see § 32); comp. *Test. xii Patr.* Nepht. 5 τὰ δώδεκα σκῆπτρα τοῦ Ἰσραήλ.

XXXII. 'If any one will consider, he may see what blessings God showers on the faithful. What great honours did He confer on this patriarch Jacob! From him was derived the priestly tribe of Levi: from him came the great high-priest, the Lord Jesus; from him are descended kings and rulers through Judah. And by the other tribes also he was the father of countless multitudes. It was God's will, not their own righteous doing, whereby they were glorified. And by His will also, not by our own piety or wisdom, are we and all men justified through faith—by His Almighty will to whom be glory for ever'.

20. Ἐάν] Previous editors read εἰ; but, though εἰ with the conjunction is possible (see *Philippians* iii. 11), it is rare and ought not to be introduced unnecessarily.

εἰλικρινῶς] '*distinctly, severally*'. It seems to be a military metaphor from εἴλη 'turma': see the note, *Philippians* i. 10.

21. ὑπ' αὐτοῦ] i.e. τοῦ Θεοῦ. There is a little awkwardness in the sudden transition to ἐξ αὐτοῦ, which must refer to Jacob; but τῶν ὑπ' αὐτοῦ δεδ. δωρεῶν can only be said of God (as in §§ 19, 23, 35), nor can ὑπ' αὐτοῦ be translated '*per* eum', as in the Latin version of Young.

22. ἐξ αὐτοῦ] i.e. from Jacob. The following clauses render it necessary

ται πάντες οἱ λειτουργ[οῦν]τες τῷ θυσιαστηρίῳ τοῦ
Θεοῦ· ἐξ αὐτοῦ ὁ Κύριος Ἰησοῦς τὸ κατὰ σάρκα· ἐξ
αὐτοῦ βασιλεῖς καὶ ἄρχοντες καὶ ἡγούμενοι, κατὰ τὸν
Ἰούδαν· τὰ δὲ λοιπὰ σκῆπτρα αὐτοῦ οὐκ ἐν μικρᾷ
δόξῃ ὑπάρχουσιν, ὡς ἐπαγγειλαμένου τοῦ Θεοῦ ὅτι 5
Ἔϲται τὸ ϲπέρμα ϲου ὡϲ οἱ ἀϲτέρεϲ τοῦ οὐρανοῦ. Πάντες
οὖν ἐδοξάσθησαν καὶ ἐμεγαλύνθησαν οὐ δι' αὐτῶν ἢ
τῶν ἔργων αὐτῶν ἢ τῆς δικαιοπραγίας ἧς κατειργά-
σαντο, ἀλλὰ διὰ τοῦ θελήματος αὐτοῦ. καὶ ἡμεῖς οὖν,

1 λειτουργοῦντες] λιτουργ...τεσ A.

to read αὐτοῦ for αὐτῶν, which might otherwise stand. For the whole passage comp. Rom. ix. 4, 5 ὧν...ἡ λατρεία καὶ αἱ ἐπαγγελίαι, ὧν οἱ πατέρες καὶ ἐξ ὧν Χριστὸς τὸ κατὰ σάρκα.

2. ὁ Κύριος Ἰησοῦς] He is mentioned in connexion with the Levitical tribe, as being the great High-priest, a favourite title in Clement: see the note § 36. Comp. *Ign. Philad.* 9 καλοὶ καὶ οἱ ἱερεῖς, κρεῖσσον δὲ ὁ ἀρχιερεύς. With Levi He is connected as a priest; from Judah He is descended as a king. Hence His name is placed between the two, as the link of transition from the one to the other. But there is no ground for assuming that by this collocation Clement implies our Lord to have *descended* from Levi, as Hilgenfeld (*Apost. Vät.* p. 103, and here) thinks. The Epistle to the Hebrews, which Clement quotes so repeatedly, and from which his ideas of Christ's high-priesthood are taken, would distinctly teach him otherwise (vii. 14, viii. 8). A double descent (from both Judah and Levi) is maintained in the *Test. xii Patr.* (see *Galatians* p. 308), but this writing travels in a different cycle of ideas. And even in this Judaic work the Virgin herself is represented as belonging to Judah. On the descent from Levi see Sinker *Test. of Twelve Patr.* p. 105 sq.

3. κατὰ τὸν Ἰούδαν] '*after Judah*,' i.e. as descended from him and thereby inheriting the attribute of royalty, Gen. xlix. 10. This idea of the royalty of the patriarch Judah runs through the *Test. xii Patr.*, e.g. Jud. 1 ὁ πατήρ μου Ἰακὼβ ηὔξατό μοι λέγων, Βασιλεὺς ἔσῃ κατευοδούμενος ἐν πᾶσι.

6. ἔσται κ.τ.λ.] Comp. Gen. xv. 5, xxii. 17, xxvi. 4. It is not an exact quotation from any of these passages, but most closely resembles the first.

7. δι' αὐτῶν] not αὐτῶν. See above the notes on §§ 9, 12, 14, 30.

11. δι' ἑαυτῶν] i.e. ἡμῶν αὐτῶν, as e.g. Rom. viii. 23, 2 Cor. i. 9, iii. 1, 5, and commonly.

σοφίας ἢ συνέσεως] The words occur together 1 Cor. i. 19 (from Is. xxix. 14), Col. i. 9; so too σοφοὶ καὶ συνετοί, Matt. xi. 25 (Luke x. 21). They are explained in Arist. *Eth. Nic.* vi. 7, 10. The first is a creative, the second a discerning faculty.

15. ἡ δόξα] See the notes on *Galatians* i. 5.

XXXIII. 'What then? If we are justified by *faith*, shall we leave off doing good? God forbid. We must

10 διὰ θελήματος αὐτοῦ ἐν Χριστῷ Ἰησοῦ κληθέντες, οὐ
δι' ἑαυτῶν δικαιούμεθα οὐδὲ διὰ τῆς ἡμετέρας σοφίας
ἢ συνέσεως ἢ εὐσεβείας ἢ ἔργων ὧν κατειργασάμεθα ἐν
ὁσιότητι καρδίας, ἀλλὰ διὰ τῆς πίστ[ε]ως, δι' ἧς
πάντας τοὺς ἀπ' αἰῶνος ὁ παντοκράτωρ Θεὸς ἐδικαίωσεν·
15 ᾧ ἔστω ἡ δόξα εἰς τοὺς αἰῶνας τῶν αἰώνων. ἀμήν.

XXXIII. Τί οὖν ποιήσωμεν, ἀδελφοί; ἀργήσωμεν
ἀπὸ τῆς ἀγαθοποιΐ[ας] καὶ ἐγκαταλείπωμεν τὴν ἀγά-

10 ἡμετέρας] ημερασ A.   13 τούς] του A.

needs *work*. The Almighty Himself rejoices in His own beneficent works. The heaven, the earth, the ocean, the living things that move on the land and in the sea, are His creation. Lastly and chiefly He made man after His own image. All these He created and blessed. As we have seen before that the righteous have ever been adorned with good works, so now we see that even the Creator thus arrayed Himself. Having such an example, let us do good with all our might'.

In § 31 we have seen Clement combining the teaching of S. Paul and S. John in the expression οὐχὶ δικαιοσύνην καὶ ἀλήθειαν διὰ πίστεως ποιήσας; So here, after declaring emphatically that men are not justified by their own works but by faith (§ 32 οὐ δι' αὐτῶν ἢ τῶν ἔργων αὐτῶν κ.τ.λ., and again οὐ διὰ...ἔργων ὧν κατειργασάμεθα ἐν ὁσιότητι καρδίας ἀλλὰ διὰ πίστεως κ.τ.λ.), he hastens to balance this statement by urging the importance of good works. The same anxiety reveals itself elsewhere. Thus, where he deals with the examples adduced in the Apostolic writings, he is careful to show that neither faith alone nor works alone were present: § 10 of Abraham διὰ πίστιν καὶ φιλοξενίαν ἐδόθη αὐτῷ υἱὸς κ.τ.λ., § 12 of Rahab διὰ πίστιν καὶ φιλοξενίαν ἐσώθη. See Westcott *Canon* p. 23. Nor is it only where doctrine is directly concerned that Clement places the teaching of the Apostles of the Circumcision and the Uncircumcision in juxtaposition, as e.g. § 49 ἀγάπη καλύπτει πλῆθος ἁμαρτιῶν, ἀγάπη πάντα ἀνέχεται κ.τ.λ. (see the note there). This studied effort to keep the balance produces a certain incongruous effect in the rapid transition from the one aspect of the antithesis to the other; but it is important when viewed in connexion with Clement's position as ruler of a community in which the two sections of the Church, Jewish and Gentile, had been in direct antagonism and probably still regarded each other with suspicion. On this position of Clement, as a reconciler, see *Galatians* p. 323.

Mai (*Script. Vet. Nov. Coll.* VII. p. 84) reports that a part of this chapter is quoted by Leontius and John *Res Sacr.* ii (see above p. 21) with considerable variations, but has not given the quotation. Dressel was unable to find the MS. See Jacobson's note.

16. τί οὖν ποιήσωμεν] evidently modeled on Rom. vi. 1 sq.

110   THE EPISTLE OF CLEMENT   [XXXIII

πην; μηθαμῶς τοῦτο ἐάσαι ὁ δεσπότ[ης] ἐφ' ἡμῖν γε
γενηθῆναι, ἀλλὰ σπεύσωμεν μετὰ ἐκτενεία[ς] καὶ προ-
θυμίας πᾶν ἔργον ἀγαθ[ὸν] ἐπιτελεῖν. αὐτὸς γὰρ ὁ
δημιουργὸς καὶ δ[εσπό]της τῶν ἁπάντων ἐπὶ τοῖς ἔρ[γοις]
αὐτοῦ ἀγαλλιᾶται. τῷ γὰρ παμμεγεθεστάτῳ αὐτ[οῦ] 5
κράτει οὐρανοὺς ἐστήρισε[ν], καὶ τῇ ἀκαταλήπτῳ αὐτοῦ
συ[νέσει διεκό]σμησεν αὐτούς· γῆν τε [διεχώ]ρισεν ἀπὸ
τοῦ περιέχον[τος αὐ]τὴν ὕδατος καὶ ἥδρασεν [ἐπὶ τὸ]ν
ἀσφαλῆ τοῦ ἰδίου βου[λήμα]τος θεμέλιον· τά τε ἐν
αὐ[τῇ ζ]ῷα φοιτῶντα τῇ ἑαυτοῦ [διατ]άξει ἐκέλευσεν 10

2 ἐκτενείας] εκτενια... A.   5 ἀγαλλιᾶται] A. ἀγάλλεται Damasc.   παμ-
μεγεθεστάτῳ] A. παμμεγεστάτῳ Damasc.   6 ἐστήρισεν] A. ἐστήριξεν Damasc.
7 συνέσει διεκόσμησεν] Wotton after Damasc.   γῆν τε διεχώρισεν] γῆν δὲ ἐχώ-
ρισεν Damasc. See below.   8 ἐπὶ τόν] Wotton after Damasc.   9 βουλή-
ματος] A. θελήματος Damasc.   10 διατάξει] or perhaps ἐπιτάξει or συντάξει.
The reading of previous editors προστάξει seems too long for the space.   Damascene
omits τά τε ἐν αὐτῇ...δυνάμει.   11 θάλασσάν τε καί] Tisch. would omit τε on

1. ἐάσαι ὁ δεσπότης κ.τ.λ.] True
to his dictum that every thing is διὰ
θελήματος αὐτοῦ and nothing δι' ἑαυτῶν, he ascribes the prevention of
this consequence solely to God's pro-
hibition. On ὁ δεσπότης see the note
above § 7. For the preposition in
ἐφ' ἡμῖν, ' in our case,' comp. John xii.
16, Acts v. 35, xxi. 24, 2 Cor. ix. 14.
3. αὐτὸς γὰρ κ.τ.λ.] This passage
as far as αὐξάνεσθε καὶ πληθύνεσθε is
quoted (with some omissions and variations) by John of Damascus Sacr.
Parall. (II. p. 310).
6. ἐστήρισεν] See the note on
στήρισον § 18.
7. διεχώρισεν] The space seems
to require διεχώρισεν, which, as being
used in Gen. i. 4 sq. several times,
was restored by Wotton here in place
of Young's διεμέρισεν.
8. περιέχοντος] This has been
thought to imply an acceptance of
the theory of the ὠκεανὸς ποταμὸς

supposed to encircle the earth: comp.
e.g. Herod. ii. 21 τὸν δ' ὠκεανὸν γῆν
περὶ πᾶσαν ῥέειν, M. Ann. Seneca Suas.
i. 1 'de Oceano dubitant utrumne
terras velut vinculum circumfluat.'
But, as Clement does not use the
word ὠκεανός, and as it is not unnatural to speak of the water 'gird-
ling' the land independently of this
theory, the inference is questionable.
See the note on § 20.
11. προδημιουργήσας] i.e. before τὰ
ἐν τῇ γῇ ζῷα φοιτῶντα, which have
been* already mentioned out of their
proper place.
12. ἐνέκλεισεν] 'inclosed within
their proper bounds': see above § 20
τὰ περικείμενα αὐτῇ κλεῖθρα.
τὸ ἐξοχώτατον κ.τ.λ.] Is this an
accusative after ἔπλασεν, ἄνθρωπον
being in apposition? Or is it a
nominative absolute, referring to the
whole sentence which follows, ἄνθρωπον...χαρακτῆρα? On the construction

εἶναι· θάλασ[σάν τε κ]αὶ τὰ ἐν αὐτῇ ζῶα προδημι[ουργή]σας. ἐνέκλεισεν τῇ ἑαυτοῦ [δυ]νάμει· ἐπὶ πᾶσι τὸ ἐξοχώτατον [καὶ] παμμέγεθες κατὰ διάνοιαν, [ἄ]νθρωπον ταῖς ἱεραῖς καὶ ἀμώμοις χερσὶν ἔπλασεν τῆς ἑαυτοῦ εἰκόνος
15 χαρακτῆρα. οὕτως γάρ φησιν ὁ Θεός· Ποιήϲωμεν ἄνθρωπον κατ' εἰκόνα καὶ καθ' ὁμοίωϲιν ἡμετέραν. καὶ ἐποίηϲεν ὁ Θεὸϲ τὸν ἄνθρωπον, ἄρϲεν καὶ θῆλυ ἐποίηϲεν αὐτούϲ. Ταῦτα οὖν πάντα τελειώσας ἐπῄνεσεν αὐτὰ καὶ ηὐλόγησεν καὶ εἶπεν· Αὐξάνεϲθε καὶ πληθύνεϲθε. Εἴδο-
20 μεν ὅτι †τό† ἐν ἔργοις ἀγαθοῖς πάντες ἐκοσμήθησαν

account of the space; but the connexion of the sentences requires it. 12 ἐνέκλεισεν] ἐνέκλισεν A. ἐπὶ πᾶσι...ἄνθρωπον] ἐπὶ τούτοις τὸν ἐξοχώτατον καὶ παμμεγέθη ἄνθρωπον Damasc. 14 ἱεραῖς] A. ἰδίαις αὐτοῦ Damasc. 16 εἰκόνα] Damasc. adds ἡμετέραν and omits it after ὁμοίωσιν. 18 ἐπῄνεσεν] A. ἐποίησεν Damasc. 19 αὐξάνεσθε] αὐξανεσθαι A. πληθύνεσθε] πληθύνεσθαι. εἴδομεν] Young (marg.). ἴδωμεν A. 20 ἔργοις] εγγοισ A.

adopted depends the sense assigned to κατὰ διάνοιαν, which will mean respectively either (1) '*in intellectual capacity*', referring to man; or (2) '*as an exercise of His creative intelligence*', referring to God. The former appears to be generally adopted; but the latter seems to me preferable; for a sentiment like Hamlet's 'How noble in reason! how infinite in faculty!' is somewhat out of place on the lips of Clement, and such a strong expression as παμμεγεθὲς κατὰ διάνοιαν jars with his language elsewhere about human intellect, e.g. §§ 13, 32, 36. The παμμεγεθὲς κατὰ διάνοιαν therefore seems to have the same bearing as τῇ ἀκαταλήπτῳ αὐτοῦ συνέσει above. John of Damascus indeed takes the sentence otherwise, but he omits κατὰ διάνοιαν.

14. ἀμώμοις] '*faultless*'. See the note on μωμοσκοπηθέν, § 41.

15. ποιήσωμεν κ.τ.λ.] A broken quotation from the LXX Gen. i. 26, 27, clauses being left out.

16. εἰκόνα, ὁμοίωσιν] These words are distinguished in reference to this text by Trench *N. T. Syn.* 1st ser. § xv.

19. αὐξάνεσθε κ.τ.λ.] From the LXX Gen. i. 28.

εἴδομεν] The sense seems to require this substitution for ἴδωμεν of the MS; see the introduction p. 25 for similar errors of transcription. 'We saw before,' says Clement, 'that all the righteous were adorned with good works (§ 32), and now I have shown that the Lord God Himself etc.' By ὁ Κύριος is meant ὁ δημιουργὸς καὶ δεσπότης τῶν ἁπάντων, as appears from οὖν and from ἐχάρη taken in connexion with what has gone before; (compare ἀγαλλιᾶται above).

20. ὅτι †τό†] If this reading be retained, we must understand a cognate accusative such as κόσμημα: e.g.

οἱ δίκαιοι· καὶ αὐτὸς οὖν ὁ Κύριος ἔργοις ἑαυτὸν κοσμήσας ἐχάρη. ἔχοντες οὖν τοῦτον τὸν ὑπογραμμὸν ἀόκνως προσέλθωμεν τῷ θελήματι αὐτοῦ, ἐξ ὅλης ἰσχύος ἡμῶν ἐργασώμεθα ἔργον δικαιοσύνης.

XXXIV. Ὁ ἀγαθὸς ἐργάτης μετὰ παρρησίας λαμ- 5
βάνει τὸν ἄρτον τοῦ ἔργου αὐτοῦ, ὁ νωθρὸς καὶ παρειμένος οὐκ ἀντοφθαλμεῖ τῷ ἐργοπαρέκτῃ αὐτοῦ. δέον οὖν ἐστιν προθύμους ἡμᾶς εἶναι εἰς ἀγαθοποιΐαν· ἐξ αὐτοῦ γάρ ἐστιν τὰ πάντα· προλέγει γὰρ ἡμῖν· Ἰδοὺ ὁ Κύριος, καὶ ὁ μιςθὸς αὐτοῦ πρὸ προςώπου αὐτοῦ, ἀποδοῦ- 10
ναι ἑκάςτῳ κατὰ τὸ ἔργον αὐτοῦ. Προτρέπεται οὖν ἡμᾶς

11 προτρέπεται] προτρεπετε A.

Soph. El. 1075 τὸν ἀεὶ πατρὸς (sc. στόνον) δειλαία στενάχουσα. This is possible; but the reading is discredited by the fact that the scribe's attention was flagging here, for he writes εγγοις for εργοις and (as we have seen) ιδωμεν for ειδομεν. All the corrections proposed however are objectionable; e.g. ὅτι τοῖς for ὅτι τὸ ἐν (Young and others), which disregards a common rule about the position of the article; ὅτι τὸ λεγόμενον ἐν ('as the saying is', Hilgenfeld after M. Schmidt), but there is no proverb here, and this very classical idiom seems out of place in Clement; ὅτι τε ἐν (Hefele and others after Birr), which makes an awkward connecting particle with the following καὶ...οὖν. This last however is the least objectionable of all the proposed corrections: and if it were adopted, we must suppose a slight anacoluthon in the connexion of the sentences. But I should be disposed to omit the τὸ boldly.

2. ὑπογραμμόν] See the note on § 5.

XXXIV. 'The good workman receives his wages boldly: but the slothful dares not face his employer. The Lord will come quickly with His reward in His hand. He will come attended by myriads of angels, hymning His praises. Let us therefore with one voice and one soul cry to Him, that we may be partakers of His glorious promises, which surpass all that man can conceive'.

7. ἀντοφθαλμεῖ] 'faces', as Wisd. xii. 14, Acts xxvii. 15, Barnab. § 5. The word occurs frequently in Polybius. Comp. ἀντωπῆσαι, Theoph. ad Autol. i. 5.

ἐργοπαρέκτῃ] 'his employer'. I have not found any other instance of this word, which is equivalent to ἐργοδότης. Compare also ἐργολάβος, ἐργοδιώκτης (Exod. iii. 7, v. 6, etc.).

8. ἐξ αὐτοῦ] i.e. τοῦ ἐργοπαρέκτου ἡμῶν.

9. ἰδοὺ ὁ Κύριος κ.τ.λ.] The beginning is a confusion of Is. xl. 10 ἰδοὺ Κύριος (ὁ θεὸς ὑμῶν ℵ) Κύριος (om. Κύριος sec. A) μετὰ ἰσχύος ἔρχεται καὶ ὁ βραχίων (add. αὐτοῦ A) μετὰ κυρίας· ἰδοὺ ὁ μισθὸς αὐτοῦ μετ' αὐτοῦ καὶ τὸ ἔργον ἐναντίον αὐτοῦ, and Is. lxii. 11 ἰδοὺ ὁ σωτήρ σοι παραγέγονεν (σοι ὁ σωτὴρ παραγίνεται ℵA) ἔχων τὸν ἑαυ-

ἐξ ὅλης τῆς καρδίας ἐπ' αὐτῷ μὴ ἀργοὺς †μήτε† παρειμένους εἶναι ἐπὶ πᾶν ἔργον ἀγαθόν· τὸ καύχημα ἡμῶν καὶ ἡ παρρησία ἔστω ἐν αὐτῷ· ὑποτασσώμεθα τῷ θελή-
5 ματι αὐτοῦ· κατανοήσωμεν τὸ πᾶν [π]λῆθος τῶν ἀγγέλων αὐτοῦ, πῶς τῷ θελήματι αὐτοῦ λειτουργοῦσιν παρεστῶτες· λέγει γὰρ ἡ γραφή· Μύριαι μυριάδες παρειστήκεισαν αὐτῷ, καὶ χίλιαι χιλιάδες ἐλειτούργουν αὐτῷ· Καὶ ἐκέκραγον· ἅγιος, ἅγιος, ἅγιος Κύριος Σαβαώθ, πλήρης πᾶσα
10 ἡ κτίσις τῆς δόξης αὐτοῦ. Καὶ ἡμεῖς οὖν, ἐν ὁμονοίᾳ ἐπὶ τὸ αὐτὸ συναχθέντες τῇ συνειδήσει, ὡς ἐξ ἑνὸς στόματος βοήσωμεν πρὸς αὐτὸν ἐκτενῶς εἰς τὸ μετόχους ἡμᾶς

16 λειτουργοῦσιν] λιτουργουσιν A.   18 ἐλειτούργουν] λιτουργουν A.

τοῦ μισθόν, καὶ τὸ ἔργον αὐτοῦ (om. αὐτοῦ A) πρὸ προσώπου αὐτοῦ: but the ending comes from Prov. xxiv. 12 ὃς ἀποδίδωσιν ἑκάστῳ κατὰ τὰ ἔργα αὐτοῦ, unless (as seems more probable from the connexion) it is taken from Rev. xxii. 12 ἰδοὺ ἔρχομαι ταχὺ καὶ ὁ μισθός μου μετ' ἐμοῦ ἀποδοῦναι ἑκάστῳ ὡς τὸ ἔργον ἔσται αὐτοῦ. Clem. Alex. *Strom.* iv. 22 (p. 625) has the same quotation, but is copying the Roman Clement.

12. ἐπ' αὐτῷ] i.e. τῷ μισθῷ, '*with our reward in view*'. The position of ἐξ ὅλης τῆς καρδίας is opposed to such corrections as ἐπ' αὐτὸ τό or ἐπὶ τό for the MS reading ἐπ' αὐτῷ; nor does any alteration seem needed.

†μήτε† παρειμένους κ.τ.λ.] Comp. 2 Tim. ii. 21 εἰς πᾶν ἔργον ἀγαθὸν ἡτοιμασμένον, ib. iii. 17, Tit. iii. 1, and see above § 2. The μήτε after μή is suspicious (see Winer § lv. p. 513, A. Buttmann p. 315), and should probably be read μηδέ; see the vv. ll. in Luke vii. 33, Eph. iv. 27.

17. μύριαι κ.τ.λ.] Dan. vii. 10 (Theodot.) χίλιαι χιλιάδες ἐλειτούργουν αὐτῷ (ἐθεράπευον αὐτόν LXX) καὶ μύριαι μυριάδες παρειστήκεισαν αὐτῷ, the clauses being transposed by Clement. The order of the clauses in the Hebrew is the same as in the Greek versions. Yet Iren. *Hær.* ii. 7. 4, Euseb. *Præp. Ev.* vii. 15 (p. 326), Greg. Nyss. *Hom. viii in Eccles.* (I. p. 463), Cyril. Hier. *Catech.* xv. 24 (p. 237), and others, give the quotation with the inverted clauses as here; but, as it is quoted with every shade of variation in different fathers and even these same fathers in some cases give the right order elsewhere, no stress can be laid on this coincidence which seems to be purely accidental.

18. καὶ ἐκέκραγον] A loose quotation from LXX Is. vi. 3. Ἐκέκραγον is an imperfect of a new verb κεκράγω formed from κέκραγα; see Buttmann *Ausf. Griech. Sprachl.* § 111 (II. p. 37).

21. τῇ συνειδήσει] '*in heart, in consciousness*': comp. Eccles. x. 20 καί γε ἐν συνειδήσει σου βασιλέα μὴ καταράσῃ i.e. 'in your secret heart'. The presence of their hearts, and not of their bodies only, is required. The commentators however either translate as though it were ἐν ἀγαθῇ συνειδήσει, or give τῇ συνειδήσει the unsupported sense 'harmony, unanimity'. Others

γενέσθαι τῶν μεγάλων καὶ ἐνδόξων ἐπαγγελιῶν αὐτοῦ. λέγει γάρ· Ὀφθαλμὸς ογκ εἶδεν καὶ ογc ογκ Ἤκογcεν, καὶ ἐπὶ καρδίαν ἀνθρώπογ ογκ ἀνέβη, ὅca ἡτοίμαcεn τοῖc ὑπομένογcιn αὐτόν.

have proposed to read συνδήσει or συνωδίᾳ.
2. ὀφθαλμὸς κ.τ.λ.] This quotation occurs also in S. Paul 1 Cor. ii. 9 (where it is introduced by καθὼς γέγραπται), in the form ἃ ὀφθαλμὸς οὐκ εἶδεν καὶ οὓς οὐκ ἤκουσεν καὶ ἐπὶ καρδίαν ἀνθρώπου οὐκ ἀνέβη ὅσα ἡτοίμασεν ὁ Θεὸς τοῖς ἀγαπῶσιν αὐτόν. It is cited again in *Clem. Rom.* ii § 11, *Mart. Polyc.* 2; see also Lagarde's *Gesamm. Abhandl.* p. 142. It is apparently taken from Isaiah lxiv. 4, which runs in the LXX ἀπὸ τοῦ αἰῶνος οὐκ ἠκούσαμεν οὐδὲ οἱ ὀφθαλμοὶ ἡμῶν εἶδον θεὸν πλὴν σοῦ καὶ τὰ ἔργα σου ἃ ποιήσεις τοῖς ὑπομένουσιν ἔλεον, but more nearly in the Hebrew, 'From eternity they have not heard, they have not hearkened, neither hath eye seen a god, [or 'O God'] save thee (who) worketh [or '(what) He shall do'] to him that awaiteth Him' (see Delitzsch *ad loc.*); combined with Is. lxv. 16, 17 οὐκ ἀναβήσεται αὐτῶν ἐπὶ τὴν καρδίαν...οὐ μὴ ἐπέλθῃ αὐτῶν ἐπὶ τὴν καρδίαν. Clement mixes up S. Paul's free translation or paraphrase from the Hebrew with the passage as it stands in the LXX; just as above, § 13, in quoting Jer. ix. 23, 24 (or 1 Sam. ii. 10) he condenses it after S. Paul. For a similar instance see above § 34 ἰδοὺ ὁ Κύριος κ.τ.λ. The passages, which Hilgenfeld suggests as the sources of the quotation (4 Esdr. x. 35 sq., 55 sq.), diverge more from the language of S. Paul and Clement, than these words of Isaiah.

The passage, if we may trust S. Jerome, occurred as given by S. Paul, both in the *Ascension of Isaiah* and in the *Apocalypse of Elias* (Hieron. *in Is.* lxiv. 4, IV. p. 761; *Prol. in Gen.* IX. p. 3). And Origen, *in Matth.* xxvii. 9 (III. p. 916), says that S. Paul quotes from the latter, 'In nullo regulari libro hoc positum invenitur, nisi (εἰ μή, 'but only') in Secretis Eliæ prophetæ'. This assertion is repeated also by later writers (see Fabricius *Cod. Ps. V. T.* I. p. 1073) doubtless from Origen, but combated by Jerome (ll. cc. and *Epist.* lvii. § 9, I. p. 314), who refers the quotation to Is. lxiv. 4. If it could be shown that these apocryphal books were prior to S. Paul, this solution would be the most probable; but they would appear to have been produced by some Christian sectarians of the second century, for Jerome terms them 'Iberæ næniæ' and connects them with the Basilideans and other Gnostics who abounded in Spain (ll. cc.; see also *c. Vigil.* II. p. 393, and comp. Fabricius p. 1093 sq.). If so they incorporated the quotation of S. Paul in their forgeries. For a similar instance of incorporation see the notes on *Galatians* vi. 15. At all events both these works appear from the extant remains to have been Christian. For the *Apocalypse of Elias* see Epiphan. *Hær.* xlii (p. 372), who says that the quotation in Eph. v. 14 (which is obviously Christian) was found there; and for the *Ascension of Isaiah*, this same father *Hær.* lxvii. 3 (p. 712), where he quotes a passage referring to the Trinity. Indeed there is every reason to believe that the work known to Epiphanius and several other fathers under this

XXXV. Ὡς μακάρια καὶ θαυμαστὰ τὰ δῶρα τοῦ
Θεοῦ, ἀγαπητοί. ζωὴ ἐν ἀθανασίᾳ, λαμπρότης ἐν δικαιοσύνῃ, ἀλήθεια ἐν παρρησίᾳ, πίστις ἐν πεποιθήσει,
ἐγκράτεια ἐν ἁγιασμῷ· καὶ ταῦτα ὑπέπιπτεν πάντα ὑπὸ

8 ἐγκράτεια] ΕΓΚΡΑΤΙΑ A.

name, is the same with the *Ascension and Vision of Isaiah* published first (by Lawrence) in an Æthiopic Version and subsequently (by Gieseler) in a Latin. The two versions represent different recensions; and the passage 'Eye hath not seen, etc.' appears in the Latin (xi. 34) but not in the Æthiopic (see Iolowicz *Himmelfahrt u. Vision des Propheten Iesaia* p. 90, Leipzig, 1854). The Latin recension therefore must have been in the hands of Jerome; though this very quotation seems to show clearly that the Æthiopic more nearly represents the original form of the work (see Lücke *Offenbarung d. Johannes* p. 279 sq.). Both recensions alike are distinctly Christian.

It was at all events a favourite text with certain early Gnostic sects, who introduced it into their formula of initiation and applied it to their esoteric teaching; see Hippol. *Hær.* v. 24, 26, 27, vi. 24. This perverted use of the text was condemned by their contemporary Hegesippus (as reported by Stephanus Gobarus in Photius *Bibl.* 232), as contradicting our Lord's own words μακάριοι οἱ ὀφθαλμοὶ ὑμῶν κ.τ.λ. In other words he complained that they would restrict to the initiated few the knowledge which Christ declared to be laid open to all. But Stephanus Gobarus himself, writing some centuries later and knowing the text only as it occurs in S. Paul, is not unnaturally at a loss to know what Hegesippus means by this condemnation (οὐκ οἶδ'

ὅ τι καὶ παθὼν μάτην μὲν εἰρῆσθαι ταῦτα λέγει κ.τ.λ.). On the use which some modern critics have made of this reference to Hegesippus in Stephanus Gobarus, see *Galatians* p. 320.

Fabricius (p. 1073) quotes a parallel from Empedocles (*Fragm. Philos.* I. p. 2, ed. Mullach) οὔτ' ἐπιδερκτὰ τάδ' ἀνδράσιν οὔτ' ἐπακουστά, οὔτε νόῳ περιληπτά.

XXXV. 'Great and marvellous are God's gifts even in the present! How then can we conceive the glory that hereafter awaits His patient servants? Let us strive to attain this reward. And to this end let us do what is well-pleasing to Him: let us shun strife and vainglory; let us lay aside all selfish and unbrotherly sins. Remember how in the Psalms God denounces those who hearken not to His warning voice, who persist in wronging their neighbours, counting on His forbearance. He tells us that the sacrifice of praise is the path of salvation'.

6. λαμπρότης] '*cheerfulness, alacrity, strenuousness*', as e.g. Plut. *Vit. Cim.* 17, Polyb. xxxii. 23. 1 (see Schweigh. *Lex.* s.v. λαμπρός). Compare the similar word φαιδρότης. The position of λαμπρότης here seems to require this sense, for all the words in the parallel clauses ζωή, ἀλήθεια, πίστις, ἐγκράτεια, refer to the moral consciousness, not to any external advantages.

7. πίστις ἐν πεποιθήσει] See the note above, § 26.

8. καὶ ταῦτα κ.τ.λ.] 'These,' Cle-

τὴν διάνοιαν ἡμῶν. τίνα οὖν ἄρα ἐστὶν τὰ ἑτοιμαζόμενα τοῖς ὑπομένουσιν; ὁ δημιουργὸς καὶ πατὴρ τῶν αἰώνων ὁ πανάγιος αὐτὸς γινώσκει τὴν ποσότητα καὶ τὴν καλλονὴν αὐτῶν. ἡμεῖς οὖν ἀγωνισώμεθα εὑρεθῆναι ἐν τῷ ἀριθμῷ τῶν ὑπομενόντων αὐτόν, ὅπως μεταλά- 5 βωμεν τῶν ἐπηγγελμένων δωρεῶν. πῶς δὲ ἔσται τοῦτο, ἀγαπητοί; ἐὰν ἐστηριγμένη ᾖ ἡ διάνοια ἡμῶν διὰ πίστεως πρὸς τὸν Θεόν· ἐὰν ἐκζητῶμεν τὰ εὐάρεστα καὶ εὐπρόσδεκτα αὐτῷ· ἐὰν ἐπιτελέσωμεν τὰ ἀνήκοντα τῇ ἀμώμῳ βουλήσει αὐτοῦ καὶ ἀκολουθήσωμεν τῇ ὁδῷ 10 τῆς ἀληθείας, ἀπορρίψαντες ἀφ' ἑαυτῶν πᾶσαν ἀδικίαν καὶ ἀνομίαν, πλεονεξίαν, ἔρεις, κακοηθείας τε καὶ δόλους, ψιθυρισμούς τε καὶ καταλαλιάς, θεοστυγίαν, ὑπερη-

6 δωρεῶν] δωραιων A.   7 διά] Young (marg.). om. A.   13 καταλαλίς] καταλιλιασ A.   14 ἀλαζονείαν] αλαζονιά A.   ἀφιλοξενίαν] φιλοξενίαν A.   16 μόνον] μον A.   19 σου] μου A. So the MS

ment argues, 'are already within our cognisance. What then are the joys in store for those who remain stedfast to the end?' comp. 1 Joh. iii. 2 νῦν τέκνα Θεοῦ ἐσμὲν καὶ οὔπω ἐφανερώθη τί ἐσόμεθα.

3. πανάγιος] Apparently the first occurrence of the word, which afterwards takes a prominent place in the language of Greek Christendom.

7. διὰ πίστεως] The omission of διὰ in the MS may perhaps be explained by the neighbourhood of διάνοια. Hilgenfeld reads πιστῶς. Lipsius (p. 15) defends πίστεως, translating 'cogitationes fidei', but this would require αἱ διάνοιαι τῆς πίστεως.

11. πᾶσαν ἀδικίαν κ.τ.λ.] The whole passage which follows is a reminiscence of Rom. i. 29 sq. ποιεῖν τὰ μὴ καθήκοντα...πάσῃ ἀδικίᾳ...πλεονεξίᾳ...ἔριδος δόλου κακοηθείας, ψιθυριστὰς καταλάλους θεοστυγεῖς... ὑπερηφάνους ἀλαζόνας...ἐπιγνόντες ὅτι οἱ τὰ τοιαῦτα πράσσοντες ἄξιοι θανάτου εἰσίν, οὐ μόνον αὐτὰ ποιοῦσιν (v.l. ποιοῦντες) ἀλλὰ καὶ συνευδοκοῦσιν (v. l. συνευδοκοῦντες) τοῖς πράσσουσιν. On the reading ποιοῦντες, συνευδοκοῦντες, supported by Clement's language here, see Tischendorf's note.

14. ἀφιλοξενίαν] This is the simplest emendation of the MS reading; see the note on μὴ ἀτημελείτω § 38. The word occurs Orac. Sibyll. viii. 304 τῆς ἀφιλοξενίης ταύτην τίσουσι τράπεζαν. Other proposed readings are φιλοτιμίαν, φιλοδοξίαν, φιλονεικίαν. The suggestion of Lipsius (p. 115), that the Corinthians had failed in the duty of providing for others, appears to be correct. But the word seems to point rather to their churlishness in not entertaining foreign Christians at Corinth, than (as he maintains) to the niggardliness of their contributions towards the needs of poor Christians abroad, though they may have

φανίαν τε καὶ ἀλαζονείαν, κενοδοξίαν τε καὶ ἀφιλο-
15 ξενίαν. ταῦτα γὰρ οἱ πράσσοντες στυγητοὶ τῷ Θεῷ
ὑπάρχουσιν· οὐ μόνον δὲ οἱ πράσσοντες αὐτά, ἀλλὰ καὶ
οἱ συνευδοκοῦντες αὐτοῖς. λέγει γὰρ ἡ γραφή· Τῷ δὲ
ἁμαρτωλῷ εἶπεν ὁ Θεός· Ἵνα τί ϲὺ διηγῇ τὰ δικαιώματά
μου, καὶ ἀναλαμβάνεις τὴν διαθήκην μου ἐπὶ ϲτόματός ϲου;
20 ϲὺ δὲ ἐμίϲηϲαϲ παιδείαν, καὶ ἐξέβαλλεϲ τοὺϲ λόγουϲ μου εἰϲ
τὰ ὀπίϲω. εἰ ἐθεώρειϲ κλέπτην, ϲυνέτρεχεϲ αὐτῷ, καὶ μετὰ
μοιχῶν τὴν μερίδα ϲου ἐτίθειϲ· τὸ ϲτόμα ϲου ἐπλεόναϲεν
κακίαν, καὶ ἡ γλῶϲϲά ϲου περιέπλεκεν δολιότητα· καθήμενοϲ
κατὰ τοῦ ἀδελφοῦ ϲου κατελάλειϲ, καὶ κατὰ τοῦ υἱοῦ τῆϲ
25 μητρόϲ ϲου ἐτίθειϲ ϲκάνδαλον· ταῦτα ἐποίηϲαϲ καὶ ἐϲίγηϲα·
ὑπέλαβεϲ, ἄνομε, ὅτι ἔϲομαί ϲοι ὅμοιοϲ· ἐλέγξω ϲε καὶ

seems clearly to read (as even the photograph shows), though Tisch. gives it σου.
20 παιδείαν] παιδιαν Α. ἐξέβαλλες] εξαβαλλεσ Α. 24 ἀδελφοῦ] αδελφουσ Α. 26 ἄνομε] ανομαι Α.

failed in this respect also (see the note § 38). The duty of entertaining the brethren from foreign churches was a recognised obligation among the early Christians. In former times the Corinthians had obtained a good report for the practice of this virtue (§ 1 τὸ μεγαλοπρεπὲς τῆς φιλοξενίας ὑμῶν ἦθος οὐκ ἐκήρυξεν;), but now all was changed. Hence the stress laid on the *hospitality* of Abraham (§ 10), of Lot (§ 11), of Rahab (§ 12); for this virtue cannot have been singled out in all three cases without some special reference.

17. τῷ δὲ ἁμαρτωλῷ κ.τ.λ.] From the LXX Ps. l. 16—23, with slight variations, of which the more important are noted below.

23. καθήμενος] implying deliberate conspiracy; see Perowne on Ps. i. 1.

26. ἄνομε] LXX ἀνομίαν (B); but א has ανομε, though it is afterwards corrected into ανομειαν (ἀνομίαν). Ἀνο-

μίαν is read by Justin *Dial.* 22 (p. 240¹), Clem. Alex. *Strom.* vi. 14 (p. 798); but ἄνομε Clem. Alex. *Strom.* iv. 24 (p. 634). The Syriac ܥܘܠܐ does not favour ἄνομε (as Wotton states), except that the existing pointing interprets it thus. The reading of our MS here shows how easy was the transition from the one to the other, ανομαι (ἄνομε) and ανομιᾱ (=ἀνο-μίαν). (See the notes on ἀναστήσομαι § 5, and ᾗ δείξω just below). Though ἄνομε makes better sense, the original reading of the LXX here must have been ἀνομίαν (not ἄνομε as Wotton thinks); for the translators must have misread דמית היות אהיה 'Thou thoughtest, I shall surely be', as if דמית הוות אהיה 'Thou thoughtest destruction (or iniquity), I shall be', since הוות is elsewhere translated by ·ἀνομία, Ps. lvii. 2, xciv. 20; and Theodotion, whose version agreed with the LXX (see Field's *Hexapl.* ad loc.),

παραστήςω ςε κατὰ πρόςωπόν ςογ. ςγνετε δή ταῦτα, οἱ ἐπιλανθανόμενοι τοῦ Θεοῦ, μήποτε ἀρπάςῃ ὡς λέων, καὶ μὴ ᾖ ὁ ῥγόμενος. θγςία αἰνέςεως δοξάςει με, καὶ ἐκεῖ ὁδὸς ᾗ δείξω αὐτῷ τὸ ςωτήριον τοῦ Θεοῦ.

XXXVI. Αὕτη ἡ ὁδός, ἀγαπητοί, ἐν ᾗ εὕρομεν τὸ σωτήριον ἡμῶν Ἰησοῦν Χριστὸν τὸν ἀρχιερέα τῶν προσφορῶν ἡμῶν, τὸν προστάτην καὶ βοηθὸν τῆς ἀσθενείας ἡμῶν. διὰ τούτου ἀτενίσωμεν εἰς τὰ ὕψη τῶν οὐρανῶν· διὰ τούτου ἐνοπτριζόμεθα τὴν ἄμωμον καὶ ὑπερτάτην

3 ᾗ] See below. ην A.   7 ἀσθενείας] ασθενιασ A.   8 τούτου] τογτογ (the erscribed Υ being *prima manu*) A.   11 ἐσκοτωμένη] A.

must have read it in the same way.
1. παραστήσω σε κ.τ.λ.] '*I will bring thee face to face with thyself*, show thee to thyself in thy true light.' The σε is omitted in אB of the LXX and doubtless had no place in the original text of this version which agreed with the Hebrew, 'I will lay in order (the matter) before thee'. Justin *Dial*. 22 (l. c.) and other writers supply an accusative τὰς ἁμαρτίας σου, which is found also in a large number of MSS (see Holmes and Parsons).
2. ὡς λέων] i.e. '*lest one seize him as it were a lion*'. The words ὡς λέων are absent from the LXX (and Justin *Dial*. 22 p. 402), as also from the Hebrew. They must have come from Ps. vii. 3, either as a gloss in Clement's text of the LXX or as inadvertently inserted by him in a quotation made from memory.
4. ᾗ δείξω] As ᾗ is read in the LXX (אB) and in Justin l. c., and as the parallelism in the opening of the next chapter (ἡ ὁδὸς ἐν ᾗ εὕρομεν τὸ σωτήριον κ.τ.λ.) seems to require it, I have restored it for ἦν. For similar corruptions in the MS see § 15 ἀναστήσομεν (note), § 36 οσων, § 41 συνει-

δησιν, ii. § 6 αἰχμαλωσιαν. If ἦν be retained, σωτήριον must be taken as a nominative in apposition with ὁδός.

XXXVI. 'On this path let us travel. This salvation is Jesus Christ our High-priest. Through Him our darkness is made light, and we see the Father: for He is the reflexion of God's person. He has a place far above all angels, being seated on God's right hand and endowed with universal dominion and made triumphant over His enemies. These enemies are they that resist God's will.'

6. τὸν ἀρχιερέα] This is founded on the teaching of the Epistle to the Hebrews (ii. 17, iii. 1, iv. 14, 15, etc.), of which Clement's language throughout this section is an echo. See again § 58. Photius (*Bibl.* 126) alludes to these two passages in his criticism of Clement, ἀρχιερέα καὶ προστάτην τὸν Κύριον ἡμῶν Ἰησοῦν ἐξονομάζων οὐδὲ τὰς θεοπρεπεῖς καὶ ὑψηλοτέρας ἀφῆκε περὶ αὐτοῦ φωνάς (see the notes § 2, 57). The term ἀρχιερεὺς is very frequently applied to our Lord by the earliest Christian writers of all schools; Polyc. *Phil*. 12, Ign. *Philad*. 9, *Test. xii Patr.* Rub. 6,

10 ὄψιν αὐτοῦ· διὰ τούτου ἠνεῴχθησαν ἡμῶν οἱ ὀφθαλμοὶ
τῆς καρδίας· διὰ τούτου ἡ ἀσύνετος καὶ ἐσκοτωμένη διάνοια ἡμῶν ἀναθάλλει εἰς τὸ θαυμαστὸν αὐτοῦ φῶς· διὰ
τούτου ἠθέλησεν ὁ δεσπότης τῆς ἀθανάτου γνώσεως
ἡμᾶς γεύσασθαι· ὃς ὢν ἀπαύγασμα τῆς μεγαλωσύνης αὐ-
15 τοῦ τοσούτῳ μείζων ἐστὶν ἀγγέλων, ὅσῳ διαφορώτερον
ὄνομα κεκληρονόμηκεν. γέγραπται γὰρ οὕτως· Ὁ ποιῶν
τοὺς ἀγγέλους αὐτοῦ πνεύματα καὶ τοὺς λειτουργοὺς αὐτοῦ
πυρὸς φλόγα. Ἐπὶ δὲ τῷ υἱῷ αὐτοῦ οὕτως εἶπεν ὁ

ἐσκοτισμένη Clem. Alex. 613.   12 θαυμαστὸν αὐτοῦ] om. Clem. Alex.
15 ὅσῳ] οσω (i.e. ὅσων) A.

Sym. 7, etc., *Clem. Recogn.* i. 48, Justin *Dial.* 116 (p. 344).

7. προστάτην] '*guardian, patron*, who protects our interests and pleads our cause'. To a Roman it would convey all the ideas of the Latin 'patronus,' of which it was the recognised rendering, Plut. *Vit. Rom.* 13, *Vit. Marii* 5. Comp. προστάτις Rom. xvi. 2.

9. ἐνοπτριζόμεθα] Christ is the mirror in whom is reflected the faultless countenance of God the Father (αὐτοῦ); comp. 2 Cor. iii. 18 τὴν δόξαν Κυρίου κατοπτριζόμενοι, Philo *Leg. All.* iii. 33 (I. p. 107) μηδὲ κατοπτρισαίμην ἐν ἄλλῳ τινὶ τὴν σὴν ἰδέαν ἢ ἐν σοὶ τῷ Θεῷ; comp. John i. 14.

ἄμωμον] '*faultless*', '*fleckless*', because the mirror is perfect. For the meaning of ἄμωμος, see the note on μωμοσκοπηθέν, § 41.

11. διὰ τούτου κ.τ.λ.] Quoted in Clem. Alex. *Strom.* iv. 16 (p. 613) ὃ ἐν τῇ πρὸς Κορινθίους ἐπιστολῇ γέγραπται, Διὰ Ἰησοῦ Χριστοῦ ἡ ἀσύνετος...ἡμᾶς γεύσασθαι.

ἡ ἀσύνετος κ.τ.λ.] Rom. i. 21 καὶ ἐσκοτίσθη ἡ ἀσύνετος αὐτῶν καρδία, Ephes. iv. 18 ἐσκοτωμένοι [*v.l.* ἐσκοτισμένοι] τῇ διανοίᾳ. These passages are sufficient to explain how Clem.

Alex. in quoting our Clement writes ἐσκοτισμένη, but not sufficient to justify the substitution of this form for ἐσκοτωμένη in our text. See A. Jahn's *Methodius* II. p. 77, note 453.

12. ἀναθάλλει κ.τ.λ.] i.e. 'Our mind, like a plant shut up in a dark closet, had withered in its growth. Removed thence by His loving care, it revives and shoots up towards the light of heaven.' Comp. 1 Pet. ii. 9 τοῦ ἐκ σκότους ὑμᾶς καλέσαντος εἰς τὸ θαυμαστὸν αὐτοῦ φῶς. It is strange that editors should have wished to alter ἀναθάλλει, which contains so striking an image.

14. ὃς ὢν κ.τ.λ.] The whole passage is borrowed from the opening of the Epistle to the Hebrews, from which expressions, arguments, and quotations alike are taken: see esp. i. 3, 4, 5, 7, 13. For the meaning see the commentators on that epistle. On ὄνομα, '*title, dignity*', see *Philippians* ii. 9.

16. ὁ ποιῶν κ.τ.λ.] From LXX Ps. civ. 4. It is quoted exactly as in Heb. i. 7, πυρὸς φλόγα being substituted for πῦρ φλέγον of the LXX (אB, but A has πυροσ φλεγα which shows the reading in a transition state).

δεσπότης· Υίός μογ εἶ cý, ἐγὼ cήμερον γεγέννηκά ce· αἴ-
τηcαι παρ' ἐμοῦ, καὶ Δώcω coι ἔθνη τὴν κληρονομίαν coy,
κ[αὶ τὴν κατά]cχεcίν coy τὰ πέρατα τ[ῆc γῆc]. καὶ πάλιν
λέγει πρὸς αὐ[τόν· Κάθογ] ἐκ Δεξιῶν μογ, ἕως ἂν [θῶ
τογc] ἐχθρογς coy ὑποπόδιο[ν τῶν πο]Δῶν coy. Τίνες οὖν 5
οἱ ἐ[χθροί]; οἱ φαῦλοι καὶ ἀντιτασσ[όμενοι] τῷ θελήματι [αὐτοῦ].

XXXVII. Στρατευσώμεθα οὖν, ἄνδ[ρες ἀδελ]φοί,
μετὰ πάσης ἐκτενεία[ς ἐν τοῖς] ἀμώμοις προστάγμασιν

6 ἐχθροί] Jacobson. This is quite enough for the space. Other editors add αὐτοῦ or Κυρίου (i.e. ΚΎ). ἀντιτασσόμενοι] Wotton. Previous editors added other words, but ἀντιτασσόμενοι is sufficient for the space. τῷ θελήματι αὐτοῦ] τωθε-λημαтιτωθελημα...... A. The MS is correctly read by Tisch. The lacuna has space for seven letters and should probably be filled up (with Tisch.) τιαυτου, the words τῷ θελήματι being written twice over. Having regard to the context, αὐτοῦ is better than τοῦ Θεοῦ (ΤΟΥΘῩ) which would fill the lacuna equally well. 11 εὐεικτικῶς]

1. υἱός μου κ.τ.λ.] From LXX Ps. ii. 7 word for word, after Heb. i. 5 : comp. Acts xiii. 33 (in S. Paul's speech at the Pisidian Antioch), where it is again quoted. In both these passages the 7th verse only is given : Clement adds the 8th, αἴτησαι κ.τ.λ.
4. κάθου κ.τ.λ.] From LXX Ps. cx. 1 word for word, after Heb. i. 13.
XXXVII. 'We are fighting as soldiers under our heavenly captain. Subordination of rank and obedience to orders are necessary conditions in an army. There must be harmonious working of high and low. So it is with the human body. The head must work with the feet and the feet with the head, for the health and safety of the whole'.
8. στρατευσώμεθα] 2 Cor. x. 3, 1 Tim. i. 18, 2 Tim. ii. 3, 4, Ign. Polyc. 6.
10. κατανοήσωμεν κ.τ.λ.] So Seneca de Tranq. An. 4 'Quid si militare nolis nisi imperator aut tribunus? etiamsi alii primam frontem tene-bunt, te sors inter triarios posuerit,

inde voce, adhortatione, exemplo, animo, milita'.
τοῖς ἡγουμένοις ἡμῶν] 'under our temporal rulers.' For this sense of οἱ ἡγούμενοι see the note § 5. On the other hand οἱ ἡγούμενοι is used else-where of the officers of the Church: see § 1 (note). For the dative after στρατεύεσθαι see Ign. Polyc. 6 ἀρέσ-κετε ᾧ στρατεύεσθε, Appian Bell. Civ. i. 42 τοῖς ἐν αὐτῇ Ῥωμαίοις...ἐκήρυξεν... στρατεύσειν ἑαυτῷ (where στρατεύσειν is transitive).
11. εὐεικτικῶς] 'submissively'. The adverb εὐείκτως is recognised in the Etym. Magn., and of the adjective εὐεικτος the Lexicons give several in-stances, e. g. Dion Cass. lxix. 20. On the other hand of εὐεικτικός,-κῶς, though legitimate forms, no examples are given in the Lexicons. If εὐεικ-τικῶς cannot stand, we may sup-pose that the traces in the MS (as I read it) exhibit a correction of εὐεκτικωσ or rather ειεκτικωσ (which had been written first) into ευεικτωσ.

10 [αὐτοῦ]· κατανοήσωμεν τοὺς στρα[τευο]μένους τοῖς ἡγουμένοις ἡ[μῶν], πῶς εὐτάκτως, πῶς εὐεικτικ[ῶς], πῶς ὑποτεταγμένως ἐπιτελο[ῦ]σιν τὰ διατασσόμενα. οὐ πάντε[s] εἰσὶν ἔπαρχοι οὐδὲ χιλίαρχοι οὐδὲ ἑκατόνταρχοι οὐδὲ πεντηκόνταρχοι οὐδὲ τὸ καθεξῆς· ἀλλ' ἕκαστος
15 ἐν τῷ ἰδίῳ τάγματι τὰ ἐπιτασσόμενα ὑπὸ τοῦ βασιλέως καὶ τῶν ἡγουμένων ἐπιτελεῖ. οἱ ΜΕΓΑΛΟΙ ΔΙΧΑ ΤῶΝ ΜΙΚΡῶΝ ΟΥ ΔΥΝΑΝΤΑΙ ΕἶΝΑΙ, ΟΥΤΕ οἱ ΜΙΚΡΟΙ ΔΙΧΑ ΤῶΝ ΜΕΓΑ-

ἐΥΕΚΤΙΙ... Α, as I read it. The first part has originally been written ΕΙΕΚΤ but the ι is prolonged and altered into an γ and an ι is superscribed between ε and κ, so that it becomes ευεικτ·. So far I agree with Tisch. prol. p. xix. After this Tisch. reads ω ('non integra'); it seems to me more like an ι with a stroke of another letter which might be κ, so that I read the part before the lacuna ευεικτικ. But the MS is so worn, that it is impossible to speak confidently. The lacuna seems too great for a single letter, and this again is an objection to ευεικτω[σ], the reading of Tisch. But the uneven length of the lines diminishes the force of this objection.

12. οὐ πάντες κ.τ.λ.] Comp. 1 Cor. xii. 29, 30.
13. ἔπαρχοι κ.τ.λ.] See Exod. xviii. 21 καταστήσεις [αὐτοὺς] ἐπ' αὐτῶν χιλιάρχους καὶ ἑκατοντάρχους καὶ πεντηκοντάρχους καὶ δεκαδάρχους (comp. ver. 25). The reference here however is to *Roman* military organization as the context shows; comp. *Clem. Hom.* x. 14 ὅνπερ γὰρ τρόπον εἰς ἐστὶν ὁ Καῖσαρ, ἔχει δὲ ὑπ' αὐτὸν τοὺς διοικητὰς (ὑπατικούς, ἐπάρχους, χιλιάρχους, ἑκατοντάρχους, δεκαδάρχους), τὸν αὐτὸν τρόπον κ.τ.λ. The ἔπαρχοι therefore are 'prefects', ἔπαρχος being used especially of the 'præfectus prætorio', e.g. Plut. *Galb.* 13, *Otho* 7; comp. Dion Cass. *Fragm.* (v. p. 203 ed. L. Dind.) αἰσχρόν ἐστι, Καῖσαρ, ἑκατοντάρχῳ σε διαλέγεσθαι τῶν ὑπάρχων ἔξω ἑστώτων. The χιλίαρχοι, ἑκαντόνταρχοι, again are the common equivalents for 'tribuni', 'centuriones', respectively. But for πεντηκόνταρχος I do not know any corresponding term in the Roman army. If it represents the 'optio' the lieutenant or the signifer 'the ensign' (see Löhr *Taktik u. Kriegswesen* p. 41), the numerical relation of 50 to 100 has become meaningless.
14. ἕκαστος κ.τ.λ.] 1 Cor. xv. 23 ἕκαστος δὲ ἐν τῷ ἰδίῳ τάγματι; comp. below § 41.
15. βασιλέως] Comp. 1 Pet. ii. 13 sq. εἴτε βασιλεῖ...εἴτε ἡγεμόσιν; comp. Joh. xix. 15, Acts xvii. 7. The official title of the emperor in Greek was αὐτοκράτωρ, but βασιλεὺς is found in common parlance, though the corresponding 'rex' would not be used except in gross flattery.
16. οἱ μεγάλοι κ.τ.λ.] See Soph. *Aj.* 158 (quoted by Jacobson) καίτοι σμικροὶ μεγάλων χωρὶς σφαλερὸν πύργου ῥῦμα πέλονται κ.τ.λ. (with Lobeck's note), Plato *Leg.* x. p. 902 E οὐδὲ γὰρ ἄνευ σμικρῶν τοὺς μεγάλους φασὶν οἱ λιθολόγοι λίθους εὖ κεῖσθαι, with the remarks of Donaldson *New Crat.* § 455, on this proverb. I have therefore ventured to print the words as a quotation, and indeed Clement's text

λων· σγκρασίς τίς ἐστιν ἐν πᾶσιν, καὶ ἐν τούτοις χρῆσις. Λάβωμεν τὸ σῶμα ἡμῶν· ἡ κεφαλὴ δίχα τῶν ποδῶν οὐδέν ἐστιν, οὕτως οὐδὲ οἱ πόδες δίχα τῆς κεφαλῆς· τὰ δὲ ἐλάχιστα μέλη τοῦ σώματος ἡμῶν ἀναγκαῖα καὶ εὔχρηστά εἰσιν ὅλῳ τῷ σώματι· ἀλλὰ πάντα συνπνεῖ 5 καὶ ὑποταγῇ μιᾷ χρῆται εἰς τὸ σώζεσθαι ὅλο[ν] τὸ σῶμα.

XXXVIII. Σωζέσθω οὖν ἡμῶν ὅλ[ον] τὸ σῶμα ἐν Χριστῷ Ἰησοῦ, καὶ ὑποτασσέσθ[ω] ἕκαστος τῷ πλησίον αὐτοῦ, καθὼ[ς] καὶ ἐτέθη ἐν τῷ χαρίσματι αὐτοῦ. ὁ 10 ἰσχυρὸς μὴ ἀτημελείτω τὸν ἀσθενῆ, ὁ δὲ ἀσθενὴς ἐν-

11 ἀτημελείτω] τμμελειτω A. See below.   15 ἐνδεικνύσθω] ενδικνυσθω A.
ἐν λόγοις] A.   λόγοις μόνον Clem. Alex. 613.   16 ταπεινοφρονῶν] A. ταπει-
νόφρων Clem. Alex.   μὴ ἑαυτῷ μαρτυρείτω] A. μαρτ. μὴ ἑαυτ. transp.
Clem. Alex.   17 ἐάτω] A. ἐν τῷ Clem. Alex.   ἑαυτόν] A. αὐτὸν Clem. Alex.

seems to embody some anapæstic fragments.

1. σύγκρασις κ.τ.λ.] This seems to be a reference to Eurip. *Fragm. Æol.* 2 ἀλλ' ἔστι τις σύγκρασις ὥστ' ἔχειν καλῶς, for Euripides is there speaking of the mutual cooperation of rich and poor: see the passage quoted from the context of Euripides on ὁ πλούσιος κ.τ.λ. just below § 38. Comp. 1 Cor. xii. 24 ἀλλὰ ὁ Θεὸς συνεκέρασεν τὸ σῶμα.

2. λάβωμεν τὸ σῶμα κ.τ.λ.] Suggested by 1 Cor. xii. 12 sq. (comp. Rom. xii. 4); see esp. ver. 22 τὰ δοκοῦντα μέλη τοῦ σώματος ἀσθενέστερα ὑπάρχειν ἀναγκαῖά ἐστιν.

XXXVIII. 'So therefore let the health of the whole body be our aim. Let weak and strong, rich and poor, work together in harmony. Let each man exercise his special gift in humility of heart and without vainglory, remembering that he owes everything to God and giving thanks to Him for His goodness.'

9. ὑποτασσέσθω ἕκαστος κ.τ.λ.] Ephes. v. 21; comp. 1 Pet. v. 5.

10. καθὼς καὶ ἐτέθη] sc. ὁ πλησίον, 'according as he was appointed with his special gift'; comp. 1 Pet. iv. 10 ἕκαστος καθὼς ἔλαβεν χάρισμα, 1 Cor. vii. 7 ἕκαστος ἴδιον ἔχει χάρισμα ἐκ Θεοῦ, Rom. xii. 6 ἔχοντες χαρίσματα κατὰ τὴν χάριν τὴν δοθεῖσαν ἡμῖν διάφορα.

11. μὴ ἀτημελείτω] This reading makes better sense than πλημμελείτω (for Clement is condemning the *depreciation* of others) and accounts more easily for the corruption; see the omission of α in ἀφιλοξενίαν § 35.

12. ὁ πλούσιος κ.τ.λ.] See Eurip. *Fragm. Æol.* 2 (of which the context is cited above, § 37) ἃ μὴ γάρ ἐστι τῷ πένητι, πλούσιος δίδωσ'· ἃ δ' οἱ πλουτοῦντες οὐ κεκτήμεθα, τοῖσιν πένησι χρώμενοι θηρώμεθα. The resemblance here confirms the conjecture that in the earlier passage Clement has the words of Euripides in his mind.

14. ἀναπληρωθῇ κ.τ.λ.] For the ex-

τρεπέτω τὸν ἰσχυρόν· ὁ πλούσιος ἐπιχορηγείτω τῷ
πτωχῷ, ὁ δὲ πτωχὸς εὐχαριστείτω τῷ Θεῷ, ὅτι ἔδωκεν
αὐτῷ δι' οὗ ἀναπληρωθῇ αὐτοῦ τὸ ὑστέρημα. ὁ σοφὸς
15 ἐνδεικνύσθω τὴν σοφίαν αὐτοῦ μὴ ἐν λόγοις ἀλλ' ἐν
ἔργοις ἀγαθοῖς· ὁ ταπεινοφρονῶν μὴ ἑαυτῷ μαρτυρεί-
τ[ω], ἀλλ' ἐάτω ὑφ' ἑτέρου ἑαυτὸν μ[αρ]τυρεῖσθαι. ὁ
ἁγνὸς ἐν τῇ σαρκὶ [ἔστω] καὶ μὴ ἀλαζονευέσθω, γινώσ-
[κων ὅτι ἕτ]ερός ἐστιν ὁ ἐπιχορηγῶν [αὐτῷ] τὴν ἐγκρά-
20 τειαν. Ἀναλογι[σώμ]εθα οὖν, ἀδελφοί, ἐκ ποίας [ὕλης]
ἐγενήθημεν, ποῖοι καὶ τί[νες εἰ]σήλθαμεν εἰς τὸν κόσμον·
[ὡς ἐκ τ]οῦ τάφου καὶ σκότους [ὁ ποιή]σας ἡμᾶς καὶ

18 ἐν] om. Clem. Alex.   ἔστω] Laurent, p. 423. The margin of the parchment is cut off, so that nothing is visible in the MS. There seems however to have been room for ἔστω, as the size of the letters is often diminished at the end of the lines. On the reading of Clem. Alex. see below.   19 ἐγκράτειαν] εγκρατιαν A.

pression see 1 Cor. xvi. 17, Phil. ii. 30: comp. Col. i. 24.

ὁ σοφὸς κ.τ.λ.] This passage down to τὴν ἐγκράτειαν is quoted in Clem. Alex. Strom. iv. 16 (p. 613) between extracts from § 40, 41 (see the notes there).

18. ἔστω] 'let him be it'. For this emphatic use compare Ign. Ephes. 15 ἄμεινόν ἐστιν σιωπᾶν καὶ εἶναι ἢ λαλοῦντα μὴ εἶναι, Iren. ii. 30. 2 οὐκ ἐν τῷ λέγειν ἀλλ' ἐν τῷ εἶναι ὁ κρείττων δείκνυσθαι ὀφείλει. I have preferred Laurent's happy emendation ἔστω to σιγάτω which has also been suggested, both because it better suits the vacant space in the MS, and because it explains why Clem. Alex. quotes the passage ὁ ἁγνὸς τῇ σαρκὶ μὴ ἀλαζονευέσθω, omitting ἔστω καὶ for the sake of getting a smoother construction. At the end of a line it is not safe to speak positively about the number of letters to be supplied, as there the letters are sometimes much smaller and extend beyond the line; but

σιγάτω seems under any circumstances too long to be at all probable. Hilgenfeld's reading, ὁ ἁγνὸς ἐν τῇ σαρκὶ καὶ [αὐτὸς] μὴ ἀλαζονευέσθω, supplies the lacuna in the wrong place. For the sentiment see Ign. Polyc. 5 εἴ τις δύναται ἐν ἁγνείᾳ μένειν εἰς τιμὴν τῆς σαρκὸς τοῦ Κυρίου, ἐν ἀκαυχησίᾳ μενέτω· ἐὰν καυχήσηται, ἀπώλετο (see above p. 9), Tertull. de Virg. Vel. 13 'Et si a Deo confertur continentiæ virtus, quid gloriaris, quasi non acceperis', passages quoted by Wotton. Clement's language is not sufficient to explain the allusions of Epiphanius and Jerome (quoted above, p. 16), which doubtless refer to the spurious Epistles on Virginity.

21. ποῖοι καὶ τίνες] 1 Pet. i. 11 εἰς τίνα ἢ ποῖον καιρόν.

εἰσήλθαμεν] See Winer § xiii. p. 86.

22. ὡς ἐκ τοῦ τάφου καὶ σκότους] rightly punctuated by Hilgenfeld with Potter on Clem. Alex. l. c. The editors generally have connected this clause with the preceding sentence.

δημιουργήσας [εἰσή]γαγεν εἰς τὸν κόσμον αὐτοῦ, [προ]ε-
τοιμάσας τὰς εὐεργεσίας [αὐτ]οῦ πρὶν ἡμᾶς γεννηθῆναι.
[ταῦ]τα οὖν πάντα ἐξ αὐτοῦ ἔχοντες [ὀ]φείλομεν κατὰ
πάντα εὐχαριστεῖν [αὐ]τῷ· ᾧ ἡ δόξα εἰς τοὺς αἰῶνας τῶν
αἰώνων. ἀμήν.   5

XXXIX. Ἄφρονες καὶ ἀσύνετοι καὶ μωροὶ καὶ
ἀπαίδευτοι χλευάζουσιν ἡμᾶς καὶ μυκτηρίζουσιν, ἑαυτοὺς
βουλόμενοι ἐπαίρεσθαι ταῖς διανοίαις αὐτῶν. τί γὰρ
δύναται θνητός; ἢ τίς ἰσχὺς γηγενοῦς; γέγραπται γάρ·
Ογκ ἦν μορφὴ πρὸ ὀφθαλμῶν μογ· ἀλλ᾽ ἢ αγρᾶν καὶ 10
φωνὴν ἤκογον. τί γάρ; μὴ καθαρὸς ἔσται βροτὸς ἔναντι
Κγρίογ; ἢ ἀπὸ τῶν ἔργων αγτογ ἄμεμπτος ἀνήρ; εἰ κατὰ

3 ὀφείλομεν] οφιλομεν A.   4 εὐχαριστεῖν] ευχαριστῖ A.   7 μυκτηρίζουσιν] μυκτιρηζουσιν A.   16 ἔπαισεν] επεσεν A.   σητός] σητον stands in A (as I

1. προετοιμάσας κ.τ.λ.] See the fragment from 'the 9th Epistle' of Clement of Rome in Leontius and John *Sacr. Rer.* ii (Mai *Script. Vet. Nov. Coll.* VII. p. 84) ἵνα καὶ γενώμεθα βουληθέντος αὐτοῦ, οὐκ ὄντες πρὶν γενέσθαι, καὶ γενόμενοι ἀπολαύσωμεν τῶν δι᾽ ἡμᾶς γενομένων· διὰ τοῦτό ἐσμεν ἄνθρωποι καὶ φρόνησιν ἔχομεν καὶ λόγον, παρ᾽ αὐτοῦ λαβόντες.

XXXIX. 'What folly is the arrogance and self-assumption of those who would make a mockery of us! Have we not been taught in the Scriptures the nothingness of man? In God's sight not even the angels are pure: how much less we frail creatures of earth! A lump of clay, a breath of air, the sinner is consumed in a moment by God's wrath: and the righteous shall inherit his forfeited blessings.'

6. ἄφρονες κ.τ.λ.] Comp. Hermas *Sim.* ix. 14 ἄφρων εἶ καὶ ἀσύνετος.

7. χλευάζουσιν κ.τ.λ.] Ps. xliv. 14 (v. l.), lxxix. 4, μυκτηρισμὸς καὶ χλευασμός.

9. γέγραπται γάρ] A long passage from the LXX Job iv. 16—v. 5, the words οὐρανὸς δὲ...αὐτοῦ being inserted from Job xv. 15 (see below). The variations from the LXX are for the most part slight.

10. οὐκ ἦν μορφὴ κ.τ.λ.] The words of Eliphaz reproving Job. He relates how a voice spoke to him in the dead of night, telling him that no man is pure in God's sight. The LXX differs materially from the Hebrew, but the general sense is the same in both. The οὐκ is not represented in the Hebrew, and it may have been inserted by the LXX to avoid an anthropomorphic expression; but the translators must also have read the preceding words somewhat differently.

12. εἰ κατὰ παίδων κ.τ.λ.] '*seeing that against His servants He is distrustful, and against* (to the discredit of) *His angels He noteth some depravity.*'

14. οὐρανὸς δὲ κ.τ.λ.] From Job xv. 15 (likewise in a speech of Eliphaz) εἰ κατὰ ἁγίων οὐ πιστεύει, οὐρανὸς δὲ οὐ

TO THE CORINTHIANS.

παίδων αὐτοῦ οὐ πιστεύει, κατὰ δὲ ἀγγέλων αὐτοῦ σκολιόν
τι ἐπενόησεν· οὐρανὸς δὲ οὐ καθαρὸς ἐνώπιον αὐτοῦ· ἔα
15 δέ, οἱ κατοικοῦντες οἰκίας πηλίνας ἐξ ὧν καὶ αὐτοὶ ἐκ τοῦ
αὐτοῦ πηλοῦ ἐσμέν· ἔπαισεν αὐτοὺς σητὸς τρόπον, καὶ ἀπὸ
πρωΐθεν ἕως ἑσπέρας οὐκ ἔτι εἰσίν· παρὰ τὸ μὴ δύνασθαι
αὐτοὺς ἑαυτοῖς βοηθῆσαι ἀπώλοντο· ἐνεφύσησεν αὐτοῖς καὶ
ἐτελεύτησαν, παρὰ τὸ μὴ ἔχειν αὐτοὺς σοφίαν. ἐπικάλεσαι
20 δέ, εἴ τίς σοι ὑπακούσεται, ἢ εἴ τινα ἁγίων ἀγγέλων ὄψῃ·
καὶ γὰρ ἄφρονα ἀναιρεῖ ὀργή, πεπλανημένον δὲ θανατοῖ
ζῆλος. ἐγὼ δὲ ἑώρακα ἄφρονας ῥίζας βαλόντας, ἀλλ᾽ εὐθέως ἐβρώθη αὐτῶν ἡ δίαιτα. πόρρω γένοιντο οἱ υἱοὶ
αὐτῶν ἀπὸ σωτηρίας· κολαβρισθείησαν ἐπὶ θύραις ἡσσόνων,

read it), by a transposition with the termination of the next word. Tisch. however gives the reading σητοσ. τρόπον] τροποσ A.

καθαρὸς ἐναντίον αὐτοῦ. The fact that nearly the same words occur as the first clause of xv. 15, which are found likewise in iv. 18, has led Clement to insert the second clause also of this same verse in the other passage to which it does not belong.

ἔα δέ, οἱ κατοικοῦντες] 'Away, ye that dwell'. In the LXX אB read τοὺς δὲ κατοικοῦντας, but A ἔα δὲ τοὺς κατοικοῦντας 'let alone those that dwell'. The latter is a better rendering of the Hebrew and must have been the original LXX text. Symmachus has πόσῳ μᾶλλον, to which ἔα with this construction is an equivalent, Job xv. 16, xxv. 6.

15. οἰκίας πηλίνας] The *houses of clay* in the original probably signify men's bodies: comp. 2 Cor. v. 1 ἡ ἐπίγειος ἡμῶν οἰκία τοῦ σκήνους, called before (iv. 7) ὀστράκινα σκεύη. But the LXX by the turn which they give to the next clause, ἐξ ὧν καὶ αὐτοὶ κ.τ.λ., seem to have understood it literally, 'We are made of the same clay as our houses'; ἐξ ὧν being ex-

plained by ἐκ τοῦ αὐτοῦ πηλοῦ.

16. καὶ ἀπὸ πρωΐθεν κ.τ.λ.] καὶ is found in אB but omitted in A. By ἀπὸ πρωΐθεν κ.τ.λ. is meant 'in the course of a single day'; comp. Is. xxxviii. 12, 13.

21. ὀργή, ζῆλος] i.e. indignation against God, such as Job had shown.

23. δίαιτα] 'their abode'; as e.g. LXX Job viii. 6, 22, xi. 14, xxxix. 6.

24. κολαβρισθείησαν] 'mocked, insulted', as Athen. viii. p. 364 A καλαβρίζουσι τοὺς οἰκέτας, ἀπειλοῦσι τοῖς πολλοῖς. Suidas after others says κολαβρισθείη· χλευασθείη, ἐκτιναχθείη, ἀτιμασθείη. κόλαβρος γὰρ καὶ κάλαβρος, ὁ μικρὸς χοῖρος· ἀντὶ τοῦ οὐδενὸς λόγου ἄξιος νομισθείη. And so Bochart *Hieroz.* ii. § 57, 1. p. 707, 'κολαβρίζειν Hellenistis *contemnere*, quia porcello apud Judæos nihil fuit contemptius'. But this derivation cannot be correct; for (to say nothing else) the word was not confined to Hellenist Jews. The same Athenæus, who furnishes the only other instance of the verb κολαβρίζω, has also two substantives, κύλα-

καὶ ογκ ἔσται ὁ ἐξαιρούμενος· ἃ γὰρ ἐκείνοις ἠτοίμασται, δίκαιοι ἔδονται· αὐτοὶ δὲ ἐκ κακῶν οὐκ ἐξαίρετοι ἔσονται.

XL. *Προδήλων οὖν ἡμῖν ὄντων τούτων, καὶ ἐγ-*

2 ἐξαίρετοι] εξερετοι A.   3 ἡμῖν ὄντων] A. ὄντων ἡμῖν Clem. Alex. 613.

βρος or κάλαβρος (iv. p. 164 E, xv. p. 697 C) 'a licentious song', and καλαβρισμός (xiv. p. 629 D) 'a certain Thracian dance'. The latter is defined by Pollux (iv. 100) Θρᾳκικὸν ὄρχημα καὶ Καρικόν. Here therefore the derivation must be sought. The jeering sallies and mocking gestures of these unrestrained songs and dances would be expressed by κολαβρίζειν. The reading of A in the LXX σκολαβρισθείησαν, compared with σκοραρκίζειν, might seem to favour the other derivation, if there were sufficient evidence that κόλαβρος ever meant χοιρίδιον.
ἐπὶ θύραις ἡσσόνων] '*at the doors of their inferiors*'. There is nothing corresponding to ἡσσόνων in the Hebrew, where 'at the gate' means 'in court, in judgment'.
1. ἃ γὰρ ἐκείνοις κ.τ.λ.] In the LXX (אB) ἃ γὰρ ἐκεῖνοι συνήγαγον (ἐθέρισαν A), δίκαιοι ἔδονται κ.τ.λ. For ἐξαίρετοι ἔσονται A has εξερεθησονται (*i.e.* ἐξαιρεθήσονται). The LXX in this verse diverges considerably from the Hebrew. ἐξαίρετοι here has the somewhat rare sense '*rescued, exempt*,' as e.g. Dion. Hal. *A. R.* vi. 50.
XL. 'This being plain, we must do all things decently and in order, as our Heavenly Master wills us. The appointed times, the fixed places, the proper ministers, must be respected in making our offerings. So only will they be acceptable to God. In the law of Moses the high-priest, the priests, the Levites, the laity, all have their distinct functions'.
The offence of the Corinthians was contempt of ecclesiastical order.

They had resisted and ejected their lawfully appointed presbyters; and—as a necessary consequence—they held their agapae and celebrated their eucharistic feasts when and where they chose, dispensing with the intervention of these their proper officers. There is no ground for supposing (with Rothe *Anfänge* p. 404 sq.), that they had taken advantage of a vacancy in the episcopate by death to mutiny against the presbyters. Of bishops, properly so called, no mention is made in this epistle (see the notes on §§ 42, 44); and, if the government of the Corinthian Church was in any sense episcopal at this time, the functions of the bishop were not yet so distinct from those of the presbyters, but that he could still be regarded as one of them and that no special designation of his office was necessary or natural. On the late development of the episcopate in Corinth, compared with the Churches of Syria and Asia Minor, see the dissertation in *Philippians* p. 213 sq.

3. προδήλων κ.τ.λ.] This passage as far as καιροὺς τεταγμένους is quoted in Clem. Alex. *Strom.* iv. 16 (p. 613).

ἐγκεκυφότες] '*peered into, pored over*'. See below §§ 45, 53, Polyc. *Phil.* 3, *Clem. Hom.* iii. 9. In all these passages it is used of searching the Scriptures. Similarly παρακύπτειν, James i. 25, 1 Pet. i. 12. The word ἐκκεκυφότες in Clem. Alex. must be regarded as an error of transcription.

4. τὰ βάθη τῆς θείας γνώσεως] The large and comprehensive spirit of Clement, as exhibited in the use

κεκυφότες εἰς τὰ βάθη τῆς θείας γνώσεως, πάντα
5 τάξει ποιεῖν ὀφείλομεν ὅσα ὁ δεσπότης ἐπιτελεῖν ἐκέλευσεν κατὰ καιροὺς τεταγμένους· τάς τε προσφορὰς

3 ἐγκεκυφότες] A.   ἐκκεκυφότες Clem. Alex.   5 ὀφείλομεν] οφιλομεν A.

of the Apostolic writers, has been already pointed out (notes on §§ 12, 31, 33, 49). Here it is seen from a somewhat different point of view. While he draws his arguments from the law of Moses and his illustrations from the Old Testament, thus showing his sympathy with the Judaic side of Christianity, he at the same time uses freely those forms of expression which afterwards became the watchwords of the Gnostic sects and were doubtless frequently heard on the lips of their forerunners his contemporaries. To this class belongs τὰ βάθη τῆς γνώσεως (comp. 1 Cor. ii. 10): see S. John's language in Rev. ii. 24 οἵτινες οὐκ ἔγνωσαν τὰ βαθέα τοῦ Σατανᾶ, ὥς λέγουσιν, which is illustrated by Iren. *Hær.* ii. 22. 3 'Profunda Dei adinvenisse se dicentes', ii. 28. 9 'Aliquis eorum qui altitudines Dei exquisisse se dicunt', Hippol. *Hær.* v. 6 ἐπεκάλεσαν ἑαυτοὺς γνωστικούς, φάσκοντες μόνοι τὰ βάθη γινώσκειν; compare the description in Tertullian *adv. Valent.* 1 'Si bona fide quæras, concreto vultu, suspenso supercilio, *Altum est* aiunt', and see *Galatians* p. 298. It is significant too that γνῶσις is a favourite word with Clement: see §§ 1, 36, 41, and especially § 48 ἤτω δυνατὸς γνῶσιν ἐξειπεῖν (with the note). Again in § 34 he repeats the favourite Gnostic text 'Eye hath not seen etc', which they misapplied to support their principle of an esoteric doctrine. See the note there.

6. τάς τε προσφορὰς κ.τ.λ.] Editors have failed to explain the reading of the MS satisfactorily. Two modes of punctuation are offered. The main stop is placed (1) after ἐκέλευσεν, so that we read κατὰ καιρ. τετ. τάς τε προσφ. κ.τ.λ.; but in this case we get an unmeaning repetition, κατὰ καιροὺς τεταγμένους and ὡρισμένοις καιροῖς κ.τ.λ. belonging to the same sentence: or (2) after ἐπιτελεῖσθαι, in which case ἐπιτελεῖσθαι must be governed by ὀφείλομεν. But, with this construction (not to urge other obvious objections) there is an awkwardness in using the middle ἐπιτελεῖσθαι in the same sense in which the active ἐπιτελεῖν has occurred just before; though the middle in itself might stand. (In James iv. 2, 3 however we have αἰτεῖν and αἰτεῖσθαι side by side). I have therefore inserted ἐπιμελῶς (perhaps ἐπιμελείᾳ), supposing that the omission was due to the similar beginnings of the two words (as e.g. αιωνιον for αινον αιωνιον ii. § 9; see also the note on ii. § 10 εὑρεῖν); comp. 1 (3) Esdr. viii. 21 πάντα κατὰ τὸν τοῦ Θεοῦ νόμον ἐπιτελεσθήτω ἐπιμελῶς τῷ Θεῷ τῷ ὑψίστῳ, Herm. *Mand.* xii. 3 τὴν διακονίαν...τέλει ἐπιμελῶς. Thus the passage reads smoothly and intelligibly. An alternative would be to omit ἐπιτελεῖσθαι, as having been inserted from below (διὰ τίνων ἐπιτελεῖσθαι), and to take τάς τε προσφορὰς καὶ λειτουργίας in apposition with ὅσα, but this does not seem so good for more than one reason. The perplexed syntax might perhaps be unravelled in a third way, by substituting something else for the doubtful ἐκέλευσεν below. I should have preferred τὰς δὲ προσφορὰς as Tischendorf deciphers the MS,

καὶ λειτουργίας ἐπιμελῶς ἐπιτελεῖσθαι καὶ οὐκ εἰκῆ ἢ
ἀτάκτως †ἐ[κέλευσεν]† γίνεσθαι, ἀλλ' ὡρισμένοις καιροῖς
καὶ ὥραις· ποῦ τε καὶ διὰ τίνων ἐπιτελεῖσθαι θέλει, αὐτὸς
ὥρισεν τῇ ὑπερτάτῳ αὐτοῦ βουλήσει· ἵν' ὁσίως πάντα
γινόμενα ἐν εὐδοκήσει εὐπρόσδεκτα εἴη τῷ θελήματι 5
αὐτοῦ. Οἱ οὖν τοῖς προστεταγμένοις καιροῖς ποιοῦντες
τὰς προσφορὰς αὐτῶν εὐπρόσδεκτοί τε καὶ μακάριοι,

1 λειτουργίας] λειτουργειασ A.   ἐπιμελῶς] om. A. The reasons for the insertion are given on p. 127.   2 †ἐκέλευσεν†] Tisch. deciphers ε...εγcεν. I have looked again and again, but could only read (and this doubtfully) the initial ε. The whole word (or words) occupies the same space as ιλομενοσαοδ (i.e. 11 letters) in the line above.   4 πάντα] παντατα A. See below.

but (unless I misread it) it certainly has τε, not δε. On the Christian sense of προσφοραί see the note on προσενεγκόντας τὰ δῶρα § 44.

2. καιροῖς καὶ ὥραις] A pleonasm, as in Dionys. *de Isocr.* 14 (p. 561) μὴ ἐν καιρῷ γίνεσθαι μηδ' ἐν ὥρᾳ, Plut. *Ages.* 36 τοῦ καλοῦ καιρὸν οἰκεῖον εἶναι καὶ ὥραν. The words differ only so far, that καιρός refers to the *fitness*, ὥρα to the *appointedness*, of the time. Demosth. *Olynth.* ii. p. 24 μηδένα καιρὸν μηδ' ὥραν παραλείπων shows that ὥρα does not refer to the '*hour of the day*', as this use of the word was only introduced long after the age of Demosthenes.

4. ὑπερτάτῳ] I have not ventured with previous editors to alter the MS reading to ὑπερτάτῃ, since even in classical writers comparatives and superlatives are sometimes of two terminations; e.g. Thucyd. iii. 89, 101, v. 71, 110. See Buttmann *Griech. Sprachl.* § 60 anm. 5. No dependence however can be placed on our scribe in such a matter; see instances of similar errors, p. 25.

πάντα γινόμενα] I have struck out τὰ before γινόμενα as a mere repetition of the last syllable of πάντα and as interfering with the sense;

see, for similar errors of transcription in our MS, p. 25.

5. ἐν εὐδοκήσει] sc. τοῦ Θεοῦ. See the note on § 2 μετ' ἐλέους καὶ εὐδοκήσεως, as I propose to read the passage. But possibly we should here for ΕΥΔΟΚΗΣΕΙΕΥΠΡΟΣΔΕΚΤΑ read ΕΥΔΟΚΗΣΕΙΘΥΠΡΟΣΔΕΚΤΑ; as in Epiphan. *Hær.* lxx 10 (p. 822) εὐδοκήσει Θεοῦ.

9. τῷ γὰρ ἀρχιερεῖ κ.τ.λ.] This is evidently an instance from the old dispensation adduced to show that God will have His ministrations performed through definite *persons*, just as below (§ 41) οὐ πανταχοῦ κ.τ.λ. Clement draws an illustration from the same source that He will have them performed in the proper *places*. There is therefore no *direct* reference to the Christian ministry in ἀρχιερεύς, ἱερεῖς, Λευῖται, but it is an argument by *analogy*. Does the analogy then extend to the *three* orders? The answer to this seems to be that, though the episcopate appears to have been widely established in Asia Minor at this time (see *Philippians* p. 209 sq.), this epistle throughout only recognises two orders, presbyters and deacons, as existing at Corinth (see esp. the notes on ἐπισκόπων § 42,

τοῖς γὰρ νομίμοις τοῦ δεσπότου ἀκολουθοῦντες οὐ δια-
μαρτάνουσιν. τῷ γὰρ ἀρχιερεῖ ἴδιαι λειτουργίαι δεδο-
μέναι εἰσίν, καὶ τοῖς ἱερεῦσιν ἴδιος ὁ τόπος προστέ-
τακται, καὶ λευΐταις ἴδιαι διακονίαι ἐπίκεινται· ὁ λαϊκὸς
ἄνθρωπος τοῖς λαϊκοῖς προστάγμασιν δέδεται.

XLI. Ἕκαστος ὑμῶν, ἀδελφοί, ἐν τῷ ἰδίῳ τάγματι εὐχαριστείτω Θεῷ ἐν ἀγαθῇ συνειδήσει ὑπάρχων,

11 ἐπικεῖνται] επικινται A.   14 συνειδήσει] συνειδησιν A.

and on ἐὰν κοιμηθῶσιν, διαδέξωνται κ.τ.λ. § 44). It has been held indeed by some (*e.g.* Lipsius p. 25) that, this being so, the analogy notwithstanding extends to the number three, Christ being represented by the highpriest (see the note § 36), the presbyters by the priests, and the deacons by the Levites. But to this it is a sufficient answer that the Highpriesthood of Christ is wholly different in kind and exempt from those very limitations on which the passage dwells. And again why should the analogy be so pressed? It would be considered ingenious trifling to seek out the Christian equivalents to ἐνδελεχισμοῦ ἢ εὐχῶν ἢ περὶ ἁμαρτίας καὶ πλημμελείας below (§ 41), or to ἔπαρχοι, χιλίαρχοι, ἑκατόνταρχοι, πεντηκόνταρχοι, κ.τ.λ. above (§ 37); nor is there any reason why a closer correspondence should be exacted from this passage than from the others. Later writers indeed did dwell on the analogy of the *threefold* ministry; but we cannot argue back from them to Clement, in whose epistle the very element of *threefoldness*, which gives force to such a comparison, is wanting.

10. ἴδιος ὁ τόπος κ.τ.λ.] '*The office assigned to the priests is special*'. On this sense of τόπος comp. below § 44 τοῦ ἱδρυμένου αὐτοῖς τόπου, and see the notes on Ign. *Polyc.* 1 ἐκδίκει σου τὸν τόπον.

11. λαϊκός] Comp. *Clem. Hom.* Epist. Cl. § 5 οὕτως ἑκάστῳ λαϊκῷ ἁμαρτία ἐστὶν κ.τ.λ., Clem. Alex. *Strom.* iii. 12 (p. 552) κἂν πρεσβύτερος ᾖ κἂν διάκονος κἂν λαϊκός, *ib.* v. 6 (p. 665) κώλυμα λαϊκῆς ἀπιστίας. In Tertullian 'laicus' is not uncommon, e.g. *de Præscr.* 41 'Nam et laicis sacerdotalia munera injungunt'. In the LXX λαός is used not only in contradistinction to 'the Gentiles' (see the note on § 29 above), but also as opposed to (1) 'The rulers', *e.g.* 2 Chron. xxiv. 10, xxx. 24, (2) 'The priests', *e.g.* Exod. xix. 24, Neh. vii. 73 (viii. 1), Is. xxiv. 2; comp. Jer. xxxiv (xli). 19 τοὺς ἄρχοντας Ἰουδα καὶ τοὺς δυνάστας καὶ τοὺς ἱερεῖς καὶ τὸν λαόν. From this last contrast comes the use of λαϊκός here. The adjective however is not found in the LXX, though in the other Greek versions we meet with λαϊκός 'laic' or 'profane' and λαϊκοῦν 'to profane', Deut. xx. 6, xxviii. 30, Ruth i. 12, 1 Sam. xxi. 4, Ezek. vii. 22. xlviii. 15.

XLI. 'Let each man therefore take his proper place in the thanksgiving of the Church. Then again, in the law of Moses the several sacrifices are not offered anywhere, but only in the temple at Jerusalem and after careful scrutiny. If then transgression was visited on the Israelites of old with death, how much greater shall be our punishment, seeing that

μὴ παρεκβαίνων τὸν ὡρισμένον τῆς λειτουργίας αὐτοῦ κανόνα, ἐν σεμνότητι. Οὐ πανταχοῦ, ἀδελφοί, προσφέρονται θυσίαι ἐνδελεχισμοῦ ἢ εὐχῶν ἢ περὶ ἁμαρτίας καὶ πλημμελείας, ἀλλ' ἢ ἐν Ἱερουσαλὴμ μόνῃ· κἀκεῖ δὲ οὐκ

1 παρεκβαίνων] παραικβαιγων A. λειτουργίας] λιτουργιασ A.

our knowledge also is greater'.

εὐχαριστείτω] The allusion here is plainly to the public services of the Church, where order had been violated. Thus εὐχαριστία will refer chiefly, though not solely, to the principal act of Christian thanksgiving, the celebration of the Lord's Supper, which at a later date was almost exclusively termed εὐχαριστία. The usage of Clement is probably midway between that of S. Paul where no such appropriation of the term appears (e.g. 1 Cor. xiv. 16, 2 Cor. ix. 11, 12, Phil. iv. 6, 1 Tim. ii. 1, etc.), and that of the Ignatian Epistles (*Philad.* 4, *Smyrn.* 7) and of Justin (*Apol.* i. § 66, p. 97 sq., *Dial.* 41, p. 260) where it is specially so applied. For the ἴδιον τάγμα of the people at the eucharistic feast see Justin *Apol.* i. § 65 (p. 97 D) οὗ (i.e. τοῦ προεστῶτος τῶν ἀδελφῶν) συντελέσαντος τὰς εὐχὰς καὶ τὴν εὐχαριστίαν πᾶς ὁ λαὸς ἐπευφημεῖ λέγων 'Αμήν... εὐχαριστήσαντος δὲ τοῦ προεστῶτος καὶ ἐπευφημήσαντος παντὸς τοῦ λαοῦ κ.τ.λ., and again *ib.* § 67 (p. 98 E). See Harnack *Der Christliche Gottesdienst* etc. (Erlangen, 1854).

ἐν ἀγαθῇ συνειδήσει] Acts xxiii. 1, 1 Tim. i. 5, 19, 1 Pet. iii. 16, 21: comp. καλὴ συνείδησις, Heb. xiii. 18. For an explanation of the MS reading συνείδησιν see above § 15.

2. κανόνα] Compare the metaphor 2 Cor. x. 13, 14, κατὰ τὸ μέτρον τοῦ κανόνος and ὑπερεκτείνομεν: see also the note on § 7.

προσφέρονται] The present tense has been thought to imply that the sacrifices were still offered and the temple yet standing, and therefore to fix the date of the epistle before the destruction of Jerusalem, i.e. about the close of Nero's reign. To this very early date however there are insuperable objections (see the introduction p. 4 and notes on §§ 1, 5, 44, 47). Clement therefore must use προσφέρονται as implying rather the *permanence of the record* and of the lesson contained therein than *the continuance of the institution* and practice itself. Indeed it will be seen that his argument gains considerably, if we suppose the practice discontinued; because then and then only is the sanction transferred from the Jewish sacrifices to the Christian ministrations, as the true fulfilment of the Divine command. If any one doubts whether such a usage is natural, let him read the account of the Mosaic sacrifices in Josephus *Ant.* iii. cc. 9, 10 (where the parallels to Clement's present tense προσφέρονται are far too numerous to be counted), remembering that the *Antiquities* were published A.D. 93, i.e. within two or three years of our epistle. Comp. Barnab. 7 sq., *Epist. ad Diogn.* 3, where also the present is used. This mode of speaking is also very common in the Talmud. See Friedmann and Graetz *Die angebliche Fortdauer des jüdischen Opfercultus* etc. in the *Theolog. Jahrb.* XVII. p. 338 sq. (1848), and the references in Derenbourg *L'Hist. et la Géogr. de la Palestine* p. 480 sq.

3. ἐνδελεχισμοῦ] '*of continuity, perpetuity*', the expression used in the LXX for the ordinary daily sacri-

5 ἐν παντὶ τόπῳ προσφέρεται, ἀλλ' ἔμπροσθεν τοῦ ναοῦ πρὸς τὸ θυσιαστήριον, μωμοσκοπηθὲν τὸ προσφερόμενον διὰ τοῦ ἀρχιερέως καὶ τῶν προειρημένων λειτουργῶν. οἱ οὖν παρὰ τὸ καθῆκον τῆς βουλήσεως αὐτοῦ

7 λειτουργῶν] λιτουργων A.

fices, as a rendering of חמים (*e.g.* Exod. xxix. 42, Neh. x. 33); and thus opposed to the special offerings, of which the two types are the freewill offerings (εὐχῶν) and expiatory offerings (περὶ ἁμαρτίας ἢ πλημμελείας). Of the last two words ἁμαρτία denotes the sin-offering (חמאת) and πλημμέλεια the trespass-offering (אשם). A similar threefold division of sacrifices is given by Philo *de Vict.* 4 (II. p. 240) τὸ ὁλόκαυτον, τὸ σωτήριον, τὸ περὶ ἁμαρτίας, and by Josephus *Ant.* iii. 9. 1 sq. ἡ ὁλοκαύτωσις, ἡ χαριστήριος θυσία, ἡ ὑπὲρ ἁμαρτάδων (passages referred to in Jacobson's notes); see also Ewald *Alterth. des Volkes Isr.* p. 52 sq. Here the θυσία ἐνδελεχισμοῦ stands for the ὁλοκαυτώματα generally, as being the most prominent type; and in the same way the θυσία εὐχῶν, as a part for the whole, represents the peace-offerings (σωτήρια in the LXX and Philo) which comprised two species (Lev. vii. 11—17), the vow or free-will offering (which Clement has selected) and the thanksgiving-offering (which Josephus takes as the type). On the other hand, when speaking of expiatory offerings, Clement gives both types.

5. ἔμπροσθεν κ.τ.λ.] The ναός is here the shrine, the holy-place; the θυσιαστήριον, the court of the altar: see the note on Ign. *Ephes.* 5. The ἱερόν comprises both. This distinction of ναός and ἱερόν is carefully observed in the N.T.: see Trench *N. T. Synon.* 1st ser. § iii.

6. μωμοσκοπηθέν] '*after inspection*', with a view to detecting blemishes.

A flaw or blemish, which vitiates a person or thing for holy purposes, is in the LXX μῶμος. Doubtless the choice of this rendering was partly determined by its similarity in sound to the Hebrew מום, for otherwise it is not a very obvious or natural equivalent. [A parallel instance is the word σκηνή, chosen for the same reasons, as a rendering of Shechinah, and carrying with it all the significance of the latter.] Hence ἄμωμος in the LXX signifies 'without blemish', being applied to victims and the like, and diverges from its classical meaning. Hence also are derived the words μωμοσκόπος, μωμοσκοπεῖν, which seem to be confined to Jewish and Christian writers: Philo *de Agric.* 29 (I. p. 320) οὕς ἔνιοι μωμοσκόπους ὀνομάζουσιν, ἵνα ἄμωμα καὶ ἀσινῆ προσάγηται τῷ βωμῷ τὰ ἱερεῖα κ.τ.λ., Polyc. *Phil.* 4 πάντα μωμοσκοπεῖται, Clem. Alex. *Strom.* iv. 18 (p. 617) ἦσαν δὲ κἂν ταῖς τῶν θυσιῶν προσαγωγαῖς παρὰ τῷ νόμῳ οἱ ἱερέων μωμοσκόποι, *Apost. Const.* ii. 3 γέγραπται γάρ, Μωμοσκοπεῖσθε τὸν μέλλοντα εἰς ἱερωσύνην προχειρίζεσθαι (a paraphrase of Lev. xxi. 17).

7. ἀρχιερέως] Wotton suggests ἱερέως, 'quum sacerdotum inferioris ordinis potius quam summi sacerdotis sit τὰς θυσίας μωμοσκοπεῖν'; but διὰ τοῦ ἀρχιερέως κ.τ.λ. belongs rather to προσφέρεται than to μωμοσκοπηθέν, as the order seems to show. The three conditions are (1) that it must be offered at the proper place, (2) that it must be examined and found without blemish, (3) that it must be sacrificed by the proper persons, the

ποιοῦντές τι θάνατον τὸ πρόστιμον ἔχουσιν. Ὁρᾶτε, ἀδελφοί, ὅσῳ πλείονος κατηξιώθημεν γνώσεως, τοσούτῳ μᾶλλον ὑποκείμεθα κινδύνῳ.

XLII. Οἱ ἀπόστολοι ἡμῖν εὐηγγελίσθησαν ἀπὸ τοῦ Κυρίου Ἰησοῦ Χριστοῦ, Ἰησοῦς ὁ Χριστὸς ἀπὸ τοῦ 5 Θεοῦ ἐξεπέμφθη. ὁ Χριστὸς οὖν ἀπὸ τοῦ Θεοῦ, καὶ οἱ ἀπόστολοι ἀπὸ τοῦ Χριστοῦ· ἐγένοντο οὖν ἀμφότερα εὐτάκτως ἐκ θελήματος Θεοῦ. παραγγελίας οὖν λαβόντες καὶ πληροφορηθέντες διὰ τῆς ἀναστάσεως τοῦ Κυρίου ἡμῶν Ἰησοῦ Χριστοῦ καὶ πιστωθέντες ἐν τῷ λόγῳ 10

2 κατηξιώθημεν] καταξιωθημεν A, as Tisch. (praef. p. xix.) reads it, but I could not see distinctly.

high priests or other priests. The διὰ τοῦ ἀρχιερέως κ.τ.λ. is comprehensive, so as to include all sacrifices.

τὸ καθῆκον κ.τ.λ.] 'the seemly ordinance of His will.' For the genitive comp. Plut. Mor. p. 617 E ἐκ τῶν Ὁμήρου τὸ θεώρημα τοῦτο λαμβάνων καθηκόντων.

1. τὸ πρόστιμον] 2 Macc. vii. 36. Ἐπιτίμιον Ἀττικῶς, πρόστιμον Ἑλληνικῶς Moeris s. v. ἐπιτίμιον. This is one among many instances of the exceptional character of the Attic dialect, for πρόστιμον occurs as early as Hippocrates; see for other examples *Galatians* vi. 6 and p. 92 (p. 89, ed. 1), *Philippians* i. 28, ii. 14.

ὁρᾶτε κ.τ.λ.] This sentence is quoted by Clem. Alex. *Strom.* iv. 16 (p. 613).

2. γνώσεως] See the note on τὰ βάθη τῆς θείας γνώσεως § 40.

XLII. 'The Apostles were sent by Christ, as Christ was sent by the Father. Having this commission they preached the kingdom of God and appointed presbyters and deacons in every place. This was no new institution, but had been foretold ages ago by the prophet.'

4. εὐηγγελίσθησαν] 'were taught the Gospel', as Matt. xi. 5 (Luke vii. 22), Heb. iv. 2, 6; for the first aorist apparently is always passive, being used with a nominative either of the person instructed or the lesson conveyed; and ἡμῖν will be 'for our sakes'. It might be a question however whether we should not read ἡμῶν, as in the opening of § 44.

6. ἐξεπέμφθη] is attached by all the editors to the following sentence. Yet I can hardly doubt that it belongs to the preceding words; for (1) The position of οὖν seems to require this; (2) The awkward expression that 'Christ was taught the Gospel by the Father' thus disappears; (3) We get in its place a forcible epigrammatic parallelism ὁ Χριστὸς οὖν κ.τ.λ. For the omission of the verb to gain terseness, and for the form of the sentence generally, comp. Rom. x. 17 ἄρα ἡ πίστις ἐξ ἀκοῆς, ἡ δὲ ἀκοὴ διὰ ῥήματος Χριστοῦ, 1 Cor. iii. 23 ὑμεῖς δὲ Χριστοῦ, Χριστὸς δὲ Θεοῦ. For the thought see Joh. xvii. 18 καθὼς ἐμὲ ἀπέστειλας εἰς τὸν κόσμον, κἀγὼ ἀπέστειλα αὐτοὺς εἰς τὸν κόσμον, xx. 21 καθὼς ἀπέσταλκέν με ὁ πατήρ, κἀγὼ

τοῦ Θεοῦ μετὰ πληροφορίας πνεύματος ἁγίου ἐξῆλθον, εὐαγγελιζόμενοι τὴν βασιλείαν τοῦ Θεοῦ μέλλειν ἔρχεσθαι. κατὰ χώρας οὖν καὶ πόλεις κηρύσσοντες καθίστανον τὰς ἀπαρχὰς αὐτῶν, δοκιμάσαντες τῷ πνεύ-
15 ματι, εἰς ἐπισκόπους καὶ διακόνους τῶν μελλόντων πιστεύειν. καὶ τοῦτο οὐ καινῶς, ἐκ γὰρ δὴ πολλῶν χρόνων ἐγέγραπτο περὶ ἐπισκόπων καὶ διακόνων· οὕτως γάρ που λέγει ἡ γραφή: Καταστήcω τοὺc ἐπιcκόπουc αὐτῶν ἐν δικαιοcύνῃ καὶ τοὺc διακόνουc αὐτῶν
20 ἐν πίcτει.

13 καθιστανον] καθεσταναν A.

πέμπω ὑμᾶς. See also the notes on *Ign. Ephes.* 6.

8. παραγγελίας] '*word of command*', received as from a superior officer that it may be passed on to others; as *e.g.* Xen. *Cyr.* ii. 4. 2, iv. 2. 27.

10. πιστωθέντες] 2 Tim. iii. 14 μένε ἐν οἷς ἔμαθες καὶ ἐπιστώθης.

11. μετὰ πληροφορίας κ.τ.λ.] '*with firm conviction* inspired *by the Holy Ghost*': comp. I Thess. i. 5 ἐν πνεύματι ἁγίῳ καὶ [ἐν] πληροφορίᾳ πολλῇ.

13. χώρας] '*country districts*', as opposed to towns; comp. Luke xxi. 21, Joh. iv. 35, Acts viii. 1, James v. 4. Hence the ancient title χωρεπίσκοπος; see *Philippians* p. 230.

14. τὰς ἀπαρχὰς αὐτῶν] '*the firstfruits of their preaching*'; or perhaps αὐτῶν refers not to the Apostles but to the χῶραι καὶ πόλεις, and is like the genitives in Rom. xvi. 5 ὅς ἐστιν ἀπαρχὴ τῆς Ἀσίας, 1 Cor. xvi. 15 ὅτι ἐστὶν ἀπαρχὴ τῆς Ἀχαΐας, which passages Clement may have had in his mind.

δοκιμάσαντες] 1 Tim. iii. 10 δοκιμαζέσθωσαν πρῶτον, εἶτα διακονείτωσαν; see below § 44 διαδέξωνται ἕτεροι δεδοκιμασμένοι ἄνδρες.

τῷ πνεύματι] '*by the Spirit*', which is the great searcher, 1 Cor. ii. 10.

15. ἐπισκόπους] i.e. πρεσβυτέρους; for Clement thrice mentions ἐπίσκοποι καὶ διάκονοι in conjunction (as in Phil. i. 1 σὺν ἐπισκόποις καὶ διακόνοις), and it is impossible that he could have omitted the presbyters, more especially as his one object is to defend their authority which had been assailed (§§ 44, 47, 54). The words ἐπίσκοπος and πρεσβύτερος therefore are synonymes in Clement, as they are in the Apostolic writers. In Ignatius and Polycarp they first appear as distinct titles. See *Philippians* p. 93 sq., 191 sq.

18. καταστήσω] loosely quoted from LXX Is. lx. 17 δώσω τοὺς ἄρχοντάς σου ἐν εἰρήνῃ καὶ τοὺς ἐπισκόπους σου ἐν δικαιοσύνῃ. Thus the introduction of the διάκονοι is due to misquotation. Irenæus also (*Hær.* iv. 26. 5) applies the passage to the Christian ministry, but quotes the LXX correctly. The force of the original is rightly given in the A.V., 'I will also make thy officers [magistrates] peace and thine, exactors [task-masters] righteousness'; i.e. 'there shall be no tyranny or oppression'. For ἐπίσκοπος, 'a task-master', see *Philippians* p. 93.

XLIII. Καὶ τί θαυμαστὸν εἰ οἱ ἐν Χριστῷ πιστευθέντες παρὰ Θεοῦ ἔργον τοιοῦτο κατέστησαν τοὺς προειρημένους; ὅπου καὶ ὁ μακάριος πιϲτὸϲ θεράπων ἐν ὅλῳ τῷ οἴκῳ Μωϋσῆς τὰ διατεταγμένα αὐτῷ πάντα ἐσημειώσατο ἐν ταῖς ἱεραῖς βίβλοις, ᾧ καὶ 5 ἐπηκολούθησαν οἱ λοιποὶ προφῆται συνεπιμαρτυροῦντες τοῖς ὑπ' αὐτοῦ νενομοθετημένοις. ἐκεῖνος γάρ, ζήλου ἐμπεσόντος περὶ τῆς ἱερωσύνης καὶ στασιαζουσῶν τῶν φυλῶν ὁποία αὐτῶν εἴη τῷ ἐνδόξῳ ὀνόματι κεκοσμημένη, ἐκέλευσεν τοὺς δώδεκα φυλάρχους προσενεγκεῖν 10 αὐτῷ ῥάβδους ἐπιγεγραμμένας ἑκάστης φυλῆς κατ' ὄνομα· καὶ λαβὼν αὐτὰς ἔδησεν καὶ ἐσφράγισεν τοῖς δακτυλίοις τῶν φυλάρχων, καὶ ἀπέθετο αὐτὰς εἰς τὴν σκηνὴν τοῦ μαρτυρίου ἐπὶ τὴν τράπεζαν τοῦ Θεοῦ· καὶ κλείσας τὴν σκηνὴν ἐσφράγισεν τὰς κλεῖδας ὡσαύ- 15

5 ἐσημειώσατο] εσημιωσατο A.   9 κεκοσμημένη] κεκοσμημενω A.
15 κλείσας] κλισασ A.   22 προέφερεν τάς] I prefer this to προσέφερεν τάς (comp. ἐξήνεγκε Num. xvii. 9, προεκύμισε Jos. *Ant.* iv. 4. 2), and apparently the traces of the last letter visible might belong equally well to an ε as to a c, though Tisch. reads a c. All previous editors (following Young) have read προσήνεγκεν without τάς;

XLIII. 'And no marvel, if the Apostles of Christ thus ordained ministers, seeing that there was the precedent of Moses. When the authority of the priests was assailed, he took the rods of the twelve tribes and placed them within the tabernacle, saying that God had chosen the tribe whose rod should bud. On the morrow when the doors were opened, Aaron's rod alone had budded, and the office of the priesthood was vindicated.'

2. πιστευθέντες] '*entrusted with*'. The construction πιστεύεσθαί τι is common in S. Paul: Rom. iii. 2, 1 Cor. ix. 17, Gal. ii. 7, 1 Thess. ii. 4, 1 Tim. i. 11, Tit. i. 3.

3. πιστὸς θεράπων κ.τ.λ.] From Heb. iii. 5 Μωϋσῆς μὲν πιστὸς ἐν ὅλῳ τῷ οἴκῳ αὐτοῦ ὡς θεράπων, where there is a reference to Num. xii. 7 οὐχ οὕτως ὁ θεράπων μου Μωϋσῆς ἐν ὅλῳ τῷ οἴκῳ μου πιστός ἐστιν. On θεράπων see above § 4. For the combination of epithets here comp. Justin *Dial.* 56 (p. 274) Μωϋσῆς οὖν ὁ μακάριος καὶ πιστὸς θεράπων Θεοῦ κ.τ.λ.

5. ἐσημειώσατο] '*recorded as a sign*': comp. § 11 εἰς κρίμα καὶ εἰς σημείωσιν πάσαις ταῖς γενεαῖς γίνονται. So in the narrative to which Clement here refers, Num. xvii. 10 ἀπόθες τὴν ῥάβδον Ἀαρών...σημεῖον τοῖς υἱοῖς τῶν ἀνηκόων.

ἱεραῖς] On this epithet see below, § 53.

7. ἐκεῖνος γὰρ κ.τ.λ.] The lesson

τως καὶ τὰς ῥάβδους· καὶ εἶπεν αὐτοῖς· Ἄνδρες ἀδελφοί,
ἧς ἂν φυλῆς ἡ ῥάβδος βλαστήςῃ, ταύτην ἐκλέλεκται ὁ
θεὸς εἰς τὸ ἱερατεύειν καὶ λειτουργεῖν αὐτῷ. πρωΐας
δὲ γενομένης συνεκάλεσεν πάντα τὸν Ἰσραήλ, τὰς
20 ἑξακοσίας χιλιάδας τῶν ἀνδρῶν, [καὶ ἐπε]δείξατο τοῖς
φυλάρχοις [τὰς σφρα]γῖδας καὶ ἤνοιξεν τὴ[ν σκηνὴν]
τοῦ μαρτυρίου καὶ προέ[φερεν τὰς] ῥάβδους· καὶ
εὑρέθη ἡ ῥ[άβδος τοῦ] Ἀαρὼν οὐ μόνον βεβλ[αστηκυῖα]
ἀλλὰ καὶ καρπὸν ἔχουσα. τί δοκεῖτε, ἀγαπητοί; οὐ
25 προ[έγνω] Μωϋσῆς τοῦτο μέλλειν [ἔσεσθαι]; μάλιστα
ᾔδει· ἀλλ' ἵνα μὴ ἀκ[αταστα]σία γένηται ἐν τῷ
Ἰσραήλ, οὕτω[ς ἐποί]ησεν εἰς τὸ δοξασθῆναι τ[ὸ ὄνο]μα
τοῦ ἀληθινοῦ καὶ μόνου [Θεοῦ]· ᾧ ἡ δόξα εἰς τοὺς
αἰῶνας τῶν αἰώνων. ἀμήν.
30 XLIV. Καὶ οἱ ἀπόστολοι ἡμῶν ἔγνωσαν διὰ τοῦ

but (1) the article is certainly wanted, and (2) more letters seem required to fill the lacuna.   23 τοῦ Ἀαρών] I have inserted the article, which previous editors have omitted, because the lacuna seems to require it; e.g. eight letters...αστηκυια occupy the same space in the next line.   24 δοκεῖτε] δοκειται A.

of this narrative is drawn out also by Joseph. *Ant.* iv. 4. 2, and by Philo *Vit. Moys.* iii. 21 (II. p. 162).

9. ὀνόματι] i.e. '*dignity, office*', sc. τῆς ἱερωσύνης; as § 44 ἐπὶ τοῦ ὀνόματος τῆς ἐπισκοπῆς. On this sense of ὄνομα see above § 36.

11. ἑκάστης φυλῆς] For the genitive of the thing inscribed after ἐπιγράφειν comp. Plut. *Mor.* 400 E τὸν ἐνταῦθα τουτονὶ θησαυρὸν ἐπιγράψαι τῆς πόλεως. Here however φυλῆς might be governed by κατ' ὄνομα.

12. ἔδησεν κ.τ.λ.] This incident, with the following ἐσφράγισεν τὰς κλεῖδας ὡσαύτως, is not given in the biblical narrative (Num. xvii). It seems however to be intended by Josephus (l.c.) τῶν τότε (τε?) ἀνδρῶν κατασημηναμένων αὐτάς, οἵπερ ἐκόμιζον,

καὶ τοῦ πλήθους, though his language is obscure. Comp. Xen. *Hell.* iii. 1. 27 κατέκλεισεν αὐτὰ καὶ κατεσημήνατο καὶ φύλακας κατέστησεν.

24. οὐ προέγνω κ.τ.λ.] This passage is loosely quoted or rather abridged and paraphrased by one Joannes. The quotation is given in *Spicil. Solesm.* I. p. 293 (see above, p. 14).

28. τοῦ ἀληθινοῦ κ.τ.λ.] Comp. Joh. xvii. 3.

XLIV. 'So likewise the Apostles foresaw these feuds. They therefore provided for a succession of tried persons, who should fulfil the office of the ministry. Thus it is no light sin of which you are guilty in ejecting men so appointed, when they have discharged their duties faithfully. Happy those presbyters who have

Κυρίου ἡμῶν Ἰησοῦ Χριστοῦ, ὅτι ἔρις ἔσται ἐπὶ τοῦ ὀνόματος τῆς ἐπισκοπῆς. Διὰ ταύτην οὖν τὴν αἰτίαν πρόγνωσιν εἰληφότες τελείαν κατέστησαν τοὺς προειρημένους, καὶ μεταξὺ ἐπιμονὴν δεδώκασιν ὅπως, ἐὰν κοιμηθῶσιν, διαδέξωνται ἕτεροι δεδοκιμασμένοι ἄνδρες 5

1 Κυρίου] ΚΥ̃, but ΧΥ̃ A.   ἔρις] ερεισ A.   4 μεταξύ] μετοξυ A.
ἐπιμονήν] επινομην A. See below   δεδώκασιν] εδωκασιν A.

departed hence, and are in no fear of removal from their proper office'.
1. ἡμῶν] Comp. 2 Pet. iii. 2 τῆς τῶν ἀποστόλων ὑμῶν ἐντολῆς, where ὑμῶν (not ἡμῶν) is the correct reading, as quoted by Hilgenfeld: so that it is an exact parallel to Clement's expression. See the note on τοὺς ἀγαθοὺς ἀποστόλους § 5.
τοῦ ὀνόματος κ.τ.λ.] On ὄνομα above §§ 36, 43. The ἐπισκοπή here is of course the 'office of presbyter', as in 1 Tim. iii. 1.
3. τοὺς προειρημένους] sc. ἐπισκόπους καὶ διακόνους, § 42.
4. μεταξύ] 'afterwards'; comp. Acts xiii. 42 εἰς τὸ μεταξὺ σάββατον, Barnab. § 13 εἶδεν δὲ Ἰακὼβ τύπον τῷ πνεύματι τοῦ λαοῦ τοῦ μεταξύ, Theoph. ad Autol. i. 8, iii. 21, 23. See also the references in Meyer's note to Acts l.c.
ἐπιμονὴν δεδώκασιν] 'have given permanence to the office': comp. Athenag. de Resurr. 18 δεῖται δὲ διαδοχῆς διὰ τὴν τοῦ γένους διαμονήν. For ἐπιμονή (which occurs occasionally also in classical writers of this age) see Epist. Gall. § 6 in Euseb. v. 1, Tatian ad Græc. 32. This reading was adopted by Bunsen, but he wrongly interpreted it 'life-tenure', (see Ignat. von Antioch. etc. p. 96 sq., Hippolytus I. p. 45 2nd ed.); and it has consequently found no favour. Other suggestions, ἐπιλογήν, ἐπιτροπήν, ἐπισκοπήν, ἐπιστολήν, ἀπονομήν, ἔτι νόμον, are either inappropriate or di-

verge too widely from the MS. It seems impossible to assign any fit sense to the reading ἐπινομήν conformably with usage or derivation. The word elsewhere has two meanings only; (1) 'encroachment or ravage', e.g. of the spread of fire (Plut. Alex. 35) or poison (Ælian H.A. xii. 32), (2) 'a bandage' Galen XVIII. 1. p. 791 (Kuhn) and frequently (see Hase in Steph. Thes.). It might also consistently with its derivation have the sense 'distribution, assignment', like ἐπινέμησις. If it is to be retained, we have the choice (1) of assuming a secondary meaning 'injunction', derived from the possible (though unsupported) sense 'assignment' (so Lipsius p. 19 sq.); or (2) of giving to ἐπινομή the known meaning of ἐπινομίς, 'an after enactment', 'a codicil' (so Rothe Anfänge p. 374 sq.; see the note on κοιμηθῶσιν). Of these alternatives the former is preferable, but both are unwarranted. I have the less hesitation in making so slight a change in the MS reading, because μετοξυ before and εδωκασιν after show that the scribe wrote carelessly at this point.
The Latin quotation already mentioned (pp. 14, 135) contains the words 'Hanc formam tenentes apostoli etc.', and Dom Pitra (Spicil. Solesm. I. p. 293) considers that 'forma' here represents ἐπινομή (so too even Ewald Gesch. VII. p. 269), congratulating himself that the sense of ἐπινομή is

τὴν λειτουργίαν αὐτῶν. τοὺς οὖν κατασταθέντας ὑπ᾽ ἐκείνων ἢ μεταξὺ ὑφ᾽ ἑτέρων ἐλλογίμων ἀνδρῶν, συνευδοκησάσης τῆς ἐκκλησίας πάσης, καὶ λειτουργήσαντας ἀμέμπτως τῷ ποιμνίῳ τοῦ Χριστοῦ μετὰ ταπεινοφρο-
10 σύνης ἡσύχως καὶ ἀβαναύσως, μεμαρτυρημένους τε πολ-

7 μεταξύ] μετοξυ A.   8 λειτουργήσαντας] λιτουργησαντασ A.
10 μεμαρτυρημένους] μεμαρτυρημενοισ A.

thus decided. A late Latin paraphrase would be worthless as an authority, even if this view of its meaning were correct. But a comparison of the order of the Latin with the original of Clement shows that the words mean 'the Apostles following this precedent set by Moses', and that 'forma' therefore has nothing to do with ἐπινομή.

For ἐδωκασιν it is a question whether we should read δεδώκασιν or ἔδωκαν. The former involves a less change, and the transition from the aorist (κατέστησαν) to the perfect (δεδώκασιν) may be explained by the fact that the consequences of this second act are permanent.

5. κοιμηθῶσιν] sc. οἱ προειρημένοι, i.e. the first generation of presbyters appointed by the Apostles themselves; and αὐτῶν too will refer to these same persons. Rothe (l.c.) refers both to the Apostles themselves. He assumes Clement to be here describing the establishment of episcopacy properly so called, and supposes ἐπινομή, which he translates 'after-enactment', to refer to a second Apostolic council convened for this purpose. I have discussed this theory at length elsewhere (*Philippians* p. 199 sq.). Of his interpretation of this particular passage it is enough to say that it interrupts the context with irrelevant matter. The Apostles, says Clement, first appointed approved persons to the ministry (καθίστανον δοκιμάσαντες § 42), and afterwards

(μεταξύ) provided for a succession so that vacancies by death should be filled by *other* approved men (ἕτεροι δεδοκιμασμένοι ἄνδρες). The presbyters at Corinth who had been rudely ejected from office, belonged to these two classes: some were appointed directly by the Apostles (κατασταθέντας ὑπ᾽ ἐκείνων); others belonged to the second generation, having been appointed by the persons thus immediately connected with the Apostles (κατασταθέντας ὑφ᾽ ἑτέρων ἐλλογίμων ἀνδρῶν).

6. τοὺς οὖν κατασταθέντας κ.τ.λ.] This notice assists to determine the chronology of the epistle. Some of those appointed by the Apostles had died (οἱ προοδοιπορήσαντες), but others were still living (οἱ κατασταθέντες ὑπ᾽ ἐκείνων). This falls in with the date assigned p. 4. Here again μεταξὺ means '*afterwards*', as above.

7. συνευδοκησάσης κ.τ.λ.] Wotton quotes Cyprian's expression 'plebis suffragium' referring to the appointment of Church officers, *Epist.* lv. (p. 243), lxviii. (p. 292). Add also the more important passage *Epist.* lxvii (p. 288), where the part of the laity in such appointments is described.

9. τῷ ποιμνίῳ τοῦ Χριστοῦ] The phrase occurs again §§ 54, 57 (comp. § 16). See also Acts xx. 28, 29, 1 Pet. v. 2, 3.

ἀβαναύσως] '*unassumingly*'. The adjective occurs *Apost. Const.* ii. 3

138   THE EPISTLE OF CLEMENT   [XLIV

λοῖς χρόνοις ὑπὸ πάντων, τούτους οὐ δικαίως νομίζομεν †ἀποβαλέσθαι† τῆς λειτουργίας. ἁμαρτία γὰρ οὐ μικρὰ ἡμῖν ἔσται, ἐὰν τοὺς ἀμέμπτως καὶ ὁσίως προσενεγκόντας τὰ δῶρα τῆς ἐπισκοπῆς ἀποβάλωμεν. μακάριοι οἱ προοδοιπορήσαντες πρεσβύτεροι, οἵτινες 5 ἔγκαρπον καὶ τελείαν ἔσχον τὴν ἀνάλυσιν· οὐ γὰρ

2 λειτουργίας] λιτουργιασ A.   8 μετηγάγετε] μεταγαγετε A.

ἔστω δὲ εὔσπλαγχνος, ἀβάναυσος, ἀγαπητικός, where again it refers to the qualifications for the ministry. See below § 49 οὐδὲν βάναυσον ἐν ἀγάπῃ, οὐδὲν ὑπερήφανον, Clem. Alex. Pæd. iii. 6 (p. 273) μεταδοτέον φιλανθρώπως, οὐ βαναύσως οὐδὲ ἀλαζονικῶς, Job xli. 26 (Theod.) υἱοὶ βαναυσίας (Heb. שחץ 'pride, arrogance'). In Arist. Eth. Nic. ii. 7, iv. 2, βαναυσία is the excess of μεγαλοπρέπεια 'lavish profusion', the result of *vulgarity*. Somewhat similar is the sense which the word has here and in the passages quoted, 'vulgar self-assertion'.

2. †ἀποβαλέσθαι†] '*that we should have rejected*'. But as the active and not the middle is used just below (τῆς ἐπισκοπῆς ἀποβάλωμεν), it is probable that we should read ἀποβάλλεσθαι and treat it as a passive.

3. ἀμέμπτως καὶ ὁσίως] So 1 Thess. ii. 10.

προσενεγκόντας τὰ δῶρα] What does Clement mean by *sacrifices*, by *gifts* (δῶρα) and *offerings* (προσφοράς)? In what sense are the presbyters said to have presented or offered the gifts? The answers to these questions must be sought in the parallel passages; § 18 θυσία τῷ Θεῷ πνεῦμα συντετριμμένον, §§ 35, 36 θυσία αἰνέσεως δοξάσει με καὶ ἐκεῖ ὁδὸς ᾗ δείξω αὐτῷ τὸ σωτήριον τοῦ Θεοῦ. Αὕτη ὁ ὁδός, ἀγαπητοί, ἐν ᾗ εὕρομεν τὸ σωτήριον ἡμῶν Ἰησοῦν Χριστὸν τὸν ἀρχιερέα τῶν προσφορῶν

ἡμῶν, τὸν προστάτην καὶ βοηθὸν τῆς ἀσθενείας ἡμῶν, § 41 ἕκαστος ὑμῶν, ἀδελφοί, ἐν τῷ ἰδίῳ τάγματι εὐχαριστείτω τῷ Θεῷ ἐν ἀγαθῇ συνειδήσει ὑπάρχων, μὴ παρεκβαίνων τὸν ὡρισμένον τῆς λειτουργίας αὐτοῦ κανόνα, § 52 θῦσον τῷ Θεῷ θυσίαν αἰνέσεως καὶ ἀπόδος τῷ ὑψίστῳ τὰς εὐχάς σου κ.τ.λ. These passages are illustrated by Heb. xiii. 15, 16, δι' αὐτοῦ οὖν (i.e. διὰ τοῦ ἀρχιερέως Ἰησοῦ, vv. 11, 12) ἀναφέρωμεν θυσίαν αἰνέσεως διὰ παντὸς τῷ Θεῷ, τουτέστιν, καρπὸν χειλέων ὁμολογούντων τῷ ὀνόματι αὐτοῦ· τῆς δὲ εὐποιίας καὶ κοινωνίας μὴ ἐπιλανθάνεσθε, τοιαύταις γὰρ θυσίαις εὐαρεστεῖται ὁ Θεός, to which epistle Clement is largely indebted elsewhere. The sacrifices, offerings, and gifts therefore are the prayers and thanksgivings, the alms, the contributions to the agape, and so forth. See esp. *Const. Apost.* ii. 25 αἱ τότε θυσίαι νῦν εὐχαὶ καὶ δεήσεις καὶ εὐχαριστίαι, αἱ τότε ἀπαρχαὶ καὶ δεκάται καὶ ἀφαιρέματα καὶ δῶρα νῦν προσφοραὶ αἱ διὰ τῶν ὁσίων ἐπισκόπων προσφερόμεναι Κυρίῳ κ.τ.λ., § 27 προσήκει οὖν καὶ ὑμᾶς, ἀδελφοί, θυσίας ὑμῶν ἤτοι προσφορὰς τῷ ἐπισκόπῳ προσφέρειν ὡς ἀρχιερεῖ κ.τ.λ., § 34 τοὺς καρποὺς ὑμῶν καὶ τὰ ἔργα τῶν χειρῶν ὑμῶν εἰς εὐλογίαν ὑμῶν προσφέροντες αὐτῷ (sc. τῷ ἐπισκόπῳ)...τὰ δῶρα ὑμῶν διδόντες αὐτῷ ὡς ἱερεῖ Θεοῦ, § 35 μηκέτι ἐάσας ὑμᾶς (ὁ Θεός) θύειν ἄλογα ζῶα...οὐ δήπου καὶ τῶν εἰσφορῶν ὑμᾶς

εὐλαβοῦνται μή τις αὐτοὺς μεταστήσῃ ἀπὸ τοῦ ἱδρυμένου αὐτοῖς τόπου. ὁρῶμεν γὰρ ὅτι ἐνίους ὑμεῖς μετηγάγετε καλῶς πολιτευομέν[ους] ἐκ τῆς ἀμέμπτως αὐτοῖς
10 †τετιμημένης† λειτουργίας.
XLV. Φιλόνεικ[οι] ἔστε, ἀδελφοί, καὶ ζηλωταὶ περὶ

10 λειτουργίας] ·λιτουργειασ A. 11 φιλόνεικοι] φιλονικοι A.
ἔστε] εσται A.   περὶ τῶν] See below.

ἠλευθέρωσεν ὧν ὀφείλετε τοῖς ἱερεῦσιν καὶ τῶν εἰς τοὺς δεομένους εὐποιϊῶν κ.τ.λ., § 53 δῶρον δέ ἐστι Θεῷ ἡ ἑκάστου προσευχὴ καὶ εὐχαριστία. These passages show in what sense the presbyters might be said to 'offer the gifts'. They led the prayers and thanksgivings of the congregation, they presented the alms and contributions to God and asked His blessing on them in the name of the whole body. Hence Clement is careful to insist (§ 40) that these offerings should be made at the right time and in the right place and through the right persons. The first day of the week had been fixed by Apostolic authority not only for common prayer and breaking of bread (Acts xx. 7) but also for collecting alms (1 Cor. xvi. 2); and the presbyters, as the officers appointed by the same authority, were the proper persons to receive and dispense the contributions. On the whole subject see Höfling *die Lehre der ältesten Kirche vom Opfer etc.* p. 8 sq. (Erlangen 1851).

6. τελείαν] i.e. '*in mature, ripe, age*', so that it has borne fruit (ἔγκαρπον). Comp. the compound τελειοκαρπεῖν which occurs several times in Theophrastus (e.g. *Hist. Pl.* i. 13. 4, *Caus. Pl.* iii. 6. 9). The work of these presbyters had not, like those Corinthian elders whose cause Clement pleads, been rudely interfered with

and prematurely ended. τὴν ἀνάλυσιν] '*their departure*'; comp. Phil. i. 23, 2 Tim. iv. 6. The metaphor seems to be taken from the breaking up of an encampment (see *Philippians* l.c.), so that it is well suited to προοδοιπορήσαντες.
οὐκ εὐλαβοῦνται μή] '*They have no fear lest*': comp. 1 Macc. iii. 30, xii. 40 (v. l.). In Acts xxiii. 10 εὐλαβηθεὶς is a false reading.

8. τόπου] On the *place* of the departed see the note on § 5. There is here also an allusion to the other sense, 'office'; see § 40 (with the note).

10. †τετιμημένης†] '*respected by them*'. But I should be disposed to read τετηρημένης: comp. 1 Thess. v. 23 ἀμέμπτως...τηρηθείη.

XLV. 'Your zeal is misplaced, my brethren. Search the Scriptures. You will indeed find that God's servants have been persecuted, but their persecutors are always the impious and unholy. Did pious men shut up Daniel in the lions' den? Or cast the three children into the fire? This was the deed of the wicked who knew not that God mightily shields His faithful people. And so He has crowned the sufferers with everlasting renown and honour'.

11. Φιλόνεικοι ἔστε κ.τ.λ.] By reading τῶν ἀνηκόντων, instead of μὴ ἀνηκόντων (with previous editors), I have changed ἔστε from an indicative to

[τῶν] ἀνηκόντων εἰς σωτηρίαν. Ἐν[κύπτε]τε εἰς τὰς γραφάς, τὰς ἀληθεῖς, [τὰς τοῦ] πνεύματος τοῦ ἁγίου· ἐπίστασθε [ὅτι οὐ]δὲν ἄδικον οὐδὲ παραπε[ποιη]μένον γέγραπται ἐν αὐταῖς. [πότε ε]ὑρήσετε δικαίους ἀποβε[βλημ]ένους ἀπὸ ὁσίων ἀνδρῶν; [ἐδι]ώχθησαν δίκαιοι, ἀλλ' ὑπὸ ἀνό[μω]ν· ἐφυλακίσθησαν, ἀλλ' ὑπὸ [ἀν]οσίων· ἐλιθάσθησαν ὑπὸ πα[ρα]νόμων· ἀπεκτάνθησαν [ὑ]πὸ τῶν μιαρὸν καὶ ἄδικον ζῆλον [ἀ]νειληφότων. ταῦτα πάσχοντες εὐκλεῶς ἤνεγκαν. [Τί] γὰρ εἴπωμεν, ἀδελφοί; Δανιὴλ ὑπὸ τῶν φοβουμένων τὸν Θεὸν [ἐ]βλήθη εἰς λάκκον λεόντων; [ἢ] Ἀνανίας καὶ Ἀζαρίας καὶ Μισαὴλ ὑπὸ τῶν θρησκευόντων τὴν μεγαλοπρεπῆ καὶ ἔνδοξον θρησ-

2 τὰς τοῦ] No better way of filling the lacuna occurs to me. The ῥήσεις of all previous editors (following Young) can hardly stand, as the usual expression is either πνεύματος ἁγίου or τοῦ πνεύματος τοῦ ἁγίου.   3 ἐπίστασθε] επιτασθαι A.
4 πότε] or perhaps ποῦ; all previous editors read οὐ γὰρ (after Young), but this is an imperative; 'Contend zealously, if you will, but let your zeal be directed to things pertaining to salvation'; comp. Gal. iv. 17, 18, 1 Pet. iii. 13. There is a Θεοῦ ζῆλος, and in some sense also a Θεοῦ φιλονεικία. Compare Barnab. § 17 ἐλπίζει μου ἡ ψυχὴ τῇ ἐπιθυμίᾳ μου μὴ παραλελοιπέναι τι τῶν ἀνηκόντων εἰς σωτηρίαν. For ἀνήκειν εἰς see also Ign. Philad. 1, Smyrn. 8, Polyc. 7, Polyc. Phil. 13.

1. ἐνκύπτετε] See the note above § 40.

3. παραπεποιημένον] 'counterfeit, spurious'. For the metaphor see Basil. (?) in Esai. i. 22 (1. p. 416 E) μήπου κίβδηλος ἢ δραχμή, τουτέστι, μήπου δόγμα παραπεποιημένον, with the whole context in which the metaphor is developed. So παραποιεῖν Justin Dial. 69, 115, παραποίησις Iren. i. 9. 2.

6. ἐφυλακίσθησαν] Many editors read ἐνεφυλακίσθησαν, but this is open to two objections; (1) There seems to be no authority for a verb ἐμφυλακίζω, and indeed such a compound is hardly possible, for φυλακίζω is derived not from φυλακή but from φύλαξ: (2) The lacuna in the MS seems insufficient for so many letters.

8. μιαρόν] I have made a slight alteration in the reading of the MS. For the confusion of o and ω in the MS compare ειπομεν just below, and see above p. 25. Here the immediate neighbourhood of τῶν would suggest the change to a transcriber. Compare § 1 μιαρᾶς καὶ ἀνοσίου στάσεως, § 3 ζῆλον ἄδικον καὶ ἀσεβῆ ἀνειληφότας.

13. θρησκείαν] The word is here used in its correct sense (see Trench N. T. Syn. 1st ser. § xlviii); for the incident turns on an act of *external worship.*

14. μηθαμῶς κ.τ.λ.] i.e. 'Let us not entertain the thought, let us not so pervert facts.'

16. ἐξήρισαν] '*persisted in strife*'. So Plut. Pomp. § 56 οὐκ ἐξερίσας ἀλλ' οἷον ἡττηθείς, Appian. Bell. Civ. ii.

κείαν τοῦ ὑψίστου κατείρχθησαν εἰς κάμινον πυρός; μηθαμῶς τοῦτο γένοιτο. Τίνες οὖν οἱ ταῦτα δράσαν-
15 τες; οἱ στυγητοὶ καὶ πάσης κακίας πλήρεις εἰς τοσοῦτο ἐξήρισαν θυμοῦ ὥστε τοὺς ἐν ὁσίᾳ καὶ ἀμώμῳ προθέσει δουλεύοντας τῷ Θεῷ εἰς αἰκίαν †περιβαλεῖν†, μὴ εἰδότες ὅτι ὁ ὕψιστος ὑπέρμαχος καὶ ὑπερασπιστής ἐστιν τῶν ἐν καθαρᾷ συνειδήσει λατρευόντων τῷ [πα]ναρέτῳ ὀνό-
20 ματι αὐτοῦ· ᾧ ἡ δόξ[α εἰ]ς τοὺς αἰῶνας τῶν αἰ[ώνων. ἀ]μήν. [Ο]ἱ δὲ ὑπο[μ]ένοντες ἐν πεποιθήσει δόξαν καὶ τιμὴν ἐκληρονόμησαν, ἐπήρθησάν τε καὶ ἔγγραφοι ἐγένοντο ἀπὸ τοῦ Θεοῦ ἐν τῷ μνημοσύνῳ αὐτῶν εἰς τοὺς αἰῶνας τῶν αἰώνων. ἀμήν.

slightly too long for the lacuna, and a question seems to be required.   εὑρήσετε]
...υρησεται A.   8 μια/όν] μιαρων A.   9 εὐκλεῶς] ευκλαιωσ A.   εἴπωμεν]
ειπομεν A.   15 στυγητοί] στυηητοι A.   22 ἔγγραφοι] Laurent p. 424.   επαφροι A.

151 φιλονεικότεροι δὲ τοῖς ἐξερίζουσιν ὄντες. So too ἐξεριστής Eur. *Suppl.* 894, ἐξεριστικός Diog. Laert. x. 143. For the whole expression comp. § 1 εἰς τόσουτον ἀπονοίας ἐξέκιυσαν.

17. †περιβαλεῖν†] '*to drive round*'. If the reading be correct, the idea of the preposition (as in περιπίπτειν) must be 'sudden and complete change'. But I cannot find any parallel; for in Eur. *Hel.* 312 φόβος γὰρ ἐς τὸ δεῖμα περιβαλών μ' ἄγει the meaning of the word is wholly different. Elsewhere (see Schweighaüser *Lex. Polyb.* s.v. περιβάλλεσθαι) περιβάλλειν has been substituted for παραβάλλειν, and this may possibly have been the case here. So Heb. xiii. 9 περιφέρεσθε and παραφέρεσθε are confused. Comp. § 55 παρέβαλεν.

18. ὑπέρμαχος κ.τ.λ.] 'Ὑπέρμαχος is said of God, 2 Macc. xiv. 34 (comp. Wisd. x. 20); ὑπερασπιστής is frequently so applied (especially in connexion with βοηθός), Ps. xviii. 2, xxviii. 7, 8, xxxiii. 20, cxiv. 17, 18, 19, etc.

19. ἐν καθαρᾷ συνειδήσει] The same expression occurs 1 Tim. iii. 9, 2 Tim. i. 3; comp. *Ign. Trall.* 7.
παναρέτῳ] See the note on § 1.

22. ἔγγραφοι] '*recorded, notable, famous*'. The word occurs also in a fragment ascribed to our Clement in Joann. Damasc. *Eclog.* i. 49 (II. p. 752 ed. Lequien) ὅθεν ἔγγραφον περὶ αὐτοῦ (i.e. τοῦ Ἀβραάμ) ἱστορίαν γενέσθαι ᾠκονόμησεν; but see especially Herm. *Sim.* v. 3 ἔσται ἡ θυσία σου δεκτὴ παρὰ τῷ Θεῷ καὶ ἔγγραφος ἔσται ἡ νηστεία αὕτη, *Apost. Can.* § 19 ὁ γὰρ ἐμπιπλῶν ὦτα μὴ νοοῦντος ἔγγραφος λογισθήσεται παρὰ τῷ Θεῷ, § 29 ὁ γὰρ θησαυρίζων ἐν τῇ βασιλείᾳ ἔγγραφος ἐργάτης λογισθήσεται παρὰ τῷ Θεῷ (Lagarde's *Rel. Jur. Eccles.* pp. 78, 79, see Hilgenfeld *Nov. Test. extr. Can.* IV. pp. 102, 104: this writing elsewhere bears traces of the influence of Clement's epistle; e.g. in § 23 which reproduces the language of Clem. § 40). The MS reading επαφροι, 'foam-flecked', is senseless, and the common emen-

XLVI. Τοιούτοις οὖν ὑποδείγμασιν κολληθῆναι καὶ ἡμᾶς δεῖ, ἀδελφοί. γέγραπται γάρ· Κολλᾶσθε τοῖς ἁγίοις, ὅτι οἱ κολλώμενοι ἀυτοῖς ἁγιασθήσονται. καὶ πάλιν ἐν ἑτέρῳ τόπῳ λέγει· Μετὰ ἀνδρὸς ἀθώου ἀθῶος ἔςη καὶ μετὰ ἐκλεκτοῦ ἐκλεκτὸς ἔςη καὶ μετὰ στρεβλοῦ διαστρέψεις. [κ]ολ- 5
ληθῶμεν οὖν τοῖς ἀθῴοις καὶ δικαίοις· εἰσὶν δὲ οὗτοι ἐκλεκτοὶ τοῦ Θεοῦ. Ἵνα τί ἔρεις καὶ θυμοὶ καὶ διχοστασίαι

2 κολλᾶσθε] κολλασθαι A.

dations, ἐλαφροί, ἐπαφρόδιτοι, ἀνέπαφοι, etc. do not commend themselves. I had conjectured ἐπάϊστοι, or ἔπαθλα (see Diod. Sic. x. fragm., IV. p. 58 Wessel., ἔστι δ᾽ ὁ μὲν ἔπαινος, ὡς ἄν τις εἴποι, ἔπαθλον ἀρετῆς ἀδάπανον κ.τ.λ : I had not then seen Wordsworth's conjecture ἐπαθλοφόροι, on Theocr. xxvi): but Laurent's neat emendation ἔγγραφοι, which is accepted by Hilgenfeld, seems preferable to either, the confusion of ΓΓ with Π and the transposition of ΡΑ being easy. It is however unnecessary to substitute ὑπό for ἀπό with Hilgenfeld : e. g. in this very chapter we have ἀποβεβλημένους ἀπὸ ὁσίων ἀνδρῶν; see also 1 Cor. i. 30, James i. 13, with the examples in Winer § xlvii. p. 389. The phrase τὸ μνημόσυνον αὐτοῦ, or αὐτῶν, is common in the LXX.

XLVI. 'Copy these bright examples. Cleave to the righteous, the elect of God. To what end are these strifes and divisions? Have you forgotten that, as there is one God, one Christ, one Spirit, so also there is one body? Would you rend asunder its limbs? Remember how the Lord denounces the man through whom the offences shall come. Already have your feuds been a scandal to many, and yet they continue.'

2. κολλᾶσθε κ.τ.λ.] This quotation is no where found in the Old Testament. The nearest approach is

Ecclus. vi. 34 τίς σοφός; αὐτῷ προσκολλήθητι. Similar words however occur in Hermas Vis. iii. 6 μηδὲ κολλώμενοι τοῖς ἁγίοις, Sim. viii. 8 οἱ ἐν ταῖς πραγματείαις ἐμπεφυρμένοι καὶ μὴ κολλώμενοι τοῖς ἁγίοις, Sim. ix. 20 οὐ κολλῶνται τοῖς δούλοις τοῦ Θεοῦ. It is perhaps another of those apocryphal quotations to which Photius alludes (see the notes on §§ 8, 13, 17, 23, 29); or possibly Clement is giving from memory the sense of some canonical text or texts. This passage is imitated by Clem. Alex. Strom. v. 8 (p. 677) γέγραπται δέ, Μετὰ ἀνδρὸς ἀθῴου ἀθῷος ἔσῃ καὶ μετὰ ἐκλεκτοῦ ἐκλεκτὸς ἔσῃ καὶ μετὰ στρεβλοῦ διαστρέψεις· κολλᾶσθαι οὖν τοῖς ἁγίοις προσήκει ὅτι οἱ κολλώμενοι αὐτοῖς ἁγιασθήσονται, where the change of form suggests that the Alexandrian Clement did not recognise the source of the quotation in his Roman namesake. Part of this passage is loosely quoted also by Nicon thus: κολληθῶμεν οὖν τοῖς ἀθῴοις καὶ δικαίοις· εἰσὶ δὲ οὗτοι ἐκλεκτοὶ τοῦ Θεοῦ· γέγραπται γάρ· Κολλᾶσθαι (κολλᾶσθε) τοῖς ἁγίοις, ὅτι οἱ κολλώμενοι αὐτοῖς ἁγιασθήσονται (see above § 14).

4. μετὰ ἀνδρὸς κ.τ.λ.] An accurate quotation from Ps. xviii. 25, 26: but the application of the passage by S. Clement to the influence of good or bad companionship is wholly wrong. The 'Thou' of the Psalmist is God

TO THE CORINTHIANS. 143

καὶ σχίσματα πόλεμός τε ἐν ὑμῖν; ἢ οὐχὶ ἕνα Θεὸν ἔχομεν
καὶ ἕνα Χριστὸν καὶ ἓν πνεῦμα τῆς χάριτος τὸ ἐκχυθὲν
10 ἐφ' ἡμᾶς; καὶ μία κλῆσις ἐν Χριστῷ; ἵνα τί διέλκομεν
καὶ διασπῶμεν τὰ μέλη τοῦ Χριστοῦ, καὶ στασιάζομεν
πρὸς τὸ σῶμα τὸ ἴδιον, καὶ εἰς τοσαύτην ἀπόνοιαν
ἐρχόμεθα ὥστε ἐπιλαθέσθαι ἡμᾶς ὅτι μέλη ἐσμὲν ἀλλήλων; μνήσθητε τῶν λόγων Ἰησοῦ τοῦ Κυρίου ἡμῶν·
15 εἶπεν γάρ· Οὐαὶ τῷ ἀνθρώπῳ ἐκείνῳ· καλὸν ἦν αὐτῷ εἰ

Himself, and the passage teaches that He deals with men according to their characters. The word ἐκλεκτός, on which Clement lays so much stress, here (as frequently in the LXX) means 'choice, excellent,' being a loose rendering of תמים, 'perfect'. For a similar misunderstanding see the application of Is. lx. 17 in § 42.

7. ἔρις κ.τ.λ.] The words are arranged in an ascending scale; see the notes on *Galatians* v. 20, 21. Θυμοὶ are 'outbursts of wrath, as in l.c. Διχοστασία is weaker than σχίσμα, as it is stronger than στάσις § 51: as στάσις developes into διχοστασία, so διχοστασία widens into σχίσμα.

8. πόλεμός τε ἐν ὑμῖν] comp. James iv. 1.

οὐχὶ ἕνα Θεὸν κ.τ.λ.] From Ephes. iv. 4 sq. ἓν σῶμα καὶ ἓν πνεῦμα, καθὼς καὶ ἐκλήθητε ἐν μιᾷ ἐλπίδι τῆς κλήσεως ὑμῶν· εἷς Κύριος, μία πίστις, ἓν βάπτισμα, εἷς Θεός...ἑνὶ δὲ ἑκάστῳ ἡμῶν ἐδόθη ἡ χάρις κ.τ.λ.; comp. 1 Cor. viii. 6, xii. 12 sq. See also Hermas *Sim.* ix. 13 ἔσονται εἰς ἓν πνεῦμα, εἰς ἓν σῶμα...καὶ ἦν αὐτῶν ἓν πνεῦμα καὶ ἓν σῶμα, ix. 18 ἔσται ἡ ἐκκλησία τοῦ Θεοῦ ἓν σῶμα, μία φρόνησις, εἷς νοῦς, μία πίστις, μία ἀγάπη, Ign. *Magn.* 7.

This mention of Θεός, Χριστός, πνεῦμα, has a parallel in the reference to the Trinity quoted by S. Basil (*de Spir. Sanct.* xxix. III. p. 16) as from

our Clement, but not found in our MS and probably belonging to the lacuna after § 57, ζῇ ὁ Θεὸς καὶ ὁ Κύριος Ἰησοῦς Χριστὸς καὶ τὸ πνεῦμα τὸ ἅγιον. See the note at the end of § 57. Owing to this parallel, I have taken ἐν πνεῦμα as an accusative and connected it with the preceding words, rather than as a nominative in which case it would be attached to the following clause, καὶ μία κλῆσις ἐν Χριστῷ; but the construction is doubtful.

13. μέλη ἐσμέν] Rom. xii. 5 οἱ πολλοὶ ἓν σῶμά ἐσμεν ἐν Χριστῷ, τὸ δὲ καθ' εἷς ἀλλήλων μέλη.

15. οὐαὶ κ.τ.λ.] Two different sayings of our Lord are here combined. The *first* is recorded in Matt. xxvi. 24, Mark xiv. 21, οὐαὶ δὲ τῷ ἀνθρώπῳ ἐκείνῳ δι' οὗ ὁ υἱὸς τοῦ ἀνθρώπου παραδίδοται· καλὸν ἦν αὐτῷ εἰ οὐκ ἐγεννήθη ὁ ἄνθρωπος ἐκεῖνος; and more briefly in Luke xxii. 22, πλὴν οὐαὶ τῷ ἀνθρώπῳ ἐκείνῳ δι' οὗ παραδίδοται. The *second* runs in Matt. xviii. 6, 7, ὃς δ' ἂν σκανδαλίσῃ ἕνα τῶν μικρῶν τούτων τῶν πιστευόντων εἰς ἐμέ, συμφέρει αὐτῷ ἵνα κρεμασθῇ μύλος ὀνικὸς περὶ τὸν τράχηλον αὐτοῦ καὶ καταποντισθῇ ἐν τῷ πελάγει τῆς θαλάσσης...οὐαὶ τῷ ἀνθρώπῳ δι' οὗ τὸ σκάνδαλον ἔρχεται: in Mark ix. 42, ὃς ἂν σκ. ἕ. τ. μ. τ. τ. π. εἰς ἐμέ, καλόν ἐστιν αὐτῷ μᾶλλον εἰ περίκειται μ. ὀν. π. τ. τρ. αὐτοῦ καὶ βέβληται εἰς τὴν θάλασσαν: in Luke xvii. 1, 2, ἀνένδεκτόν ἐστιν τοῦ τὰ σκάνδαλα μὴ

ογκ ἐγεννήθη, ἢ ἕνα τῶν ἐκλεκτῶν μογ σκανδαλίσαι· κρεῖττον ἦν αγτῷ περιτεθῆναι μγλον καὶ καταποντισθῆναι εἰς
τὴν θάλασσαν, ἢ ἕνα τῶν μικρῶν μογ σκανδαλίσαι. τὸ
σχίσμα ὑμῶν πολλοὺς διέστρεψεν, πολλοὺς εἰς ἀθυμίαν
ἔβαλεν, πολλοὺς εἰς δισταγμόν, τοὺς πάντας ἡμᾶς εἰς 5
λύπην· καὶ ἐπίμονος ὑμῶν ἐστιν ἡ στάσις.

XLVII. Ἀναλάβετε τὴν ἐπιστολὴν τοῦ μακαρίου
Παύλου τοῦ ἀποστόλου. τί πρῶτον ὑμῖν ἐν ἀρχῇ τοῦ
εὐαγγελίου ἔγραψεν; ἐπ᾽ ἀληθείας πνευματικῶς ἐπέ-

12 πρόσκλισίς] προσκλησεισ A.

ἐλθεῖν, πλὴν οὐαὶ δι᾽ οὗ ἔρχεται· λυσι-
τελεῖ αὐτῷ εἰ λίθος μυλικὸς περίκειται
π. τ. τρ. αὐτοῦ καὶ ἔρριπται εἰς τὴν
θάλασσαν, ἢ ἵνα σκανδαλίσῃ τῶν μικρῶν
τούτων ἕνα. Hermas *Vis.* iv. 2 has
οὐαὶ τοῖς ἀκούσασιν τὰ ῥήματα ταῦτα καὶ
παρακούσασιν· αἱρετώτερον ἦν αὐτοῖς τὸ
μὴ γεννηθῆναι : and in *Clem. Hom.*
xii. 29 a saying of our Lord is quoted,
τὰ ἀγαθὰ ἐλθεῖν δεῖ, μακάριος δὲ δι᾽ οὗ
ἔρχεται· ὁμοίως καὶ τὰ κακὰ ἀνάγκη
ἐλθεῖν, οὐαὶ δὲ δι᾽ οὗ ἔρχεται. S. Clement here may be quoting from our
canonical gospels (confusing them
together), or from oral tradition, or
possibly (though this seems the least
probable supposition) from some
written account no longer extant, e.g.
the Gospel of the Hebrews. The
first solution presents no difficulties ;
for the insertion of ἢ ἕνα τῶν ἐκλεκτῶν
μου σκανδαλίσαι is not a more violent
change than is found in many of his
Old Testament quotations ; e.g. the
perversion of Is. lx. 17 at the end of
§ 42. See also the fusion of different
passages in §§ 18, 26, 29, 32, 35, 39,
50, 52, 53. The quotation of Clem.
Alex. *Strom.* iii. 18 (p. 561) is not an
independent authority, for it is evidently taken from the Roman Clement, and in the words ἢ ἕνα τῶν
ἐκλεκτῶν μου διαστρέψαι the Alexandrian father has confused his predecessor's application (πολλοὺς διέστρεψεν) with the quotation itself (ἢ
ἕνα τῶν ἐκλεκτῶν σκανδαλίσαι).

5. δισταγμόν] The word is rare,
but occurs in Hermas *Sim.* ix. 28,
Plut. *Mor.* 214 F.

XLVII. 'Read the epistle which
Paul the Apostle wrote to you long
ago. See how he condemns strife and
party spirit in you. Yet then you
had this excuse, that you chose as
leaders Apostles and Apostolic men.
Now even this palliation of your
offence is wanting. It is sad indeed
that two or three ringleaders should
sully the fair fame of the Corinthian
Church and bring dishonour on the
name of Christ.'

7. τὴν ἐπιστολήν] It must not be
inferred from this expression that Clement was unacquainted with the 2nd
Epistle to the Corinthians; for exactly
in the same way Irenæus (iv. 27. 4)
quotes from 2 Thessalonians as 'ea
quæ est ad Thessalonicenses epistola', and Chrysostom in his preface to
the Colossians (XI. p. 322 B, ed. Bened.)
refers to 2 Timothy as ἡ πρὸς Τιμό-
θεον (ἐπιστολή). Where the context
clearly shows which epistle is meant,
no specification is needed. On the
other hand I have not observed any

10 ἔστειλεν ὑμῖν περὶ αὑτοῦ τε καὶ Κηφᾶ τε καὶ Ἀπολλώ,
διὰ τὸ καὶ τότε προσκλίσεις ὑμᾶς πεποιῆσθαι· ἀλλ' ἡ
πρόσκλισις ἐκείνη ἧττον ἁμαρτίαν ὑμῖν προσήνεγκεν·
προσεκλίθητε γὰρ ἀποστόλοις μεμαρτυρημένοις καὶ
ἀνδρὶ δεδοκιμασμένῳ παρ' αὐτοῖς. νυνὶ δὲ κατανοήσατε
15 τίνες ὑμᾶς διέστρεψαν καὶ τὸ σεμνὸν τῆς περιβοήτου
φιλαδελφίας ὑμῶν ἐμείωσαν. αἰσχρά, ἀγαπητοί, καὶ
λίαν αἰσχρά, καὶ ἀνάξια τῆς ἐν Χριστῷ ἀγωγῆς,
ἀκούεσθαι τὴν βεβαιοτάτην καὶ ἀρχαίαν Κορινθίων ἐκ-

16 ἐμείωσαν] εμιωσαν A.

distinct traces of the influence of 2 Corinthians on Clement's language or thoughts.

μακαρίου] Polyc. *Phil.* § 3 τοῦ μακαρίου καὶ ἐνδόξου Παύλου, *ib.* § 11 'beatus Paulus.' This passage of Clement is perhaps the earliest instance of the specially Christian sense of μακάριος: comp. Rev. xiv. 13 μακάριοι οἱ νεκροὶ οἱ ἐν Κυρίῳ ἀποθνήσκοντες ἀπάρτι. In § 43 he applies the epithet to Moses; in § 55 to Judith. The word continues to be used occasionally of the living, e. g. Alex. Hieros. in Euseb. H. E. vi. 11 διὰ Κλήμεντος τοῦ μακαρίου πρεσβυτέρου, and even in later writers.

8. ἐν ἀρχῇ κ.τ.λ.] i.e. 'in the first days of the Gospel, soon after your conversion.' The expression occurs in S. Paul himself, Phil. iv. 15. See also the note on Polyc. *Phil.* 11 'in principio'. It is quite impossible that ἀρχὴ τοῦ εὐαγγελίου can mean (as Young, Cotelier, and others suppose), 'the beginning of his epistle' as containing his evangelical teaching (Iren. iv. 34. 1 'Legite diligentius id quod ab apostolis est evangelium nobis datum').

10. περὶ αὑτοῦ τε κ.τ.λ.] 1 Cor. i. 10 sq. The party whose watchword was ἐγὼ Χριστοῦ is passed over in silence by Clement, because the mention of them would only have complicated his argument. Moreover it is not probable that their exact theological position was known to him or his contemporaries.

11. προσκλίσεις] See above on § 21.

13. μεμαρτυρημένοις] 'attested, famous': see the note on § 17. So *Ign. Eph.* 12 Παύλου...τοῦ μεμαρτυρημένου.

14. ἀνδρὶ δεδοκιμασμένῳ] Apollos therefore is not regarded as an Apostle. See *Galatians* pp. 96, 98.

15. τὸ σεμνὸν κ.τ.λ.] Comp. § 1 ὥστε τὸ σεμνὸν καὶ περιβόητον καὶ πᾶσιν ἀνθρώποις ἀξιαγάπητον ὄνομα ὑμῶν μεγάλως βλασφημηθῆναι.

16. αἰσχρά καὶ λίαν αἰσχρά] Comp. § 53 ἐπίστασθε καὶ καλῶς ἐπίστασθε. See also Theoph. *ad Autol.* i. 17 καλὰ καὶ καλὰ λίαν, Hippol. p. 36 (Lagarde) πάντα μὲν καλὰ καὶ καλὰ λίαν τὰ τοῦ Θεοῦ, Clem. *Recogn.* iii. 25 'Ignoras, O Simon, et valde ignoras', and perhaps Hermas *Mand.* viii οὐ δοκεῖ σοι ταῦτα πονηρὰ εἶναι καὶ λίαν πονηρὰ τοῖς δούλοις τοῦ Θεοῦ; (if this be the right punctuation). The very words αἰσχρὰ καὶ λίαν αἰσχρὰ occur in Maximus (?) on Jude 7 in *Cramer's Catena* p. 157.

18. ἀκούεσθαι] i.e. 'It is a disgraceful state of things, that *it should be*

κλησίαν δι' ἓν ἢ δύο πρόσωπα στασιάζειν πρὸς τοὺς πρεσβυτέρους. καὶ αὕτη ἡ ἀκοὴ οὐ μόνον εἰς ἡμᾶς ἐχώρησεν ἀλλὰ καὶ εἰς τοὺς ἑτεροκλινεῖς ὑπάρχοντας ἀφ' ἡμῶν, ὥστε καὶ βλασφημίας ἐπιφέρεσθαι τῷ ὀνόματι Κυρίου διὰ τὴν ὑμετέραν ἀφροσύνην, ἑαυτοῖς δὲ κίνδυνον 5 ἐπεξεργάζεσθαι.

XLVIII. Ἐξάρωμεν οὖν τοῦτο ἐν τάχει καὶ προσπέσωμεν τῷ δεσπότῃ καὶ κλαύσωμεν ἱκετεύοντες αὐτόν, ὅπως ἵλεως γενόμενος ἐπικαταλλαγῇ ἡμῖν καὶ ἐπὶ τὴν

reported,' the word ἀκούεσθαι being dependent on αἰσχρὰ...καὶ ἀνάξια. I mention this, because the construction is generally mistaken; some editors wanting to understand δεῖ and others substituting ἀκούεται for ἀκούεσθαι. For the plural αἰσχρὰ κ.τ.λ. see Jelf's *Gramm.* § 383.

ἀρχαίαν] This epithet seems hardly consistent with the very early date which some critics would assign to Clement's epistle: see p. 4, and the notes on §§ 5, 44.

1. πρόσωπα] '*persons*', or rather '*ringleaders*'; as in § 1. See the note on *Ign. Magn.* 6.

3. ἑτεροκλινεῖς] See the note on § 11.

4. ὥστε...βλασφημίας ἐπιφέρεσθαι] '*so that you heap blasphemies*'; ἐπιφέρεσθαι being middle as frequently elsewhere, and the subject being ὑμᾶς or possibly τοὺς ἑτεροκλινεῖς ὑπάρχοντας. Comp. Rom. ii. 24 τὸ γὰρ ὄνομα τοῦ Θεοῦ δι' ὑμᾶς βλασφημεῖται ἐν τοῖς ἔθνεσιν, καθὼς γέγραπται.

5. κίνδυνον] i.e. the danger of incurring God's wrath, as § 14 κίνδυνον ὑποίσομεν μέγαν, § 41 τοσούτῳ μᾶλλον ὑποκείμεθα κινδύνῳ.

6. ἐπεξεργάζεσθαι] '*withal to create*'; for this is the force of ἐπί, as in Demosth. *de Cor.* p. 274 ἐν δ' ἐπεξειργάσατο τοιοῦτον ὃ πᾶσι τοῖς προτέροις

ἐπέθηκε τέλος. Here ἑαυτοῖς will be equivalent to ὑμῖν αὐτοῖς: see the note on § 32 and Winer § xxii. p. 163.

XLVIII. 'Let us put our sin away. Let us fall on our knees and implore God's pardon. Righteousness in Christ is the only gate which leads to life. Is any one faithful, wise, learned, energetic, pure? He should be the more humble in proportion as he is greater. He should work for the common good'.

9. τὴν σεμνὴν κ.τ.λ.] The expression is copied by Clem. Alex. *Strom.* iv. 17 (p. 613) ἡ σεμνὴ οὖν τῆς φιλανθρωπίας καὶ ἁγνὴ ἀγωγὴ κατὰ τὸν Κλήμεντα τὸ κοινωφελὲς ζητεῖ, where the insertion of καὶ relieves the sentence. Comp. the words at the close of this chapter. Ἀγωγὴ is '*conduct*', as in § 47: see also 2 Tim. iii. 10, Esth. ii. 20, x. 3, 2 Macc. iv. 16, vi. 8, xi. 24.

12. ἀνοίξατε κ.τ.λ.] From the LXX Ps. cxviii. 19, 20, word for word. This passage, as far as ἤτω γοργὸς ἐν ἔργοις, is loosely quoted with interpolations of his own by Clem. Alex. *Strom.* i. 7 (p. 338 sq.), who gives his authority as ὁ Κλήμης ἐν τῇ πρὸς Κορινθίους ἐπιστολῇ. Elsewhere *Strom.* vi. 8 (p. 772), after quoting Ps. cxviii. 19, 20, he adds (by a lapse of memory) ἐξηγούμενος δὲ τὸ ῥητὸν τοῦ προφήτου Βαρνάβας ἐπιφέρει, Πολλῶν πυλῶν

10 σεμνὴν τῆς φιλαδελφίας ἡμῶν ἁγνὴν ἀγωγὴν ἀποκαταστήσῃ ἡμᾶς. πύλη γὰρ δικαιοσύνης ἀνεῳγυῖα εἰς ζωὴν αὕτη, καθὼς γέγραπται· Ἀνοίξατέ μοι πύλας Δικαιοσύνης, εἰσελθὼν ἐν αὐταῖς ἐξομολογήσωμαι τῷ Κυρίῳ· αὕτη ἡ πύλη τοῦ Κυρίου, Δίκαιοι εἰσελεύσονται ἐν αὐτῇ. Πολλῶν
15 οὖν πυλῶν ἀνεῳγυιῶν, ἡ ἐν δικαιοσύνῃ αὕτη ἐστὶν ἡ ἐν Χριστῷ, ἐν ᾗ μακάριοι πάντες οἱ εἰσελθόντες καὶ κατευθύνοντες τὴν πορείαν αὐτῶν ἐν ὁσιότητι καὶ δικαιοσύνῃ, ἀταράχως πάντα ἐπιτελοῦντες. ἤτω τις πιστός, ἤτω δυνατὸς γνῶσιν ἐξειπεῖν, ἤτω σοφὸς ἐν

ἀνεῳγυιῶν...οἱ εἰσελθόντες, though a few sentences below he cites the words ἔστω τοίνυν πιστός ... μᾶλλον μείζων εἶναι, as from 'Clement in the letter to the Corinthians'. His two quotations do not agree exactly either with the original text of Clement or with one another. These facts make it clear that he cites chiefly from memory, and this must be borne in mind in using his quotations to correct the text of the Roman Clement.

13. ἐξομολογήσωμαι] The best MSS of the LXX have ἐξομολογήσομαι, which is substituted for the conjunctive by most editors here, but ἐξομολογήσωμαι will stand; see Winer § xli. p. 300. Hilgenfeld inserts ἵνα before εἰσελθών, following Clem. Alex. *Strom.* i. 7 (p. 338); but the quotation of the later Clement is much too loose to be a guide here, and he probably inserted the ἵνα to improve the grammar of the sentence.

14. πολλῶν οὖν πυλῶν κ.τ.λ.] Perhaps a reference to our Lord's saying, Matt. vii. 13, 14.

16. ἡ ἐν Χριστῷ] John x. 9 ἐγώ εἰμι ἡ θύρα, Hermas *Sim.* ix. 12 ἡ πύλη ὁ υἱὸς τοῦ Θεοῦ ἐστί (and the whole section), *Ign. Philad.* 9 αὐτὸς ὢν θύρα τοῦ πατρός, *Clem. Hom.* iii. 52 διὰ τοῦτο

αὐτὸς ἀληθὴς ὢν προφήτης ἔλεγεν, 'Εγώ εἰμι ἡ πύλη τῆς ζωῆς κ.τ.λ., Hegesipp. in Euseb. *H. E.* ii. 23 ἀπάγγειλον ἡμῖν τίς ἡ θύρα τοῦ Ἰησοῦ.

17. ὁσιότητι κ.τ.λ.] The usual combination of ὅσιος and δίκαιος. See the note on ii. § 5.

18. ἤτω τις πιστός κ.τ.λ.] i.e. 'If a man has any special gift, let him employ it for the common good, and not as a means of self-assertion.' The same gifts of the Spirit are enumerated, though in the reverse order, in 1 Cor. xii. 8, 9 ᾧ μὲν γὰρ διὰ τοῦ πνεύματος δίδοται λόγος σοφίας, ἄλλῳ δὲ λόγος γνώσεως κατὰ τὸ αὐτὸ πνεῦμα, ἑτέρῳ πίστις ἐν τῷ αὐτῷ πνεύματι. Unless Clement is using this language without warrant, the temper of the factious Corinthians of his time must have closely resembled that of their predecessors in S. Paul's age.

19. γνῶσιν ἐξειπεῖν] '*to utter, expound a* γνῶσις', i.e. 'to bring out the hidden meaning of a scripture'. For this sense of γνῶσις see the note on Barnabas § 6. The possession of γνῶσις was an old boast of the factious Corinthians, 1 Cor. viii. 1, 10, 11, xiii. 2, 8; and the vaunt has not without reason been attributed espe-

10—2

διακρίσει λόγων, ἤτω γοργὸς ἐν ἔργοις, ἤτω ἀγνός·
τοσούτῳ γὰρ μᾶλλον ταπεινοφρονεῖν ὀφείλει, ὅσῳ
δοκεῖ μᾶλλον μείζων εἶναι, καὶ ζητεῖν τὸ κοινωφελὲς
πᾶσιν καὶ μὴ τὸ ἑαυτοῦ.

XLIX. Ὁ ἔχων ἀγάπην ἐν Χριστῷ ποιησάτω τὰ 5

1 διακρίσει] διακριακρισει A, as read by Tisch.; see Prol. p. xix. As far as the C he appears to me to have deciphered the MS correctly. Jacobs., instead of CEI, reads it CIN. This seemed to me more like the traces in the MS, but I could not see it distinctly. On Clem. Alex. see below.
ἤτω γοργὸς ἐν ἔργοις, ἤτω ἀγνός] Clem. Alex. (see below). ητωαγνοσενεργοισ A.

cially to the party among them which claimed as its leader Apollos, the learned *Alexandrian*, 'mighty in the scriptures' (Acts xviii. 24).

1. διακρίσει] As the passage is twice so quoted by Clem. Alex., this is the probable reading, the reading of the MS (if it be correctly given διακριακρισιν) being a corruption of διακρισιν (=διακρισι) which itself arose out of διακρισι and this out of διακρισει: see for other instances of a like error the note on ἀναστήσομαι § 15. Otherwise διακρίσεσιν might be read (see above, p. 25, for similar corruptions), as the plural διακρίσεις occurs Rom. xiv. 1 διακρίσεις διαλογισμῶν, 1 Cor. xii. 10 διακρίσεις πνευμάτων.

‹ ἤτω γοργός] 'let him be energetic'. In later writers γοργὸς is 'active, quick, strenuous'; e.g. Dion. Hal. *de Comp. Verb.* p. 133 (Reiske) τὸ μὲν αὐτῶν [τῶν κώλων] γοργότερον τὸ δὲ βραδύτερον. Epict. *Diss.* ii. 16. 20 ἐν μὲν τῇ σχολῇ γοργοὶ καὶ κατάγλωσσοι, iii. 12. 10 ἄσκησον, εἰ γοργὸς εἶ, λοιδορούμενος ἀνέχεσθαι κ.τ.λ., M. Antonin. xii. 6 εἰ οὖν γοργὸς εἶ, ταύτην θεράπευσον. The departure in the later usage of the word from its Attic sense 'terrible' is noted by the old lexicographers. The passage is twice quoted by Clem. Alex., *Strom.* i. 7 (p. 339) αὐτίκα ὁ Κλήμης ἐν τῇ πρὸς Κορινθίους ἐπιστολῇ κατὰ λέξιν φησί, τὰς διαφορὰς ἐκτιθέμενος τῶν κατὰ τὴν ἐκκλησίαν δοκίμων, Ἤτω τις πιστός, ἤτω δυνατός τις γνῶσιν ἐξειπεῖν, ἤτω σοφὸς ἐν διακρίσει λόγων, ἤτω γοργὸς ἐν ἔργοις, and *Strom.* vi. 8 (p. 722 sq.) ἔστω τοίνυν πιστὸς ὁ τοιοῦτος, ἔστω δυνατὸς γνῶσιν ἐξειπεῖν, ἤτω σοφὸς ἐν διακρίσει λόγων, ἤτω γοργὸς ἐν ἔργοις, ἤτω ἁγνός· τοσούτῳ γὰρ μᾶλλον ταπεινοφρονεῖν ὀφείλει, ὅσῳ δοκεῖ μᾶλλον μείζων εἶναι· ὁ Κλήμης ἐν τῇ πρὸς Κορινθίους φησί. The correction adopted in the text (after Hilgenfeld) seems to be justified by these two quotations. The reading of the MS may be explained as arising out of a confusion, the transcriber's eye passing from one similar ending to another.

3. μᾶλλον μείζων] For the double comparative see the note on *Philippians* i. 23. Antonius Melissa *Loc. Comm.* ii. 73 (34) and Maximus *Serm.* 49 both quote this sentence as from Clement in a somewhat different form, τοσοῦτόν τις μᾶλλον ὀφείλει ταπεινοφρονεῖν, ὅσον δοκεῖ μᾶλλον εἶναι: but they cannot be regarded as *independent* authorities for omitting μείζων, since in such collections of excerpts the later compiler generally borrows directly from his predecessor: see *Philippians* p. 251, note 2.

ζητεῖν κ.τ.λ.] 1 Cor. x. 24 μηδεὶς τὸ ἑαυτοῦ ζητείτω ἀλλὰ τὸ τοῦ ἑτέρου

τοῦ Χριστοῦ παραγγέλματα. τὸν δεσμὸν τῆς ἀγάπης τοῦ Θεοῦ τίς δύναται ἐξηγήσασθαι; τὸ μεγαλεῖον τῆς καλλονῆς αὐτοῦ τίς ἀρκετὸς ἐξειπεῖν; τὸ ὕψος εἰς ὃ ἀνάγει ἡ ἀγάπη ἀνεκδιήγητόν ἐστιν. ἀγάπη κολλᾷ
10 ἡμᾶς τῷ Θεῷ· ἀγάπη καλύπτει πλῆθος ἁμαρτιῶν· ἀγάπη πάντα ἀνέχεται, πάντα μακροθυμεῖ· οὐδὲν βά-

2 τοσούτῳ γάρ] A, Clem. Alex. τοσοῦτόν τις Ant. Mel., Max. ταπεινοφρονεῖν ὀφείλει] A, Clem. Alex. ὀφείλει ταπεινοφρονεῖν Ant. Mel., Max. ὅσῳ] A, Clem. Alex. ὅσον Ant. Mel., Max. 3 μείζων] A, Clem. Alex.; om. Ant. Mel., Max. 5 ποιησάτω] So Tisch. reads the MS. Other collators give it τηρησάτω. I could not satisfy myself. On the first two inspections I inclined to τηρησατω, but on the last to ποιησατω.

and *ib.* ver. 33 μὴ ζητῶν τὸ ἐμαυτοῦ σύμφορον ἀλλὰ τὸ τῶν πολλῶν. For ζητεῖν τὸ ἑαυτοῦ see also 1 Cor. xiii. 5, Phil. ii. 21.

3. τὸ κοινωφελές] '*the common advantage*'; comp. Philo *de Joseph.* II. p. 47 M διὰ τὸ κοινωφελὲς φθάνοντα τοὺς ἄλλους, M. Anton. iii. 4 χωρὶς μεγάλης καὶ κοινωφελοῦς ἀνάγκης.

XLIX. 'Who shall tell the power and the beauty of love? Love unites us to God: love is all enduring: love is free from pride and vulgarity: love brooks no strife or discord. In love all the saints were perfected. In love God took us to Himself. In love Christ gave His body for our bodies and His life for our lives'.

5. Ὁ ἔχων κ.τ.λ.] resembles our Lord's saying in John xiv. 15 ἐὰν ἀγαπᾶτέ με, τὰς ἐντολὰς τὰς ἐμὰς τηρήσετε (v.l. τηρήσατε): comp. 1 Joh. v. 1—3.

6. τὸν δεσμόν] i.e. the binding power: comp. Col. iii. 14 τὴν ἀγάπην ὅ ἐστιν σύνδεσμος τῆς τελειότητος. This clause is quoted by Jerome *ad Ephes.* iv. 1 (VII. p. 606) 'Cujus rei et Clemens ad Corinthios testis est, scribens *Vinculum charitatis Dei qui (quis) poterit enarrare?*'

8. ἀρκετὸς ἐξειπεῖν] Previous editors have misread the MS, and written

ἀρκεῖ, ὡς ἔδει, εἰπεῖν. For the construction of ἀρκετός see 1 Pet. iv. 3. The word occurs also Matt. vi. 34, x. 25, Hermas *Vis.* iii. 8.

τὸ ὕψος κ.τ.λ.] See the elaborate metaphor in Ign. *Ephes.* 9 ἀναφερόμενοι εἰς τὰ ὕψη διὰ τῆς μηχανῆς Ἰησοῦ Χριστοῦ κ.τ.λ. The passage of Clement from this point as far as τῆς βασιλείας τοῦ Χριστοῦ (§ 50) is loosely quoted and abridged by Clem. Alex. *Strom.* iv. 17 (p. 613 sq.).

10. ἀγάπη καλύπτει κ.τ.λ.] '*throws a veil over, omits to notice, forgets, forgives*'. The expression is taken from 1 Pet. iv. 8 (comp. James v. 20), which again seems to be a loose quotation from Prov. x. 12, where the original has בָּל־פְּשָׁעִים 'all sins' for 'a multitude of sins', and the LXX rendering is still wider, πάντας δὲ τοὺς μὴ φιλονεικοῦντας καλύπτει φιλία. For this Hebrew metaphor of 'covering' see Ps. xxxii. 1, lxxxv. 3, Neh. iii. 37 (iv. 6).

11. ἀγάπη πάντα ἀνέχεται] An imitation of 1 Cor. xiii. 4, 7, ἡ ἀγάπη μακροθυμεῖ...πάντα στέγει...πάντα ὑπομένει: and indeed the whole passage is evidently inspired by S. Paul's praise of love. The juxtaposition of the language of S. Paul and the lan-

ναῦσον ἐν ἀγάπῃ, οὐδὲν ὑπερήφανον· ἀγάπη σχίσμα
οὐκ ἔχει, ἀγάπη οὐ στασιάζει, ἀγάπη πάντα ποιεῖ ἐν
ὁμονοίᾳ· ἐν τῇ ἀγάπῃ ἐτελειώθησαν πάντες οἱ ἐκλεκτοὶ
τοῦ Θεοῦ· δίχα ἀγάπης οὐδὲν εὐάρεστόν ἐστιν τῷ Θεῷ·
ἐν ἀγάπῃ προσελάβετο ἡμᾶς ὁ δεσπότης· διὰ τὴν 5
ἀγάπην, ἣν ἔσχεν πρὸς ἡμᾶς, τὸ αἷμα αὐτοῦ ἔδωκεν
ὑπὲρ ἡμῶν Ἰησοῦς Χριστὸς ὁ Κύριος ἡμῶν ἐν θελήματι
Θεοῦ, καὶ τὴν σάρκα ὑπὲρ τῆς σαρκὸς ἡμῶν καὶ τὴν
ψυχὴν ὑπὲρ τῶν ψυχῶν ἡμῶν.

12 ἐξήγησις] εξηγησεισ A.   οὒς ἂν καταξιώσῃ] Tisch. seems to have rightly deciphered the MS ΟΥΓΚΑΤΑΞΙΩΟΗ, though the superscribed N is not distinct.   13 δεώμεθα] So I would read, as better fitted to the lacuna than

guage of S. Peter is a token of the large and comprehensive sympathies of one who paid equal honour to both these great Apostles (§ 5), though rival sectarians claimed them for their respective schools. See *Galatians* p. 323, with notes above §§ 12, 33.

1. βάναυσον] '*coarse, vulgar, self-asserting, arrogant*'. See the note on ἀβαναύσως § 44.

σχίσμα οὐκ ἔχει κ.τ.λ.] The expressions are in an ascending scale (1) 'knows nothing of outward schisms'; (2) 'does not even foster a factious spirit'; (3) 'nay, preserves entire and universal harmony'.

3. ἐτελειώθησαν] 1 John iv. 18 ὁ δὲ φοβούμενος οὐ τετελείωται ἐν τῇ ἀγάπῃ.

5. διὰ τὴν ἀγάπην κ.τ.λ.] Comp. John xv. 12, Gal. ii. 20, Ephes. v. 2.

8. καὶ τὴν σάρκα] Wotton quotes Iren. v. 1. 1 τῷ ἰδίῳ αἵματι λυτρωσαμένου ἡμᾶς τοῦ Κυρίου καὶ δόντος τὴν ψυχὴν ὑπὲρ τῶν ἡμετέρων ψυχῶν καὶ τὴν σάρκα τὴν ἑαυτοῦ ἀντὶ τῶν ἡμετέρων σαρκῶν, which seems to have been taken from this passage of Clement.

L. 'In this marvellous love let us pray God that we may live. We can only do so by His grace. Past

generations, thus perfected in love, now dwell in the abodes of bliss, awaiting His kingdom : for He has promised to raise them again. Happy are we, if we pass our time here in harmony and love. For then our sins will be forgiven us: we shall inherit the blessing promised to the elect of God through Christ'.

12. ἐν αὐτῇ εὑρεθῆναι] Comp. Phil. iii. 9.

15. αἱ γενεαὶ πᾶσαι] Comp. § 7 εἰς τὰς γενεὰς πάσας. Clem. Alex. adds ἀπὸ Ἀδάμ, but, as there seems to be no room for so many letters in the lacuna of the MS, the words are probably his own. Yet as the lines in this part of the MS were clearly of very uneven lengths, it is impossible to speak positively on this point. Tischendorf's language however (præf. p. xix), 'Verba απο αδαμ vel απ αρχησ spatio certe satis conveniunt', is too strong, for the ασ of πᾶσαι stand directly over the ρη of παρῆλθον and the θε of τελειωθέντες.

17. χῶρον εὐσεβῶν] '*the place assigned to the pious*', like τὸν ὀφειλόμενον τόπον τῆς δόξης § 5, or τοῦ ἱδρυμένου αὐτοῖς τόπου § 44. See the note

L.] TO THE CORINTHIANS. 151

10 L. Ὁρᾶτε, ἀγαπητοί, πῶς μέγα καὶ θαυμαστόν
ἐστιν ἡ ἀγάπη, καὶ τῆς τελειότητος αὐτῆς οὐκ ἔστιν
ἐξήγησις· τίς ἱκανὸς ἐν αὐτῇ εὑρ[εθῆναι], εἰ μὴ οὓς ἂν
καταξιώσῃ [ὁ Θεός; δεώμε]θα οὖν καὶ αἰτώμεθα ἀπ[ὸ
τοῦ ἐλέ]ους αὐτοῦ, ἵνα ἐν ἀγάπῃ [ζῶμεν] δίχα προσ-
15 κλίσεως ἀνθρω[πίνης] ἄμωμοι. Αἱ γενεαὶ πᾶσ[αι] ἕως
τῆσδε ἡμέρας παρῆ[λθον], ἀλλ' οἱ ἐν ἀγάπῃ τελειωθέν-
[τες] κατὰ τὴν τοῦ Θεοῦ χάριν ἔχο[υσιν] χῶρον εὐσεβῶν·
οἳ φανερ[οὶ ἔσον]ται ἐν τῇ ἐπισκοπῇ τῆς βασιλ[είας]
τοῦ Χριστοῦ. γέγραπται γάρ· Εἰcελ[θε] εἰc τὰ ταμεῖα

εὐχώμεθα which previous editors supply.   18 φανεροὶ ἔσονται] See below.
19 Χριστοῦ] At least Tisch. reads the MS X͞Υ. I could only see Υ̅, the first letter being hopelessly blurred.

on § 5, and comp. Iren. v. 31. 2 (quoted by Wotton here) αἱ ψυχαὶ ἀπέρχονται εἰς τὸν [ἀόρατον] τόπον τὸν ὡρισμένον αὐταῖς ἀπὸ τοῦ Θεοῦ, κἀκεῖ μέχρι τῆς ἀναστάσεως φοιτῶσι, περιμένουσαι τὴν ἀνάστασιν κ.τ.λ. For χῶρον εὐσεβῶν the existing text of Clem. Alex. has χώραν εὐσεβῶν, 'the country, the realms of the pious', which suggests a more sensuous image, conveying a notion similar to the 'Elysian fields'. The one might be translated 'locus piorum', the other 'campus piorum'. But χῶρος, rather than χώρα, accords with the language of the Roman Clement elsewhere. A place in Sicily, named after two brothers famous for their piety, was called indifferently Εὐσεβῶν χώρα and Εὐσεβῶν χῶρος; see Bentley's *Dissert. on Phalar.* v (I. p. 238, ed. Dyce).

18. φανεροὶ ἔσονται] I have preferred this to φανερωθήσονται, the reading of Clem. Alex., as taking up less room [φανεροιεσσται] and therefore better adapted to the lacuna: comp. Luke viii. 17, 1 Cor. iii. 13. The reading φανεροῦνται, which is generally adopted, cannot well stand,

as a future tense seems to be wanted. ἐν τῇ ἐπισκοπῇ κ.τ.λ.] 1 Pet. ii. 12 δοξάσωσιν τὸν Θεὸν ἐν ἡμέρᾳ ἐπισκοπῆς, Wisd. iii. 7 καὶ ἐν καιρῷ ἐπισκοπῆς αὐτῶν ἀναλάμψουσιν, Polycrates in Euseb. *H.E.* v. 24 περιμένων τὴν ἀπὸ τῶν οὐρανῶν ἐπισκοπὴν ἐν ᾗ ἐκ νεκρῶν ἀναστήσεται.

19. εἴσελθε κ.τ.λ.] A combination of passages. The opening is taken from the LXX Is. xxvi. 20 εἴσελθε εἰς τὰ ταμεῖά σου, ἀπόκλεισον τὴν θύραν σου, ἀποκρύβηθι μικρὸν ὅσον ὅσον, ἕως ἂν παρέλθῃ ἡ ὀργὴ Κυρίου: the close probably from Ezek. xxxvii. 12 ἀνάξω ὑμᾶς ἐκ τῶν μνημάτων ὑμῶν. The intermediate words καὶ μνησθήσομαι ἡμέρας ἀγαθῆς are not found anywhere. They may possibly be intended to give the general purport of the promise which they introduce: see a parallel instance in § 52. The combination of the two passages from different prophets was probably suggested by the verse in Isaiah which immediately precedes the words quoted, ἀναστήσονται οἱ νεκροὶ καὶ ἐγερθήσονται οἱ ἐν τοῖς μνημείοις (Is. xxvi. 19).

152 THE EPISTLE OF CLEMENT [L

μικρὸν ὅσον ὅσο[ν], ἕως οὗ παρέλθῃ ἡ ὀργὴ καὶ θυ[μός] μου, καὶ μνησθήσομαι ἡμέρ[ας] ἀγαθῆς καὶ ἀναστήσω ὑμᾶς [ἐκ] τῶν θηκῶν ὑμῶν. Μακάριοί ἐσμεν, ἀγαπητοί, εἰ τὰ [προσ]τάγματα τοῦ Θεοῦ ἐποιοῦμεν ἐ[ν ὁ]μονοίᾳ ἀγάπης, εἰς τὸ ἀφεθῆ[ναι] ἡμῖν δι' ἀγάπης τὰς ἁμαρτίας. γέ- 5 γραπται γάρ· Μακάριοι ὧν ἀ[φέ]θησαν αἱ ἀνομίαι καὶ ὧν ἐπεκα[λύ]φθησαν αἱ ἁμαρτίαι· μακάριος ἀ[νὴρ] οὗ οὐ μὴ λογίσηται Κύριος ἁμαρτία[ν], οὐδέ ἐστιν ἐν τῷ στόματι αὐτ[οῦ] δόλος. Οὗτος ὁ μακαρισμὸς ἐ[γέ]νετο ἐπὶ τοὺς ἐκλελεγμένους ὑπὸ τοῦ Θεοῦ διὰ Ἰησοῦ Χριστοῦ τοῦ Κυρίου 10 ἡμ[ῶν], ᾧ ἡ δόξα εἰς τοὺς αἰῶνας τῶν α[ἰώ]νων. ἀμήν.

5^b μακάριοι] μακακαριοι A. enclosed in brackets I could not see at all, to me uncertain though highly probable.   12 τινος τῶν τοῦ ἀντικειμένου] The letters Even τινοσ (except the final C) seemed The traces of a letter before ΑΝ appeared

1. ταμεῖα] 'the inner chamber', חדר. On the form see Lobeck *Phryn.* p. 493, *Paral.* p. 28. The same tendency to elide the ι before ει appears in ὑγεία § 20. In § 21 however our MS writes ταμιεια.

ὅσον ὅσον] Comp. Heb. x. 37 (with Bleek's note).

ὀργὴ καὶ θυμός] ὀργή is the settled temper, '*anger*'; θυμός the sudden outburst, '*wrath*'. See the distinction in Trench's *N. T. Syn.* 1st ser. § xxxvii, and to the passages there collected add Joseph. *B. J.* ii. 8. 6 ὀργῆς ταμίαι δίκαιοι θυμοῦ καθεκτικοί, Hermas *Mand.* v. 2 ἐκ δὲ τῆς πικρίας θυμός, ἐκ δὲ τοῦ θυμοῦ ὀργή, κ.τ.λ.

4. ἐποιοῦμεν] If the reading be correct, the point of time denoted in ἐσμέν must be the second advent, so that the deeds of this present life are regarded as past.

ἐν ὁμονοίᾳ ἀγάπης] § 49 ἀγάπη πάντα ποιεῖ ἐν ὁμονοίᾳ.

5. δι' ἀγάπης] '*through* God's *love*',

of which we become partakers by ourselves living in love. There is the same transition from the believer's love to God's love in § 49 δίχα ἀγάπης κ.τ.λ.

6. μακάριοι κ.τ.λ.] From the LXX of Ps. xxxii. 1, 2, word for word, as read in A (א writes αφειθησαν). For οὗ B has ᾧ. In Rom. iv. 8 it is a question whether οὗ or ᾧ is the correct reading.

9. οὗτος ὁ μακαρισμός] Suggested by Rom. iv. 9, where after quoting the same passage from the Psalms S. Paul continues, ὁ μακαρισμὸς οὖν οὗτος ἐπὶ τὴν περιτομὴν κ.τ.λ. For μακαρισμός see also Rom. iv. 6, Gal. iv. 15 (note).

LI. 'We must therefore ask pardon for our sins. Above all ought the leaders of these factions to deny themselves for the common good. It is well always to confess our wrong-doings, and not to harden our hearts. Let us take warning by the fate of the factious opponents of

LI] TO THE CORINTHIANS. 153

LI. Ὅσα [οὖ]ν παρέβ[η]μεν διά †τινος τῶν [το]ῦ†
ἀν[τικειμέ]νου, ἀξιώσωμεν [†συγγνώμην†]· καὶ ἐκεῖνοι δέ,
οἵτι[νες] ἀρχηγ[οὶ τῆς] στάσεως καὶ διχοστασίας ἐγεν[ή]-
15 θησαν, ὀφείλουσιν τὸ κοινὸν τῆς ἐλπίδος σκοπεῖν. οἱ
γὰρ μετὰ φόβου καὶ ἀγάπης πολιτευόμενοι ἑαυτοὺς
θέλουσιν μᾶλλον αἰκίαις περιπίπτειν ἢ τοὺς πλησίον,
μᾶλλον δὲ ἑαυτῶν κατάγνωσιν φέρουσιν ἢ τῆς παραδε-
δομένης ἡμῖν καλῶς καὶ δικαίως ὁμοφωνίας. καλὸν
20 γ[ὰ]ρ ἀνθρώπῳ ἐξομολογεῖσθαι περὶ τῶ[ν] παραπτωμά-
των ἢ σκληρῦναι τὴν καρδίαν αὐτοῦ, καθὼς ἐσκληρύνθη
ἡ καρδία τῶν στασιαζόντων πρὸς τὸν θεράποντα τοῦ

to resemble part of β or ρ but certainly not γ. Tisch. however deciphers τινοστων...
ναντικ...νου. See the lower note. 13. †συγγνώμην†] See below.
17 αἰκίαις] οικιαισ A. Tisch. (prol. p. xix) considers that it is altered into αικιαισ
prima manu, but I could not distinctly see this correction.

Moses who were swallowed up alive in the pit, by the fate of Pharaoh and his host who were overwhelmed in the Red Sea, because they hardened their hearts.'

12. διά τινος κ.τ.λ.] '*by any of the wiles* (or *of the ministers*) *of the adversary*'. In a quotation or rather a paraphrase of this sentence in Clem. Alex. *Strom.* iv. 17, p. 614, we have ἦν δὲ καὶ περιπέσῃ ἄκων τοιαύτῃ τινὶ περιστάσει διὰ τὰς παρεμπτώσεις τοῦ ἀντικειμένου. It may be therefore that παρεμπτώσεων has fallen out from our text: but the Alexandrian father's quotation is very loose. I am disposed to think that the indistinct parts of the MS have been wrongly deciphered and that the remedy must be sought in a different reading. See the upper note.

τοῦ ἀντικειμένου] So ὁ ἀντίδικος 1 Pet. v. 8, and perhaps ὁ ἀντενεργῶν Barnab. § 2. Ὁ ἀντικείμενος itself is not so used in the New Testament (except possibly in 1 Tim. v. 14), but

occurs *Mart. Polyc.* 17.

13. ἀξιώσωμεν †συγγνώμην†] '*let us claim pardon*'. The instances however where ἀξιοῦν appears to govern an accusative of the thing claimed (e. g. Dan. ii. 23, Esth. v. 6, ix. 12, Xen. *Mem.* iii. 11. 12) are not decisive. It would therefore be better to supply the lacuna otherwise, ἐλέους τυχεῖν or ἀφεθῆναι, or perhaps ἀποθέσθαι. Tischendorf indeed believes that he sees the lower part of the letters ΓΝωΜ (prol. p. xix), but I have looked again and again and cannot identify a single letter.

14. διχοστασίας] See the note on § 46.

15. τὸ κοινὸν τῆς ἐλπίδος] Comp. Ign. *Ephes.* 1 ὑπὲρ τοῦ κοινοῦ ὀνόματος καὶ ἐλπίδος with the note.

19. καλόν...ἤ] Matt. xviii. 8, Mark ix. 43, 45; see Winer *Gramm.* § xxxv p. 255.

21. σκληρῦναι κ.τ.λ.] Ps. xcv. 8; comp. Heb. iii. 8, 15, iv. 7.

22. τὸν θεράποντα] See the note § 4.

Θεοῦ Μωϋσῆν· ὧν τὸ [κρί]μα πρόδηλον ἐγενήθη. κατέ-
β[η]σαν γὰρ εἰς ᾄδου ζῶ[ν]τες, καὶ θά[νατος κατέπιεν
α]ὐτούς. Φαραὼ καὶ ἡ στρα[τιὰ αὐτ]οῦ καὶ πάντες
οἱ ἡγούμε[νοι Αἰγ]ύπτου, τά τε ἅρματα καὶ οἱ [ἀναβά]ται
αὐτῶν, οὐ δι' ἄλλην τινὰ [αἰτία]ν ἐβυθίσθησαν εἰς θά- 5
λασσαν [ἐρυθρ]ὰν καὶ ἀπώλοντο, ἀλλὰ διὰ [τὸ σκλ]η-
ρυνθῆναι αὐτῶν τὰς ἀσυ[νέτου]ς καρδίας μετὰ τὸ
γενέσθαι [τὰ σημ]εῖα [καὶ] τὰ τέρατα ἐν γῇ Αἰγύ[πτου]
διὰ [τοῦ θ]εράποντος τοῦ Θεοῦ [Μ]ωϋσέω[ς].

LII. Ἀπροσδεής, ἀδελφοί, [ὁ] δεσπότης ὑπάρχει 10
τῶν ἁπάντων, [οὐ]δὲν οὐδενὸς χρῄζει εἰ μὴ τὸ [ἐξ]ομο-
λογεῖσθαι αὐτῷ. φησὶν γὰρ [ὁ ἐ]κλεκτὸς Δαυείδ·

4 ἀναβάται] Wotton.   5 οὗ] οἱ A.   8 τὰ σημεῖα] Wotton.   9 τοῦ] Wotton. om. Young.   12 Δαυείδ] δᾷδ A. See above, § 4.   14 νέον] ναιον A.   16 ἐπικάλεσαι] επικαλεσε A.   19 ἐπίστασθε] επιστασθαι A.
21 δέχεσθε] I have substituted this as better adapted to the lacuna than the λάβετε

1. κατέβησαν γὰρ κ.τ.λ.] Num. xvi. 32, 33 ἠνοίχθη ἡ γῆ καὶ κατέπιεν αὐτούς ...καὶ κατέβησαν αὐτοὶ καὶ ὅσα ἐστὶν αὐτῶν ζῶντα εἰς ᾄδου.

4. τά τε ἅρματα καὶ οἱ ἀναβάται] The expression is borrowed from the Mosaic narrative, where it occurs several times, Exod. xiv. 23, 26, 28, comp. xv. 19, Jer. li (xxviii). 22, Hagg. ii. 22.

7. τὰς ἀσυνέτους καρδίας] As Rom. i. 21 ἐσκοτίσθη ἡ ἀσύνετος αὐτῶν καρδία.

LII. 'The Lord of the universe wants nothing. He demands of us only confession. He asks no sacrifice, but the sacrifice of praise and thanksgiving; for so the Psalmist teaches us.'

10. ἀπροσδεής] 'wants nothing besides'. Comp. Joseph. Ant. viii. 4. 3 ἀπροσδεὲς γὰρ τὸ θεῖον ἁπάντων (with the context), Act. Paul. et Thecl. § 17 (p. 47 Tisch.) Θεὸς ἀπροσδεής, Clem. Hom. xi. 9 ὁ Θεὸς γὰρ ἀνενδεὴς

ὢν αὐτὸς οὐδενὸς δεῖται, Epist. ad Diogn. 3 ὁ ποιήσας τὸν οὐρανὸν καὶ τὴν γῆν καὶ πάντα τὰ ἐν αὐτοῖς...οὐδενὸς ἂν αὐτὸς προσδέοιτο τούτων κ.τ.λ., A-thenag. Suppl. § 13 ὁ τοῦδε τοῦ παντὸς δημιουργὸς καὶ πατήρ...ἀνενδεὴς καὶ ἀπροσδεής, § 29 ἀνενδεές...τὸ θεῖον, Resurr. § 12 παντὸς γάρ ἐστιν ἀπροσδεής, Tatian. ad Graec. 4 ὁ γὰρ πάντων ἀνενδεὴς οὐ διαβλητέος ὑφ' ἡμῶν ὡς ἐνδεής, Theophil. ad Aut. ii. 10 ἀνενδεὴς ὤν. See also Acts xvii. 25 with the passages from heathen writers collected there by Wetstein. This was a favourite mode of speaking with the Stoics. The parallel passages quoted above would support the connexion of τῶν ἁπάντων either with ἀπροσδεὴς or with ὁ δεσπότης. The latter seems more forcible and more natural here, besides that ὁ δεσπότης τῶν ἁπάντων is a common phrase in Clement, §§ 8, 20, 33.

13. ἐξομολογήσομαι κ.τ.λ.] Comp. Ps. lxix. 31, 32, καὶ ἀρέσει τῷ Θεῷ ὑπὲρ

ἘΣΟΜΟΛΟΓΗCΟ[Μ]ΑΙ τῷ Κυρίῳ, καὶ ἀρέcει αὐτῷ ὑπὲρ μόcχον
νέον κέρατα ἐκφέροντα καὶ ὁπλάc· ἰδέτωcαν πτωχοὶ καὶ
15 εὐφρανθήτωcαν. καὶ π[ά]λιν λέγει· Θῦcον τῷ Θεῷ θυcίαν
αἰ[νέ]cεωc καὶ ἀπόδοc τῷ ὑψίcτῳ τὰc εὐχάc coy· καὶ ἐπικά-
λεcαί με ἐν ἡμέρᾳ θλίψεώc coy, καὶ ἐξελοῦμαί ce, καὶ δοξάcειc
με· θυcία γὰρ τῷ Θεῷ πνεῦμα cyντετριμμένον.

LIII. Ἐπίστασθε γὰρ καὶ καλῶς ἐπίστασ[θε τὰ]ς
20 ἱερὰς γραφάς, ἀγαπητοί, [καὶ ἐγκ]εκύφατε εἰς τὰ λόγια
τοῦ [Θεοῦ· εἰς ἀ]νάμνησιν οὖν ταῦτα [δέχεσθε]. Μωϋ-
σέως γὰρ ἀναβαί[νοντος εἰ]ς τὸ ὄρος καὶ ποιήσαν[τος
τεσσερ]άκοντα ἡμέρας καὶ τεσ[σεράκοντ]α νύκτας ἐν
νηστείᾳ [καὶ ταπειν]ώσει, εἶπεν πρὸς αὐτὸν [ὁ Θεός·

of previous editors. The final ι (δέχεσθε being written δεχεσθαι) is visible in the MS (though Tisch. says 'ante Μωυσεως præcedit punctum, non ι quod Jacobsonus videre sibi visus est'). Or perhaps read λέλεκται.   22 ἀναβαίνοντος] A, not ἀναβάντος as Jacobson would read. The ι is distinct and cannot have formed the first stroke of a N as he supposes. See Tisch.   24 ὁ Θεός] Wotton.

μόσχον νέον κέρατα ἐκφέροντα καὶ ὁπλάς· ἰδέτωσαν κ.τ.λ. The introductory words ἐξομολογήσομαι τῷ Κυρίῳ are not found in the context, though they express the *sense* of the preceding verse αἰνέσω τὸ ὄνομα κ.τ.λ. and occur frequently elsewhere.
15. θῦσον κ.τ.λ.] The first part θῦσον...δοξάσεις με occurs in Ps. l. 14, 15 word for word (except that the LXX has ἐπικάλεσαι for ἐπικαλέσει and that the second σου is omitted in the best MSS): the last clause is taken from Ps. li. 17 θυσία τῷ Θεῷ πνεῦμα συντετριμμένον.
17. ἐξελοῦμαι] For this future see Buttmann *Gr. Sprachl.* II. p. 100, Winer *Gramm.* § xciv. Clem. Alex. *Strom.* iv. 18 (p. 614), after διὰ τὰς παρεμπτώσεις τοῦ ἀντικειμένου (already quoted p. 153), goes on μιμησάμενος τὸν Δαβὶδ ψαλεῖ Ἐξομολογήσομαι κ.τ.λ. ......συντετριμμένον, stringing together the same quotations as in this chapter of the Roman Clement.

LIII. 'You are well versed in the Scriptures. I therefore quote them only to remind you. Remember how Moses entreated God for the people, how he would accept no honour for himself, but asked to be blotted out with them, if they might not be forgiven.'
19. ἐπίστασθε κ.τ.λ.] For the form of the sentence see the note on § 47 αἰσχρά, ἀγαπητοί, καὶ λίαν αἰσχρά.
τὰς ἱερὰς γραφάς] Comp. Polyc. *Phil.* 12 'Confido enim vos bene exercitatos esse in sacris literis et nihil vos latet'. So 2 Tim. iii. 15 [τὰ] ἱερὰ γράμματα, the only passage in the New Testament where this epithet is applied to the Scriptures. It occurs above § 43, and in 2 Macc. viii. 23, and is so used both by Philo and by Josephus.
20. ἐγκεκύφατε] See the note on § 40.
24. εἶπεν πρὸς αὐτὸν κ.τ.λ.] The first part, as far as μᾶλλον ἢ τοῦτο, is taken from Deut. ix. 12—14, which how-

Μωϋ]cH, Μωϋcῆ, κατάβηθι [τὸ τάχοc] ἐντεῦθεν, ὅτι ἠνόμηcεν
[ὁ λαόc c]ου οὓc ἐξήγαγεc ἐκ γῆc [Αἰγύπτο]γ· παρέβηcαν ταχὺ
ἐκ [τῆc ὁδοῦ] ἧc ἐνετείλω αὐτοῖc, [ἐποίηcα]ν ἑαυτοῖc χω-
νεύματα. ʼ[Καὶ εἶπε]ν Κύριος πρὸς αὐτόν· Λελάλη[κα
πρόc] cε ἅπαξ καὶ δὶc λέγων, [ʼΕώρακα] τὸν λαὸν τοῦτον, καὶ 5
ἰδοὺ [λαὸc c]κληροτράχηλοc· ἔαcόν [με ἐξολ]εθρεῦcαι αὐτούc,
καὶ ἐξα[λείψω τ]ὸ ὄνομα αὐτῶν ὑποκά[τωθεν] τοῦ οὐρανοῦ
καὶ ποιήcω [cε εἰc ἔ]θνοc μέγα καὶ θαυμαcτὸν [καὶ πολ]ὺ

ever commences somewhat differently καὶ εἶπε Κύριος πρός με· ʼΑνάστηθι, κατά- βηθι τὸ τάχος, the remainder following the LXX very closely (compare also Exod. xxxii. 7, 8). After μᾶλλον ἢ τοῦτο the parallel narrative in Exod. xxxii is taken up, and the substance of vv. 11, 31, 32 is given in a compressed form. See Barnab. § 4 λέγει γὰρ οὕτως Κύριος, Μωῦσῆ, Μωῦσῆ, κατάβηθι τὸ τάχος, ὅτι ἠνόμησεν ὁ λαός σου οὓς ἐξήγαγες ἐκ γῆς Αἰγύπτου, and again § 14 εἶπεν Κύριος πρὸς Μωῦσῆν, Μωῦσῆ, Μωῦσῆ, κατάβηθι τὸ τάχος ὅτι ὁ λαός σου ὃν ἐξήγαγες ἐκ γῆς Αἰγύπτου ἠνόμησεν. The coincidence in the repetition of the name Μωῦσῆ, Μωῦσῆ, is not sufficient to show that the one writer was indebted to the other (as Hilgenfeld seems to think, here and p. xx); for, though the name is not repeated at this place in either of the Mosaic narratives, it may very easily have been inserted independently by both writers from Exod. iii. 4.

8. πολὺ μᾶλλον ἢ τοῦτο] i.e. πλεῖον τούτου; an attempt to render the Hebrew idiom רב ממנו, 'greater than it'. See ii. § 2 from Is. liv. 1.

Clem. Alex. *Strom.* iv. 19 (p. 617) αὐτίκα οὐχ ὁ Μωῦσῆς κ.τ.λ., paraphrases the remainder of this chapter from καὶ εἶπεν κ.τ.λ., giving the same quotations as the Roman Clement.

LIV. 'Is any one noble, tender-hearted, loving? Let him declare his willingness to withdraw, that the flock of Christ may be at peace. He will not want a place of retirement. The whole earth will be ready to receive him, for *The earth is the Lord's and the fulness thereof.* This has been the conduct of the true citizens of God's kingdom in all ages.'

15. τίς οὖν κ.τ.λ.] This passage, as far as καθεσταμένων πρεσβυτέρων, is quoted in a collection of extracts in a Syriac MS in the British Museum. I owe the following account of it to the kindness of Dr W. Wright, the eminent Syriac scholar.

'Add. 14, 533, fol. 172 a, a MS of the 8th or 9th cent. Here there is a section entitled:

ܟ̈ܬܒܐ ܕܪ̈ܫܐ ܕܐܗܠ ܩܘܪ̈ܝܐ
ܚ̈ܬܡܐ ܕܐܦܠܘܓܣ̈ܐ.

'Charges brought by the followers of Paul [of Beth-Ukkāmē, patriarch of Antioch], with replies to them, and chapters against them'; and in it occurs the citation from Clement, fol. 176 b;'

ܟܬܒܐ ܗܟܝܠ ܕܩ̈ܕܡܝܐ ܐܦ ܩܠܡܝܣ
ܬܠܡܝܕܗ ܕܦܛܪܘܣ ܫܠܝܚܐ
ܐܡܪ ܒܗܠܢ ܕܠܘܬ ܩܘܪ̈ܢܬܝܐ

TO THE CORINTHIANS.

μᾶλλον ἢ τοῦτο. [εἶπεν δὲ Μ]ωϋσῆς· Μηθαμῶς Κύριε· [ἄφες
10 τὴν] ἁμαρτίαν τῷ λαῷ τούτῳ ἢ κἀμὲ ἐξάλειψον ἐκ βίβλου
ζώντων. ὦ μεγάλης ἀγάπης, ὦ τελειότητος ἀνυπερ-
βλήτου· παρρησιάζεται θεράπων πρὸς κύριον, αἰτεῖται
ἄφεσιν τῷ πλήθει ἢ καὶ ἑαυτὸν ἐξαλειφθῆναι μετ'
αὐτῶν ἀξιοῖ.
15 LIV. Τίς οὖν ἐν ὑμῖν γενναῖος; τίς εὔσπλαγχνος;
τίς πεπληροφορημένος ἀγάπης; εἰπάτω· Εἰ δι' ἐμὲ

[Syriac text]

The Syriac follows the Greek closely and presents no various readings of consequence. It is translated in Cowper's *Syriac Miscell.* p. 56. Epiphanius also (*Hær.* xxvii. 6, p. 107) quotes a few words, but incorrectly and at second hand (see above p. 16). He had read them in some ὑπομνηματισμοί, i.e. in some such collection of extracts as those of the Syriac MS which contains this passage. The passage suggests to Epiphanius a solution of the difficulty attending the lists of the early Roman bishops. He conjectures that Clement, after being consecrated by S. Peter, may have acted as he here advises others to act, and have refrained from active ministrations (παραιτησάμενος ἤργει) till the deaths of Linus and Cletus. Compare Cic. *pro Mil.* § 93 (to which Fell refers) 'Tranquilla republica cives mei (quoniam mihi cum illis non licet) sine me ipsi, sed per me tamen, perfruantur. Ego cedam atque abibo.' It would seem (from the reference to patriotic kings and rulers in the next chapter), as though Clement had read this passage.

16. †πεπληροφορημένος†] In the New Testament this verb has only the following senses: (1) 'to fulfil', 2 Tim. iv. 5, 17; (2) in the passive 'to be fully believed' (e.g. Luke i. 1), or 'to be fully persuaded' (e.g. Rom. iv. 21). Here, if the reading be correct, it must be equivalent to πεπληρωμένος, 'filled full'; but of this sense, though natural in itself, the lexicons do not furnish any example nor have I succeeded in finding a distinct instance. In the only passage however where it occurs in the LXX, Eccles. viii. 11 ἐπληροφορήθη καρδία υἱῶν τοῦ ἀνθρώπου ἐν αὐτοῖς τοῦ ποιῆσαι τὸ πονηρόν, the corresponding Hebrew is מָלֵא לֵב, 'the heart was full to do etc.' The word seems to be confined

στάσις καὶ ἔρις καὶ σχίσματα, ἐκχωρῶ, ἄπειμι οὗ ἐὰν βούλησθε, καὶ ποιῶ τὰ προστασσόμενα ὑπὸ τοῦ πλήθους· μόνον τὸ ποίμνιον τοῦ Χριστοῦ εἰρηνευέτω μετὰ τῶν καθεσταμένων πρεσβυτέρων. τοῦτο ὁ ποιήσας ἑαυτῷ μέγα κλέος ἐν Χριστῷ περιποιήσεται, καὶ 5 πᾶς τόπος δέξεται αὐτόν. τοῦ ρὰρ Κγρίογ ἡ ΓΗ κὰὶ τὸ πλήρωμα ἀγτῆc. ταῦτα οἱ πολιτευόμενοι τὴν ἀμεταμέλητον πολιτείαν τοῦ Θεοῦ ἐποίησαν καὶ ποιήσουσιν.

LV. Ἵνα δὲ καὶ ὑποδείγματα ἐθνῶν ἐνέγκωμεν· πολλοὶ βασιλεῖς καὶ ἡγούμενοι, λοιμικοῦ τινος ἐνστάν- 10

2 βούλησθε] βούλησθαι A.   5 κλέος] κλαιοσ A.

almost exclusively to biblical and ecclesiastical writings.
4. καθεσταμένων] *'duly appointed,'* as described in the earlier chapters, § 43, 44 (τοὺς κατασταθέντας ὑπ' ἐκείνων).
6. τοῦ γὰρ Κυρίου κ.τ.λ.] A noble application of Ps. xxiv. 1. He retires in God's cause, and there is room for him everywhere on God's earth.
7. πολιτευόμενοι...πολιτείαν] The idea of a spiritual polity to which the several members owe a duty is prominent in the context (e.g. ὑπὸ τοῦ πλήθους), and is still further developed by the comparison with secular states and statesmen in the following chapter.
LV. 'Even heathen nations have set bright examples of this self-denial. Kings and rulers have died for the common weal: statesmen have of their free will withdrawn into exile to lull factions. Among ourselves many have become slaves to ransom or to feed others. Even women, strengthened by God's grace, have been brave as men. Judith and Esther by their patriotic courage delivered the people from slavery and destruction.'
10. πολλοὶ βασιλεῖς κ.τ.λ.] Such feats of patriotism as were exhibited by Codrus, by Bulis and Sperthias, by M. Curtius; 'Quantus amor patriæ Deciorum in pectore, quantum dilexit Thebas, si Græcia vera, Menœceus.' The λοιμικός τις καιρός is a type of the sort of crisis which called forth these deeds of heroic self-sacrifice. Origen (*in Joann.* vi. § 36, IV. p. 153) refers to this passage, μεμαρτύρηται καὶ παρὰ τοῖς ἔθνεσιν ὅτι πολλοί τινες, λοιμικῶν ἐνσκηψάντων νοσημάτων, ἑαυτοὺς σφάγια ὑπὲρ τοῦ κοινοῦ παραδεδώκασι · καὶ παραδέχεται ταῦθ' οὕτως γεγονέναι οὐκ ἀλόγως πιστεύσας ταῖς ἱστορίαις ὁ πιστὸς Κλήμης ὑπὸ Παύλου μαρτυρούμενος. In several other passages also (*c. Cels.* i. 31, I. p. 349; *in Joann.* xxviii. § 14, IV. p. 393; *ad Rom.* iv. § 11, IV. p. 541) he uses similar language, but without mentioning Clement's name.
13. πολλοὶ ἐξεχώρησαν κ.τ.λ.] Like Lycurgus at Sparta, or Scipio Africanus at Rome. Of the latter it is reported (Seneca *Epist.* 86) that 'Clementis nostri fere verbis urbi valedixit, dicens *Exeo, si plus quam tibi* [*tibi quam*] *expedit crevi*' (Fell).
14. ἐν ἡμῖν] Gundert (*Zeitschr. f. Luther. Theol.* 1853, p. 649 sq.) explains this 'among us Romans,' supposing that Clement is still referring to examples of heathen self-devotion.

LV]   TO THE CORINTHIANS.   159

τος καιροῦ, χρησμοδοτηθέντες παρέδωκαν ἑαυτοὺς εἰς
θάνατον, ἵνα ῥύσωνται διὰ τοῦ ἑαυτῶν αἵματος τοὺς
πολίτας. πολλοὶ ἐξεχώρησαν ἰδίων πόλεων, ἵνα μὴ
στασιάζωσιν ἐπὶ πλεῖον. ἐπιστάμεθα πολλοὺς ἐν ἡμῖν
15 παραδεδωκότας ἑαυτοὺς εἰς δεσμά, ὅπως ἑτέρους λυτρώ-
σονται. πολλοὶ ἑαυτοὺς παρέδωκαν εἰς δουλείαν, καὶ
λαβόντες τὰς τιμὰς αὐτῶν ἑτέρους ἐψώμισαν. πολλαὶ
γυναῖκες ἐνδυναμωθεῖσαι διὰ τῆς χάριτος τοῦ Θεοῦ
ἐπετελέσαντο πολλὰ ἀνδρεῖα. Ἰουδὶθ ἡ μακαρία, ἐν

6 τόπος] τοπωσ A.   19 Ἰουδίθ] ιουδειθ A.

This view is adopted by Lipsius (p. 155), Hilgenfeld, and others. But, whatever may have been the miseries inflicted on the Roman citizens by the civil wars and by imperial despotism, the mention of slavery and ransom seems to be decisive against this interpretation. Here, as in the parallel passage § 6, ἐν ἡμῖν may refer indeed to Romans but to Christian Romans, of whom a considerable number belonged to the slave class and the lower orders. The ransom of slaves and the support of captives were regarded as a sacred duty by the early Christians generally, and the brethren of Rome especially were in early times honourably distinguished in this respect: see the notes on *Ign. Smyrn.* 6 and on Ign. *Rom.* 1.

15 †λυτρώσονται†] This construction of ὅπως with a future is possible (see Winer § xii. p. 304), though it does not occur in the New Testament, where ἵνα is several times so used. But, as the MS elsewhere confuses o and ω (see p. 25, and §§ 33, 44), we ought perhaps to read λυτρώσωνται.

17. τὰς τιμὰς αὐτῶν] '*the value of themselves*.' The form αὑτῶν (adopted by Hilgenfeld) must certainly be rejected from the New Testament, and probably from Clement also: see above 9, 12, 14, 30, 32.

ἐψώμισαν] The word is used several times in the LXX and generally as a translation of הַאֲכִיל 'to give to eat': comp. also 1 Cor. xiii. 3. Like so many other words (e.g. χορτάζεσθαι, see the note *Philippians* iv. 12), it has in the later language lost the sense of ridicule or meanness, which belonged to it in its origin; and Coleridge's note on its 'half satirical' force in 1 Cor. xiii. 3 (quoted in Stanley's *Corinthians* l. c.) seems to be overstrained. On the other hand, it is especially appropriate of feeding the poor and helpless, the sick man or the child.

πολλαὶ γυναῖκες κ.τ.λ.] The whole of this passage about Judith and Esther is paraphrased by Clem. Alex. *Strom.* iv. 19 (p. 617), immediately after the paragraph relating to Moses (already quoted p. 156); and sometimes he gives the very words of the elder Clement, e.g. ἡ τελεία κατὰ πίστιν Ἐσθήρ. But he does not acknowledge his obligation in this passage, though in the preceding chapter he has directly quoted the Roman Clement.

19. Ἰουδίθ] This passage has a critical value as containing the first reference to the Book of Judith,

συγκλεισμῷ οὔσης τῆς πόλεως, ἠτήσατο παρὰ τῶν
πρεσβυτέρων ἐαθῆναι αὐτὴν ἐξελθεῖν εἰς τὴν παρεμβο-
λὴν τῶν ἀλλοφύλων· παραδοῦσα οὖν ἑαυτὴν τῷ κινδύνῳ ἐξῆλθεν δι' ἀγάπην τῆς πατρίδος καὶ τοῦ λαοῦ
τοῦ ὄντος ἐν συγκλεισμῷ, καὶ παρέδωκεν Κύριος Ὀλο- 5
φέρνην ἐν χειρὶ θηλείας. οὐχ ἧττον καὶ ἡ τελεία κατὰ
πίστιν Ἐσθὴρ κινδύνῳ ἑαυτὴν παρέβαλεν, ἵνα τὸ δωδεκάφυλον τοῦ Ἰσραὴλ μέλλον ἀπολέσθαι ῥύσηται· διὰ

1 συγκλεισμῷ] συγκλισμω A.   6 θηλείας] θηλιασ A.

which was apparently unknown to, as it is unmentioned by, Josephus. Volkmar (*Theol. Jahrb.* 1856 p. 362 sq. and 1857 p. 441 sq., *Einl. in die Apokr.* I. I. p. 28, and elsewhere), followed by Baur (*Lehrb. der Christl. Dogmeng.* ed. 2. p. 82, and in other places), Hitzig (*Zeitschr. für Wissensch. Theol.* 1860, III. p. 240 sq.), and Graetz (*Gesch. der Juden vom Untergang etc.* p. 132 sq. ed. 2, 1866), places the writing of that book after the Jewish war of Trajan, and as a consequence denies the authenticity of the epistle of Clement. More sober critics however date the Book of Judith about the second century before the Christian era, e.g. Fritzsche *Einl.* p. 127 sq. in the *Kurzgef. Handb. zu den Apokr.*, Ewald *Gesch. des Volkes Isr.* IV. pp. 396, 541 sq., Westcott in *Smith's Dictionary of the Bible* I. p. 1174, besides R. A. Lipsius (*Zeitschr. f. Wissensch. Theol.* 1859, I. p. 39 sq.) and Hilgenfeld (ib. 1858, p. 247 sq., 1861, IV. p. 335 sq.), who both have directly refuted Volkmar's theory; and indeed the date and authenticity of Clement's Epistle are established on much more substantial grounds than the shadowy and fanciful argument by which it is attempted to postdate the Book of Judith. On this book see also an article of Lipsius *Jüdische Quellen zur Judithsage* (*Zeitschr. f. Wissensch. Theol.* 1867, x. p. 337 sq.).

4. τοῦ λαοῦ] '*the chosen people*' (see the note on § 29), and thus opposed to ἀλλόφυλοι.

6. ἐν χειρὶ θηλείας] Taken from Judith xiii. 15 ἐπάταξεν αὐτὸν ὁ Κύριος ἐν χειρὶ θηλείας, xvi. 5 Κύριος παντοκράτωρ ἠθέτησεν αὐτοὺς ἐν χειρὶ θηλείας. The expression ἐν χειρὶ therefore would seem to be the common Aramaism, equivalent to διά: see the note on *Galatians* iii. 19. On the other hand the construction παραδοῦναι ἐν χειρί (or ἐν χερσίν) is common in the LXX as an equivalent to παραδοῦναι εἰς χεῖρας: e.g. the same expression ויתן ביד is translated first καὶ παρέδωκεν ἐν χειρί (A) and then καὶ παρέδωκεν εἰς χεῖρας in Josh. x. 30, 32.

7. τὸ δωδεκάφυλον] So Acts xxvi. 7, *Protev. Jacob.* § 1; see above τὸ δωδεκάσκηπτρον § 31 with the note.

9. ἠξίωσεν] '*desired, entreated*', with an accusative of the person and without any dependent case or clause expressing the thing asked: as e.g. 1 Macc. xi. 62 καὶ ἠξίωσαν οἱ ἀπὸ Γάζης τὸν Ἰωνάθαν, καὶ ἔδωκεν αὐτοῖς δεξιάς, *Clem. Hom.* iii. 55 πρὶν αὐτὸν ἀξιώσητε. With an infinitive or a final clause added this use of ἀξιοῦν τινα is more common. On another more

γὰρ τῆς νηστείας καὶ τῆς ταπεινώσεως αὐτῆς ἠξίωσεν
10 τὸν παντεπόπτην δεσπότην, Θεὸν τῶν αἰώνων· ὃς ἰδὼν
τὸ ταπεινὸν τῆς ψυχῆς αὐτῆς ἐρύσατο τὸν λαόν, ὧν
χάριν ἐκινδύνευσεν.

LVI. Καὶ ἡμεῖς οὖν ἐντύχωμεν περὶ τῶν ἔν τινι
παραπτώματι ὑπαρχόντων, ὅπως δοθῇ αὐτοῖς ἐπιείκεια
15 καὶ ταπεινοφροσύνη εἰς τὸ εἶξαι αὐτοὺς μὴ ἡμῖν ἀλλὰ
τῷ θελήματι τοῦ Θεοῦ. οὕτως γὰρ ἔσται αὐτοῖς ἔγκαρπος καὶ τελεία ἡ πρὸς τὸν Θεὸν καὶ τοὺς ἁγίους μετ᾽

6 ἥττονι] ηττονει A.   15 ἐπιείκεια] επιεικια A.

questionable construction of ἀξιοῦν see above § 51.

10. παντεπόπτην] So below § 58, Polyc. *Phil.* 7, Clem. *Hom.* iv. 14, 23, v. 27, viii. 19. The word is not found in the LXX or New Testament. In the *Orac. Sibyll.* proœm. 4 πανεπόπτης occurs; and in heathen writers παν-όπτης is a common epithet of Zεύς.

Θεὸν τῶν αἰώνων] '*the God of* all *the ages*': comp. πατὴρ τῶν αἰώνων § 35, ὁ βασιλεὺς τῶν αἰώνων 1 Tim. i. 17: comp. Ps. cxlv. 13 ἡ βασιλεία σου βασιλεία πάντων τῶν αἰώνων. The devil on the other hand is the god (2 Cor. iv. 4) or the ruler (Ign. *Ephes.* 19) of this age or æon (τοῦ αἰῶνος τούτου). See also the passage in *Clem. Hom.* xx. 2 sq.

LVI. 'Let us intercede for offenders, that they may submit in meekness and humility. Let us be ever ready to give and to take admonition. The Scriptures teach us that chastisement is an instrument of mercy in the hands of God, that He inflicts it as a fatherly correction, that it is a blessing to be so chastised, that the man who endures patiently shall be restored again, shall be delivered from all perils, shall end his days in peace, and be gathered into the garner like the ripe sheaf, in due season.'

13. ἔν τινι παραπτώματι κ.τ.λ.] See Gal. vi. 1, of which this passage is perhaps a reminiscence. The ἡμεῖς and ἡμῖν seem to refer especially to the rulers of the Church and to contrast with the ὑμεῖς, the leaders of the feuds, at the beginning of § 57.

14. ἐπιείκεια] See Trench *N. T. Syn.* 1st ser. § xliii, and notes on *Philippians* iv. 5. The context here points to its derivation and primary meaning, εἰς τὸ εἶξαι αὐτοὺς κ.τ.λ.

16. ἔγκαρπος καὶ τελεία] See the note on § 44, where there is the same combination of epithets.

17. ἡ πρὸς τὸν Θεὸν κ.τ.λ.] i.e. The record of them before God and the Church will redound to their benefit, and they will receive pity. The expression ἡ πρὸς τὸν Θεὸν μνεία is almost equivalent to the Old Testament phrase μνημόσυνον ἔναντι Κυρίου, Exod. xxviii. 23, xxx. 16, Is. xxiii. 18, Ecclus. l. 16, comp. Acts x. 4. See also § 45 ἔγγραφοι ἐγένοντο ἀπὸ τοῦ Θεοῦ ἐν τῷ μνημοσύνῳ αὐτῶν.

τοὺς ἁγίους] 'the Christian brotherhood', as in the Apostolic writers: comp. *Ign. Smyrn.* 1, *Mart. Polyc.* 20. See 2 Cor. viii. 21. Two other interpretations have been proposed: (1) '*the saints*', i.e. the beatified dead, in which case ἡ πρὸς τοὺς ἁγίους μνεία

162   THE EPISTLE OF CLEMENT   [LVI

οἰκτιρμῶν μνεία. ἀναλάβωμεν παιδείαν, ἐφ' ᾗ οὐδεὶς
ὀφείλει ἀγανακτεῖν, ἀγαπητοί. ἡ νουθέτησις, ἣν ποιούμεθα εἰς ἀλλήλους, καλή ἐστιν καὶ ὑπεράγαν ὠφέλιμος·
κολλᾷ γὰρ ἡμᾶς τῷ θελήματι τοῦ Θεοῦ. οὕτως γάρ
φησιν ὁ ἅγιος λόγος· Παιδεύων ἐπαίδευσέν με ὁ Κύ- 5
ριος, καὶ τῷ θανάτῳ οὐ παρέδωκέν με. Ὃν γὰρ ἀγαπᾷ Κύριος
παιδεύει, μαστιγοῖ δὲ πάντα υἱὸν ὃν παραδέχεται· Παιδεύσει
με γάρ, φησιν, δίκαιος ἐν ἐλέει καὶ ἐλέγξει με, ἔλεος δὲ
ἁμαρτωλῶν μὴ λιπανάτω τὴν κεφαλὴν μου. Καὶ πάλιν
λέγει· Μακάριος ἄνθρωπος ὃν ἤλεγξεν ὁ Κύριος, νου- 10
θέτημα δὲ παντοκράτορος μὴ ἀπαναίνου· αὐτὸς γὰρ ἀλγεῖν
ποιεῖ, καὶ πάλιν ἀποκαθίστησιν· ἔπαισεν, καὶ αἱ χεῖρες
αὐτοῦ ἰάσαντο. ἑξάκις ἐξ ἀναγκῶν ἐξελεῖταί σε, ἐν δὲ τῷ

1 οἰκτιρμῶν μνεία] οικτειρμωνμνια A.   παιδείαν] παιδιαν A.   2 ὀφείλει]
ὀφιλει A.   νουθέτησις] νουθετησεισ A.   8 ἔλεος] ελαιοσ A.   See below.

is supposed to refer to invocation of saints. It is needless to say that this idea would be an anachronism in Clement and for some generations after. (2) '*the holy angels*', a sense which οἱ ἅγιοι frequently has, e. g. Job xv. 15, Zach. xiv. 5, Ecclus. xlv. 2, Tobit viii. 15, 1 Thess. iii. 13 (passages quoted by Hilgenfeld). This is a possible interpretation (comp. 1 Tim. v. 21 διαμαρτύρομαι ἐνώπιον τοῦ Θεοῦ καὶ Χριστοῦ Ἰησοῦ καὶ τῶν ἐκλεκτῶν ἀγγέλων), but the common usage of οἱ ἅγιοι in the Apostolic writings is a safer guide.

1. ἀναλάβωμεν παιδείαν] '*Let us receive correction*': comp. Heb. xii. 7 εἰς παιδείαν ὑπομένετε κ.τ.λ.

2. ἡ νουθέτησις] On the difference between νουθεσία (νουθέτησις) and παιδεία, see Trench *N. T. Syn.* 1st ser. § xxxii; comp. Ephes. vi. 4. On the forms νουθεσία, νουθέτησις, see Lobeck *Phryn.* p. 512.

5. παιδεύων κ.τ.λ.] From the LXX Ps. cxviii. 18 word for word.

6. ὃν γὰρ ἀγαπᾷ κ.τ.λ.] From LXX Prov. iii. 12 word for word, as אA; but for παιδεύει B has ἐλέγχει. The Syro-Hexaplar text wavers, giving the equivalent to παιδεύει in the text and to ἐλέγχει in the margin. In Heb. xii. 6 it is quoted with παιδεύει as here: in Rev. iii. 19 both words are combined, ἐγὼ ὅσους ἐὰν φιλῶ, ἐλέγχω καὶ παιδεύω. Clem. Alex. *Pæd.* I. 9 (p. 145) has παιδεύει, but his quotation is perhaps not independent of the Roman Clement. On the other hand Philo *de Conj. Erud. grat.* § 31 (I. p. 544) quotes it with ἐλέγχει. This, which corresponds with the Hebrew, was probably the original reading of the LXX, and all the texts with παιδεύει may perhaps have been derived directly or indirectly from the quotation in the Epistle to the Hebrews.

7. παιδεύσει κ.τ.λ.] From Ps. cxli. 5, word for word, if we read ἔλαιον. Our MS however has ελαιοσ, i. e. ἔλεος (for so our scribe generally writes the word: see p. 25). On the other hand,

TO THE CORINTHIANS.

ἐβδόμῳ οὐχ ἄψεταί coy κακόν· ἐν λιμῷ ῥύσεταί ce ἐκ θανά-
5 τοy, ἐν πολέμῳ δὲ ἐκ χειρὸc cιδήροy λύcει ce· καὶ ἀπὸ
μάcτιγοc γλώccηc cὲ κρύψει, καὶ οὐ μὴ φοβηθήcῃ κακῶν
ἐπερχομένων· ἀδίκων καὶ ἀνόμων καταγελάcῃ, ἀπὸ δὲ
θηρίων ἀγρίων οὐ μὴ φοβηθῇc. θῆρεc γὰρ ἄγριοι εἰρηνεύ-
coycίν coι· εἶτα γνώcῃ, ὅτι εἰρηνεύcει coy ὁ οἶκοc· ἡ δὲ
ὁ δίαιτα τῆc cκηνῆc coy οὐ μὴ ἁμάρτῃ, γνώcῃ δὲ ὅτι πολὺ
[τὸ cπέρμα coy], τὰ δὲ τέκνα coy ὥcπερ [τὸ παμβό]τανον
τοῦ ἀγροῦ· ἐλεύcῃ [δὲ ἐν τά]φῳ ὥcπερ cῖτοc ὥριμο[c
κατὰ και]ρὸν θεριζόμενοc, ἢ ὥc[περ θημω]νιὰ ἅλωνοc
καθ᾿ ὥραν cy[νκομι]cθεῖcα. Βλέπετε, ἀγαπη[τοί, ὅτι]
5 ὑπερασπισμός ἐστιν τ[οῖς παιδευ]ομένοις ὑπὸ τοῦ δεσπό-

14 οὐχ ἄψεται] ουκοψεται A.

the original reading of the LXX was unquestionably ἔλαιον (ἔλαιον is the oil, ἔλαιος the olive-tree and therefore out of place here) as it is in אAB, and apparently in all existing MSS of the LXX, the Hebrew being שֶׁמֶן; but ἔλαιος (i.e. ἔλεος) might not unnaturally be substituted by some early transcriber on account of the preceding ἐν ἐλέει. It is therefore not improbable that Clement found this reading in his text of the LXX, so that I have not ventured to correct it. See another instance of the same error above, § 18 (note).

10. μακάριος κ.τ.λ.] From LXX Job v. 17—26 as read in אB, with slight and unimportant differences. The text of A presents considerable variations, chiefly in adding clauses which are found in the Hebrew but wanting in אB. The points in which Clement's quotation agrees with A, as against אB (e.g. οὐχ ἄψεται for οὐ μὴ ἄψηται), are insignificant.

13. ἑξάκις κ.τ.λ.] For this Hebraism where two successive numbers are given to denote magnitude and in-

crease, see Prov. vi. 16 Hebr. (six, seven, as here); Micah v. 5, Eccles. xi. 2 (seven, eight); Exod. xx. 5, etc. (three four); Job xxxiii. 29 Hebr. (two, three).

16. κακῶν] The LXX text prefixes ἀπό (אAB).

18. θῆρες γὰρ κ.τ.λ.] As in the vision of Hermas Vis. iv. 1, 2, where the wild beast is thus pacified.

19. ἡ δὲ δίαιτα] 'the abode': see above § 39. The Hebrew is quite different.

21. τὸ παμβότανον] 'the manifold herbage'. It seems to be a ἅπαξ λεγόμενον till quite a late period. There is nothing in the Hebrew (עָלֶה) to explain the adoption of so unusual a word.

22. ἐν τάφῳ] A Hebraism for εἰς τάφον: see another instance on § 55 παρέδωκεν ἐν χειρί.

23. θημωνιά] A word, it would appear, almost confined to the LXX, though θημών is as old as Homer, Od. v. 368.

25. ὑπερασπισμός] 'protection', 2 Sam. xxii. 36, Ps. xviii. 35, Lam. iii. 64,

[τοῦ· καὶ γάρ] ἀγαθὸς ὢν παιδε[ύει Θεός] εἰς τ[ὸ νουθετ]ηθῆναι ἡμᾶς διὰ τῆς ὁσίας π[αι]δείας αὐτοῦ.

LVII. Ὑμεῖς οὖν, οἱ τὴν καταβολὴν [τῆς] στάσεως ποιήσαντες, ὑποτά[γη]τε τοῖς πρεσβυτέροις καὶ παι-[δεύ]θητε εἰς μετάνοιαν, κάμψαν[τες] τὰ γόνατα τῆς 5 καρδίας ὑμῶν· μάθετε ὑποτάσσεσθαι, ἀποθέμενοι τὴν ἀλαζόνα καὶ ὑπερήφανον τῆς γλώσσης ὑμῶν αὐθά-δ[εια]ν· ἄμεινον γάρ ἐστιν ὑμῖν [ἐν] τῷ ποιμνίῳ τοῦ

1 παιδεύει Θεός] There is not room in the lacuna for more letters than γειθc, if for so many (see Tisch. prol. xix). I have therefore read Θεός in place of ὁ Θεός, the reading of previous editors (following Wotton). 2 παιδείας] π .. διασ A.

Eccles. xxxi (xxxiv). 19. It does not occur in the New Testament. See the note on ὑπερασπιστής above, § 45.
1. ἀγαθὸς ὤν] 'of His kindness' (as e.g. Ps. lxxiii. 1), corresponding to ὃν γὰρ ἀγαπᾷ κ.τ.λ. above.
LVII. 'And do you leaders of the schism submit to the elders, and ask pardon of God on your knees. It is far better that you should be of no account, so that the flock of Christ may have peace. Remember how sternly Wisdom rebukes the disobedient in the Book of Proverbs. She will laugh them to scorn when destruction cometh as a tempest. They mocked at her counsels before, and she will not hear them then.'
4. ὑποτ. τοῖς πρεσβ.] The same expression occurs, 1 Pet. v. 5.
5. κάμψαντες κ.τ.λ.] Compare the expression in the prayer of Manasses (*Apost. Const.* ii. 22) νῦν κλίνω γόνυ καρδίας. A strong oriental metaphor like 'girding the loins of the mind' (1 Pet. i. 13), or 'rendering the calves of the lips' (Hosea xiv. 2).
7. ἀλάζονα καὶ ὑπερήφανον] See Trench *N. T. Syn.* 1st ser. § xxix.
10. δοκοῦντας] '*held in repute*': see the note on *Galatians* ii. 2.
τῆς ἐλπίδος αὐτοῦ] i.e. τοῦ Χρι-

στοῦ, either a subjective or an objective genitive, 'the hope which He holds out' or 'the hope which reposes in Him'.
11. ἡ πανάρετος σοφία] The Book of Proverbs, besides the title commonly prefixed to the LXX Version, Παροιμίαι or Παροιμίαι Σαλομῶντος, is frequently quoted by early Christian writers as ἡ πανάρετος σοφία 'the Wisdom which comprises all virtues' (for πανάρετος comp. § 1); see esp. Euseb. *H.E.* iv. 22, where speaking of Hegesippus he says, οὐ μόνος δὲ οὗτος ἀλλὰ καὶ Εἰρηναῖος καὶ ὁ πᾶς τῶν ἀρχαίων χορὸς πανάρετον σοφίαν τὰς Σολομῶνος παροιμίας ἐκάλουν. Sometimes it bears the name σοφία simply; e.g. in Just. Mart. *Dial.* § 129 (p. 359 A), Melito in Euseb. *H.E.* iv. 26, Clem. Alex. *Protr.* § 8 (pp. 67, 68), *Paed.* ii. 2 (p. 182 ἡ θεία σοφία), *Strom.* ii. 18 (p. 472), Orig. *Hom. xiv in Gen.* § 2 (II. p. 97), besides others quoted in Cotelier. It is a probable inference from Eusebius (ll. cc.) that both Melito and Hegesippus derived the name from Jewish sources, and this is borne out by the fact that the book is called הכמה, 'Wisdom', by rabbinical writers (see Fürst *Kanon des Alten Testaments*,

TO THE CORINTHIANS.

Χριστοῦ μικροὺς καὶ ἐλλογίμους εὑρεθῆναι, ἢ καθ' ὑ-
10 περοχὴν δοκοῦντας ἐκριφῆναι ἐκ τῆς ἐλπίδος αὐτοῦ.
οὕτως γὰρ λέγει ἡ πανάρετος σοφία· ἸΔΟΫ́ ΠΡΟΉϹΟΜΑ[Ι
ϒ̔ΜῖΝ ἘΜΗ͂ϹΠΝΟΗ͂ϹῬΗ͂ϹΙΝ, ΔΙΔΆΞΩ [ΔῈϒ̔ΜΑ͂]ϹΤῸΝἘΜῸΝΛΌΓΟΝ·
ἘΠ[ΕΙΔῊΕΚΆΛΟΫΝ] ΚΑῚΟΫ̓ΧΫ̔ΠΗΚΟΫ́ϹΑ[ΤΕ, ΚΑῚἘΞΈΤΕΙ]ΝΟΝΛΌΓΟΫϹ
ΚΑῚΟΫ̓ [ΠΡΟϹΕΊΧΕΤΕ], ἈΛΛᾺἈΚΫ́ΡΟΫϹἘΠΟ[ΙΕῖΤΕἘΜᾺϹ] ΒΟΫΛΆϹ
15 ΤΟῖϹ ΔῈἘΜ[ΟῖϹἘΛΈΓΧΟΙϹ] ἨΠΕΙΘΉϹΑΤΕ· ΤΟΙΓΑ[ΡΟΫ͂ΝΚἈΓῺ] ΤΗ͂
ϒ̔ΜΕΤΈΡΑ ἈΠΩΛΕΊ[Α ἘΠΙΓΕΛΆϹΟ]ΜΑΙ, ΚΑΤΑΧΑΡΟΫ͂ΜΑΙ ΔῈ [ΗΝΙΚΑ
ΑΝ] ἜΡΧΗΤΑΙ ϒ̔ΜῖΝ ΟΛΕΘΡΟ[Ϲ ΚΑῚ ὩϹ ΑΝ Α]ΦΊΚΗΤΑΙ ϒ̔ΜῖΝ ἈΦΝΩ

14 *ἐποιεῖτε ἐμᾶς*] Tisch. (prol. xix) says 'Rectius suppletur ιειτε τασ εμασ quam ιειτε εμασ'; but ιειται εμασ is better suited to the space than either, and εποιειτε would as likely as not be written εποιειται. This reading also accords with the LXX.

1868, p. 73 sq.). The personification of Wisdom in the opening would lead naturally to this designation; e.g. Iren. iv. 20. 3, v. 20. 1, Philo *de Ebr.* 8 (I. p. 362), though Philo himself quotes the book as παροιμίαι *ib.* § 20 (I. p. 369). Whether the epithet πανάρετος was first used by Clement and derived from him by later writers, or not, it is impossible to say. At the same time the title ἡ πανάρετος σοφία is given, not only to the canonical Book of Wisdom, but also to the apocryphal Wisdom of Solomon (Method. *Symp.* i. 3, ii. 7, noted by Hilgenfeld; Epiphan. *de Mens. et Pond.* § 4, II. p. 162 ed. Petau; Greg. Nyss. *c. Eunom.* vii, II. p. 638, Paris 1638; [Athanas.] *Synops.* § 45, II. p. 132 F, τῆς σοφίας Σολομῶντος τῆς λεγομένης παναρέτου; and others: and its title in the list of books prefixed to A is σοφία ἡ πανάρετος), and to the apocryphal Ecclesiasticus or Wisdom of Jesus the Son of Sirach (Euseb. *Chron.* OL cxxxvii 'quem vocant Panareton, *Dem. Evang.* viii. 2 p. 393 Ἰησοῦς ὁ τοῦ Σειρὰχ ὁ τὴν καλουμένην πανάρετον σοφίαν συντάξας, Hieron. *Prol. in Libr. Sal.*, IX. p.

1293, etc.). Joannes Damasc. *de Fid. Orth.* iv. 17 (I. p. 284) says ἡ πανάρετος, τουτέστιν ἡ Σοφία τοῦ Σολομῶντος καὶ ἡ Σοφία τοῦ Ἰησοῦ, thus including both these apocryphal books under the term, but excluding Proverbs which he has before mentioned as παροιμίαι; and so Jerome *Praef. in Libr. Salom.* (IX. p. 1293) 'Fertur et πανάρετος Jesu filii Sirach liber et alius ψευδεπίγραφος qui Sapientia Salomonis inscribitur'. Moreover the name of 'Wisdom' is occasionally given also to Ecclesiastes (Fürst l.c. p. 91) and to the Song of Songs (Fürst l.c. p. 85, and Cotelier here). And still more generally the third group of the Old Testament writings, the ἁγιόγραφα or γραφεῖα, is sometimes called הכמה 'Wisdom' (Fürst l.c. p. 55), because it comprises Proverbs and the allied books, as it is elsewhere called ψαλμοὶ or ὕμνοι (see above § 28) from another most important component element.

11. *ἰδοὺ κ.τ.λ.*] A close quotation from the LXX Prov. i. 23—31. The variations are unimportant, and not greater than between one MS and another of the LXX.

θ[όρυβος, ἡ δὲ] καταστροφὴ ὁμοία κ[αταιγίδι πα]ρῇ, ἡ
ὅταν ἔρχηται ὑμ[ῖν θλῖψις] καὶ πολιορκία. ἔσται γ[άρ, ὅταν
ἐπι]καλέσησθέ με, ἐγὼ δὲ [οὐκ εἰσα]κούσομαι ὑμῶν· ζη-
τ[ήσουσί] με κακοὶ καὶ οὐχ εὑρή[σουσιν]· ἐμίσησαν γὰρ σοφίαν,
[τὸν δὲ φό]βον τοῦ Κυρίου οὐ προείλα[ντο, οὐδὲ] ἤθελον 5

2 ὅταν] οταρ A.   3 ἐπικαλέσησθε] επικαλεσησθαι A.   5 προείλαντο]
I read the MS προειλα..., as in the LXX, but Tisch. gives it προσιλα...

8. πλησθήσονται] The letters πλησθησον occur towards the end of the last line in a page, fol. 167 b. The margin is torn, so that a few letters have disappeared. There is not room however for many more than three letters, and probably the page ended with πλησθήσονται, so that a new subject would begin with the following page. All this the photograph shows clearly.

It is now established beyond a doubt that one leaf, and one leaf only, of the MS has disappeared: see the introduction p. 23. The first leaf of this epistle (fol. 159) extends from the beginning to καὶ σεμνὸν...§ 7; the second (fol. 160) from ...σεως ἡμῶν κανόνα § 7 to οὕτως κριθήσε[ται] § 13. These examples will show the average contents of a leaf. The preceding 57 chapters in fact have taken up nine leaves, so that nearly a tenth of the whole epistle is lost. This lacuna therefore gives ample room for the passages from Clement's epistle which are quoted in ancient writers but not found in the MS. These are now gathered together.

(i) If there were no independent reason for inserting this fragment in our epistle, we might hesitate; for (1) I have shown above (§ 47) that ἐν τῇ πρὸς Κορινθίους ἐπιστολῇ might mean the Second Epistle; and to the Second Epistle Ussher and others after him have referred it; (2) The

suggestion of Cotelier (Jud. de Epist. II) that for καθώς φησιν we should read καί ὡς φησιν, or better καὶ καθώς φησιν, would be very plausible. But Cotelier himself points out (l.c.) that the statement of the Pseudo-Justin is confirmed from another source. Irenæus (iii. 3. 3) describes this epistle of Clement as preserving the tradition recently received from the Apostles, 'annuntiantem unum Deum omnipotentem, factorem cœli et terræ, plasmatorem hominis, qui induxerit cataclysmum et advocaverit Abraham, qui eduxerit populum de terra Ægypti, qui collocutus sit Moysi, qui legem disposuerit et prophetas miserit, qui *ignem præparaverit diabolo et angelis ejus*'. This description corresponds with the contents of our epistle, excepting the last clause which I have italicised; and the insertion of a statement so remarkable could not have been an accidental error on the part of Irenæus. Wotton indeed supposes that these words do not give the contents of Clement's epistle, but that Irenæus is describing in his own language the general substance of the Apostolic tradition. To this interpretation however the subjunctive *præparaverit* is fatal, for it shows that the narrative is oblique and that Irenæus is speaking in the words of another.

It seems then that Clement towards the close of the epistle dwelt upon

ἐΜΑῖc προcέχ[ειν Βογλαῖc], ἐΜΥΚΤΉριζοΝ Δὲ ἐΜΟΫ́[c ἐλέΓχΟΥc]·
τοιΓΑΡΟῦΝ ἔΔΟΝΤΑΙ τῆ[c ἑΑΥΤῶΝ] ὁΔΟΫ́ ΤΟῪc ΚΑΡΠΟΫ́c, [ΚΑὶ
τῆc ἑΑΥΤῶΝ] ἀceBeίΑc πληcθΉcΟΝ[ΤΑΙ]...

(i) εἰ Τῆς παρούσης καταστάσεως τὸ τέλος ἐστὶν
10 ἡ διὰ τοῦ πυρὸς κρίσις τῶν ἀσεβῶν, καθά φασιν αἱ
γραφαὶ προφητῶν τε καὶ ἀποστόλων ἔτι δὲ καὶ τῆς

the end of all things, the destruction of the world by fire. For such an allusion the threats taken from the Book of Proverbs (§ 57) would prepare the way; and it would form a fit termination to a letter of warning.

And for this statement he appealed to the authority, not only of the Apostles and prophets, but also of the Sibyl. There is no difficulty in this. The oldest Jewish Sibylline Oracle, of which a large part is preserved in the 3rd book of the extant Sibylline collection and in quotations of the early fathers, appears to have been written in the 2nd century B.C. by an Alexandrian Jew (see esp. Bleek in Schleiermacher's *Theolog. Zeitschr.* I. p. 120 sq., II. p. 172 sq.; Ewald *Enstehung etc. der Sibyll. Bücher* Gottingen, 1858; and Alexandre *Oracula Sibyllina*, Paris, 1841, 1856). It is quoted and accepted as a genuine oracle of the Sibyl by Josephus (*Ant.* i. 4. 3), in the early apocryphal *Prædicatio Petri et Pauli* (Clem. Alex. *Strom.* vi. 5, p. 761 sq), by the Christian Fathers Melito(Cureton's *Spicil. Syr.* pp. 43, 86), Athenagoras (*Legat.* § 30), Theophilus (*ad Autol.* ii. 3, 9, 31, 36, 38), and Clement of Alexandria (very frequently), in the *Cohort. ad Græc.* ascribed to Justin (§ 37), and in a Peratic document quoted by Hippolytus (*Hær.* v. 16), besides allusions in Hermas (*Vis.* ii. 4) and in Justin (*Apol.* i. §§ 20, 44). Justin in the last passage (§ 44) says that the reading of the Sibylline oracles had been forbidden under penalty of death but that the Christians nevertheless read them and induced others to read them; and Celsus tauntingly named the Christians Sibyllists (Orig. *c. Cels.* v. 61, I. p. 625; comp. vii..56, I. p. 734). Clement therefore might very well have quoted the Sibyl as an authority.

After the enforcement of monotheism and the condemnation of idolatry, the main point on which the Sibyllines dwelt was the destruction of the world by fire. To this end the authority of the Sibyl is quoted in Justin (*Apol.* i. 20), *Apost. Const.* (v. 7), Theophilus (ii. 38), Lactantius (*Div. Inst.* vii. 15 sq.), and others. The impending destruction by fire is connected in these oracles with the past destruction by water, as in 2 Pet. iii. 6, 7, 10, 11, 12. The juxta-position of the two great catastrophes in Melito (Cureton's *Spicil. Syr.* pp. 50, 51) is derived from the Sibyllines, as the coincidence of language shows, and not from 2 Pet. iii. 6 sq., as Cureton (§ 95) supposes: see Westcott *Hist. of the Canon* p. 195 2nd ed. I have pointed out above (§§ 7, 9) that Clement's language respecting the 'regeneration' by the flood and Noah's 'preaching of repentance' seems to be taken from the Sibylline Oracles, and this affords an additional presumption that he may have referred to the Sibyl as his authority for the ἐκπύρωσις and παλιγγενεσία at the end of all things. It is a slight

Σιβύλλης, καθώς φησιν ὁ μακάριος Κλήμης ἐν τῇ πρὸς Κορινθίους ἐπιστολῇ, κ.τ.λ.

PSEUDO-JUSTINUS *Quæst. ad Orthod.* 74.

(ii) ἀλλὰ καὶ Κλήμης ἀρχαϊκώτερον, Ζῇ, φησίν, ὁ Θεὸς καὶ ὁ Κύριος Ἰησοῦς Χριστὸς καὶ τὸ πνεῦμα τὸ ἅγιον.

BASILIUS *de Spir. Sanct.* c. xxix (III. p. 61 A).

confirmation too, that the word παντεπόπτης at the beginning of § 58 seems to be derived from Sibylline diction (see the note on § 55, where also it occurs). The passage of Theophilus (ii. 38) shows how it might occur to an early father to combine the testimonies of the prophets and the Sibyl to the ἐκπύρωσις, just as a similar combination is found in the far-famed medieval hymn, 'Dies iræ, dies illa, solvet sæclum in favilla, Teste David cum Sibylla': see the note in Trench's *Sacred Latin Poetry* p. 297. For the passages in the Sibyllines relating to the conflagration of the universe see Alexandre II. p. 518 sq.

(ii) S. Basil in the context defines the Clement from whom he thus quotes, as Κλήμης ὁ Ῥωμαῖος. Though ἀρχαϊκώτερος appears in some texts, Garnier reads ἀρχαϊκώτερον after the best MSS accessible to him. Nolte also (*Patrist. Miscell.* p. 276 in the *Theol. Quartalschr.* XLI, 1859) states that ἀρχαϊκώτερον is the reading of all the MSS of S. Basil which he inspected. The contrast seems to be between the simple and archaic language of Clement, and the more technical expressions of Dionysius of Alexandria who has been quoted just before as speaking of the τρεῖς ὑποστάσεις and of the μονὰς and τριὰς in enunciating the same doctrine. The passage can hardly have belonged to any other Clementine writing besides the genuine First Epistle to the Corinthians; for (1) The Second Epistle to the Corinthians is not quoted as genuine till a much later date: (2) The passage is not contained in the Epistles to Virgins, which it might be thought that Basil, like Epiphanius and Jerome, would possibly have accepted as genuine; (3) The Clementine Homilies and Recognitions with other works of this cycle were so manifestly heretical, that they could not possibly have misled the keen theological perceptions of the orthodox Basil or have been quoted by him as genuine; and the orthodox recension of these seems to have been made at a much later date. On the other hand such words as Basil quotes would be appropriate at the close of our epistle, and may well have occurred in the lacuna. Compare § 46 ἢ οὐχὶ ἕνα Θεὸν ἔχομεν καὶ ἕνα Χριστὸν καὶ ἐν Πνεῦμα τῆς χάριτος τὸ ἐκχυθὲν ἐφ' ἡμᾶς (with the note). It might perhaps be supposed that Basil refers to the passage just quoted; but this seems impossible, as he obviously professes to give the exact words of Clement and not the general sense only.

Other passages, wrongly supposed to be quoted from this portion of the genuine epistle, will be considered in treating of the fragments at the end; p. 215 sq.

TO THE CORINTHIANS.

5   LVIII. [λο]ιπὸν ὁ παντεπόπτης Θεὸς [καὶ] δεσπότης τῶν πνευμάτων καὶ Κύριος [πά]σης σαρκός, ὁ
ἐκλεξάμενος [τὸ]ν Κύριον Ἰησοῦν Χριστὸν καὶ ἡμᾶς δι'
αὐτοῦ [εἰ]ς λαὸν περιούσιον, δῴη πάσῃ [ψ]υχῇ ἐπικεκλημένῃ τὸ μεγαλο[π]ρεπὲς καὶ ἅγιον ὄνομα αὐτοῦ
10 [π]ίστιν, φόβον, εἰρήνην, ὑπομονήν, μακροθυμίαν, ἐγκράτειαν, ἁγνείαν καὶ σωφροσύνην, εἰς εὐαρέστησιν τῷ
ὀνόματι αὐτοῦ διὰ τοῦ ἀρχιερέως καὶ προστάτου ἡμῶν

5 λοιπόν] Vansittart. See below, and p. 26.   11 ἁγνείαν] αγνιαν Λ.

LVIII. 'Finally, may the God of all spirits and all flesh, who hath chosen us in Christ Jesus, grant us all graces through Christ, our Highpriest, through whom be glory and honour to Him. Amen.'

5. λοιπόν] For λοιπὸν or τὸ λοιπόν, with which S. Paul frequently ushers in the close of his epistles, see *Philippians* iii. 1. I cannot doubt that one or other should be read here, and λοιπὸν is perhaps better than τὸ λοιπόν, for the initial λ (as is usual in the MS) would be enlarged and the word thus written would be sufficient to fill up the vacant space.

παντεπόπτης] See the note on § 55.
Θεός...τῶν πνευμάτων κ.τ.λ.] Num. xxvii. 16 Κύριος ὁ Θεὸς τῶν πνευμάτων καὶ πάσης σαρκός (comp. xvi. 22): see also Heb. xii. 9 τῷ πατρὶ τῶν πνευμάτων, Rev. xxii. 6 Κύριος ὁ Θεὸς τῶν πνευμάτων τῶν προφητῶν.

7. ἡμᾶς δι' αὐτοῦ] Ephes. i. 4 καθὼς ἐξελέξατο ἡμᾶς ἐν αὐτῷ (i.e. ἐν Χριστῷ).

8. εἰς λαὸν περιούσιον] Deut. xiv. 4 καὶ σὲ ἐξελέξατο Κύριος ὁ Θεός σου γενέσθαι σε. λαὸν αὐτῷ περιούσιον; comp. *ib.* vii. 6, xxvi. 18, Exod. xix. 5, Ps. cxxxiv. 4, Tit. ii. 14 καθαρίσῃ ἑαυτῷ λαὸν περιούσιον. In the LXX λαὸς περιούσιος is a translation of עַם סְגֻלָּה, the expression doubtless present to S. Peter's mind when he spoke of λαὸς εἰς περιποίησιν (1 Pet. ii. 9). In Mal. iii. 17 סְגֻלָּה is translated εἰς περιποίησιν in the LXX, and περιούσιος by Aquila. As סְגֻלָּה is 'peculium', 'opes', (סָגַל 'acquisivit'), περιούσιος would seem to mean 'acquired over and above', and hence 'specially acquired' with a meaning similar to the classical ἐξαίρετος. It was rendered at once literally and effectively in the Latin Bible by 'peculiaris'.

ἐπικεκλημένη] 'which hath invoked his name'; comp. Acts ii. 21, ix. 14, 21, xxii. 16, etc. Or is it rather, as the perfect tense suggests, '*which is called by his name*'? This latter makes better sense, especially in connexion with λαὸς περιούσιος; but with this meaning the common constructions in biblical Greek would be ἐφ' ἣν (or ἐφ' ᾗ) ἐπικέκληται τὸ ὄνομα αὐτοῦ (e.g. Acts xv. 17, James ii. 7, and freq. in the LXX), or τῇ ἐπικεκλημένῃ τῷ ὀνόματι αὐτοῦ (Is. xliii. 7).

11. ἁγνείαν καὶ σωφροσύνην] So too Ign. *Ephes.* 10: comp. Tit. ii. 5 σώφρονας, ἁγνάς.

εὐαρέστησιν] The word occurs *Test. xii Patr.* Is. 4.

12. ἀρχιερέως καὶ προστάτου] See the note on § 36 above, where the expression is expanded.

Ἰησοῦ Χριστοῦ· δι' οὗ αὐτῷ δόξα καὶ μεγαλωσύνη, κράτος, τιμή, καὶ νῦν καὶ εἰς πάντας τοὺς αἰῶνας τῶν αἰώνων. ἀμήν.

LIX. Τοὺς δὲ ἀπεσταλμένους ἀφ' ἡμῶν Κλαύδιον Ἔφηβον καὶ Οὐαλέριον Βίτωνα σὺν καὶ Φορτουνάτῳ 5 ἐν εἰρήνῃ μετὰ χαρᾶς ἐν τάχει ἀναπέμψατε πρὸς ἡμᾶς, ὅπως θᾶττον τὴν εὐκταίαν καὶ ἐπιποθήτην ἡμῖν εἰρήνην

6 ἀναπέμψατε] ανεπεμψατε A.

1. δόξα καὶ μεγαλωσύνη] See the note on § 20, where also these two words occur together in a doxology: comp. also § 59, where nearly the same combination of words as here is repeated. In Rev. v. 13 we have ἡ τιμὴ καὶ ἡ δόξα καὶ τὸ κράτος εἰς τοὺς αἰῶνας τῶν αἰώνων.

LIX. 'We have sent Claudius Ephebus and Valerius Bito to you. Let them return to us quickly accompanied by Fortunatus, and bear glad tidings of harmony and peace restored among you. The grace of our Lord Jesus Christ be with you and with all. Through Him be glory to God for ever.'

4. Κλαύδιον κ.τ.λ.] These two names, Claudius and Valerius, suggest some connexion with the imperial household; as the fifth Cæsar with his two predecessors belonged to the Claudian gens and his empress Messalina to the Valerian. Hence it happens that during and after the reign of Claudius we not unfrequently find the names Claudius (Claudia) and Valerius (Valeria) in conjunction, referring to slaves or retainers of the Cæsars; e.g. D.M. CLAVDIAE. AVG. LIB. NEREIDI. M. VALERIVS. FVTIANS. MATRI. CARISSIMAE (*Accad. di Archeol.* XI. p. 376, no. 35), or VALERIA. HILARIA. NVTRIX. OCTAVIAE. CAESARIS. AVGVSTI. REQVIESCIT. CVM. TI. CLAVDIO.

FRVCTO. VIRO (Orelli *Inscr.* 4492). It is not impossible therefore that these two delegates of the Roman Church were among the members of 'Cæsar's household' mentioned in Phil. iv. 22, and fairly probable that they are in some way connected with the palace; see the dissertation in *Philippians* p. 169 sq. Of the two cognomina Ephebus is not so uncommon. On the other hand Bito is very rare. As a man's name, I have only succeeded in finding one instance of it, and there, by a strange coincidence, it is connected with the nomen Claudius; see Mommsen's *Inscr. Regn. Neap.* p. 370, 'Originis incertæ no. 6472; extat in Mus. Borb.; DIIS. MANIBVS. TI. CLAVDIO. BITONI.RVTILIA. MARGARIS. CONJVGI. BENEMERENTI. F. VIX. ANNIS. LXXXV'. In Muratori, 1367 no. 12, it occurs as a woman's name, LONGINVS. BITONI. VXORI. AMENTO.

5. σὺν καὶ Φορτουνάτῳ] For the position of καὶ comp. Phil. iv. 3 μετὰ καὶ Κλήμεντος (quoted by Laurent p. 425). Hilgenfeld adds 'from the *Assumption of Moses*' Clem. Alex. *Strom.* vi. 15 (p. 806) σὺν καὶ τῷ Χαλέβ. The clever emendation of Davies σὺν Γαίῳ Φορτουνάτῳ is therefore unnecessary. The form of expression seems to separate Fortunatus from Ephebus and Bito: and, if so, he was perhaps not a Roman

καὶ ὁμόνοιαν ἀπαγγέλλωσιν· εἰς τὸ τάχιον καὶ ἡμᾶς χαρῆναι περὶ τῆς εὐσταθείας ὑμῶν.
10 Ἡ χάρις τοῦ Κυρίου ἡμῶν Ἰησοῦ Χριστοῦ μεθ' ὑμῶν καὶ μετὰ πάντων πανταχῆ τῶν κεκλημένων ὑπὸ τοῦ Θεοῦ καὶ δι' αὐτοῦ· δι' οὗ αὐτῷ δόξα, τιμή, κράτος καὶ μεγαλωσύνη, θρόνος αἰώνιος, ἀπὸ τῶν αἰώνων εἰς τοὺς αἰῶνας τῶν αἰώνων. ἀμήν.

8 ἀπαγγέλλωσιν] The first λ is supplied above the line but *primâ manu*.
τάχιον] ταχειῶ A.   9 εὐσταθείας] ευσταθιασ A.
The subscription is ΚΛΗΜΕΝΤΟC ΠΡΟC ΚΟΡΙΝΘΙΟΥC ʃA. See above p. 22.

who accompanied the letter, but a Corinthian from whom Clement was expecting a visit. In this case there is no improbability in identifying him with the Fortunatus of 1 Cor. xvi. 17; for Fortunatus seems to be mentioned by S. Paul (A. D. 57) as a younger member of the household of Stephanas, and might well be alive less than forty years after, when Clement wrote. It must be remembered however, that Fortunatus is a very common name.

6. ἐν εἰρήνῃ κ.τ.λ.] 1 Cor. xvi. 11 προπέμψατε δὲ αὐτὸν ἐν εἰρήνῃ.

7. θᾶττον] This form is doubly strange here, as it does not occur in the New Testament, and Clement uses the usual τάχιον just below. Θᾶττον however is found in *Mart. Ign.* 3, 5, *Mart. Polyc.* 13, in which latter passage θᾶττον and τάχιον occur in consecutive sentences as here.

εὐκταίαν] The word does not occur in the LXX or New Testament, though common in classical Greek.

ἐπιποθήτην] as an adjective of two terminations; comp. Barnab.

§ 1 ἡ ἐπιποθήτη ὄψις ὑμῶν (MS), where Hilgenfeld unnecessarily reads ἐπιπόθητος. The feminine does not occur in the LXX or New Testament. For similar instances of adjectives of three terminations in the New Testament see A. Buttmann p. 22 sq.; and on the whole subject refer to Lobeck *Paral.* p. 455 sq., especially p. 473 sq.

9. εὐσταθείας] '*tranquillity*': comp. Wisd. vi. 26, 2 Macc. xiv. 6. On εὐσταθεῖν see the notes to Ign. *Polyc.* 4.

11. καὶ μετὰ πάντων κ.τ.λ.] For a benediction similarly extended see 1 Cor. i. 2 σὺν πᾶσι τοῖς ἐπικαλουμένοις τὸ ὄνομα κ.τ.λ.

13. θρόνος αἰώνιος] This doxology is imitated in *Mart. Polyc.* 21 Ἰησοῦ Χριστοῦ ᾧ ἡ δόξα, τιμή, μεγαλωσύνη, θρόνος αἰώνιος, ἀπὸ γενεᾶς εἰς γενεάν. Here θρόνος αἰώνιος seems to be thrown in as an after thought, the ascription having ended with καὶ μεγαλωσύνη; and the idea of αἰώνιος is prolonged by the thrice repeated αἰώνων, αἰῶνας, αἰώνων.

THE SO CALLED

SECOND EPISTLE OF CLEMENT

TO THE

CORINTHIANS.

I.

WE have seen (pp. 22, 23) that the table of contents prefixed to the MS ascribes to Clement the Second Epistle equally with the First. On the other hand it ought to be noticed that there is no heading προc κορινθιογc β̄, as the corresponding title of the first would lead us to expect. This omission is perhaps not accidental. Though the scribe of our MS held the Second Epistle to be not only a letter of Clement, but also (as we may perhaps infer) a letter to the Corinthians; yet the absence of such a title may have been transmitted from an earlier copy, where the work was anonymous and not intended to be ascribed to this father.

While the First Epistle is universally attributed to Clement, the balance of external testimony is strongly opposed to his being regarded as the author of the Second. It is first mentioned by Eusebius, who throws serious doubts on its genuineness (*H.E.* iii. 37). After describing the First he adds, 'I should mention also that there is said to be a Second Epistle of Clement (ἰστέον δ' ὡς καὶ δευτέρα τις εἶναι λέγεται τοῦ Κλήμεντος ἐπιστολή): but we do not know that this is recognised like the former (οὐ μὴν ἔθ' ὁμοίως τῇ προτέρᾳ καὶ ταύτην γνώριμον ἐπιστάμεθα); for we do not find the older writers making any use of it (ὅτι μηδὲ καὶ τοὺς ἀρχαίους αὐτῇ κεχρημένους ἴσμεν).' Then after summarily rejecting other pretended Clementine writings, because 'they are never once mentioned by the ancients' and 'do not preserve the stamp of Apostolic orthodoxy intact', he concludes by referring again to the First Epistle, which he calls 'the acknowledged writing of Clement (ἡ τοῦ Κλήμεντος ὁμολογουμένη γραφή).' And in other passages, where he has occasion to speak of it, he uses similar expressions, '*the* Epistle of Clement', the *acknowledged* Epistle of Clement (*H. E.* iii. 16, iv. 22, 23, vi. 13). The statement of Eusebius is more than borne out by facts. Not only is a Second Epistle of Clement not mentioned by early writers; but it is a reasonable inference from the language of Hegesippus and Dionysius of Corinth[1] (as reported by Eusebius), and of Irenæus and Clement of Alexandria (as read in their extant writings), that they cannot have known or at least accepted any such epistle. Rufinus and Jerome use still more decisive language. The former professedly translates Eusebius, 'Dicitur esse et alia Clementis epistola *cujus nos notitiam non accepimus*'; the latter tacitly paraphrases him, 'Fertur et secunda ejus nomine epistola *quæ a veteribus reprobatur*' (*de Vir. Ill.* 15). These writers are not independent witnesses, but the strength, which they consciously or unconsciously add to the language of the Greek original, has at least a negative value; for they could not have so written, if any Second Epistle of Clement which might be accepted as genuine had fallen within the range of their knowledge.

Early in the 9th century Georgius Syncellus still speaks of 'the *one genuine* letter to the Corinthians' (*Chronog.* A.D. 78, I. p. 651 ed. Dind.); and later in the same century Photius (*Bibl.* 113) writes, 'The so called Second Epistle (of Clement) to the same persons (the Corinthians) is rejected as spurious (ὡς νόθος ἀποδοκιμάζεται).'

Meanwhile however this epistle had been gradually gaining recognition as a genuine work of Clement. The first distinct mention of it as such is in our MS, which belongs probably to the fifth century: but the notice of Eusebius implies that even in his day some persons were disposed to accept it. At a later period its language and teaching made it especially welcome to the Monophysites (Hilgenfeld p. xxiv),

---

[1] Hegesippus, *H. E.* iii. 16, iv. 22: Dionysius, *H. E.* iv. 23. The words of the latter are τὴν σήμερον οὖν κυριακὴν ἁγίαν ἡμέραν διηγάγομεν, ἐν ᾗ ἀνέγνωμεν ὑμῶν τὴν ἐπιστολήν, ἣν ἕξομεν ἀεί ποτε ἀναγινώσκοντες νουθετεῖσθαι, ὡς καὶ τὴν προτέραν ἡμῖν διὰ Κλήμεντος γραφεῖσαν. He is writing in the name of the Corinthians to the Romans, acknowledging a letter which they had received from the brethren in Rome written apparently by their bishop Soter; and he declares that his Church will preserve and read from time to time this second letter from the Romans, as they do the former which was written by Clement. Thus he seems to know of only one letter of Clement to the Corinthians. The passage however has been strangely misinterpreted, as though τὴν προτέραν meant *the former of Clement's two epistles* — a meaning which the context does not at all favour and which the grammar excludes, for then we should require τὴν προτέραν τῶν διὰ Κλήμεντος γραφεισῶν.

and from the close of the 5th century it is frequently quoted as genuine. Thus citations are found in SEVERUS of ANTIOCH (Cureton *Corp. Ign.* pp. 215, 246, 365) and in TIMOTHEUS of ALEXANDRIA (*ib.* pp. 212, 244) in the early part of the 6th century, besides the Syriac collections mentioned below (see the note on § 1) which perhaps belong to about the same age. To this century also may perhaps be ascribed the APOSTOLICAL CANONS, where (can. 85) 'Two Epistles of Clement' are included among the books of the New Testament (see above, p. 12). About the opening of the 7th century again it is quoted by DOROTHEUS the ARCHIMANDRITE (see the note, § 7); in the 8th century by JOANNES DAMASCENUS (see the fragments at the end of the epistle); and in the 11th by NICON of RHÆTHUS (see the notes, § 3). If NICEPHORUS († 828) in his *Stichometria* (see above, p. 13) places it with the First Epistle among the apocrypha, he does not by this classification question its genuineness but merely denies its canonicity.

But what is the external authority for considering it an *Epistle to the Corinthians*? We have seen that it is called an *Epistle* from the first; but the designation *to the Corinthians* is neither so early nor so universal. It was not so designated in our MS (so far as we know), nor by Eusebius or Jerome or Timotheus (see above, p. 22). But in SEVERUS of ANTIOCH (c. A.D. 520) for the first time a quotation is distinctly given as 'from the Second Epistle to the Corinthians' (*Corp. Ign.* pp. 215, 246, comp. p. 365). The Syriac MS itself which contains the extract from Severus (Brit. Mus. *Add. MSS* 12, 157) 'can hardly,' in Cureton's opinion (p. 355), 'have been transcribed later than the commencement of the 8th century and might have been written about the end of the 6th.' In other Syriac extracts also (*Corp. Ign.* pp. 364 sq., Cowper's *Syr. Miscell.* p. 57: see the note § 1), which perhaps belong to the 6th century, it is quoted in this way. In the copy used by Photius again (see above, p. 27) it appears to have been so entitled (*Bibl.* 126 βιβλιδάριον ἐν ᾧ Κλήμεντος ἐπιστολαὶ πρὸς Κορινθίους β΄ ἐνεφέροντο, compared with *Bibl.* 113 ἡ λεγομένη δευτέρα πρὸς τοὺς αὐτούς); and John Damascene twice cites it as 'the Second Epistle to the Corinthians' (see the fragments at the end of the epistle).

2.

Passing from external to internal evidence, we have to seek an answer to three several questions: (1) Was it written by Clement of Rome? (2) Is it an epistle? (3) Was it addressed to the Corinthians?

1. The indications of authorship contained in the writing itself do not encourage us to assign it to the same author as the First or indeed to any contemporary. (i) The writer delights to identify himself and his hearers with Gentile Christianity. He speaks of a time when he and they worshipped stocks and stones, gold and silver and bronze (§ 1). He and they are prefigured by the prophet's image of the barren woman who bore many more children than she that had the husband, *i.e.*, as he explains it, than the Jewish people 'who seem to have God' (§ 2). On the other hand the genuine Clement never uses such language. On the contrary he looks upon himself as a descendant of the patriarchs, as an heir of the glories of the Israelite race; and (what is more important) he is thoroughly imbued with the feelings of an Israelite, has an intimate knowledge of the Old Testament Scriptures (though not in the original tongue), and is even conversant with the apocryphal literature of the race and with the traditional legends and interpretations. In short his language and tone of thought proclaim him a Jew, though a Hellenist. (ii) On the difference in style I do not lay great stress; because, where there is much play for fancy, there is much room also for self-deception, and criticism is apt to become hypercritical. Yet I think it will be felt by all that the language of this Second Epistle is more Hellenic and less Judaic, though at the same time more awkward and less natural, than the First. This argument against the identity of authorship gains strength if we assume the writing to be not only the same kind of composition as the other, but also addressed to the same persons, i.e. if we suppose it to be strictly a Second Epistle to the Corinthians. (iii) The argument from the theology is perhaps a little stronger than the argument from the style, but not very strong. There is a more decided dogmatic tone in the Second Epistle than in the First. More especially the pre-existence and divinity of Christ are stated with a distinctness (§§ 1, 9) which is wanting in the First, and in a form which perhaps the writer of the First would have hesitated to adopt. (iv) The position of the writer with respect to the Scriptures is changed. In the First Epistle Clement draws his admonitions and his examples chiefly from the Old Testament. The direct references to the evangelical history are very few in comparison. On the other hand in the Second Epistle the allusions to and quotations from gospel narratives (whether canonical or apocryphal) very decidedly preponderate. This seems to indicate a somewhat later date, when gospel narratives were more generally circulated and when appeal could safely be made to a *written* Christian literature. The *form* of quotation too is more mature; 'Another

TO THE CORINTHIANS. 177

scripture[1] saith, I came not to call the righteous etc. (§ 2)'; 'The Lord *saith*, No servant can serve two masters (§ 6)'; 'The Lord *saith in the Gospel*, If ye kept not that which is small, who shall give you that which is great (§ 8)'. (v) The indications of the condition of the Church when the epistle was written have been thought to point very clearly to the time of persecution under M. Aurelius A.D. 161—180 (see Hilgenfeld *Apost. Vät.* p. 115 sq.). To myself they seem far too indefinite to settle the date even with this degree of precision. The writer urges his hearers not to cling too fondly to this life, to remember the Lord's forewarning respecting those who might kill the body but could not hurt the soul, to strive hard for the incorruptible crown, to lay aside all fear of men, all craving after earthly enjoyment (§§ 4, 5, 7, 10). Such language, I conceive, might well be used at almost any time during the first half of the second century. Again he cautions them against evil teachers (κακοδιδασκαλοῦντες), who (as we may gather from the context) dissuaded their disciples from undergoing suffering as a testimony to their faith (§ 10). This charge we know to have been brought against the Basilideans and other Gnostics (see the notes there); and to such the writer probably alludes; but even this condition would be satisfied by an earlier date, and after all the language is sufficiently vague to leave the allusion doubtful. Lastly he puts them on their guard against the heresy which denies that this flesh is judged and rises again; and, as connected therewith, urges them to 'keep the flesh pure and the seal (of baptism) undefiled', to 'guard the flesh as a temple of God' (§§ 8, 9). Here the writer seems certainly to be denouncing Gnostic immorality as the consequence of Gnostic error; but the Pastoral Epistles and the Apocalypse show that even in its earliest stages the same speculative opinions of Gnosticism tended to produce the same practical evils. But, though some of the arguments adduced will appear too weak to support any hypothesis, yet in the aggregate they create a strong presumption that the epistle was written at least a generation later than Clement.

2. I have hitherto spoken of this writing as an epistle, because our authorities so call it. But is this its proper description? If we examine it throughout, we find nothing which would lead to this inference. It is not addressed to any one and contains no personal allusion of any kind. This argument would have had much more force, if the end had

[1] Too much stress however must not be laid on the fact that a gospel is quoted as γραφή. It is now placed beyond any reasonable doubt that this mode of quotation occurs in the very early epistle ascribed to Barnabas § 4; and this is possibly the correct interpretation of 1 Tim. v. 18 also (see the note on § 2).

not been wanting; but still it is a sufficient starting point for the opinion of Grabe and others, that we have here not a letter but a fragment of a treatise or a homily. The inference however is not safe, for the same might have been inferred of the Epistle to the Hebrews, if its conclusion had been mutilated in the same way. Only one thing seems clear that, if in any sense an epistle, it was written in the name not of a church, like the First Epistle of Clement, but of the individual writer; for he throughout addresses his hearers as 'my brethren' (ἀδελφοί μου, §§ 7, 10). Of the bearing of this fact I shall have to speak presently.

3. Was it written to the Corinthians? With one exception the language is colourless in this respect and might have been addressed to any church. But the exceptional passage strikingly confirms the traditional view. Like S. Paul writing to these same Corinthians, the author refers at length to the athletic games of the Greeks (§ 7). This fact is not very important in itself, as he obviously has the passage of S. Paul in his mind. Nor can much stress be laid on the circumstance that he is apparently well acquainted with the rules of such contests. But there is one piece of local colouring which seems to point especially to Corinth and to the Isthmian games: he speaks of 'crowds who land' (καταπλέουσιν πολλοί) to take part in such contests, using such language as a writer or a preacher would naturally use, who counted on hearers able to appreciate his allusion.

The conclusions therefore at which we seem to have arrived from an investigation of the internal evidence are these; (1) That it was not written by Clement or in Clement's age; (2) That it bears no traces of the epistolary form, though it may possibly have been a letter; (3) That on the whole it appears to have been addressed to the Corinthian Church.

3.

In the light of this evidence, external and internal, we may pronounce judgment on the opinions which modern critics have entertained respecting the authorship of the epistle.

1. Cotelier, Bull, Galland, Lumper, and many others, have contended that it is what tradition declares it to be—an Epistle from Clement to the Corinthians. They have differed only about the time when it was written, Cotelier placing it before the First Epistle, while most writers have dated it after. As no allusion is made to dissensions (and it may be inferred from the silence of Photius, *Bibl.* 126, that the lost

ending was equally without any such reference), it cannot have been written about the same time with the First, nor after it (as Cotelier thinks). Indeed, if the date assigned above (p. 4) to the First Epistle be correct, and if Clement died at the time when he is reputed to have died (A.D. 95 or 100), the interval is hardly long enough for the feuds to have passed out of mind. Yet the objections above stated (pp. 176, 177) are considerably enhanced, if we assign an earlier date to it than to the First. Thus the difficulty of finding a time for it is an additional argument against its genuineness. And generally it may be said that, if the internal or the external evidence alone were insufficient to condemn it, yet the combination of the two must be considered fatal.

Recently the defence of the Clementine authorship has assumed a new form. Hagemann (*Ueber den 2ten Brief des Clemens* etc. in the *Theolog. Quartalschr.* XLIII. p. 509 sq. 1861) supposes it to have been a letter of Clement sent to accompany the Shepherd of Hermas. He refers to the direction given by the angelic messenger to Hermas (*Vis.* ii. 4) that Clement shall circulate his book among foreign cities, and he postulates an accompanying letter of recommendation written by Clement. This however is a mere assumption. Moreover our epistle bears no traces of this purpose, and Photius (who had it unmutilated) evidently did not discern any such object. Hagemann again points to a few coincidences between our epistle and the Shepherd, but these are far less striking than might be expected under the supposed circumstances, and indeed are not closer than may often be found between early Christian documents written about the same time. Thus, except its ingenuity, this hypothesis has nothing to recommend it; and we should do better to fall back on the traditional view and regard the epistle as addressed to the Church of Corinth, for its Corinthian destination is somewhat favoured (as we have seen) by internal evidence.

2. Grabe (*Spicil. Patr.* I. pp. 268, 30c) supposes it to be a fragment of a homily forged in Clement's name; and points to a passage in Anastasius *Quæst.* 96 (p. 526 ed. Gretser), who quotes from 'the sacred and apostolic doctor Clement in his first discourse (λόγῳ) concerning providence and righteous judgment', as showing that such homilies existed. But against this view several objections may be urged. (1) The quotation in Anastasius is taken not from Clement of Rome, but from Clement of Alexandria, as Hagemann has shown (l. c. p. 514 sq.); and therefore the ground for assuming the existence of such homilies is cut away. (2) The writing bears no traces of forgery. The author does

indeed appear to have read Clement and to have borrowed from him (see the notes on §§ 3, 11), but there is no attempt at impersonation: so that its ascription to this early Roman bishop would seem to be the error of a later age. (3) Lastly, this theory fails to account for its being called an epistle to *the Corinthians*. It should be added also that in ascribing this writing to the middle of the third century after the time of Origen (l. c. p. 269) Grabe has shown a disregard of its characteristic features (see the next paragraph), which require us to assign to it a date not later, or not much later, than the middle of the second century.

3. Dodwell (*Dissert. in Iren.* i. § xxix. p. 53) professed to see in this epistle a resemblance to the style of Clement of Alexandria in the fragments of the *Hypotyposeis*, and suggested that the two Clements had been confused. This suggestion is thrown out casually among other speculations, and it is not clear what weight its author attached to it, or what inference he intended to draw. At all events the opinion has found no favour, and may be briefly dismissed. Few will be able to trace this resemblance of style; and the quotations from the evangelical history bear testimony to an earlier period, when the four canonical Gospels had not yet established that exclusive authority which they have in the age of the younger Clement. In our epistle the Gospel of the Egyptians is a main source of quotation (see § 11), and is employed in a manner quite foreign to Clement of Alexandria who, though acquainted with this apocryphal book and even quoting from it (though perhaps only at second hand), yet recognises only the four canonical Gospels as authoritative.

4. Hilgenfeld (*Proleg.* p. xxxviii sq.) has recently propounded the view, to which casual suggestions of previous writers seemed to lead up, that this is the letter written by the Church of Rome to the Church of Corinth during the episcopate of Soter. Addressing the Romans in reply to this letter Dionysius of Corinth, as quoted by Eusebius (*H. E.* iv. 23; see above, p. 174 note), says that on the day on which he writes, being the Lord's day, the Corinthian brethren had read the Roman letter publicly, and would continue to do so from time to time, as also their former epistle sent through Clement. This hypothesis therefore has two very strong recommendations. (1) It accounts for the fact that our epistle is found appended to a MS of the New Testament, as being read from time to time in the public services of the Church. (2) An explanation is thus suggested how Clement's name came to be attached to it: for it thus became the second of two letters from the Church of Rome to the Church of Corinth; and,

TO THE CORINTHIANS. 181

as Clement was the acknowledged author of the first, so not unnaturally his name would be extended to the second. On the other hand this theory seems to me to be open to one fatal objection. Dionysius speaks distinctly of a letter not from the Roman bishop, but from the Roman church. He does not even mention Soter's name in connexion with the letter (though he had spoken of him just before), but uses the plural in describing its authorship, ὑμῶν τὴν ἐπιστολήν. On the other hand our fragment, whether it be regarded as part of a letter or of a homily, professes to come from *one* person. The writer more than once addresses his hearers as '*my* brethren' (§§ 7, 10), and it contains no indication that others were associated with him in the writing. It therefore fails to satisfy the primary test which alone the very brief fragment of Dionysius enables us to apply.

5. Lastly, Wocher (*der Brief des Clemens* etc. p. 204) suggested that the author is Dionysius of Corinth. This suggestion has the advantage of connecting our epistle with Clement's genuine letter (though not very directly), and it moreover accounts for the local colouring which has been noticed above, p. 178. Beyond this, it has nothing to recommend it. Eusebius was well acquainted with the letters of Dionysius; and there is a presumption that he would in this case have known or detected the authorship of this epistle.

As all theories fail us, we must be content to accept this as an anonymous writing; but it will remain nevertheless an important monument of Christian antiquity, as dating probably before or about the middle of the second century. In the notes on § 12 I have pointed out an indication that it may have emanated from Egypt.

The theological position of the writer has been much canvassed, and some difference of opinion exists. Schwegler (*Nachap. Zeit.* 1. p. 448 sq.) characteristically maintains that the work was written towards the end of the second century by a Roman Ebionite, whose aim it was to reconcile the older and more rigorous Ebionism with the now rapidly developing Catholic doctrine. He assumes it as a recognised fact that the mode of thought in this epistle is Ebionite (p. 450). Yet notwithstanding this boldness of assertion, it is difficult to see how even a *prima facie* case can be made out from such a perverse view. The writer's avowed position as a Gentile Christian, his uncompromising attack upon the Jews, his lofty conception of the person of Christ, his constant reference to the teaching of our Lord and total silence about the Mosaic ordinances, his habit of appealing to the Prophets and not to the Law, all give a direct negative to this theory. On the other hand, if the writer protests against the defects of Ebionism, he is equally severe on the errors of Gnosticism. And this double-edged antagonism points to his true position. He belongs to Catholic Christianity, which is equidistant from the one and the other. Yet the *form* of his teaching differs widely from the definite and systematic type of the post-Nicene age, when the opposition to Arian and Apollinarian heresies had led to a more precise statement of Catholic doctrine, and even falls short of the comparative distinctness which characterises the writers of the third century, when the prevalence of Monarchian and Sabellian views had produced the same effect in a smaller degree. Our Second Epistle is clearly Catholic: but Catholic doctrine is still held in solution; it has not yet coalesced into dogma. At the same time, though Catholic, the teaching is not markedly Pauline in type; for though the writer is obviously acquainted with S. Paul's Epistles and imitates them (e.g. §§ 2, 7), yet he never adopts the modes of stating Christian doctrine which are characteristic of the Apostle. This is substantially the view maintained by Ritschl (*Entst. d. Altkath. Kirche* p. 286 sq.), Hilgenfeld (*Apost. Vät.* p. 118 sq.), and others. The remarks of the first mentioned, which still further define the writer's position, may be read as a supplement to what is said here.

4.

The following is an analysis of the fragment:

'My brethren, we must look on Christ as God. We must not think mean things of Him who has been so merciful to us, who has given us life and all things (§ 1). In *us* is fulfilled the saying that the barren woman hath many children. The Gentile Church was once unfruitful, but now has a numerous offspring. *We* are those sinners whom Christ came especially to save (§ 2). Therefore we owe all recompense to Him. And the return which he asks is that we should confess Him in our *deeds*. The worship, not of the lips only, but of the heart, must be yielded to Him (§ 3). He has denounced those who, while they obey Him not, yet call Him Lord. He has declared that, though they be gathered into His bosom, He will reject them (§ 4). Let us therefore remember that we are sojourners here, and let us not fear to quit this world. Rather let us call to mind His warning, and fear not those who kill the body but Him who can destroy body and soul together. All things earthly we must hold foreign to us (§ 5). On this there must be no wavering. We cannot serve two masters. This world and the other are deadly foes. It must be our choice to do Christ's will. Even Noah, Job, and Daniel could not have rescued their own children from destruction. How shall we then, if we keep not the baptismal seal intact, present ourselves in God's kingdom? (§ 6) The lists are open; the struggle approaches. Let us crowd thither to take our part. Let us fight to win the immortal chaplet. But, so doing, we must observe the laws of the contest, if we would escape chastisement. A horrible fate awaits those who break the seal (§ 7). Now is the time for repentance. Now we can be moulded like clay in the hands of the potter. After death it will be too late. If we keep not small things, how shall we be trusted with great? If we guard not the seal intact, how shall we inherit eternal life? (§ 8).'

'Deny not, that men shall rise in their bodies. As Christ came in the flesh, so also shall we be judged in the flesh. Let us give ourselves to God betimes. He reads our very inmost thoughts. To those who do His will Christ has given the name of brothers (§ 9). This will let us ever obey. If we fear men and choose present comfort, we shall purchase brief pleasure at the price of eternal joy. They who lead others astray herein are doubly guilty (§ 10). We must not falter. The prophetic word denounces the double-minded; it foretels how the course of things is maturing to its consummation, as the vine grows and ripens. God is faithful; and, as He has promised, so will He give joys unspeakable to the righteous (§ 11). The signs, which shall herald the approach of His kingdom, Christ has foretold. *The two shall be one* in universal peace. *The outside shall be as the inside* in strict sincerity. *The male shall be as the female* in'.........

'Be not dismayed at seeing the rich prosperous and the faithful straitened. If our reward were immediate, piety would be changed into merchandise'......

'Things are not what they seem. Our fondest desires, when granted, often bring grievous calamity'......

5.

Information respecting the single MS which contains this epistle has been given already, p. 22 sq.

6.

An account of the *literature* will be found in the introduction to the First Epistle p. 27 sq. To the list of works there given should be added (as referring to this epistle alone):

1861 *Ueber den zweiten Brief des Clemens von Rom;* HAGEMANN. in the *Theologische Quartalschrift* (XLIII. Hft. 4. p. 509 sq.).

[ΠΡΟC ΚΟΡΙΝΘΙΟΥC Β.]

I. Ἀδελφοί, οὕτως δεῖ ἡμᾶς φρονεῖν περὶ Ἰησοῦ

[προc κορινθιογc B.] The authorities for this title will be found on p. 175. For the designation of this epistle in the MS, where it has no heading, see pp. 22, 23, 173.

1. 'My brethren, we must think of Christ as God, as judge of all men. It is no light crime to have mean views of Him by whom we were called and who suffered for us. What worthy recompense can we pay to Him, who has given us light and life, who has rescued us from the worship of stocks and stones, has scattered the dark cloud that hung over us, has brought back our straying footsteps, and thus has called us into being?'

1. Ἀδελφοί κ.τ.λ.] The opening of the epistle, as far as παθεῖν ἕνεκα ἡμῶν, is quoted by Severus of Antioch (c. A.D. 515) and by Timotheus of Alexandria († A.D. 535) in extracts preserved in a Syriac translation. By Severus it is given as 'from the Second Epistle to the Corinthians' (Cureton's *Corp. Ign.* pp. 215, 246); by Timotheus as 'from the beginning of the Third Epistle' (*Corp. Ign.* pp. 212, 244) immediately after a quotation 'from the First Epistle on Virginity' (see above pp. 17, 22). Of the Syriac MSS containing these extracts, the former may date from the 6th to the 8th century (*Corp. Ign.* p. 355), and the latter was written not later than A.D. 562 (*ib.* p. 353). Moreover the opening words Ἀδελφοί...νεκρῶν are found in several Syriac extracts, of which one is given by Cureton (*Corp. Ign.* p. 365) and another by Cowper (*Syriac Miscell.* p. 57). Of these Dr Wright of the British Museum sends me the following account:

'There are in the Syriac collection several large volumes ranging from the 7th or 8th cent. to the 10th, and entitled ܟܬܒܐ ܕܬܚܘܝܬܐ or *Books of Demonstrations*, i.e. extracts from the Fathers to be used in combating various heresies. They are all Monophysite compilations. The extract occurs in several of these volumes. I send the text copied from *Add.* 17, 214, fol. 77 a, which MS seems to be of the 7th century'.

ܡܢ ܐܓܪܬܐ ܕܬܪܬܝܢ ܕܠܘܬ
ܩܘܪܢܬܝܐ܂ ܡܢ ܗܘ ܕܐܝܬܘ̈ܗܝ
ܐܚܝ̈܂ ܗܟܢܐ ܘܠܐ ܠܢ
ܕܢܬܪܥܐ ܥܠ ܝܫܘܥ ܡܫܝܚܐ܂
ܐܝܟ ܕܥܠ ܐܠܗܐ܂

Χριστοῦ, ὡς περὶ Θεοῦ, ὡς περὶ κριτοῦ ζώντων καὶ νεκρῶν. καὶ οὐ δεῖ ἡμᾶς μικρὰ φρονεῖν περὶ τῆς σωτηρίας ἡμῶν· ἐν τῷ γὰρ φρονεῖν ἡμᾶς μικρὰ περὶ αὐτοῦ, μικρὰ καὶ ἐλπίζομεν λαβεῖν. Καὶ †οἱ† ἀκούοντες ὡς περὶ μικρῶν ἁμαρτάνομεν, οὐκ εἰδότες πόθεν ἐκλήθημεν 5

4 ὡς περί] Sever., Timoth.; see below. ὥσπερ A.

[Syriac text]

After this follows a passage from § 9 καὶ μὴ λεγέτω...τὸν μισθόν.

[Syriac text]

'For ܥܠܝܢ Cowper reads ܥܠܝܢ, *ye live*, which I find in another MS of the 8th cent., but a 3rd later MS has also ܥܠܝܢ, *ye see*. Again Cowper's MS has ܠܢ ܩܪܐ, *called us*; the other two ܩܪܟܘܢ, *called you*.'

Photius (*Bibl*. 126) remarks on the opening of this epistle, contrasting it with the First as respects its Christology, ἡ δὲ δευτέρα καὶ αὐτὴ νουθεσίαν καὶ παραίνεσιν κρείττονος εἰσάγει βίου καὶ ἐν ἀρχῇ Θεὸν τὸν Χριστὸν κηρύσσει: see the notes on §§ 2, 36, 57 of the First Epistle.

1. κριτοῦ κ.τ.λ.] The expression occurs in Acts x. 42 (in a speech of S. Peter): comp. 2 Tim. iv. 1, 1 Pet. iv. 5. See also Barnab. § 7, Polyc. *Phil*. 2.

2. μικρὰ φρονεῖν] '*to have mean views*.' The Ebionites, whom the writer of this epistle attacks, were said to have earned the title of 'poor' by their mean and beggarly conception of the Person of Christ; see esp. Origen *de Princ*. iv. 22 (I. p. 183) οἱ πτωχοὶ τῇ διανοίᾳ Ἐβιωναῖοι τῆς πτωχείας τῆς διανοίας ἐπώνυμοι, ἐβιὼν [אביון] γὰρ ὁ πτωχὸς παρὰ Ἑβραίοις ὀνομάζεται, *c. Cels*. ii. 1 (I. p. 385), *in Matth*. t. xvi. § 12 (III. p. 734) τῷ Ἐβιωναίῳ καὶ πτωχεύοντι περὶ τὴν εἰς Ἰησοῦν πίστιν, and again *in Gen. iii Hom*. § 5 (II. p. 68); Euseb. *H. E*. iii. 27 Ἐβιωναίους τούτους οἰκείως ἐπεφήμιζον οἱ πρῶτοι πτωχῶς καὶ ταπεινῶς

καὶ ὑπὸ τίνος καὶ εἰς ὃν τόπον, καὶ ὅσα ὑπέμεινεν
Ἰησοῦς Χριστὸς παθεῖν ἕνεκα ἡμῶν. τίνα οὖν ἡμεῖς
αὐτῷ δώσομεν ἀντιμισθίαν; ἢ τίνα καρπὸν ἄξιον οὗ
ἡμῖν αὐτὸς ἔδωκεν; πόσα δὲ αὐτῷ ὀφείλομεν ὅσια; τὸ
10 φῶς γὰρ ἡμῖν ἐχαρίσατο, ὡς πατὴρ υἱοὺς ἡμᾶς προση-

9 ὀφείλομεν] οφιλομεν A.

τὰ περὶ τοῦ Χριστοῦ δοξάζοντας, *Eccl.*
Theol. i. 14 οἱ πρωτοκήρυκες Ἐβιωναίους
ὠνόμαζον Ἐβραϊκῇ φωνῇ πτωχοὺς τὴν
διάνοιαν ἀποκαλοῦντες τοὺς ἕνα μὲν Θεὸν
λέγοντας εἰδέναι καὶ τοῦ σωτῆρος τὸ
σῶμα μὴ ἀρνουμένους τὴν δὲ τοῦ υἱοῦ
θεότητα μὴ εἰδότας, with other passages collected in Schliemann *Clement.* p. 471 sq. Origen's language perhaps does not necessarily imply that he gives this as a serious account of the term, but only that they were fitly called 'poor'. Eusebius however, mistaking his drift, supposes this name to have been a term of reproach imposed upon these heretics by the orthodox; instead of being, as doubtless it was and as perhaps Origen knew it to be, self-assumed in allusion to their voluntary poverty. The idea of a heresiarch named Ebion, which is found first in Tertullian (*de Præscr.* 33, and elsewhere), is now generally allowed to be a mistake.

4. † οἱ † ἀκούοντες] '*we who hear*'. For the article compare Clem. Rom. § 6 αἱ ἀσθενεῖς τῷ σώματι; but the expression is awkward and misplaced. Young suggested καίτοι which others have adopted, but this is not the particle required. The Syriac quotations of Timotheus and Severus have ܘܟܕ ܡܢ '*and when we hear*', as though the article were absent from their text; but, allowance being made for the license of translation, no stress can be laid on

this fact. Photius (*Bibl.* 126) remarks on the looseness and inconsequence of expression in this Second Epistle (or rather in the two epistles, but he must be referring especially to the Second), τὰ ἐν αὐταῖς νοήματα ἐρριμμένα πως καὶ οὐ συνεχῆ τὴν ἀκολουθίαν ὑπῆρχε φυλάττοντα. Several instances of this will be noted below; and this passage, if the text be correct, furnishes another illustration.

8. ἀντιμισθίαν] The word occurs Rom. i. 27, 2 Cor. vi. 13, Theoph. *ad Autol.* ii. 9. Though apparently not common, it is a favourite word with our author; see just below and §§ 9, 11. The sentiment is taken from Ps. cxvi. 12 τί ἀνταποδώσω τῷ Κυρίῳ κ.τ.λ.

9. ὅσια] '*mercies, kindnesses*', as it is used in the LXX Is. lv. 3 (quoted in Acts xiii. 34 δώσω ὑμῖν τὰ ὅσια Δαυεὶδ τὰ πιστά) for חסדים: see Wolf *Cur. Philol.* p. 1197. In a parallel passage 2 Chron. vi. 42 the LXX has τὰ ἐλέη. In this case ὀφείλομεν will have a pregnant sense, '*we have received and should repay*'. Perhaps however it is simpler to take ὅσια as '*religious duties*' (e.g. Eur. *Suppl.* 368 ὅσια περὶ θεούς). The distinction between ὅσια 'what is due to God' and δίκαια 'what is due to men' is as old as Plato (*Gorg.* p. 507 B) and runs through Greek literature: comp. Trench *N. T. Syn.* 2nd ser. § xxxviii, and Steph. *Thes.* s. vv. δίκαιος and ὅσιος. See also below, §§ 5, 6.

10. ὡς πατὴρ κ.τ.λ.] The refer-

γόρευσεν, ἀπολλυμένους ἡμᾶς ἔσωσεν. ποῖον οὖν αἶνον αὐτῷ δώσωμεν ἢ μισθὸν ἀντιμισθίας ὧν ἐλάβομεν; πηροὶ ὄντες τῇ διανοίᾳ, προσκυνοῦντες λίθους καὶ ξύλα καὶ χρυσὸν καὶ ἄργυρον καὶ χαλκόν, ἔργα ἀνθρώπων· καὶ ὁ βίος ἡμῶν ὅλος ἄλλο οὐδὲν ἦν εἰ μὴ θάνατος. ἀμαύρω- 5 σιν οὖν περικείμενοι καὶ τοιαύτης ἀχλύος γέμοντες ἐν τῇ ὁράσει, ἀνεβλέψαμεν ἀποθέμενοι ἐκεῖνο ὃ περικείμεθα νέφος τῇ αὐτοῦ θελήσει. ἠλέησεν γὰρ ἡμᾶς καὶ σπλαγχνισθεὶς ἔσωσεν, θεασάμενος ἐν ἡμῖν πολλὴν πλάνην καὶ ἀπώλειαν, καὶ μηδεμίαν ἐλπίδα ἔχοντας 10 σωτηρίας, εἰ μὴ τὴν παρ' αὐτοῦ. ἐκάλεσεν γὰρ ἡμᾶς

1 ποῖον οὖν] ποιουν Α.   10 ἐλπίδα ἔχοντας] ελπιδανεχοντεσ Α.

ence is perhaps to Hosea ii. 1 καὶ ἔσται ἐν τῷ τόπῳ οὗ ἐρρέθη αὐτοῖς Οὐ λαός μου ὑμεῖς, ἐκεῖ κληθήσονται υἱοὶ Θεοῦ ζῶντος, more especially as applied by S. Paul Rom. ix. 26. See also the quotation in 2 Cor. vi. 18 καὶ ἔσομαι ὑμῖν εἰς πατέρα καὶ ὑμεῖς ἔσεσθέ μοι εἰς υἱοὺς καὶ θυγατέρας (a combination of 2 Sam. vii. 14 and Is. xliii. 6), and 1 Joh. iii. 1 ἴδετε ποταπὴν ἀγάπην δέδωκεν ἡμῖν ὁ πατὴρ ἵνα τέκνα Θεοῦ κληθῶμεν.

2. δώσωμεν] 'can we give?' The editors tacitly read δώσομεν, though the MS has δωσωμεν, and a conjunctive is more forcible: comp. e.g. Matt. xxiii. 33 πῶς φύγητε, xxvi. 54 πῶς οὖν πληρωθῶσιν αἱ γραφαί; and see Winer § xli. p. 301.

πηροὶ ὄντες κ.τ.λ.] Arist. *Eth. Nic.* i. 10 τοῖς μὴ πεπηρωμένοις πρὸς ἀρετήν, Ptolemæus *ad Flor.* (in Epiphan. *Hær.* xxxiii. 3 p. 217) μὴ μόνον τὸ τῆς ψυχῆς ὄμμα ἀλλὰ καὶ τὸ τοῦ σώματος πεπηρωμένων. In the New Testament πηροῦν, πήρωσις, occur occasionally as various readings for πωροῦν, πώρωσις, but are not well supported: see Fritzsche *Rom.* II. p. 451 sq.

3. προσκυνοῦντες κ.τ.λ.] The writer of this epistle therefore is plainly a Gentile Christian: comp. § 2 ἡ ἐκκλησία ἡμῶν, and the introduction p. 176.

4. ὁ βίος] Their βίος was not ζωὴ but θάνατος: see the note on Ign. *Rom.* 7. Comp. 1 Tim. v. 6 ζῶσα τέθνηκεν.

7. ἀνεβλέψαμεν] Comp. § 9.

ἀποθέμενοι κ. τ. λ.] The language here, though not the thought, is coloured by Heb. xii. 1 τοσοῦτον ἔχοντες περικείμενον ἡμῖν νέφος μαρτύρων, ὄγκον ἀποθέμενοι πάντα κ.τ.λ. For the construction περικεῖσθαί τι 'to be enveloped in or surrounded by a thing,' see Acts xxviii. 20, Heb. v. 2.

10. ἔχοντας] sc. ἡμᾶς. If this reading be correct it is perhaps governed by θεασάμενος rather than by ἔσωσε, 'and this though we had no hope'. But ἔχοντες may be the right reading after all: in which case a word or words may have fallen out from the text; or this may be one of the awkward expressions to which allusion has been already made (on οἱ ἀκούοντες).

TO THE CORINTHIANS.

οὐκ ὄντας καὶ ἠθέλησεν ἐκ μὴ ὄντος εἶναι ἡμᾶς.
II. Εγφράνθητι, cτεῖρα ἡ ογ τίκτογcα· ῥῆξον καὶ
βόηcον, ἡ ογκ ὠδίνογcα, ὅτι πολλὰ τὰ τέκνα τῆc ἐρήμογ
15 μᾶλλον ἢ τῆc ἐχογcηc τὸν ἄνδρα. "Ο εἶπεν εὐφράνθητι
cτεῖρα ἡ ογ τίκτογcα, ἡμᾶς εἶπεν· στεῖρα γὰρ ἦν ἡ
ἐκκλησία ἡμῶν πρὸ τοῦ δοθῆναι αὐτῇ τέκνα. ὁ δὲ εἶπεν
βόηcον ἡ ογκ ὠδίνογcα, τοῦτο λέγει· τὰς προσευχὰς
ἡμῶν ἁπλῶς ἀναφέρειν πρὸς τὸν Θεὸν μή, ὡς αἱ
20 ὠδίνουσαι, ἐγκακῶμεν. ὃ δὲ εἶπεν ὅτι πολλὰ τὰ τέκνα
τῆc ἐρήμογ μᾶλλον ἢ τῆc ἐχογcηc τὸν ἄνδρα, ἐπεὶ ἔρημος
ἐδόκει εἶναι ἀπὸ τοῦ Θεοῦ ὁ λαὸς ἡμῶν, νυνὶ δὲ πισ-
τεύσαντες πλείονες ἐγενόμεθα τῶν δοκούντων ἔχειν

11. ἐκάλεσεν γὰρ κ.τ.λ.] Rom. iv. 17 καλοῦντος τὰ μὴ ὄντα ὡς ὄντα, Philo de Creat. Princ. 7 (II. p. 367) τὰ γὰρ μὴ ὄντα ἐκάλεσεν εἰς τὸ εἶναι: comp. Hermas Vis. I. 1 κτίσας ἐκ τοῦ μὴ ὄντος τὰ ὄντα, Mand. 1 ποιήσας ἐκ τοῦ μὴ ὄντος εἰς τὸ εἶναι τὰ πάντα, Clem. Hom. iii. 32 τῷ τὰ μὴ ὄντα εἰς τὸ εἶναι συστησαμένῳ.

II. 'For what is the meaning of the scripture, *Rejoice thou barren that bearest not?* It has been fulfilled in us—the Gentile Church, which is even now more numerous than the Jewish. In like manner also it is written elsewhere, *I came not to call just men but sinners.* Such sinners were we.'

13. εὐφράνθητι κ.τ.λ.] From the LXX Is. liv. 1, word for word. See the notes on *Galatians* iv. 27. The same application is also made in Justin *Apol.* i. 53 p. 88 c. Philo also allegorizes this text (*quod Omn. Prob. lib.* 2, II. p. 449), but in a wholly different way.

16. ἡ ἐκκλησία ἡμῶν] i.e. the Gentile Church, called ὁ λαὸς ἡμῶν below. Our author's application seems so far to differ from S. Paul's, that he makes the contrast between Gentile and Judaic Christendom, whereas in the Apostle it is between the new and the old dispensation. Justin uses the text in the same way as our Pseudo-Clement.

19. μὴ ὡς κ.τ.λ.] If the order of the words be correct they can only mean 'let us not grow weary, as women in travail grow weary'; but it is strange that the writer should have confused his application of the text by this fanciful account of ἡ οὐκ ὠδίνουσα, of which the natural explanation is so obvious. For ἐγκακῶμεν Cotelier and other editors would substitute ἐκκακῶμεν: but this is a mistake, as authority is against ἐκκακεῖν and for ἐγκακεῖν: see the note on *Galatians* vi. 9.

22. ἀπὸ τοῦ Θεοῦ] For the preposition after ἔρημος comp. Jer. xxxiii (xl). 10 (ἀπὸ ἀνθρώπων καὶ κτηνῶν), xxxiv (xli). 22 (ἀπὸ τῶν κατοικούντων), xliv (li). 2 (ἀπὸ ἐνοίκων). The word involves a secondary idea of *severance*, and so takes ἀπό.

23. πλείονες] Writing about this

Θεόν. καὶ ἑτέρα δὲ γραφὴ λέγει ὅτι Ογκ Ἦλθον κα-
λέcαι Δικαίογc, ἀλλὰ ἁμαρτωλούc. τοῦτο λέγει, ὅτι δεῖ
τοὺς ἀπολλυμένους σώζειν· ἐκεῖνο γάρ ἐστιν μέγα καὶ
θαυμαστόν, οὐ τὰ ἑστῶτα στηρίζειν ἀλλὰ τὰ πίπ-
τοντα. οὕτως καὶ ὁ Χριστὸς ἠθέλησεν σῶσαι τὰ 5
ἀπολλύμενα, καὶ ἔσωσεν πολλούς, ἐλθὼν καὶ καλέσας
ἡμᾶς ἤδη ἀπολλυμένους.

III. Τοσοῦτον οὖν ἔλεος ποιήσαντος αὐτοῦ εἰς
ἡμᾶς· πρῶτον μέν, ὅτι ἡμεῖς οἱ ζῶντες τοῖς νεκροῖς
θεοῖς οὐ θύομεν καὶ οὐ προσκυνοῦμεν αὐτοῖς, ἀλλὰ 10
ἔγνωμεν δι' αὐτοῦ τὸν πατέρα τῆς ἀληθείας· τίς ἡ
γνῶσις ἡ πρὸς αὐτόν, ἢ τὸ μὴ ἀρνεῖσθαι δι' οὗ ἔγνωμεν
αὐτόν; λέγει δὲ καὶ αὐτός· Τὸν ὁμολογήcαντά με ἐνώ-

8 ἔλεος] ελαιοσ Α.   12 γνῶσις] γνωσεισ Α.

same time, Justin Martyr gives a similar account of the greater numbers of the Gentile Christians: *Apol.* i. 53 (p. 88 B) πλείονάς τε καὶ ἀληθεστέρους τοὺς ἐξ ἐθνῶν τῶν ἀπὸ Ἰουδαίων καὶ Σαμαρέων Χριστιανοὺς εἰδότες.

τῶν δοκούντων ἔχειν Θεόν] Hilgenfeld quotes from the *Prædicatio Petri* in Clem. Alex. *Strom.* vi. 5 (p. 760) μηδὲ κατὰ Ἰουδαίους σέβεσθε· καὶ γὰρ ἐκεῖνοι, μόνοι οἰόμενοι τὸν Θεὸν γινώσκειν, οὐκ ἐπίστανται (comp. Orig. *in Joann.* xiii. § 17, IV. p. 226).

1. ἑτέρα δὲ γραφή] Thus the Gospel, treated as a written document, is regarded as Scripture like the Old Testament. Comp. Barnab. § 4, and possibly 1 Tim. v. 18. See above, the introduction p. 177.

οὐκ ἦλθον κ.τ.λ.] The quotation agrees exactly with S. Mark ii. 17, but might also be taken from S. Matthew ix. 13 οὐ γὰρ ἦλθον κ.τ.λ. On the other hand in S. Luke (v. 32) the form is different, οὐκ ἐλήλυθα κα-

λέσαι δικαίους ἀλλὰ ἁμαρτωλοὺς εἰς μετάνοιαν. Comp. also Barnab. § 5 οὐκ ἦλθεν καλέσαι δικαίους ἀλλὰ ἁμαρτωλούς (where the words εἰς μετάνοιαν, added in the late MSS, are wanting in ℵ), and Justin *Apol.* i. p. 62 C οὐκ ἦλθον κ. δ. ἀ. ἀμ. εἰς μετάνοιαν.

5. σῶσαι κ.τ.λ.] Luke xix. 10 ἦλθεν ὁ υἱὸς τοῦ ἀνθρώπου ζητῆσαι καὶ σῶσαι τὸ ἀπολωλός (compare the interpolation in Matt. xviii. 11), 1 Tim. i. 15 Ἰ. Χ. ἦλθεν εἰς τὸν κόσμον ἁμαρτωλοὺς σῶσαι.

III. 'Seeing then that He has been so merciful and has brought us to know God, wherein does this knowledge consist but in not denying Him by whom we were brought? If we confess Him, He will confess us before the Father. This we must do, not with lips only but in our lives.'

9. τοῖς νεκροῖς θεοῖς] Wisd. xv. 17 θνητὸς δὲ ὢν νεκρὸν ἐργάζεται χερσὶν ἀνόμοις· κρείττων γάρ ἐστι τῶν σεβασμάτων αὐτοῦ, ὧν αὐτὸς μὲν ἔζησεν ἐκεῖνα δὲ οὐδέποτε.

πιον τῶν ἀνθρώπων, ὁμολογήϲω αὐτὸν ἐνώπιον τοῦ πατρόϲ
15 μογ. Οὗτος οὖν ἐστὶν ὁ μισθὸς ἡμῶν, ἐὰν οὖν ὁμο-
λογήσωμεν δι' οὗ ἐσώθημεν. ἐν τίνι δὲ αὐτὸν ὁμολο-
γοῦμεν; ἐν τῷ ποιεῖν ἃ λέγει καὶ μὴ παρακούειν αὐτοῦ
τῶν ἐντολῶν, καὶ μὴ μόνον χείλεϲιν αὐτὸν τιμᾶν ἀλλὰ
ἐξ ὅληϲ καρδίαϲ καὶ ἐξ ὅληϲ τῆϲ διανοίαϲ. λέγει δὲ καὶ
20 ἐν τῷ Ἡσαΐᾳ· Ὁ λαὸϲ οὗτοϲ τοῖϲ χείλεϲίν με τιμᾷ, ἡ δὲ
καρδία αὐτῶν πόρρω ἄπεϲτιν ἀπ' ἐμοῦ.
IV. Μὴ μόνον οὖν αὐτὸν καλῶμεν Κύριον, οὐ
γὰρ τοῦτο σώσει ἡμᾶς. λέγει γάρ· Οὐ πᾶϲ ὁ λέγων
μοι, Κύριε, Κύριε, ϲωθήϲεται, ἀλλ' ὁ ποιῶν τὴν δικαιοϲύνην.
25 ὥστε οὖν, ἀδελφοί, ἐν τοῖς ἔργοις αὐτὸν ὁμολογῶμεν,
ἐν τῷ ἀγαπᾶν ἑαυτούς, ἐν τῷ μὴ μοιχᾶσθαι μηδὲ

20 ὁ] ὅ (i.e. οὗ) A.   25 αὐτόν] αυτων A.

13. λέγει δὲ καὶ αὐτὸς κ.τ.λ.] Nicon (see above on the First Epistle §§ 14, 15) quotes portions of this passage; καὶ ὁ Κύριος λέγει Τὸν ὁμολογήσαντα... τοῦ πατρός μου· ἐν τίνι δέ...τῶν ἐντολῶν. τὸν ὁμολογήσαντα κ.τ.λ.] A free quotation of Matt. x. 32 (comp. Luke xii. 8).

15. ἐὰν οὖν] 'if after all, if only.' For similar instances of the use of οὖν see Hartung Partikel. II. 11.

19. ἐξ ὅλης κ.τ.λ.] A reference ultimately to Deut. vi. 5; but as both words διανοίας and καρδίας do not seem to occur in that passage in any one text of the LXX, we must suppose that the writer had in his mind the saying rather as it is quoted in the Gospels, esp. Mark xii. 30 ἐξ ὅλης τῆς καρδίας σου καὶ ἐξ ὅλης τῆς ψυχῆς σου καὶ ἐξ ὅλης τῆς διανοίας σου καὶ ἐξ ὅλης τῆς ἰσχύος σου (comp. Matt. xxii. 37, Luke x. 27).

20. ὁ λαὸς οὗτος κ.τ.λ.] From Is. xxix. 13, modified by the form in which it is quoted in the Gospels;

see the note on the genuine Epistle of Clement § 15, where again it is quoted in almost exactly the same form as here.

IV. 'It is not enough to call Him Lord. We must confess Him by our works, by love and purity and guilelessness. We must not fear men but God. For Christ Himself has warned us that, though we be His most familiar friends, yet if we do not His commandments, He will reject us.'

23. οὐ πᾶς ὁ λέγων κ.τ.λ.] From Matt. vii. 21 οὐ πᾶς ὁ λέγων μοι, Κύριε, Κύριε, εἰσελεύσεται εἰς τὴν βασιλείαν τῶν οὐρανῶν, ἀλλ' ὁ ποιῶν τὸ θέλημα τοῦ πατρός μου, τοῦ ἐν τοῖς οὐρανοῖς (comp. Luke vi. 46 quoted below). Justin (Apol. i. 16, p. 64 A) gives the exact words of S. Matthew (except οὐχὶ for οὐ). Clem. Hom. viii. 7 has τί με λέγεις Κύριε, Κύριε, καὶ οὐ ποιεῖς ἃ λέγω; which closely resembles Luke vi. 46 τί δέ με καλεῖτε, Κύριε, Κύριε, καὶ οὐ ποιεῖτε ἃ λέγω; comp.

καταλαλεῖν ἀλλήλων μηδὲ ζηλοῦν, ἀλλ' ἐγκρατεῖς εἶναι, ἐλεήμονας, ἀγαθούς· καὶ συμπάσχειν ἀλλήλοις ὀφείλο[μεν], καὶ μὴ φιλαργυρεῖν. ἐν τ[οιού]τοις ἔργοις ὁμολογῶμεν [αὐτὸν] καὶ μὴ ἐν τοῖς ἐναντίοις· καὶ οὐ δεῖ ἡμᾶς φοβεῖσθαι το[ὺς] ἀνθρώπους μᾶλλον ἀλλὰ τὸν 5 Θεόν. δ[ιὰ] τοῦτο, ταῦτα ὑμῶν πρασσόν[των], εἶπεν ὁ Κύριος· Ἐὰν ἦτε μετ' ἐμο[ῦ] cγνηγμένοι ἐν τῷ κόλπῳ μ[ου] καὶ μὴ ποιῆτε τὰc ἐντολάc μο[γ], ἀποβαλῶ ὑμᾶc καὶ ἐρῶ

3 ὀφείλομεν] οφιλομεν A.   τοιούτοις] Tisch. (prol. p. xix).

Clem. Hom. viii. 5 οὐδὲ ἐν τῷ πιστεύειν διδασκάλοις καὶ κυρίους αὐτοὺς λέγειν ἡ σωτηρία γίνεται.

1. μηδὲ καταλαλεῖν κ.τ.λ.] James iv. 11 μὴ καταλαλεῖτε ἀλλήλων. See also Hermas *Mand.* 2 πρῶτον μὲν μηδενὸς καταλάλει, with the whole section.

2. ἀγαθούς] '*kindly, beneficent*', as Tit. ii. 5, 1 Pet. ii. 18; and so probably 1 Thess. iii. 6.

4. οὐ δεῖ ἡμᾶς κ.τ.λ.] Comp. Acts iv. 19, v. 29.

7. ἐὰν ἦτε κ.τ.λ.] Not found in the canonical Gospels, and perhaps taken from the Gospel of the Egyptians, which is quoted below; see §§ 5, 8, 12. The image and expressions are derived from Is. xl. 11 τῷ βραχίονι αὐτοῦ συνάξει ἄρνας καὶ ἐν τῷ κόλπῳ αὐτοῦ βαστάσει. The latter clause, though absent in אAB, is found in several MSS (see Holmes and Parsons), in other Greek Versions, and in the original; and must be supposed to have been known to the writer of the Gospel in question. For the expression συνάγειν ἐν κόλπῳ, '*to gather in the lap*', see LXX Prov. xxx. 4 (xxiv. 27). The image is carried out in the language of the next chapter, ἔσεσθε ὡς ἀρνία κ.τ.λ.

9. ὑπάγετε κ.τ.λ.] The parallel passage in S. Luke xiii. 27 runs καὶ ἐρεῖ, λέγω ὑμῖν, οὐκ οἶδα [ὑμᾶς] πόθεν ἐστέ· ἀπόστητε ἀπ' ἐμοῦ πάντες ἐργάται ἀδικίας. This is much closer than Matt. vii. 23. The denunciation is taken from Ps. vi. 9 ἀπόστητε ἀπ' ἐμοῦ πάντες οἱ ἐργαζόμενοι τὴν ἀνομίαν. Compare the quotations in Justin *Apol.* i. 16 (p. 64 B) καὶ τότε ἐρῶ αὐτοῖς· Ἀποχωρεῖτε ἀπ' ἐμοῦ, ἐργάται τῆς ἀνομίας, *Dial.* 76 (p. 301 D) καὶ ἐρῶ αὐτοῖς· Ἀναχωρεῖτε ἀπ' ἐμοῦ. See Westcott *Canon* p. 125 sq. (2nd ed.).

V. 'We must break loose from the ties of this world. The Lord has warned us, that here we shall be as lambs among wolves; that we have cause to fear the perdition of our souls rather than the murder of our bodies. Our life here is brief and transitory; our life in heaven is eternal rest. Therefore should we look upon ourselves as aliens to the world.'.

11. τὴν παροικίαν] '*our sojourning in*', i.e. 'our dalliance with': see the note on παροικοῦντες in the opening of the First Epistle.

14. ἔσεσθε κ.τ.λ.] This is a close parallel to Luke x. 3 ἀποστέλλω ὑμᾶς ὡς ἄρνας ἐν μέσῳ λύκων (comp. Matt. x. 16). As however Peter is not mentioned in the context, and as the con-

ὑμῖν· ὑπάγετε ἀπ' ἐμοῦ, ογκ οἶδα ὑμᾶc πόθεν ἐcτέ, ἐργάται
10 ἀνομίαc.

V. Ὅθεν, ἀδελφοί, καταλείψαντες τὴν παροικίαν τοῦ κόσμου τούτου ποιήσωμεν τὸ θέλημα τοῦ καλέσαντος ἡμᾶς, καὶ μὴ φοβηθῶμεν ἐξελθεῖν ἐκ τοῦ κόσμου τούτου. λέγει γὰρ ὁ Κύριος Ἔcecθε ὡc ἀρνία ἐν 15 μέcῳ λύκων· ἀποκριθεὶс δὲ ὁ Πέτρος αὐτῷ λέγει· Ἐὰν ογν διαcπαράξωсιν οἱ λύκοι τὰ ἀρνία; εἶπεν ὁ Ἰηcοῦc τῷ Πέτρῳ· Μὴ φοβεícθωcan τὰ ἀρνία τοὺc λύκοyc μετὰ τὸ ἀποθανεῖν αὐτά. καὶ ὑμεῖc μὴ φοβεῖcθε τοὺc ἀποκτέννον-

4 αὐτόν] Tisch. (prol. p. xix).   18 φοβεῖσθε] φοβεισθαι A.

tinuation of the quotation is not found in the canonical Gospels, the whole passage was probably taken from some apocryphal source, perhaps the Gospel of the Egyptians: see the note on §§ 4, 8, 12. As the same metaphor of the lambs occurs in the apocryphal quotation just above (§ 4), they were probably taken from the same context. Photius (*Bibl.* 126) remarks on the number of apocryphal quotations in this Second Epistle, πλὴν ὅτι ῥητά τινα ὡς ἀπὸ τῆς θείας γραφῆς ξενίζοντα παρεισάγει, ὧν οὐδ' ἡ πρώτη ἀπήλλακτο παντελῶς. (For apocryphal quotations in the First, which however are chiefly from the Old Testament and therefore not so prominent, see the notes §§ 8, 13, 17, 23, 29, 46).

18. καὶ ὑμεῖς κ.τ.λ.] The apocryphal citation again runs parallel to the canonical Gospels, Matt. x. 28 καὶ μὴ φοβεῖσθε ἀπὸ τῶν ἀποκτεννόντων τὸ σῶμα, τὴν δὲ ψυχὴν μὴ δυναμένων ἀποκτεῖναι· φοβήθητε δὲ μᾶλλον τὸν δυνάμενον [καὶ] ψυχὴν καὶ σῶμα ἀπολέσαι ἐν γεέννῃ, Luke xii. 4, 5 μὴ φοβηθῆτε ἀπὸ τῶν ἀποκτεννόντων τὸ σῶμα καὶ μετὰ ταῦτα μὴ ἐχόντων περισσότερόν τι ποιῆσαι· ὑποδείξω δὲ ὑμῖν τίνα φοβηθῆτε. φοβήθητε τὸν μετὰ τὸ ἀποκτεῖναι ἔχοντα ἐξουσίαν ἐμβαλεῖν εἰς τὴν γέενναν· ναί, λέγω ὑμῖν, τοῦτον φοβήθητε. The saying is quoted also in *Clem. Hom.* xvii. 4 μὴ φοβήθητε ἀπὸ τοῦ ἀποκτέννοντος τὸ σῶμα τῇ δὲ ψυχῇ μὴ δυναμένου τι ποιῆσαι· φοβήθητε δὲ τὸν δυνάμενον καὶ σῶμα καὶ ψυχὴν εἰς τὴν γέενναν τοῦ πυρὸς βαλεῖν, and in Justin *Apol.* i. 19 (p. 66 B) μὴ φοβεῖσθε τοὺς ἀναιροῦντας ὑμᾶς καὶ μετὰ ταῦτα μὴ δυναμένους τι ποιῆσαι, εἶπε, φοβήθητε δὲ τὸν μετὰ τὸ ἀποθανεῖν δυνάμενον καὶ ψυχὴν καὶ σῶμα εἰς γέενναν ἐμβαλεῖν. The points of coincidence in the quotations of the Clementine Homilies and Justin with our pseudo-Clement are worthy of notice, but they seem to be accidental. The expression εἰς τὴν γέενναν τοῦ πυρὸς (in the quotation of the Homilies) might have come from Matt. xviii. 9 (interpolated in the parallel passage Mark ix. 47). For the amount of variation which may arise accidentally, see a parallel instance given by Westcott *Canon* p. 116; and it is instructive to observe the variations in two quotations of this very saying in Clem. Alex. *Exc. Theod.* p. 972 φοβήθητε γοῦν, λέγει, τὸν μετὰ θάνατον δυνάμενον

τὰς ὑμᾶς καὶ μηδὲν ὑμῖν δυναμένους ποιεῖν, ἀλλὰ φοβεῖσθε τὸν μετὰ τὸ ἀποθανεῖν ὑμᾶς ἔχοντα ἐξουσίαν ψυχῆς καὶ σώματος, τοῦ βαλεῖν εἰς γέενναν πυρός. Καὶ γινώσκετε, ἀδελφοί, ὅτι ἡ ἐπιδημία ἡ ἐν τῷ κόσμῳ τούτῳ τῆς σαρκὸς ταύτης μικρά ἐστιν καὶ ὀλιγοχρόνιος· ἡ δὲ 5 ἐπαγγελία τοῦ Χριστοῦ μεγάλη καὶ θαυμαστή ἐστιν, καὶ ἀνάπαυσις τῆς μελλούσης βασιλείας καὶ ζωῆς αἰωνίου. τί οὖν ἐστὶν ποιήσαντας ἐπιτυχεῖν αὐτῶν, εἰ μὴ τὸ ὁσίως καὶ δικαίως ἀναστρέφεσθαι, καὶ τὰ κοσμικὰ ταῦτα ὡς ἀλλότρια ἡγεῖσθαι καὶ μὴ ἐπιθυμεῖν 10 αὐτῶν; ἐν γὰρ τῷ ἐπιθυμεῖν ἡμᾶς κτήσασθαι ταῦτα ἀποπίπτομεν τῆς ὁδοῦ τῆς δικαίας.

VI. Λέγει δὲ ὁ Κύριος· Οὐδεὶς οἰκέτης δύναται δυσὶ

1 φοβεῖσθε] φοβεισθαι A.   6 ἐπαγγελία] επαγγελεια A.

καὶ ψυχὴν καὶ σῶμα εἰς γέενναν βαλεῖν, and p. 981 ὁ σωτὴρ λέγει φοβεῖσθαι δεῖν τὸν δυνάμενον ταύτην τὴν ψυχὴν καὶ τοῦτο τὸ σῶμα τὸ ψυχικὸν ἐν γεέννῃ ἀπολέσαι: comp. also Iren. iii. 18. 5 'Nolite timere eos qui occidunt corpus, animam autem non possunt occidere; timete autem magis eum qui habet potestatem et corpus et animam mittere in gehennam.'

ἀποκτέννοντας] The passages quoted in the last note show that the substitution of ἀποκτείνοντας is quite unnecessary. For the form ἀποκτέννειν see Winer § xv. p. 95 (note), A. Buttmann p. 54.

4. ἡ ἐπιδημία] 'sojourn': comp. παρεπίδημοι Heb. xi. 13, 1 Pet. i. 1, ii. 11. See the note on παροικίαν above, which contains the same idea.

7. καὶ ἀνάπαυσις] 'namely, rest'. For this use of καὶ see the notes on *Galatians* vi. 16.

8. τί οὖν κ.τ.λ.] '*What then is it possible for us to do that we may obtain them, but to walk holily and righteously*'. Thus τῷ, which some would substitute for τό, interferes with the construction. For ὁσίως καὶ δικαίως, implying duties to God and to man respectively, see the note on ὅσια § 1: comp. § 6 ἔχοντες ὅσια καὶ δίκαια.

VI. 'Our Lord has told us that no man can serve two masters. There is a direct antagonism between the world present and the world to come. We cannot keep the friendship of both. Let us then, if we would deliver ourselves from eternal misery, obey the command of Christ and follow after the heavenly life. Even Noah, Job, and Daniel, it is written, could not by their righteous deeds rescue their own children. How then shall we enter the kingdom of God, if we keep not our baptismal vows?'

13. οὐδεὶς κ.τ.λ.] Luke xvi. 13 οὐδεὶς οἰκέτης δύναται δυσὶ κυρίοις δουλεύειν...οὐ δύνασθε Θεῷ δουλεύειν καὶ μαμωνᾷ. The words are the same in Matt. vi. 24, excepting the omission of οἰκέτης.

κγρίοιc δογλεγε[ιν]. ἐὰν ἡμεῖς θέλωμεν καὶ Θεῷ δ[ουλ]-
15 εύειν καὶ μαμωνᾷ, ἀσύμφο[ρ]ον ἡμῖν ἐστίν. τί γὰρ τὸ
ὄφελος, ἐάν τις τὸν κόσμον ὅλον κερΔήσῃ τὴν Δὲ ψγχὴν
ζημιωθῇ; ἔστιν δὲ οὗτος ὁ αἰὼν καὶ ὁ μέλλων δύο
ἐχθροί· οὗτος λέγει μοιχείαν καὶ φθορὰν καὶ φιλαρ-
γυρίαν καὶ ἀπάτην, ἐκεῖνος δὲ τούτοις ἀποτάσσεται.
20 οὐ δυνάμεθα οὖν τῶν δύο φίλοι εἶναι· δεῖ δὲ ἡμᾶς τούτῳ
ἀποταξαμένους ἐκείνῳ χρᾶσθαι. οἰώμεθα ὅτι βέλτιόν
ἐστιν τὰ ἐνθάδε μισῆσαι, ὅτι μικρὰ καὶ ὀλιγοχρόνια καὶ
φθαρτά· ἐκεῖνα δὲ ἀγαπῆσαι, τὰ ἀγαθὰ καὶ ἄφθαρτα.
ποιοῦντες γὰρ τὸ θέλημα τοῦ Χριστοῦ εὑρήσομεν ἀνά-
25 παυσιν· εἰ δὲ μήγε, οὐδὲν ἡμᾶς ῥύσεται ἐκ τῆς αἰωνίου
κολάσεως, ἐὰν παρακούσωμεν τῶν ἐντολῶν αὐτοῦ.
λέγει δὲ καὶ ἡ γραφὴ ἐν τῷ Ἰεζεκιήλ, ὅτι Ἐὰν ἀναστῇ

11 ἐπιθυμῶν] ἐπιθυμεῖ A. 21 οἰώμεθα] οιομεθα A.

15. τί γὰρ τὸ ὄφελος κ.τ.λ.] See Matt. xvi. 26, Mark viii. 36, Luke ix. 25. The quotation here may have been derived from either S. Matthew or S. Mark, though it differs slightly from both. The divergence from S. Luke is greater. The saying is quoted also by Justin *Apol.* i. 15; but Justin's quotation, while combining different features of the three canonical Gospels, does not reproduce the special peculiarity (τί τὸ ὄφελος;) of our pseudo-Clement.

17. ἔστιν δὲ οὗτος ὁ αἰὼν κ.τ.λ.] See the notes on *Galatians* i. 4. Compare also *Clem. Hom.* viii. 21, xx. 2.

18. φθοράν] Either (1) *corruptness, profligacy* generally, as in 2 Pet. i. 4, ii. 12, 19; or (2) in a more special sense, as Plut. *Crass.* 1 τὴν αἰτίαν τῆς φθορᾶς ἀπολυσάμενος, *Mor.* p. 89 B κριθῆναι φθορᾶς. The connexion with μοιχεία here points to this latter sense; comp. Barnab. 10 οὐ μὴ γένῃ μοῖχος οὐδὲ φθορεύς, Philo *de Spec. Leg.* 11

(II. p. 310 M) ἀδελφὸν μὲν καὶ συγγενὲς ἀδίκημα μοιχείας φθορά, Epictet. *Diss.* ii. 22. 28 ἀκρατεῖς καὶ μοιχοὺς καὶ φθορεῖς, Iren. *Hær.* i. 28. 1, *Clem. Hom.* iv. 16, 24.

21. ἀποταξαμένους τούτῳ] '*bidding farewell to this*'. *Act. Paul. et Thecl.* 5 οἱ ἀποταξάμενοι τῷ κόσμῳ τούτῳ, Ign. *Philad.* 11 ἀποταξάμενος τῷ βίῳ. The word is fairly common in the New Testament; see Lobeck *Phryn.* p. 23.

χρᾶσθαι] '*consort with* as a friend', according to a common sense of the word. The editors have substituted χρῆσθαι for the MS reading; but there is sufficient authority for χρᾶσθαι in later writers: see Lobeck *Phryn.* p. 61, Buttmann *Ausf. Sprachl.* § 105 (I. p. 487), Veitch *Irregular Verbs* s.v. χράομαι.

25. αἰωνίου κολάσεως] The expression occurs Matt. xxv. 46.

27. ἐν τῷ Ἰεζεκιήλ] Abridged from Ezek. xiv. 14—20, being taken especially from ver. 14 ἐὰν ὦσιν οἱ τρεῖς

Νῶε καὶ Ἰὼβ καὶ Δανιήλ, οὐ ῥύσονται τὰ τέκνα αὐτῶν ἐν
τῇ αἰχμαλωσίᾳ. εἰ δὲ καὶ οἱ τοιοῦτοι δίκαιοι οὐ
δύνανται ταῖς αὐτῶν δικαιοσύναις ῥύσασθαι τὰ τέκνα
αὐτῶν· ἡμεῖς, ἐὰν μὴ τηρήσωμεν τὸ βάπτισμα ἁγνὸν
καὶ ἀμίαντον, ποίᾳ πεποιθήσει εἰσελευσόμεθα εἰς τὸ 5
βασίλειον τοῦ Θεοῦ; ἢ τίς ἡμῶν παράκλητος ἔσται,

2 αἰχμαλωσίᾳ] αιχμαλωσια A.

ἄνδρες οὗτοι ἐν μέσῳ αὐτῆς Νῶε καὶ Δανιὴλ καὶ Ἰώβ, and ver. 18 οὐ μὴ ῥύσονται υἱοὺς καὶ θυγατέρας. The words ἐν τῇ αἰχμαλωσίᾳ are the writer's own addition and should not be treated as part of the quotation. It is worth noticing also that the order of the three names, which has given rise to so much speculation among modern critics, is changed by the pseudo-Clement, and a chronological sequence is produced. Chrysostom makes the same change in two passages quoted by Cotelier, *Hom. xliii in Gen.* (IV. p. 436) and *Exp. in Ps.* xlviii (V. p. 210).

3. δικαιοσύναις] The plural, as in Deut. ix. 4 (v. l.), 6, 1 Sam. xxvi. 23, Ezek. iii. 20, xxxiii. 13, Ecclus. xliv. 10.

5. τὸ βασίλειον] 'the kingdom,' as in *Test. xii Patr.* Jud. 17, 22, 23, *Orac. Sib.* iii. 159, Caius (Hippolytus?) in Euseb. *H. E.* iii. 28, Hippol. *Fragm.* 59, 103, 105 (pp. 162, 181, 182, Lagarde), Euseb. *H. E.* viii. 17, Epiphan. *Hær.* li. 9 (p. 432). Thus there is ample authority for this sense of βασίλειον. Galland, desirous of retaining the more usual meaning 'a palace,' supposes the writer to refer to the parable of the marriage feast given by the king, Matt. xxii. 11, 12. If so, we might suppose that he explained the wedding garment of baptism, which is mentioned just before. But the reference seems improbable.

6. παράκλητος] '*advocate*,' as it should always be translated in the New Testament. This is one coincidence of language in our pseudo-Clement with S. John: see esp. 1 Joh. ii. 1 παράκλητον ἔχομεν πρὸς τὸν πατέρα. So above § 3 τὸν πατέρα τῆς ἀληθείας, and see on this subject Westcott *Canon* p. 157 sq.

7. ὅσια καὶ δίκαια] See the notes on §§ 1, 5.

VII. 'Therefore let us prepare for the struggle. In the Isthmian games many enter the lists, but not many are crowned. In this our immortal race we should all strive to win. In the earthly contests he who breaks the rules is scourged. What then shall befall those who in their heavenly course swerve from the right path? Their worm, it is written, dieth not, and their fire is not quenched.'

9. ἐν χερσὶν ὁ ἀγών] '*The contest is at hand*,' as Xen. *Cyr.* ii. 3. 2 "Ανδρες φίλοι, ὁ μὲν ἀγὼν ἐγγὺς ἡμῖν: comp. Clem. Rom. 7 ὁ αὐτὸς ἡμῖν ἀγὼν ἐπίκειται. The emendation of ΑΓωΝ for ΑΙωΝ is doubtless correct, and this is not the only instance of the confusion of the two words: see Hase and Dindorf *Steph. Thes.* p. 593 s. v. ἀγών, and to the references there given add Æsch. *Agam.* 495. For ἐν χερσίν, 'at hand,' see Plut. *Vit. Cleom.* 22 οὐκ ἐλάττονα τῆς ἐν χερσὶ δυστυχίαν, *Vit. Brut.* 36 ἐν χερσὶν

ἐὰν μὴ εὑρεθῶμεν ἔργα ἔχοντες ὅσια καὶ δίκαια;
VII. "Ὥστε οὖν, ἀδελφοί μου, ἀγωνισώμεθα, εἰδότες ὅτι ἐν χερσὶν ὁ ἀγών, καὶ ὅτι εἰς τοὺς φθαρ-
10 τοὺς ἀγῶνας καταπλέουσιν πολλοί, ἀλλ᾽ οὐ πάντες στεφανοῦνται, εἰ μὴ οἱ πολλὰ κοπιάσαντες καὶ καλῶς ἀγωνισάμενοι. ἡμεῖς οὖν ἀγωνισώμεθα, ἵνα πάντες στεφανωθῶμεν. ὥστε θέωμεν τὴν ὁδὸν τὴν εὐθεῖαν,

9 ἀγών] Cotelier. αιων A.   11 εἰ] θι A.   13 θέωμεν] θωμεν A.

ἔχων τὰς ὑπὲρ τῶν ὅλων πράξεις, etc.: compare ὑπὸ χεῖρα, Hermas *Vis.* iii. 10 (with the note).
ὅτι εἰς τοὺς φθαρτοὺς κ.τ.λ.] An echo of 1 Cor. ix. 24, 25 πάντες μὲν τρέχουσιν, εἷς δὲ λαμβάνει τὸ βραβεῖον and ἐκεῖνοι μὲν οὖν ἵνα φθαρτὸν στέφανον λάβωσιν, ἡμεῖς δὲ ἄφθαρτον. Comp. Lucian *Anachars.* 13 εἰπέ μοι, πάντες αὐτὰ λαμβάνουσιν οἱ ἀγωνισταί; Σ. οὐδαμῶς ἀλλὰ εἷς ἐξ ἁπάντων ὁ κρατήσας αὐτῶν (a passage of which the context presents several coincidences with S. Paul; see Clark's *Peloponnesus* p. 50), Seneca *Ep.* lxxviii. § 16 'Athletæ quantum plagarum ore, quantum toto corpore excipiunt? ferunt tamen omne tormentum gloriæ cupiditate; nec tantum, quia pugnant, ista patiuntur, sed ut pugnent... nos quoque evincamus omnia, quorum præmium non corona nec palma est etc.'
10. καταπλέουσιν] '*resort*'; comp. Plut. *Mor.* p. 81 Ε καταπλεῖν γὰρ ἔφη τοὺς πολλοὺς ἐπὶ σχολὴν Ἀθήναζε. Compounds of πλεῖν are sometimes used metaphorically, as ἐκπλεῖν (Herod. iii. 155 ἐξέπλωσας τῶν φρενῶν), ἀποπλεῖν (Aristoph. *Fr.* II. p. 907 Meineke ἀποπλευστέ᾽ οὖν ἐπὶ τὸν νυμφίον), διαπλεῖν (Plato *Phæd.* 85 D διαπλεῦσαι τὸν βίον). But καταπλεῖν can hardly be so explained here; and we must therefore suppose that the allu-

sion is to the ἀλιερκὴς Ἰσθμοῦ δειράς (Pind. *Isthm.* i. 10), which would naturally be approached by sea. Livy (xxxiii. 32) describes the Isthmian games as 'propter opportunitatem loci, per duo diversa maria omnium rerum usus ministrantis, humano generi concilium.' In these later days of Greece they seem to have surpassed even the Olympian in importance, or at least in popularity: comp. Aristid. *Isthm.* p. 45 ἐν τῇ καλλίστῃ τῶν πανηγύρεων τῇδε καὶ ὀνομαστοτάτῃ κ.τ.λ. (see Krause *Hellen.* II. 2. p. 205 sq.). If this epistle or homily (whichever it be) of the so-called Clement were really addressed to the Corinthians (see above p. 178), there would be singular propriety in this image, as in S. Paul's contrast of the perishable and imperishable crown likewise addressed to them, or again in the lessons which Diogenes the Cynic is reported to have taught in this city during the Isthmian games, maintaining the superiority of a moral over an athletic victory (Dion Chrysost. *Orat.* viii, ix).
11. κοπιάσαντες] A word used especially of training for the contest: see the notes on Ign. *Polyc.* 6 and *Philippians* ii. 16. For the connexion here comp. 1 Tim. iv. 10 καὶ κοπιῶμεν καὶ ἀγωνιζόμεθα (the correct reading).
13. θέωμεν] For the accusative

ἀγῶνα τὸν ἄφθαρτον, καὶ πολλοὶ εἰς αὐτὸν καταπλεύσωμεν καὶ ἀγωνισώμεθα, ἵνα καὶ στεφανωθῶμεν· καὶ εἰ μὴ δυνάμεθα πάντες στεφα[ν]ωθῆναι, κἂν ἐγγὺς τοῦ στεφάνου γενώμεθα. εἰδέναι ἡμᾶς δεῖ, ὅτι ὁ τὸν φθαρτὸν ἀγῶνα ἀγωνιζόμενος, ἐὰν εὑρεθῇ φθείρων, 5 μαστιγωθεὶς αἴρεται καὶ ἔξω βάλλεται τοῦ σταδίου. τί δοκεῖτε; ὁ τὸν τῆς ἀφθαρσίας ἀγῶνα φθείρας, τί παθεῖται; τῶν γὰρ μὴ τηρησάντων, φησίν, τὴν σφρα-

7 δοκεῖτε] δοκειται A.

after this verb see Lobeck *Paral.* p. 511: comp. also Cic. *Off.* iii. 10 'stadium currit' (from Chrysippus). The reading of the MS, θῶμεν, can hardly stand. It is explained as referring to the ἀγωνοθεσία; but in this case the ἀγωνοθέτης should be God Himself (see Tertull. *ad Mart.* 3); and moreover θῶμεν τὴν ὁδόν is in itself an awkward expression.

2. καὶ εἰ μὴ δυνάμεθα κ.τ.λ.] This seems to point to some public recognition of those who came next after the victor. In the Olympian chariot races there were second, third, and fourth prizes; but in the foot races the notices of any inferior prize or honourable mention are vague and uncertain: see Krause *Hellen.* II. 1. p. 170 sq. This passage is quoted loosely by Dorotheus *Doctr.* xxiii ὡς λέγει καὶ ὁ ἅγιος Κλήμης, Κἂν μὴ στεφανωταί τις, ἀλλὰ σπουδάσει μὴ μακρὰν εὑρεθῆναι τῶν στεφανουμένων.

5. φθείρων] '*vitiating*'. The word is used of violating the conditions of the contest, e.g. by making a false start or cutting off a corner or tripping up an adversary or taking any underhand advantage: comp. Epiphan. *Hæres.* lxi. 7 παραφθείρας ἀγῶνα ὁ ἀθλητὴς μαστιχθεὶς ἐκβάλλεται τοῦ ἀγῶνος (quoted by Cotelier). The word is specially chosen here for the sake of the neighbouring φθαρτόν, ἀφθαρσίας. See Chrysippus in Cic. *Off.* iii. 10 'Qui stadium currit, eniti et contendere debet, quam maxime possit, ut vincat; supplantare eum quicum certet aut manu depellere nullo modo debet: sic in vita etc.', Lucian *Cal. non tem. cred.* 12 ὁ μὲν ἀγαθὸς δρομεύς...τῷ πλησίον οὐδὲν κακουργεῖ...ὁ δὲ κακὸς ἐκεῖνος καὶ ἄναθλος ἀνταγωνιστής...ἐπὶ τὴν κακοτεχνίαν ἐτράπετο κ.τ.λ. The turn given to the image in φθείρων was perhaps suggested by 2 Tim. ii. 5 οὐ στεφανοῦται ἐὰν μὴ νομίμως ἀθλήσῃ (comp. Epictet. *Diss.* iii. 10. 8 δός μοι ἀπόδειξιν εἰ νομίμως ἤθλησας).

6. μαστιγωθείς] i.e. by the ῥαβδοῦχοι or, as they are sometimes called (e.g. Lucian *Hermot.* 40), μαστιγοφόροι. Pollux (iii. 153) furnishes also a third name, μαστιγονόμοι. Compare Herod. viii. 59 ἐν τοῖς ἀγῶσι οἱ προεξανιστάμενοι ῥαπίζονται, Thucyd. v. 50 ἐν τῷ ἀγῶνι ὑπὸ τῶν ῥαβδούχων πληγὰς ἔλαβεν, Lucian *adv. Indoct.* 9, *Piscat.* 33. On these police see Krause *Hellen.* II. 1. pp. 112 sq., 139, 142, 144, II. 2. p. 46 sq.

αἴρεται] '*is removed.*'

8. τὴν σφραγῖδα] By a comparison with § 6 ἐὰν μὴ τηρήσωμεν τὸ βάπτισμα, it appears that baptism is here meant by the seal. So again § 8 τη-

γῖδα ὁ cκώληξ αὐτῶν οὐ τελευτήcει καὶ τὸ πῦρ αὐτῶν
10 οὐ cβεcθήcεται, καὶ ἔcονται εἰc ὅραcιν πάcῃ capκί.
VIII. 'Ὡς οὖν ἐσμὲν ἐπὶ γῆς, μετανοήσωμεν·
πηλὸς γάρ ἐσμεν εἰς τὴν χεῖρα τοῦ τεχνίτου. ὃν
τρόπον γὰρ ὁ κεραμεύς, ἐὰν ποιῇ σκεῦος καὶ ἐν ταῖς
χερσὶν αὐτοῦ διαστραφῇ ἢ συντριβῇ, πάλιν αὐτὸ
15 ἀναπλάσσει· ἐὰν δὲ προφθάσῃ εἰς τὴν κάμινον τοῦ
πυρὸς αὐτὸ βαλεῖν, οὐκέτι βοηθήσει αὐτῷ· οὕτως καὶ

ρήσατε τὴν σφραγῖδα ἄσπιλον. Comp. Hermas *Sim.* viii. 6 εἰληφότες τὴν σφραγῖδα καὶ τεθλάκοτες αὐτὴν καὶ μὴ τηρήσαντες ὑγιῆ κ.τ.λ., *Sim.* ix. 16 ὅταν δὲ λάβῃ τὴν σφραγῖδα...ἡ σφραγὶς. οὖν τὸ ὕδωρ ἐστίν κ.τ.λ., also *Sim.* viii. 2, ix. 17, 31, *Clem. Hom.* xvi. 19 τὸ σῶμα σφραγῖδι μεγίστῃ διαστετυπωμένον (with the context), *Act. Paul. et Thecl.* 25 μόνον δός μοι τὴν ἐν Χριστῷ σφραγῖδα, Hippol. *Antichr.* 42 (p. 119, Lagarde), Cureton's *Ancient Syriac Documents* p. 44. Suicer *s. v.* quotes Clem. Alex. *Quis div. salv.* 39 (p. 957), *Strom.* ii. 3 (p. 434), and other later writers. In like manner Barnabas § 9 speaks of circumcision as a σφραγὶς after S. Paul, Rom. iv. 11. But it may be questioned whether S. Paul (σφραγισάμενος 2 Cor. i. 22, comp. Ephes. iv. 30) or S. John (Rev. ix. 4 τὴν σφραγῖδα τοῦ Θεοῦ ἐπὶ τῶν μετώπων) used the image with any direct reference to baptism.

9. ὁ σκώληξ κ.τ.λ.] An accurate quotation from the LXX of the last verse of Isaiah (lxvi. 24) ὁ γὰρ σκώληξ αὐτῶν κ.τ.λ. The denunciation is uttered against τῶν ἀνθρώπων τῶν παραβεβηκότων, and the context does not contain any reference to the broken seal.

VIII. 'We are as clay in the hands of the potter. At present, if we are crushed or broken, He can mould us again; but when we have been once thrown into the furnace, nothing will avail us. Therefore let us repent in time. After death repentance is too late. Let us keep the flesh pure now, that we may inherit eternal life hereafter. This is our Lord's meaning, when He says, *If ye kept not that which is small, who shall give you that which is great?*'

11. ὡς οὖν] '*While then.*' For this sense of ὡς see § 9 ὡς ἔχομεν καιρόν, with the note.

12. πηλὸς γάρ ἐσμεν κ.τ.λ.] The image of Jeremiah xviii. 4—6, adopted by S. Paul Rom. ix. 21. The present passage is suggested rather by the prophet than by the Apostle. The image is drawn out in *Test. xii Patr.* Nepht. 2, and in Athenag. *Suppl.* 15.

14. συντριβῇ] Rev. ii. 27 ὡς τὰ σκεύη τὰ κεραμικὰ συντρίβεται.

πάλιν αὐτὸ ἀναπλάσσει] Hilgenfeld refers to Theoph. *ad Autol.* ii. 26 καθάπερ σκεῦός τι, ἐπὰν πλασθὲν αἰτίαν τινα σχῇ, ἀναχωνεύεται ἢ ἀναπλάσσεται εἰς τὸ γενέσθαι καινὸν καὶ ὁλόκληρον; see the references there given by Otto.

15. ἐὰν δὲ προφθάσῃ κ.τ.λ.] '*When He has once cast it into the fiery furnace, He will no more come to its rescue.*' προφθάνειν occurs Matt. xvii. 25 and several times in the LXX.

ἡμεῖς, ἕως ἐσμὲν ἐν τούτῳ τῷ κόσμῳ, ἐν τῇ σαρκὶ
ἃ ἐπράξαμεν πονηρὰ μετανοήσωμεν ἐξ ὅλης τῆς καρδίας, ἵνα σωθῶμεν ὑπὸ τοῦ Κυρίου, ἕως ἔχομεν καιρὸν μετανοίας· μετὰ γὰρ τὸ ἐξελθεῖν ἡμᾶς ἐκ τοῦ
κόσμου, οὐκέτι δυνάμεθα ἐκεῖ ἐξομολογήσασθαι ἢ με- 5
τανοεῖν ἔτι. ὥστε, ἀδελφοί, ποιήσαντες τὸ θέλημα
τοῦ πατρὸς καὶ τὴν σάρκα ἁγνὴν τηρήσαντες καὶ τὰς
ἐντολὰς τοῦ Κυρίου φυλάξαντες ληψόμεθα ζωὴν αἰώ-

7 σάρκα] σαρκαν A.

7. τὴν σάρκα ἁγνὴν κ.τ.λ.] *Act. Paul. et Thecl.* 5 μακάριοι οἱ ἁγνὴν τὴν σάρκα τηρήσαντες, 12 τὴν σάρκα μὴ μολύνητε ἀλλὰ τηρήσητε ἁγνήν.

9. εἰ τὸ μικρὸν κ.τ.λ.] Probably a quotation fused from Luke xvi. 10 ὁ πιστὸς ἐν ἐλαχίστῳ καὶ ἐν πολλῷ πιστός ἐστιν, καὶ ὁ ἐν ἐλαχίστῳ ἄδικος καὶ ἐν πολλῷ ἄδικός ἐστιν· εἰ οὖν ἐν τῷ ἀδίκῳ μαμωνᾷ πιστοὶ οὐκ ἐγένεσθε, τὸ ἀληθινὸν τίς ὑμῖν πιστεύσει; and Matt. xxv. 21, 23, ἐπὶ ὀλίγα ἦς πιστός, ἐπὶ πολλῶν σε καταστήσω. Irenæus (ii. 34. 3) cites it somewhat similarly, 'Si in modico fideles non fuistis, quod magnum est quis dabit vobis?' The quotation of our Clementine writer may perhaps be taken from an apocryphal gospel (see the notes on §§ 4, 5, 12); but the passage of Irenæus, who can hardly have borrowed from an apocryphal source, shows how great divergences are possible in quotations from memory, and lessens the probability of this solution. Hilgenfeld's inference (p. xxxix), 'Irenæus hac epistula quamvis nondum Clementi Romano adscripta usus esse videtur', seems to me quite unwarranted by the coincidence. We have in fact a similar coincidence in Hippol. *Hær.* x. 33 (p. 336) ἵνα ἐπὶ τῷ μικρῷ πιστὸς εὑρεθεὶς καὶ τὸ μέγα πιστευθῆναι δυνηθῇς.

12. ἄρα οὖν] A favourite colloca-tion of particles in S. Paul: see Fritzsche on Rom. v. 18. The accentuation ἄρα οὖν is erroneous.

τοῦτο λέγει] '*He means this*': as in § 2 (twice), § 12. See the note on *Galatians* iii. 17. The words therefore which follow ought not to be treated as an apocryphal quotation, as they are by several editors and others.

13. ἄσπιλον] For τηρεῖν ἄσπιλον comp. 1 Tim. vi. 14, James i. 27.

14. ἀπολάβωμεν] '*secure.*' The preposition implies that it is already potentially our own, so that we are only *recovering* a right: see *Galatians* iv. 5 with the note.

IX. 'Do not deny the resurrection of the body. As we were called in the flesh, so also shall we be judged in the flesh. As Christ being spirit became flesh for us, so shall we in the flesh receive our recompense. Let us love one another; let us make a return to God for His goodness. What must this return be? Sincere repentance and unceasing praise—the praise not of our lips only, but of our hearts and of our actions.'

15. καὶ μὴ λεγέτω τις κ.τ.λ.] This passage, as far as ἀποληψόμεθα τὸν μισθόν, is quoted in several collections of Syriac fragments, immediately after the opening sentence of this epistle: see the note on the beginning of § 1,.

νιον. λέγει γὰρ ὁ Κύριος ἐν τῷ εὐαγγελίῳ· Εἰ τὸ
10 μικρὸν οὐκ ἐτηρήσατε, τὸ μέγα τίς ὑμῖν δώσει; λέγω
γὰρ ὑμῖν ὅτι ὁ πιστὸς ἐν ἐλαχίστῳ καὶ ἐν πολλῷ πιστός ἐστιν. ἄρα οὖν τοῦτο λέγει· τηρήσατε τὴν
σάρκα ἁγνὴν καὶ τὴν σφραγῖδα ἄσπιλον, ἵνα τὴν
αἰώνιον ζωὴν ἀπολάβωμεν.
15 IX. Καὶ μὴ λεγέτω τις ὑμῶν, ὅτι αὕτη ἡ σὰρξ
οὐ κρίνεται οὐδὲ ἀνίσταται. γνῶτε· ἐν τίνι ἐσώθητε,

where the Syriac quotation is given. The sentence εἷς Χριστός...ἡμᾶς ἐκάλεσεν is also quoted by Timotheus of Alexandria (preserved in Syriac, Cureton *Corp. Ignat.* p. 212, 244).

αὕτη ἡ σὰρξ κ.τ.λ.] Difficulties on this point were very early felt and met by S. Paul, 1 Cor. xv. 12 sq. A little later the precursors of Gnosticism boldly maintained that the only resurrection was a spiritual resurrection (2 Tim. ii. 18). It afterwards became a settled tenet of the Gnostic sects to deny the resurrection of the body: see Polyc. *Phil.* 7 ὃς ἂν μεθοδεύῃ τὰ λόγια τοῦ Κυρίου πρὸς τὰς ἰδίας ἐπιθυμίας καὶ λέγῃ μήτε ἀνάστασιν μήτε κρίσιν εἶναι, Justin *Dial.* 80 (p. 306 D) εἰ γὰρ καὶ συνεβάλετε ὑμεῖς τισὶ λεγομένοις Χριστιανοῖς...οἳ καὶ λέγουσι μὴ εἶναι νεκρῶν ἀνάστασιν ἀλλ' ἅμα τῷ ἀποθνήσκειν τὰς ψυχὰς αὐτῶν ἀναλαμβάνεσθαι εἰς τὸν οὐρανόν, μὴ ὑπολάβητε αὐτοὺς Χριστιανούς κ.τ.λ., Iren. ii. 31. 2 τοσοῦτον δὲ ἀποδέουσι τὸν νεκρὸν ἐγείραι...ut ne quidem credant hoc in totum posse fieri; esse autem resurrectionem a mortuis agnitionem ejus, quae ab eis dicitur, veritatis' (comp. v. 31. 1, 2), *Act. Paul. et Thecl.* 14 ἡμεῖς σε διδάξομεν, ἣν λέγει οὗτος ἀνάστασιν γενέσθαι, ὅτι ἤδη γέγονεν ἐφ' οἷς ἔχομεν τέκνοις, καὶ ἀνιστάμεθα Θεὸν ἐπεγνωκότες ἀληθῆ, Tertull. *de Res. Carn.* 19 'Nacti quidam sollemnissimam eloquii prophetici formam, allegorici et figurati, non tamen semper, resurrectionem quoque mortuorum manifeste annuntiatam in imaginariam significationem distorquent etc.', with the following chapters.

From this doctrine the antinomian Gnostics deduced two consequences; (1) That the defilement of the flesh is a matter of indifference, provided that the spirit has grasped the truth. Against this error is directed the warning Hermas *Sim.* v. 7 τὴν σάρκα σου ταύτην φύλασσε καθαρὰν καὶ ἀμίαντον, ἵνα τὸ πνεῦμα τὸ κατενοικοῦν ἐν αὐτῇ μαρτυρήσῃ αὐτῇ καὶ δικαιωθῇ σου ἡ σάρξ· βλέπε μήποτε ἀναβῇ ἐπὶ τὴν καρδίαν σου τὴν σάρκα σου ταύτην φθαρτὴν εἶναι καὶ παραχρήσῃ αὐτῇ ἐν μιασμῷ τινί κ.τ.λ. This practical consequence our writer seems to have distinctly in view §§ 8, 9. (2) That it is legitimate to decline martyrdom and to avoid persecution by a denial of Christ with a mental reservation. Rightly or wrongly this charge is constantly brought against them by their antagonists. Thus Agrippa Castor, writing against Basilides (Euseb. *H.E.* iv. 7), represented him as teaching ἀδιαφορεῖν εἰδωλοθύτων ἀπογευομένους καὶ ἐξομνυμένους ἀπαραφυλάκτως τὴν πίστιν κατὰ τοὺς τῶν διωγμῶν καιρούς: and Iren. *Haer.* iii. 18. 5 'Ad tantam temeritatem pro-

ἐν τίνι ἀνεβλέψατε, εἰ μὴ ἐν τῇ σαρκὶ ταύτῃ ὄντες; δεῖ οὖν ἡμᾶς ὡς ναὸν Θεοῦ φυλάσσειν τὴν σάρκα· ὃν τρόπον γὰρ ἐν τῇ σαρκὶ ἐκλήθητε, καὶ ἐν τῇ σαρκὶ ἐλεύσεσθε. εἰ Χριστὸς ὁ Κύριος, ὁ σώσας ἡμᾶς, ὢν μὲν τὸ πρῶτον πνεῦμα, ἐγένετο σὰρξ καὶ 5 οὕτως ἡμᾶς ἐκάλεσεν, οὕτως καὶ ἡμεῖς ἐν ταύτῃ τῇ σαρκὶ ἀποληψόμεθα τὸν μισθόν. ἀγαπῶμεν οὖν ἀλλήλους, ὅπως ἔλθωμεν πάντες εἰς τὴν βασιλείαν τοῦ Θεοῦ. ὡς ἔχομεν καιρὸν τοῦ ἰαθῆναι, ἐπιδῶμεν ἑαυ-

4 ἐλεύσεσθε] ελευσεσθαι A. εἰ] Syr. Fragm. εισ A, Timoth. See below.
7 ἀποληψόμεθα] αποληψομαιθα A.

gressi sunt quidam ut etiam martyres spernant et vituperent eos qui propter Domini confessionem occiduntur etc.'; (comp. i. 24. 6). This is a constant charge in Tertullian. See on this subject Ritschl *Altkath. Kirche* p. 495 sq. This view again seems to be combated by our writer, §§ 4, 5, 7, 10.

Schwegler *Nachap. Zeitalt.* I. p. 453 sq. maintained that the expression in our text is directed against docetic Ebionism. He is well refuted by Hilgenfeld *Apost. Vät.* p. 115 sq.

1. ἐν τίνι] '*in what*', not '*in whom*', as the following εἰ μὴ ἐν τῇ σαρκὶ shows.

ἀνεβλέψατε] '*ye recovered your sight*'; comp. § 1 τοιαύτης ἀχλύος γέμοντες ἐν τῇ ὁράσει ἀνεβλέψαμεν κ.τ.λ.

2. ὡς ναὸν Θεοῦ κ.τ.λ.] See Ign. *Philad.* 7 τὴν σάρκα ὑμῶν ὡς ναὸν Θεοῦ τηρεῖτε: comp. 1 Cor. iii. 16, 17, vi. 19, 2 Cor. vi. 16, and see *Ign. Ephes.* 9, 15 (with the notes).

4. εἰ Χριστὸς κ.τ.λ.] The reading of the Syriac fragments (εἰ for εἶς), which seems to have escaped Jacobson and Hilgenfeld, is evidently required by the context. Mill and others would have read ὡς, which gives the same sense. Editors quote as a parallel *Ign. Magn.* 7 εἷς ἐστὶν Ἰησοῦς Χριστός, but εἷς is quite out of place here, though appropriate there where the writer is dwelling on *unity*. It is possible that the reading of the MS ΕΙC arose out of ΕIIC i.e. εἰ Ἰησοῦς, or ΕΙΟΙC i.e. εἰ ὁ Ἰησοῦς. The confusion would be easier, as the preceding word ends in Ε. Young read the MS ΟΙC i.e. ὁ Ἰησοῦς, but this is wrong.

5. ὢν μέν] as though the sentence were intended to be continued in a participial form γενόμενος δέ.

τὸ πρῶτον πνεῦμα] The doctrine of the pre-existence of the Son, as the Logos, is here presented in a somewhat unusual form; comp. however Hermas *Sim.* v. 6 τὸ πνεῦμα τὸ ἅγιον, τὸ προόν, τὸ κτίσαν πᾶσαν τὴν κτίσιν, κατῴκισεν ὁ Θεὸς εἰς σάρκα ἣν ἐβούλετο, ix. 1 ἐκεῖνο γὰρ τὸ πνεῦμα ὁ υἱὸς τοῦ Θεοῦ ἐστίν, Theoph. *ad Autol.* ii. 10 οὗτος οὖν ὢν πνεῦμα Θεοῦ καὶ ἀρχὴ καὶ σοφία καὶ δύναμις ὑψίστου κατήρχετο εἰς τοὺς προφήτας καὶ δι' αὐτῶν ἐλάλει κ.τ.λ., Tertull. *adv. Marc.* iii. 16 'Spiritus Creatoris qui est Christus', Hippol. *c. Noet.* 4 (p. 47 Lagarde) λόγος σὰρξ ἦν, πνεῦμα ἦν,

10 τοὺς τῷ θεραπεύοντι Θεῷ, ἀντιμισθίαν αὐτῷ διδόντες·
ποίαν; τὸ μετανοῆσαι ἐξ εἰλικρινοῦς καρδίας· προ-
γνώστης γάρ ἐστιν τῶν πάντων καὶ εἰδὼς ἡμῶν τὰ
ἐν καρδίᾳ. δῶμεν οὖν αὐτῷ αἶνον αἰώνιον, μὴ ἀπὸ
στόματος μόνον ἀλλὰ καὶ ἀπὸ καρδίας, ἵνα ἡμᾶς
15 προσδέξηται ὡς υἱούς. καὶ γὰρ εἶπεν ὁ Κύριος·
Ἀδελφοί μου οὗτοί εἰcιν οἱ ποιοῦντες τὸ θέλημα τοῦ
πατρός μου.

11 εἰλικρινοῦς] ιλικρινους A. 13 αἶνον] om. A. 16 ποιοῦντες] πουντεσ A.

δύναμις ἦν κ.τ.λ. See especially Dorner *Lehre von der Person Christi* I. p. 205 sq.

9. ὡς ἔχομεν καιρόν] 'while we have opportunity': comp. Gal. vi. 10 (with the note), Ign. *Smyrn*. 9 ὡς ἔτι καιρὸν ἔχομεν. Another instance of ὡς, '*while*', occurs above, § 8.

11. προγνώστης] Justin *Apol*. i. 44 (p. 82 B), Tatian *ad Grac.* 19, Theoph. *ad Autol.* ii. 15.

12. τὰ ἐν καρδίᾳ] 2 Chron. xxxii. 31 εἰδέναι τὰ ἐν τῇ καρδίᾳ αὐτοῦ, Deut. viii. 2 διαγνωσθῇ τὰ ἐν τῇ καρδίᾳ σου, 1 Sam. ix. 19, etc. Hilgenfeld reads τὰ ἐνκάρδια, saying 'ἐνκάρδια (s. ἐγκάρδια) c. cod., Jun., ἐν καρδίᾳ ceteri edd.' But, inasmuch as an iota subscript or adscript never appears in MSS of this date, the transcriber could not have written ἐν καρδίᾳ otherwise than he has done. Moreover, since ἐν καρδίᾳ and ἐν τῇ καρδίᾳ occur numberless times in the LXX, whereas the adjective ἐγκάρδιος is not once found there, this reading seems to me improbable. In Clem. Al. *Pæd.* i. 3 (p. 103) I should be disposed conversely to read διορῶν τὰ ἐν καρδίᾳ (for ἐγκάρδια) λόγος. The word ἐγκάρδιος however is legitimate in itself.

13. αἶνον αἰώνιον] This is doubtless the right emendation: see above p. 25 and the note on εὑρεῖν below § 9.

16. ἀδελφοί μου κ.τ.λ.] Matt. xii. 49 ἰδοὺ ἡ μήτηρ μου καὶ οἱ ἀδελφοί μου· ὅστις γὰρ ἂν ποιήσῃ τὸ θέλημα τοῦ πατρός μου τοῦ ἐν οὐρανοῖς, αὐτός μου ἀδελφὸς καὶ ἀδελφὴ καὶ μήτηρ ἐστίν (comp. Mark iii. 35); Luke viii. 21 μήτηρ μου καὶ ἀδελφοί μου οὗτοί εἰσιν, οἱ τὸν λόγον τοῦ Θεοῦ ἀκούοντες καὶ ποιοῦντες. Epiphanius, *Hær.* xxx. 14 (p. 139), gives the saying Οὗτοί εἰσιν οἱ ἀδελφοί μου καὶ ἡ μήτηρ, οἱ ποιοῦντες τὰ θελήματα τοῦ πατρός μου, as it is assumed, from an Ebionite gospel (Westcott *Canon* p. 160, Hilgenfeld *Apost. Vät.* p. 122); but I do not think his language implies more than that the Ebionites allowed the saying to stand in their recension of the Gospel, and he may be quoting loosely from the canonical Evangelists. A still wider divergence from the canonical passages is in Clem. Alex. *Ecl. Proph.* 20 (p. 994) ἄγει οὖν εἰς ἐλευθερίαν τὴν τοῦ πατρὸς συγκληρονόμους υἱοὺς καὶ φίλους· Ἀδελφοί μου γάρ, φησὶν ὁ Κύριος, καὶ συγκληρονόμοι οἱ ποιοῦντες τὸ θέλημα τοῦ πατρός μου, where the context shows that συγκληρονόμοι is deliberately given as part of the quotation. Omitting καὶ συγκληρονόμοι, it will be seen that this form of the saying agrees exactly

X. Ὥστε, ἀδελφοί μου, ποιήσωμεν τὸ θέλημα
τοῦ πατρὸς τοῦ καλέσαντος ἡμᾶς, ἵνα ζήσωμεν, καὶ
διώξωμεν μᾶλλον τὴν ἀρετήν, τὴν δὲ κακίαν κατα-
λείψωμεν ὡς προοδοίπορον τῶν ἁμαρτιῶν ἡμῶν, καὶ
φύγωμεν τὴν ἀσέβειαν, μὴ ἡμᾶς καταλάβῃ κακά. ἐὰν 5
γὰρ σπουδάσωμεν ἀγαθοποιεῖν, διώξεται ἡμᾶς εἰρήνη.
Διὰ ταύτην γὰρ τὴν αἰτίαν οὐκ ἔστιν †εὑρεῖν† ἄνθρωπον, οἵτινες παράγουσι φόβους ἀνθρωπίνους, προῃ-
ρημένοι μᾶλλον τὴν ἐνθάδε ἀπόλαυσιν ἢ τὴν μέλ-

with our pseudo-Clement's quotation.

X. 'Let us therefore fulfil the will of our Father. Let us flee from vice, lest evil overtake us. Let us do good, that peace may pursue us. They who teach the fear of men rather than the fear of God, are duly punished. And, if they themselves alone suffered, it were tolerable. But now they shall have a double condemnation, for they lead others besides themselves into ruin.'

2. ἵνα ζήσωμεν] to be connected not with τοῦ καλέσαντος ἡμᾶς, but with ποιήσωμεν.

4. προοδοίπορον] 'a forerunner'; for κακία is the evil disposition, while ἁμαρτία is the actual sin. On κακία see Trench *N. T. Syn.* 1st ser. § xi, where he quotes the definition of Calvin (on Ephes. iv. 32) '*Animi pravitas* quæ humanitati et æquitati est opposita et malignitas vulgo nuncupata'. The substantive προοδοίπορος seems to be very rare, though the verb προοδοιπορεῖν occurs occasionally.

6. ἀγαθοποιεῖν] See the note on the First Epistle § 2 ἀγαθοποιΐαν.

7. †εὑρεῖν†] sc. εἰρήνην; 'For this reason a man cannot find peace'. If we take the reading of the MS, no other meaning seems possible; but it can hardly be correct. Previous editors have supposed the error to lie in ἄνθρωπον, written ΑΝΟΝ in the MS. Accordingly ΑΝΘΝ (i. e. ἂν θεόν) has been suggested by Wotton; ΟΥΝΟΝ (i. e. οὐρανόν) by Davies; and ΑΙΝΟΝ (αἶνον) by Hilgenfeld. But in the first correction the ἂν is grammatically inexplicable; and the second and third give unnatural expressions. I believe the mistake is in ΕΥΡΕΙΝ, and should suggest ΕΙΡΗΝΗΝΕΥΡΕΙΝ or ΕΙΡΗΝΕΥΕΙΝ, or still better ΕΥΗΜΕ-ΡΕΙΝ. If εὐημερεῖν '*to prosper*' be adopted, the writer seems to have in mind Ps. xxxiv. 9 sq. φοβήθητε τὸν Κύριον πάντες...οὐκ ἔστιν ὑστέρημα τοῖς φοβουμένοις αὐτόν...φόβον Κυρίου διδάξω ὑμᾶς. τίς ἐστιν ἄνθρωπος ὁ θέλων ζωήν, ἀγαπῶν ἡμέρας ἰδεῖν ἀγαθάς;...ἔκκλινον ἀπὸ κακοῦ καὶ ποίησον ἀγαθόν, ζήτησον εἰρήνην καὶ δίωξον αὐτήν, where the coincidences are striking. The contrast between the *fear of men* and *the fear of God*, which underlies this passage, would naturally suggest to our author the words in which the Psalmist emphatically preaches the fear of the Lord. For εὐημερεῖν, εὐημερία, comp. 2 Macc. v. 6, viii. 8, x. 28, xii. 11, xiii. 16, xiv. 14. For the manner in which our transcriber drops letters (more.

x] TO THE CORINTHIANS. 205

10 λουσαν ἐπαγγελίαν. ἀγνοοῦσιν γὰρ ἡλίκην ἔχει βάσανον
ἡ ἐνθάδε ἀπόλαυσις, καὶ οἵαν τρυφὴν ἔχει ἡ μέλλουσα
ἐπαγγελία. καὶ εἰ μὲν αὐτοὶ μόνοι ταῦτα ἔπρασσον,
ἀνεκτὸν ἦν· νῦν δὲ ἐπιμένουσιν κακοδιδασκαλοῦντες
τὰς ἀναιτίους ψυχάς, οὐκ εἰδότες ὅτι δισσὴν ἕξουσιν
15 τὴν κρίσιν, αὐτοί τε καὶ οἱ ἀκούοντες αὐτῶν.
XI. Ἡμεῖς οὖν ἐν καθαρᾷ καρδίᾳ δουλεύσωμεν
τῷ Θεῷ, καὶ ἐσόμεθα δίκαιοι· ἐὰν δὲ μὴ δουλεύσωμεν διὰ τοῦ μὴ πιστεύειν ἡμᾶς [τῇ] ἐπαγγελίᾳ τοῦ
Θεοῦ, ταλαίπωρ[οι] ἐσόμεθα. λέγει γὰρ καὶ ὁ προ-

10 ἐπαγγελίαν] επαγγελειαν A.   ἡλίκην] ηληκην A.
12 ἐπαγγελία] επαγγελεια A.   14 ἀναιτίους] ανετιουσ A.

especially where there is a proximity of similar forms) comp. § 9 αιωνιον for αἰνον αἰώνιον, πουντεσ for ποιοῦντες, § 11 ασουκ for ἃς οὓς οὐκ. See also in the First Epistle § 11 ετερογνωμοσ, § 25 τελευτηκοτοσ, § 32 ημερασ (for ἡμετέρας), etc., and (if my conjecture be correct) § 40 the omission of ἐπιμελῶς before ἐπιτελεῖσθαι.

8. οἵτινες] 'men who,' the antecedent being the singular ἄνθρωπον. This grammatical irregularity is not uncommon: see Jelf's Gramm. § 819. 2. a.

παράγουσι κ.τ.λ.] 'introduce (instil) fears of men': comp. § 4 οὐ δεῖ ἡμᾶς φοβεῖσθαι τοὺς ἀνθρώπους μᾶλλον ἀλλὰ τὸν Θεόν. The passages in the lexicons will show that Hilgenfeld's correction παρεισάγουσι for παράγουσι is unnecessary. He rightly explains the words (Apost. Vät. p. 118) to refer to those Gnostics who taught that outward conformity to heathen rites was indifferent and that persecution might thus be rightly escaped: comp. κακοδιδασκαλοῦντες below, and see the note above on § 9 αὕτη ἡ σάρξ κ.τ.λ.

10. ἐπαγγελίαν] i.e. the subject, the fulfilment, of the promise, as e.g. Acts i. 4, Gal. iii. 14, Heb. vi. 15.

13. ἀνεκτὸν ἦν] For the imperfect see Winer § xlii. p. 321.

κακοδιδασκαλοῦντες] Ign. Philad. 2 κακοδιδασκαλίας. So καλοδιδασκάλους, Tit. ii. 3.

14. δισσήν κ.τ.λ.] For the form of the sentence comp. Gen. xliii. 11 καὶ τὸ ἀργύριον δισσὸν λάβετε.

XI. 'Let us therefore serve God and believe His promise. If we waver, we are lost. Remember how the word of prophecy denounces the distrustful, how it compares the fulfilment of God's purpose to the gradual ripening of the fruit on the vine, how it promises blessings at the last to His people. God is faithful and He will perform. Let us therefore work patiently, and we shall inherit such good things as pass man's understanding.'

16. καθαρᾷ καρδίᾳ] 1 Tim. i. 5, 2 Tim. ii. 22 (comp. Matt. v. 8), Hermas Vis. iii. 9.

19. ὁ προφητικὸς λόγος] From some apocryphal source, perhaps Eldad and Modad: see the notes on

[φη]τικὸς λόγος· Ταλαίπωροί εἰς[ιν] οἱ δίψυχοι, οἱ διστάζοντες τ[ῇ] καρδίᾳ, οἱ λέγοντες· Ταῦτα πά[ντα] ἠκούσαμεν καὶ ἐπὶ τῶν πατ[έ]ρων ἡμῶν, ἡμεῖς δὲ ἡμέραν ἐξ ἡμέρας προσδεχόμενοι οὐδὲν τούτων ἑωράκαμεν. Ἀνόητοι, συμβάλετε ἑαυτοὺς ξύλῳ, λάβετε 5 ἄμπελον· πρῶτον μὲν φυλλοροεῖ, εἶτα βλαστὸς γίνεται, μετὰ ταῦτα ὄμφαξ, εἶτα σταφυλὴ παρεστηκυῖα· οὕτως καὶ ὁ λαός μου ἀκαταστασίας καὶ θλίψεις ἔσχεν· ἔπειτα ἀπολήψεται τὰ ἀγαθά. *Ὥστε, ἀδελφοί μου, μὴ διψυχῶμεν, ἀλλὰ ἐλπίσαντες ὑπομείνωμεν, ἵνα καὶ τὸν μισθὸν* 10

8 ἔπειτα] επιτα A.

the First Epistle § 23, where also the passage is quoted. The variations from the quotation in the First Epistle are these : (1) τῇ καρδίᾳ] τὴν ψυχήν (2) πάντα] om. (3) ἡμεῖς δέ... ἑωράκαμεν] καὶ ἰδοὺ γεγηράκαμεν καὶ οὐδὲν ἡμῖν τούτων συνβέβηκεν (4) ἀνόητοι] ὦ ἀνόητοι. (5) γίνεται] add. εἶτα φύλλον, εἶτα ἄνθος καί (6) οὕτως καὶ κ.τ.λ.] this close of the quotation not given. These variations are sufficient to show that the writer of the Second Epistle cannot have derived the passage solely from the First. At the same time the coincidence of two remarkable quotations in this very chapter (see below on οὓς οὐκ ἤκουσεν κ.τ.λ.), which occur also in the First Epistle, besides other resemblances (e. g. § 3), seems to prove that our writer was acquainted with and borrowed from the genuine Clement.

The additions which some editors introduce into the text here (υἱοὶ after ἡμεῖς δέ, and ἔτι after ἑωράκαμεν) are due to a mistake. The traces, which they have wrongly so read, are the reversed impressions of letters on the opposite leaf (now lost).

The photograph shows this clearly.

3. ἡμέραν ἐξ ἡμέρας] '*day after day*' : Num. xxx. 15, 2 Pet. ii. 8. This additional coincidence of the passage quoted with the language of 2 Peter (see the notes on the First Epistle, § 23) is worthy of notice. It seems hardly possible that the two can be wholly independent, though we have no means of determining their relation.

9. μὴ διψυχῶμεν] See the note on the First Epistle § 11.

11. πιστὸς γάρ κ.τ.λ.] Heb. x. 23 πιστὸς γὰρ ὁ ἐπαγγειλάμενος.

12. ἀποδιδόναι ἑκάστῳ κ.τ.λ.] Matt. xvi. 27, Rom. ii. 6, Rev. xxii. 12. See also the quotation given in the First Epistle, § 34.

14. εἰσήξομεν] 'Vocem εἰσήκειν non agnoscunt Lexica', Jacobson. It occurs as early as Æschylus, and several instances of it are given in Steph. Thes.

15. οὓς κ.τ.λ.] See the note on the First Epistle § 34, where the same passage occurs. The ἁς should not be treated as part of the quotation.

XII. 'Let us then patiently wait for the kingdom of God. The time

κομισώμεθα. πιστὸς γάρ ἐστιν ὁ ἐπαγγειλάμενος τὰς
ἀντιμισθίας ἀποδιδόναι ἑκάστῳ τῶν ἔργων αὐτοῦ. ἐὰν
οὖν ποιήσωμεν τὴν δικαιοσύνην ἐναντίον τοῦ Θεοῦ,
εἰσήξομεν εἰς τὴν βασιλείαν αὐτοῦ καὶ ληψόμεθα
15 τὰς ἐπαγγελίας, ἃς οὓς οὐκ ἤκογςεν οὐδὲ ὀφθαλμὸς
εἶδεν, οὐδὲ ἐπὶ καρδίαν ἀνθρώπογ ἀνέβη.
XII. Ἐκδεχώμεθα οὖν καθ' ὥραν τὴν βασιλείαν
τοῦ Θεοῦ ἐν ἀγάπῃ καὶ δικαιοσύνῃ, ἐπειδὴ οὐκ οἴ-
δαμεν τὴν ἡμέραν τῆς ἐπιφανείας τοῦ Θεοῦ. ἐπερω-
20 τηθεὶς γὰρ αὐτὸς ὁ Κύριος ὑπό τινος, πότε ἥξει

15 ἃς οὓς οὐκ] ασουκ A.   19 ἐπιφανείας] επιφανιασ A.

of its coming is uncertain. Our Lord's answer to Salome says that it shall be delayed till *the two shall be one, and the outward as the inward, and the male with the female, neither male nor female*. By this saying He means that mutual harmony must first prevail, that the soul must be manifested in good works, and that...

17. καθ' ὥραν] '*betimes*', 'tempestive', according to its usual meaning; e.g. Job v. 26, Zach. x. 1. It is commonly translated here 'in horas', '*from hour to hour*'.

19. ἐπιφανείας] This word, as a synonym for the παρουσία, occurs in the New Testament only in the Pastoral Epistles, 1 Tim. vi. 14, 2 Tim. i. 10, iv. 1, 8, Tit. ii. 13; compare the indirect use in 2 Thess. ii. 8 τῇ ἐπιφανείᾳ τῆς παρουσίας αὐτοῦ.

20. ὑπό τινος] by Salome. This incident was reported in the Gospel of the Egyptians, as we learn from Clem. Alex. *Strom.* iii. 13, p. 553 (in a passage quoted from Julius Cassianus), where the narrative is given thus: πυνθανομένης τῆς Σαλώμης, πότε γνωσθήσεται τὰ περὶ ὧν ἥρετο, ἔφη ὁ Κύριος, Ὅταν οὖν τὸ τῆς αἰσχύνης ἔνδυ-

μα πατήσητε, καὶ ὅταν γένηται τὰ δύο ἕν, καὶ τὸ ἄρρεν μετὰ τῆς θηλείας οὔτε ἄρρεν οὔτε θῆλυ. To this Clement adds ἐν τοῖς παραδεδομένοις ἡμῖν τέτταρσιν εὐαγγελίοις οὐκ ἔχομεν τὸ ῥητὸν ἀλλ' ἐν τῷ κατ' Αἰγυπτίους. Similar passages from this gospel and apparently from the same context are quoted by Clement previously, *Strom.* iii. 6 (p. 532) τῇ Σαλώμῃ ὁ Κύριος πυνθανομένῃ μέχρι πότε θάνατος ἰσχύσει...Μέχρις ἄν, εἶπεν, ὑμεῖς αἱ γυναῖκες τίκτετε, and *Strom.* iii. 9 (p. 539 sq.) κἀκεῖνα λέγουσι τὰ πρὸς Σαλώμην εἰρημένα, ὧν πρότερον ἐμνήσθημεν (*Strom.* iii. 6, just quoted)· φέρεται δέ, οἶμαι, ἐν τῷ κατ' Αἰγυπτίους εὐαγγελίῳ· φασὶ γὰρ ὅτι αὐτὸς εἶπεν ὁ σωτήρ, Ἦλθον καταλῦσαι τὰ ἔργα τῆς θηλείας...ὅθεν εἰκότως περὶ συντελείας μηνύσαντος τοῦ Λόγου, ἡ Σαλώμη φησί· Μέχρι τίνος οἱ ἄνθρωποι ἀποθανοῦνται; παρατετηρημένως ἀποκρίνεται ὁ Κύριος, Μέχρις ἂν τίκτωσιν αἱ γυναῖκες...τί δέ; οὐχὶ καὶ τὰ ἑξῆς τῶν πρὸς Σαλώμην εἰρημένων ἐπιφέρουσιν οἱ πάντα μᾶλλον ἢ τῷ κατὰ τὴν ἀλήθειαν εὐαγγελικῷ στοιχήσαντες κάνονι; φαμένης γὰρ αὐτῆς, Καλῶς οὖν ἐποίησα μὴ τεκοῦσα...ἀμείβεται λέγων ὁ Κύριος, Πᾶσαν φάγε βοτάνην, τὴν δὲ

αὐτοῦ ἡ βασιλεία, εἶπεν· Ὅταν ἔςται τὰ Δύο ἕν, καὶ τὸ
ἔξω ὡς τὸ ἔςω, καὶ τὸ ἄρςεν μετὰ τῆς θηλείας, οὔτε
ἄρςεν οὔτε θῆλυ. Τὰ Δύο δὲ ἕν ἐστιν, ὅταν λαλῶ-
μεν ἑαυτοῖς ἀλήθειαν, καὶ ἐν δυσὶ σώμασιν ἀνυποκρί-

2 θηλείας] θηλιασ A.   4 ἑαυτοῖς] αυτοισ A.

πικρίαν ἔχουσαν μὴ φάγῃς. One of the sayings in the last passage is again referred to in *Exc. Theod.* 67, p. 985, ὅταν ὁ σωτὴρ πρὸς Σαλώμην λέγῃ μέχρι τότε εἶναι θάνατον ἄχρις ἂν αἱ γυναῖκες τίκτωσιν. There is nothing in these passages to suggest that Clement himself had read this gospel (unless indeed, as has occurred to me, we should read τί δὲ οὐχὶ κ.τ.λ.; for τί δέ; οὐχὶ κ.τ.λ. in *Strom.* iii. 9), and the expressions λέγουσι, οἶμαι, φασί, seem to imply the contrary; though it is generally assumed that he was acquainted with it. Of the historical value of this narrative we may remark: (1) The mystical colouring of these sayings is quite alien to the character of our Lord's utterances as reported in the authentic Gospels, though entirely in keeping with the tone of Greco-Egyptian speculation. Epiphanius thus describes this apocryphal gospel (*Hær.* lxii. 2, p. 514) πολλὰ τοιαῦτα ὡς ἐν παραβύστῳ μυστηριωδῶς ἐκ προσώπου τοῦ σωτῆρος ἀναφέρεται. (2) The only external fact which can be tested—the reference to Salome as childless—is in direct contradiction to the canonical narratives. This contradiction however might be removed by an easy change of reading, καλῶς οὖν ἂν ἐποίησα for καλῶς οὖν ἐποίησα. The Egyptian Gospel was highly esteemed by certain Gnostic sects as the Ophites (Hippol. *Hær.* v. 7, p. 99), by the Encratites (Clem. Alex. *Strom.* ll. cc.), and by the Sabellians (Epiphan. *Hær.* l. c.). The Encratites especially valued it, alleging the passages above quoted as discountenancing marriage and thus favouring their own ascetic views. This was possibly the tendency of the Egyptian Gospel, as is maintained by Schneckenburger (*Ueber das Evang. des Ægypt.* Bern 1834, p. 5 sq.) and M. Nicolas (*Evangiles Apocryphes* p. 119 sq.); but the inference is at least doubtful. Clement of Alexandria refuses to accept the interpretations of the Encratites; and though his own are sometimes fanciful, still all the passages quoted may reasonably be explained otherwise than in an Encratite sense.

This quotation has a special interest as indicating something of the unknown author of our Second Epistle. As several of his quotations cannot be referred to the canonical Gospels (see §§ 4, 5, 8), it seems not unnatural to assign them to the apocryphal source which in this one instance he is known to have used. This suspicion is borne out by a fact to which I have called attention above. One of our Lord's sayings quoted by him (§ 9) bears a close resemblance to the words as given in the *Excerpta Theodoti;* and we have just seen that the Gospel of the Egyptians was quoted in this collection. Thus our pseudo-Clement would seem to have employed this apocryphal gospel as a principal authority for the sayings of our Lord. Now this gospel was in character,

5 τως εἴη μία ψυχή. καὶ τὸ ἔξω ὡc τὸ ἔcω, τοῦτο
λέγει· τὴν ψυχὴν λέγει τὸ ἔσω, τὸ δὲ ἔξ[ω] τὸ σῶμα λέγει. ὃν τρόπον οὖν σου τὸ σῶμα φαίνεται, οὕτως καὶ ἡ ψυχή σου δῆλος ἔστω ἐν τ[οῖς] καλοῖς ἔργοις.
καὶ τὸ ἄρceν μετὰ τῆc θηλείαc, ογτε ἄρceν ογτε θῆλγ,
10 τοῦτο....

as in name, essentially Egyptian; it is known chiefly through Alexandrian writers and its principal circulation was probably in Egypt: and thus a presumption is created that he was not unconnected with this country.

3. τὰ δύο δὲ ἕν] i.e. when peace and harmony shall reign. So the opposite is thus expressed in Seneca *de Ira* iii. 8 'Non tulit Cælius adsentientem et exclamavit, *Dic aliquid contra, ut duo simus*'; comp. Plato *Symp.* 191 D ὁ ἔρως...ἐπιχειρῶν ποιῆσαι ἓν ἐκ δυοῖν καὶ ἰάσασθαι τὴν φύσιν τὴν ἀνθρωπίνην (quoted by Lagarde *Rel. Jur. Eccl.* p. 75).

4. ἑαυτοῖς] '*to one another*', as e.g. Ephes. iv. 32, Col. iii. 13, 16, 1 Pet. iv. 8, 10. If the reading of the MS be correct, it must be aspirated αὑτοῖς, and this form is perhaps less unlikely than in the earlier and genuine epistle (see the notes there on §§ 9, 12, 14, etc.). The expression occurs in Ephes. iv. 25 λαλεῖτε ἀλήθειαν ἕκαστος μετὰ τοῦ πλησίον αὐτοῦ.

5. τὸ ἔξω ὡς τὸ ἔσω] perhaps meaning originally '*when the outside corresponds with the inside*, when men appear as they are, when there is no hypocrisy or deception.' The pseudo-Clement's interpretation is slightly but not essentially different. This clause is omitted in the quotation of Julius Cassianus (*Strom.* iii. 13, p. 553, quoted above), who thus appears to have connected τὰ δύο ἐν closely with τὸ ἄρρεν μετὰ τῆς θηλείας and interpreted the expression similarly.

See Hippol. *Hær.* v. 18 (p. 173 sq.) καὶ ἔστιν ἀρσενόθηλυς δύναμις καὶ ἐπίνοια, ὅθεν ἀλλήλοις ἀντιστοιχοῦσιν...ἐν ὄντες...ἔστιν οὖν οὕτως καὶ τὸ φανὲν ἀπ' αὐτῶν, ἓν ὄν, δύο εὑρίσκεσθαι, ἀρσενόθηλυς ἔχων τὴν θήλειαν ἐν ἑαυτῷ, a passage quoted by this father from the *Great Announcement* of the Simonians. We may perhaps infer from a comparison of Cassianus' quotation with our pseudo-Clement's, that Cassianus strung together detached sentences, omitting all that could not be interpreted to bear on his Encratite views. Compare pseudo-Linus *de Pass. Petr. Apost.* (Bigne's *Magn. Bibl. Patr.* I. p. 72 E) 'Unde Dominus in mysterio dixerat: Si non feceritis dextram sicut sinistram et sinistram sicut dextram, et quæ sursum sicut deorsum et quæ ante sicut retro, non cognoscetis regnum Dei', which 'appears to contain another version of this saying' (Westcott *Introd. to Gospels* p. 427).

8. δῆλος] The lexicons give only one instance of this feminine, Eurip. *Med.* 1197 δῆλος ἦν κατάστασις. Compare τέλειον in Ign. *Philad.* 1.

9. καὶ τὸ ἄρσεν κ.τ.λ.] This supposed saying of our Lord was interpreted by Julius Cassianus, as forbidding marriage. Whether this was its true bearing, we cannot judge, as the whole context and the character of this gospel are not sufficiently known. It might have signified no more than that 'in the kingdom of heaven there is neither marrying nor

(i) Μὴ ταρασσέτω τὴν καρδίαν ὑμῶν, ὅτι βλέπομεν τοὺς ἀδίκους πλουτοῦντας, καὶ στενοχωρουμέ-
νους τοὺς τοῦ Θεοῦ δούλους. οὐδεὶς γὰρ τῶν δικαίων
ταχὺν καρπὸν ἔλαβεν, ἀλλ' ἐκδέχεται αὐτόν. εἰ γὰρ
τὸν μισθὸν τῶν δικαίων ὁ Θεὸς εὐθέως ἀπεδίδου, ἐμπο- 5

giving in marriage (Matt. xxii. 30)', or that the distinctive moral excellences of each sex shall belong to both equally. Clement of Alexandria, answering Julius Cassianus, gives the following interpretation of the passage: The male represents θυμός, the female ἐπιθυμία, according to the well-known Platonic distinction; these veil and hinder the operations of the reason; they produce shame and repentance; they must be stripped off, before the reason can assume its supremacy; then at length ἀποστᾶσα τοῦδε τοῦ σχήματος ᾧ διακρίνεται τὸ ἄρρεν καὶ τὸ θῆλυ, ψυχὴ μετατίθεται εἰς ἕνωσιν, οὐδέτερον οὖσα. Whether our author's explanation was more closely allied to the interpretation of Cassianus or to that of Clement, it is impossible to say. What has gone before, is a presumption in favour of the latter. Nor is there any sufficient ground independently of this for supposing that his views were Encratite in the matter of marriage. I have shown above (p. 16 sq.) that the statements of Epiphanius and Jerome, who speak of Clement as teaching virginity, do not refer to this epistle, as many suppose. And the references elsewhere in the epistle to the duty of keeping the flesh pure (§§ 6, 8, 9) are as applicable to the purity of wedded as of celibate life. Comp. e. g. *Clem. Hom.* iii. 26 γάμον νομιτεύει...εἰς ἁγνείαν πάντας ἄγει.

This saying of the Egyptian Gospel, if it had any historical basis at all (which may be doubted), was perhaps founded on some utterance of our Lord similar in meaning to S. Paul's οὐκ ἔνι ἄρσεν καὶ θῆλυ, Gal. iii. 28. It is worth observing that Clement of Alexandria, in explaining the saying of the Egyptian Gospel, refers to these words of S. Paul and explains them similarly of the θυμός and ἐπιθυμία. See also the views of the Ophites on the ἀρσενόθηλυς (Hippol. *Hær.* v. 6, 7), whence it appears that they also perverted S. Paul's language to their purposes. The name and idea of ἀρσενόθηλυς had their origin in the cosmical speculations embodied in heathen mythology; see *Clem. Hom.* vi. 5, 12, *Clem. Recogn.* i. 69, Athenag. *Suppl.* 21, Hippol. *Hær.* v. 14 (p. 128).

It is equally questionable whether the other sayings attributed to our Lord in this context of the Egyptian Gospel have any bearing on Encratite views. The words 'so long as women bear children' seem to mean nothing more than 'so long as the human race shall be propagated', and 'I came to abolish the works of the female' may have the same sense. The clinching utterance, πᾶσαν φάγε βοτάνην, τὴν δὲ πικρίαν ἔχουσαν μὴ φάγῃς, which has been alleged as showing decisively the Encratite tendencies of the gospel, appears to me to admit of a very different interpretation. It would seem to mean very much the same as S. Paul's πάντα μοι ἔξεστιν ἀλλ' οὐ πάντα συμφέρει, and to accord with the Apostle's injunctions respecting marriage.

In the *Stichometria* of Nicephorus

TO THE CORINTHIANS. 211

ρίαν ἠσκοῦμεν καὶ οὐκ εὐσέβειαν. ἐδοκοῦμεν γὰρ εἶναι
δίκαιοι, οὐ διὰ τὸ εὐσεβές, ἀλλὰ τὸ κερδάλεον διώκοντες.

(ii) Ὁ τῶν παρόντων αἰσθητικὸς συνίησιν ὡς οὔτε
ἃ λογίζονταί τινες εἶναι τερπνά, ξένα καὶ μακράν ἐστι

(see Credner *zur Gesch. des Kanons* p. 122) the Epistles of Clement are described as Κλήμεντος α΄. β΄. στίχοι ,βχ΄. Though other copies read λβ' for α'. β'. (a reading which is reproduced in some MSS of the Latin version by Anastasius Bibliothecarius; Credner *ib*. p. 126, Westcott *Canon* p. 504, ed. 2), and some critics have busied themselves with conjecturing what these 32 books of Clement can have been, there can be no reasonable doubt that the other is the correct text and that the two Epistles to the Corinthians are meant. Thus, as Nicephorus assigns exactly the same number of lines, 2600, to the Gospel of St Luke (Credner *ib*. p. 119), on a rough estimate we may suppose that our two epistles together were about as long as this Gospel. Now in our MS (A) this Gospel occupies 22 leaves and the existing portion of the two Clementine epistles only 12 (including the one which has been accidentally lost between fol. 167 and fol. 168; see p. 23), so that the missing end of the Second Epistle must have taken up about 10 leaves, while the extant portion comprises only 1¾. Thus it would appear that about ⅝ths of the whole epistle have been lost. Of this lost ending two fragments are preserved.

(i) 'Be not dismayed at the prosperity of the unrighteous and the affliction of the saints. The fruits of righteousness are not reaped at once. If it were so, then the pursuit of it would be a matter of traffic and not of piety'.

This fragment is given by Joannes Damascenus *Sacr. Par.* (MS Rupef.) II. p. 783 (Le Quien) with the heading τοῦ ἁγίου Κλήμεντος ἐπισκόπου Ῥώμης ἐκ τῆς β΄ πρὸς Κορινθίους ἐπιστολῆς. As it is closely connected in subject with the topics at which our MS breaks off, it probably followed at no long interval.

1. μὴ ταρασσέτω] John xiv. 1, 27, μὴ ταρασσέσθω ὑμῶν ἡ καρδία κ.τ.λ. ὅτι βλέπομεν κ.τ.λ.] Ps. xlix. 18.

5. ἐμπορίαν κ.τ.λ.] Compare 1 Tim. vi. 5 νομιζόντων πορισμὸν εἶναι τὴν εὐσέβειαν. For the imperfects ἠσκοῦμεν, ἐδοκοῦμεν, without ἄν, see Winer § xlii. p. 320 sq.

(ii) 'Far-sighted men know that apparent goods are very far from being really such. Even health and wealth sometimes are more baneful than their opposites. The most eager wishes fulfilled often lead to the greatest calamity'.

This fragment again, which in subject is allied to the former, is preserved in the same Joannes Damascenus *Sac. Par.* (MS Rupef.) II. p. 787 (Le Quien), with the heading τοῦ ἁγίου Κλήμεντος ἐκ τῆς πρὸς Κορινθίους β΄.

8. ὁ αἰσθητικός] '*one who is quick at apprehending*': see a similar use of the word in Prov. xiv. 10, 30. οὔτε] If the reading be correct, the construction is irregular. See the note on § 1.

14—2

τῶν ἀπεχθῶν, ἀλλὰ καὶ πλοῦτος πολλάκις μᾶλλον
πενίας ἔθλιψε, καὶ ὑγεία πλέον ἠνίασε νόσου. καὶ
καθόλου τῶν λυπηρῶν καὶ φευκτῶν πάντων ὑπόθεσις
καὶ ὕλη ἡ τῶν ἀσπαστῶν καὶ κατ' εὐχὴν περιβολὴ
γίνεται.   5

2. ἠνίασε] ἀνιάω, ἀνιάζω, are not found either in the LXX or in the New Testament.

καὶ καθόλου κ.τ.λ.] 'and, speaking generally, acquisition of things desirable and eagerly sought after turns out to be the foundation and material of everything that is painful and to be avoided.' The expression κατ' εὐχὴν is common in Aristotle, e.g. *Polit.* ii. 6, iv. 1, 20, vii. 4, 5, where it stands for ideal perfection. Περιβολὴ must mean '*the surrounding or investiture with*', and so here '*the acquisition of*'; comp. Xen. *Hell.* vii. 1. 40 (τῆς ἀρχῆς), Polyb. xvi. 20. 9, Porphyr. *Vit. Pyth.* 54 τῇ τε τῶν φίλων περιβολῇ καὶ τῇ τοῦ πλούτου δυνάμει, Aristid. *Or.* 14. (I. 208) περιβολῇ τε ἀρχῆς καὶ ὄγκῳ πραγμάτων; and the translation 'affluentia' (as if ὑπερβολή) appears to be wrong.

On some Clementine Fragments.

BESIDES the fragments which are distinctly quoted as belonging to the First or Second Epistle to the Corinthians or may with high probability be assigned to either, and which in this edition are printed in their proper places (pp. 167 sq., 210 sq.), other assumed quotations from Clementine Epistles have been included · in the collections of previous editors, and will now deserve consideration.

I.

A passage has been already noticed (pp. 21, 124) as cited by Leontius and John *Sacr. Rer. Lib. ii* (Mai *Script. Vet. Nov. Coll.* VII. p. 84), with the heading τοῦ ἁγίου Κλήμεντος ἐκ τῆς θ´ ἐπιστολῆς.

"Ἵνα καὶ γενώμεθα βουληθέντος αὐτοῦ, οὐκ ὄντες πρὶν γενέσθαι, καὶ γενόμενοι ἀπολαύσωμεν τῶν δι᾽ ἡμᾶς γενομένων. διὰ τοῦτό ἐσμεν ἄνθρωποι καὶ φρόνησιν ἔχομεν καὶ λόγον, παρ᾽ αὐτοῦ λαβόντες.

The resemblance of these words to a passage in the genuine epistle has been pointed out already (see the note on § 38). I have hazarded the conjecture that for Θ we should read Є (see p. 21). In this case the five epistles in the collection referred to might have been (1) the Epistle to James, (2), (3) the Two Epistles to Virgins, (4), (5) the Two Epistles to the Corinthians, so that the fragment may have been taken from the lost end of our Second Epistle. A second hypothesis would be, that it is intended for the passage in the First Epistle (§ 38) which it resembles, especially as we are told (see above pp. 21, 109) that these same writers just before have quoted a fragment from the First Epistle (§ 33) with very considerable variations from our existing text. But if so, the quotation is very loose indeed; and moreover the form of the heading seems to show that it was taken from a *different* epistle from the preceding passage. Another and very obvious alternative is that other spurious Clementine epistles were known to the ancients, which have not come down to us.

2.

Several quotations are included by preceding editors, which really belong to some recension of the Petro-Clementine writings (i. e. the *Homilies* or *Recognitions* with the letters prefixed). I have here placed them side by side with the parallel passages in these writings, that the resemblance may be seen.

(1)

Καὶ ὁ μέγας ἀπόστολος Κλήμης παρὰ τοῦ ἁγίου καὶ πρωτοκορυφαίου Πέτρου.	Ἐπιστολὴ Κλήμεντος πρὸς Ἰάκωβον.
Cὺ μὲν δήσεις ἃ δεῖ, φησίν, δεθῆναι καὶ λύσεις ἃ δεῖ λυθῆναι· οὐ δήσεις τὸν πταίσαντα, ἀλλ' ὃν δεῖ κατὰ τοὺς κανόνας ἡμῶν, τὸν παρανομοῦντα καὶ μὴ στέργοντα αὐτούς.	Πέτρος ... ἔφη ... Κλήμεντα τοῦτον ἐπίσκοπον ὑμῖν χειροτονῶ .... δήσει γὰρ ὃ δεῖ δεθῆναι καὶ λύσει ὃ δεῖ λυθῆναι, ὡς τὸν τῆς ἐκκλησίας εἰδὼς κανόνα (§ 2). σὺ δὲ δήσεις ἃ δεῖ δεθῆναι καὶ λύσεις ἃ δεῖ λυθῆναι (§ 9).
BIBL. VINDOB. *MSS Jurid. Græc.* vii, fol. 225 a.	*Clem. Hom.* Ep. Clem. ad Jac.

This passage was first published by Jacobson from a Vienna MS (described in Nessel's Catalogue P. 2, p. 18). Its source was pointed out by Nolte *Patrist. Miscell.* in the *Theolog. Quartalschr.* XLI. p. 277 (1859).

(ii)

Τοῦ ἁγίου Κλήμεντος ἐπισκόπου Ῥώμης.

Αὐτάρκης εἰς σωτηρίαν ἡ εἰς Θεὸν ἀνθρώπου ἀγάπη. εὐγνωμοσύνης γάρ ἐστι τὸ πρὸς τὸν τοῦ εἶναι ἡμᾶς αἴτιον ἀποσώζειν στοργήν, ὑφ' ἧς καὶ εἰς δεύτερον καὶ ἀγήρω αἰῶνα διασωζόμεθα.

Αὐτάρκης οὖν εἰς σωτηρίαν ἡ εἰς Θεὸν ἀνθρώπων στοργή (§ 8). δι' εὐγνωμοσύνην οὐ θελήσουσι κατὰ τοῦ τὰ πάντα κτίσαντος Θεοῦ κ.τ.λ. (§ 4). τοσοῦτον ὁ Θεὸς ὑπὲρ πάντας εὐεργέτηκεν τὸν ἄνθρωπον ἵνα εἰς τὸ πλῆθος τῶν εὐεργεσιῶν τὸν εὐεργέτην ἀγαπήσας ὑπὸ αὐτῆς ἀγάπης καὶ εἰς δεύτερον αἰῶνα διασωθῆναι δυνηθῇ (§ 7).

Clem. Hom. iii. 7, 8.

τοῦ αὐτοῦ.

Ἐπείρασεν ὁ Θεὸς τὸν Ἀβραάμ, οὐκ ἀγνοῶν τίς ἦν, ἀλλ' ἵνα τοῖς μετὰ ταῦτα δείξῃ καὶ μὴ κρύψῃ τὸν τοιοῦτον καὶ διεγείρῃ εἰς μίμησιν τῆς ἐκείνου πίστεως καὶ ὑπομονῆς, καὶ πείσῃ καὶ τέκνων στοργῆς ἀμελεῖν πρὸς ἐκπλήρωσιν θείου προστάγματος· ὅθεν ἔγγραφον περὶ αὐτοῦ ἱστορίαν γενέσθαι ᾠκονόμησεν.

JOANN. DAMASC. Sacr. Par. a. 49 (II. p. 752).

ὁ Σίμων .. ἔφη ...
τὸ δὲ πειράζειν, ὡς γέγραπται καὶ ἐπείρασεν Κύριος τὸν Ἀβραάμ, κακοῦ καὶ τὸ τέλος τῆς ὑπομονῆς ἀγνοοῦντος (§ 39).

καὶ ὁ Πέτρος ... ψεῦδός ἐστι τὸ γέγραφθαι κ.τ.λ. ... ἔτι μὴν καὶ εἰ ἐπείραζεν Κύριος τὸν Ἀβραάμ, ἵνα γνῷ εἰ ὑπομενεῖ (§ 43). ... τὰς ἀποδείξεις ἐγγράφους ἔχει παρασχεῖν (§ 10).

Clem. Hom. iii. 10, 39, 43.

The source of the quotations is pointed out in part by Nolte l. c. p. 276, though he has not put the case as strongly as he might have done. Hilgenfeld however twice denounces Nolte's reference as 'rash' (pp. 61, 90), and himself throws these fragments into the lacuna after § 57 of the First Epistle. Taking Hilgenfeld's text, I had without due consideration, yet not without misgiving, placed them there in my analysis of the genuine epistle (p. 8); but I am now convinced that this is wrong. The following facts will explain both the coincidences with and the variations from the extant text of the Homilies. (1) It seems quite clear that an orthodox recension of the Clementine writings was in common use when these collections of extracts were made. For instance Nicephorus (*Hist. Eccl.* iii. 18) hesitates about identifying the *Clementines* which were known to him, and which he describes as τῇ ἐκκλησίᾳ καὶ εὐπαράδεκτα, with the *Dialogue of Peter and Apion* mentioned by Eusebius, because the latter is described as heretical in its tendencies; and a scholiast on Eusebius (*H. E.* iii. 38; see Valois' note) protests indignantly against this historian's depreciation of a work whose merits were well known to the orthodox (ὅσον τὸ ὄφελος, οἱ ὀρθοδόξως καὶ εἰλικρινῶς ἐντετυχηκότες σαφῶς ἴσασιν). Thus it is plain that these writers knew the Clementines only in their orthodox dress. On this subject see Schliemann *Clement*. p. 338 sq., Uhlhorn *die Hom. u. Recogn.* p. 51 sq. (2) The quotations show that this orthodox recension followed the *Homilies* rather than the *Recognitions*. (3) Nevertheless, where the Homilies are distinctly heretical, very considerable changes would be necessary. This is especially the case in the passage before us where St Peter maintains in reply to Simon Magus that all the parts of the Old Testament which use objectionable language in speaking of God, and among them the passage which represents Him as *tempting Abraham*, are spurious interpolations, and that it is the duty of the faithful to discriminate between the genuine and the counterfeit. This idea occurs again and again in the Homilies. The orthodox redactor therefore would have to remodel all such passages in the Homilies, answering the objections of Simon in a wholly different way so as to preserve the integrity of the Scriptures. (3) We have other evidence that he did so alter them. Thus in *Clem. Hom.* ii. 50 St Peter is made to say to Clement ὡμολογημένου ἡμῖν ὅτι ὁ Θεὸς πάντα προγινώσκει, ἀνάγκη πᾶσα τὰς λεγούσας αὐτὸν γραφὰς ἀγνοεῖν ψεύδεσθαι, τὰς δὲ γινώσκειν αὐτὸν λεγούσας ἀληθεύειν...εἰ οὖν τῶν γραφῶν ἃ μέν ἐστιν ἀληθῆ ἃ δὲ ψευδῆ, εὐλόγως ὁ διδάσκαλος ἡμῶν ἔλεγεν Γίνεσθε τραπεζῖται δόκιμοι, ὡς τῶν ἐν ταῖς γραφαῖς τινῶν μὲν δοκίμων ὄντων λόγων τινῶν δὲ κιβδήλων κ.τ.λ.; but the same passage (for a lengthy context shows it to be the same) is differently quoted in the *Sacr. Par.* bearing the name of Joannes Damascenus (as given by Cotelier on the *Clem. Hom.* l. c.) εἰ οὖν ὁ Θεὸς μόνος πάντα, ὡς ἀποδέδεικται, προγινώσκει, ἀνάγκη πᾶσα τὰς λεγούσας αὐτὸν γραφὰς ἀγνοεῖν τι μὴ νοεῖσθαι παρά τινων, πῶς ταῦτα εἴρηται περὶ Θεοῦ τοῦ διδάσκοντος ἄνθρωπον γνῶσιν. The manipulation of the work is just the same in both cases. The orthodox recension *interprets* the passages, which the original Ebionite writing *rejects*. (4) Where the Homilies were not heretical, the orthodox reviser seems to have kept close to his original, as will appear from the fragments which follow.

(iii)

Κλήμεντος Ῥώμης.

Διαφορὰ τυγχάνει ἀληθείας καὶ συνηθείας. ἡ μὲν γὰρ ἀλήθεια γνησίως ζητουμένη εὑρίσκεται· τὸ δὲ ἔθος, ὁποῖον ἂν παραληφθῇ, εἴτε ἀληθὲς εἴτε ψευδές, ἀκρίτως ὑφ᾽ ἑαυτοῦ κρατύνεται. Ἐν αἷς γὰρ ἕκαστος ἐκ παιδόθεν ἐθίζεται, ταύταις ἐμμένειν ἥδεται. Ὁ γὰρ μισεῖ τις διὰ τὴν ἐπιοῦσαν τῇ ἡλικίᾳ σύνεσιν, τοῦτο διὰ τὴν πολυχρόνιον τῶν κακῶν συνήθειαν πράττειν συναναγκάζεται, δεινὴν σύνοικον τὴν ἁμαρτίαν παρειληφώς. Μηδαμῶς τὴν φύσιν αἰτιώμεθα· πάντα γὰρ βίον ἡδὺν (ἡδὺ MS) ἢ ἀηδῆ ἡ συνήθεια ποιεῖ.

BIBL. BODL. *MSS Barocc.* 143, fol. 136 b.

Πολλή τις, ὦ ἄνδρες Ἕλληνες, ἡ διαφορὰ τυγχάνει ἀληθείας τε καὶ συνηθείας. ἡ μὲν γὰρ ἀλήθεια γνησίως ζητουμένη εὑρίσκεται· τὸ δὲ ἔθος, ὁποιον ἂν παραληφθῇ, εἴτε ἀληθὲς εἴτε ψευδές, ἀκρίτως ὑφ᾽ ἑαυτοῦ κρατύνεται (§ 11). Ἐν οἷς γὰρ ἕκαστος ἐκ παίδων ἐθίζεται, τούτοις ἐμμένειν ἥδεται (§ 18).

Clem. Hom. iv. 11, 18.

This passage is taken from a Bodleian MS containing a collection of sentences from the Fathers and others, and occurs in a chapter περὶ συνηθείας καὶ ἔθους. It was first published by Grabe *Spicil. Patr.* I. 289. Nolte (l. c. p. 276), who first pointed out the source, remarks that the fragment is found also in a Paris MS ' *Cod. Reg.* 923 f. 368 vers. sec. col.', but with many variations. Grabe unaccountably stops short at παρειληφώς, and in this he is followed by all the editors of Clement. I collated the Bodleian MS and added the final words μηδαμῶς κ.τ.λ. The sentence, ὃ γὰρ μισεῖ...παρειληφώς, is quoted also as Κλήμεντος Ῥώμης by Maximus *Serm.* lxii (p. 673). I do not understand what Jacobson means by 'a Maximo incerta jam habebatur'. The words, ὃ μισεῖ...συνήθεια ποιεῖ, appear not to occur in the extant Homilies; but may possibly have been inserted by the reviser who produced the orthodox recension. The poetic character in both the language and the rhythm should be noticed; e. g. δεινὴν σύνοικον τὴν ἁμαρτίαν.

(iv)

Κλήμεντος.

Ἄνθρωπος κατ' εἰκόνα θείαν καὶ καθ' ὁμοίωσιν γεγονὼς ἄρχειν καὶ κυριεύειν κατεστάθη· ὅτε μέντοι δίκαιος ἐτύγχανε, πάντων παθημάτων ἀνώτερος ἦν. καὶ ἀθάνατος σώματι κατὰ θείαν μεγαλοδωρεὰν τοῦ κτίσαντος, τοῦ ἀλγεῖν πεῖραν λαβεῖν μὴ δυνάμενος. ὅτε δὲ ἥμαρτεν, ὡς δοῦλος γεγονὼς ἁμαρτίας πᾶσιν ὑπέπεσε τοῖς παθήμασι, πάντων καλῶν δικαίᾳ κρίσει στερηθείς. οὐ γὰρ εὔλογον ἦν, τοῦ δεδωκότος ἐγκαταλειφθέντος, τὰ δοθέντα παραμένειν τοῖς ἀγνώμοσι.

BIBL. BODL. *MSS Canon. Gr.* 56 fol. 187.

Ὁ ἄνθρωπος κατ' εἰκόνα καὶ καθ' ὁμοίωσιν γεγονὼς ἄρχειν τε καὶ κυριεύειν κατεστάθη (§ 3)... ὅτε μέντοι δίκαιος ἐτύγχανεν, καὶ πάντων παθημάτων ἀνώτατος ἦν, ὡς ἀθανάτῳ σώματι τοῦ ἀλγεῖν πεῖραν λαβεῖν μὴ δυνάμενος· ὅτε δὲ ἥμαρτεν (ὡς ἐχθὲς καὶ τῇ πρὸ αὐτῆς ἐδείξαμεν) ὡς δοῦλος γεγονὼς ἁμαρτίας πᾶσιν ὑπέπεσεν τοῖς παθήμασιν, πάντων καλῶν δικαίᾳ κρίσει στερηθείς. οὐ γὰρ εὔλογον ἦν, τοῦ δεδωκότος ἐγκαταλειφθέντος τὰ δοθέντα παραμένειν τοῖς ἀγνώμοσιν (§ 4).

Clem. Hom. x. 3, 4.

CLEMENTINE FRAGMENTS. 219

The whole of this extract is published now, I believe, for the first time. Previous editors (following Grabe *Spic. Patr.* I. 288) have included among the Clementine fragments the last sentence only, and this in the form οὐ δίκαιόν ἐστι κ.τ.λ. for οὐ γὰρ εὔλογον ἦν κ.τ.λ., as it is found in Maximus *Serm.* viii (II. p. 556, ed. Combefis), and also in another Bodleian MS, *Barocc.* 143 fol. 29 a, in both which places it is designated Κλήμεντος 'Ρώμης. I believe also that I am the first to point out whence it is taken. Nolte (l. c. p, 276) remarks that the quotation has points of accord (Anklänge) with several places in the Homilies, and Hilgenfeld writes 'confero *Clem. Recogn.* iv. 12 variasque hujus libri recensiones exstitisse moneo': but neither has noticed the passage in the Homilies from which it is taken word for word. I have little doubt however (considering where it is found) that it came through the medium of the orthodox recension, which here kept close to the extant Ebionite Homilies.

3.

A fragment of another stamp is included in Bp. Jacobson's collection (no. VIII). It was first published by Cotelier in his notes to *Clem. Recogn.* i. 24, from a Paris MS, *Bibl. Reg.* 1026.

Τοῦ ἁγίου Κλήμεντος ἐπισκόπου 'Ρώμης μετὰ τὸν ἀπόστολον Πέτρον τοῦ ἀποστολικοῦ θρόνου ἡγησαμένου, εἰς τὸ ἅγιον πνεῦμα.

Μακάριος ὁ κεκλεισμένους ὀφθαλμοὺς ἀνοίξας καὶ διωκόμενον ἄσθματι πνεῦμα διὰ τοῦ ἐγεῖραι ἀναλαβών. τὸ χαμαὶ κεῖσθαι τοῦτο ἦν, καὶ τὸ ἐπὶ ποδῶν μὴ ἑστάναι, τὸ τὴν ἀλήθειαν οὐκ ἔχειν. ἀνάστασις δέ ἐστι πατρὸς ἡ ἐπίγνωσις καὶ ἐπιφάνεια τοῦ υἱοῦ, ᾗ τὰς αἰσθήσεις ἐφανέρωσε. μακάριος ἀνὴρ ὁ γινώσκων τὴν τοῦ πατρὸς δόσιν δι' ἐκπορεύσεως τοῦ παναγίου πνεύματος. μακάριος ὁ γινώσκων καὶ λαβών, ὅτι τὸ ἅγιον πνεῦμά ἐστιν ἡ δόσις αὐτοῦ. καὶ τοῦτο ἐν τύπῳ περιστερᾶς παρέσχε. τὸ γὰρ ζῶον ἀκακίαν ἔχει καὶ ἄχολόν ἐστιν, ἄκακος δὲ ὁ πατὴρ πνεῦμα ἔδωκεν ἄκακον, ἀόργητον, ἀπίκραντον, τέλειον, ἀμίαντον, ἀπὸ σπλάγχνων ιδίων προϊέμενος, ἵνα ῥυθμήσῃ τοὺς αἰῶνας καὶ τοῦ ἀοράτου δῷ τὴν ἐπίγνωσιν. ἔστιν οὖν τοῦτο ἅγιον καὶ εὐθές, τὸ ἀπ' αὐτοῦ προελθόν, καὶ δύναμις αὐτοῦ καὶ θέλημα αὐτοῦ, εἰς πλήρωμα δόξης αὐτοῦ φανερωθέν. τοῦτο οἱ λαβόντες τυποῦνται ἀληθείας τύπῳ, χάριτος τελείας.

Hilgenfeld justly rejects the pretensions of this fragment to belong to our Clementine letters. I am disposed myself to believe that an officious transcriber has wrongly defined the Clement who wrote these words, and that the fragment belongs not to the Roman but to the Alexandrian. The converse error of ascribing passages of the Roman Clement to the Alexandrian has been made more than once (see Hilgenfeld p. 75), nor is this less likely to have occurred, and indeed we have already had an instance of it above (p. 179). In an extant writing *Strom.* v. 13 (p. 699) Clement of Alexandria promises to consider the subject elsewhere, ὅ τι ποτέ ἐστι τὸ ἅγιον πνεῦμα, ἐν τοῖς περὶ προφητείας κἀν τοῖς περὶ ψυχῆς ἐπιδειχθήσεται ἡμῖν; and the fragment before us may have been taken from one or other of the two works there mentioned. It accords entirely with his tone of thought, and even resembles extant passages where he speaks on this subject.

16, BEDFORD STREET, COVENT GARDEN, LONDON.
January, 1870.

MACMILLAN & Co.'S GENERAL CATALOGUE of Works in the Departments of History, Biography, Travels, Poetry, and Belles Lettres. With some short Account or Critical Notice concerning each Book.

SECTION I.

HISTORY, BIOGRAPHY, and TRAVELS.

Baker (Sir Samuel W.).—THE NILE TRIBUTARIES OF ABYSSINIA, and the Sword Hunters of the Hamran Arabs. By SIR SAMUEL W. BAKER, M.A., F.R.G.S. With Portraits, Maps, and Illustrations. Third Edition, 8vo. 21s.

Sir Samuel Baker here describes twelve months' exploration, during which he examined the rivers that are tributary to the Nile from Abyssinia, including the Atbara, Settite, Royan, Salaam, Angrab, Rahad, Dinder, and the Blue Nile. The interest attached to these portions of Africa differs entirely from that of the White Nile regions, as the whole of Upper Egypt and Abyssinia is capable of development, and is inhabited by races having some degree of civilization; while Central Africa is peopled by a race of savages, whose future is more problematical.

THE ALBERT N'YANZA Great Basin of the Nile, and Exploration of the Nile Sources. New and cheaper Edition, with Portraits, Maps, and Illustrations. Two vols. crown 8vo. 16s.

"*Bruce won the source of the Blue Nile; Speke and Grant won the Victoria source of the great White Nile; and I have been permitted to succeed in completing the Nile Sources by the discovery of the great reservoir of the equatorial waters, the Albert N'yanza, from which the river issues as the entire White Nile.*"—PREFACE.

NEW AND CHEAP EDITION OF THE ALBERT N'YANZA. 1 vol. crown 8vo. With Maps and Illustrations. 7s. 6d.

GENERAL CATALOGUE.

Baker (Sir Samuel W.) (*continued*)—
CAST UP BY THE SEA; or, The Adventures of NED GREY. By SIR SAMUEL W. BAKER, M.A., F.R.G.S. Second Edition. Crown 8vo. cloth gilt, 7s. 6d.

"*A story of adventure by sea and land in the good old style. It appears to us to be the best book of the kind since 'Masterman Ready,' and it runs that established favourite very close.*"—PALL MALL GAZETTE.

"*No book written for boys has for a long time created so much interest, or been so successful. Every parent ought to provide his boy with a copy.*"
DAILY TELEGRAPH.

Barker (Lady).—STATION LIFE IN NEW ZEALAND. By LADY BARKER. Crown 8vo. 7s. 6d.

"*These letters are the exact account of a lady's experience of the brighter and less practical side of colonization. They record the expeditions, adventures, and emergencies diversifying the daily life of the wife of a New Zealand sheep-farmer; and, as each was written while the novelty and excitement of the scenes it describes were fresh upon her, they may succeed in giving here in England an adequate impression of the delight and freedom of an existence so far removed from our own highly-wrought civilization.*"—PREFACE.

Baxter (R. Dudley, M.A.).—THE TAXATION OF THE UNITED KINGDOM. By R. DUDLEY BAXTER, M.A. 8vo. cloth, 4s. 6d.

The First Part of this work, originally read before the Statistical Society of London, deals with the Amount of Taxation; the Second Part, which now constitutes the main portion of the work, is almost entirely new, and embraces the important questions of Rating, of the relative Taxation of Land, Personalty, and Industry, and of the direct effect of Taxes upon Prices. The author trusts that the body of facts here collected may be of permanent value as a record of the past progress and present condition of the population of the United Kingdom, independently of the transitory circumstances of its present Taxation.

HISTORY, BIOGRAPHY, & TRAVELS.

Baxter (R. Dudley, M.A.) (*continued*)—
NATIONAL INCOME. With Coloured Diagrams. 8vo. 3s. 6d.

PART I.—*Classification of the Population, Upper, Middle, and Labour Classes.* II.—*Income of the United Kingdom.*

"*A painstaking and certainly most interesting inquiry.*"—PALL MALL GAZETTE.

Bernard.—FOUR LECTURES ON SUBJECTS CONNECTED WITH DIPLOMACY. By MOUNTAGUE BERNARD, M.A., Chichele Professor of International Law and Diplomacy, Oxford. 8vo. 9s.

Four Lectures, dealing with (1) *The Congress of Westphalia;* (2) *Systems of Policy;* (3) *Diplomacy, Past and Present;* (4) *The Obligations of Treaties.*

Blake.—THE LIFE OF WILLIAM BLAKE, THE ARTIST. By ALEXANDER GILCHRIST. With numerous Illustrations from Blake's designs, and Fac-similes of his studies of the "Book of Job." Two vols. medium 8vo. 32s.

These volumes contain a Life of Blake; Selections from his Writings, including Poems; Letters; Annotated Catalogue of Pictures and Drawings; List, with occasional notes, of Blake's Engravings and Writings. There are appended Engraved Designs by Blake: (1) *The Book of Job, twenty-one photo-lithographs from the originals;* (2) *Songs of Innocence and Experience, sixteen of the original Plates.*

Bright (John, M.P.).—SPEECHES ON QUESTIONS OF PUBLIC POLICY. By JOHN BRIGHT, M.P. Edited by Professor THOROLD ROGERS. Two Vols. 8vo. 25s. Second Edition, with Portrait.

"*I have divided the Speeches contained in these volumes into groups. The materials for selection are so abundant, that I have been constrained to omit many a speech which is worthy of careful perusal. I have*

naturally given prominence to those subjects with which Mr. Bright has been especially identified, as, for example, India, America, Ireland, and Parliamentary Reform. But nearly every topic of great public interest on which Mr. Bright has spoken is represented in these volumes."
EDITOR'S PREFACE.

AUTHOR'S POPULAR EDITION. Extra fcap. 8vo. cloth. Second Edition. 3s. 6d.

Bryce.—THE HOLY ROMAN EMPIRE. By JAMES BRYCE, B.C.L., Fellow of Oriel College, Oxford. [*Reprinting.*

CAMBRIDGE CHARACTERISTICS. *See* MULLINGER.

CHATTERTON: A Biographical Study. BY DANIEL WILSON, LL.D., Professor of History and English in University College, Toronto. Crown 8vo. 6s. 6d.

The Author here regards Chatterton as a Poet, not as a mere " resetter and defacer of stolen literary treasures." Reviewed in this light, he has found much in the old materials capable of being turned to new account; and to these materials research in various directions has enabled him to make some additions.

Clay.—THE PRISON CHAPLAIN. A Memoir of the Rev. JOHN CLAY, B.D., late Chaplain of the Preston Gaol. With Selections from his Reports and Correspondence, and a Sketch of Prison Discipline in England. By his Son, the Rev. W. L. CLAY, M.A. 8vo. 15s.

"*Few books have appeared of late years better entitled to an attentive perusal. . . . It presents a complete narrative of all that has been done and attempted by various philanthropists for the amelioration of the condition and the improvement of the morals of the criminal classes in the British dominions.*"—LONDON REVIEW.

HISTORY, BIOGRAPHY, & TRAVELS.

Cooper.—ATHENÆ CANTABRIGIENSES. By CHARLES HENRY COOPER, F.S.A., and THOMPSON COOPER, F.S.A. Vol. I. 8vo., 1500—85, 18*s.* Vol. II., 1586—1609, 18*s.*

This elaborate work, which is dedicated by permission to Lord Macaulay, contains lives of the eminent men sent forth by Cambridge, after the fashion of Anthony à Wood, in his famous "Athenæ Oxonienses."

Dilke.—GREATER BRITAIN. A Record of Travel in English-speaking Countries during 1866-7. (America, Australia, India.) By Sir CHARLES WENTWORTH DILKE, M.P. Fourth and Cheap Edition. Crown 8vo. 6*s.*

"*Mr. Dilke has written a book which is probably as well worth reading as any book of the same aims and character that ever was written. Its merits are that it is written in a lively and agreeable style, that it implies a great deal of physical pluck, that no page of it fails to show an acute and highly intelligent observer, that it stimulates the imagination as well as the judgment of the reader, and that it is on perhaps the most interesting subject that can attract an Englishman who cares about his country.*"
SATURDAY REVIEW.

Dürer (Albrecht).—HISTORY OF THE LIFE OF ALBRECHT DÜRER, of Nürnberg. With a Translation of his Letters and Journal, and some account of his works. By Mrs. CHARLES HEATON. Royal 8vo. bevelled boards, extra gilt. 31*s.* 6*d.*

This work contains about Thirty Illustrations, ten of which are productions by the Autotype (carbon) process, and are printed in permanent tints by Messrs. Cundall and Fleming, under license from the Autotype Company, Limited; the rest are Photographs and Woodcuts.

EARLY EGYPTIAN HISTORY FOR THE YOUNG. *See* "JUVENILE SECTION."

Elliott.—LIFE OF HENRY VENN ELLIOTT, of Brighton. By JOSIAH BATEMAN, M.A., Author of "Life of Daniel Wilson, Bishop of Calcutta," &c. With Portrait, engraved by JEENS. Crown 8vo. 8s. 6d. Second Edition, with Appendix.

"*A very charming piece of religious biography; no one can read it without both pleasure and profit.*"—BRITISH QUARTERLY REVIEW.

Forbes.—LIFE OF PROFESSOR EDWARD FORBES, F.R.S. By GEORGE WILSON, M.D., F.R.S.E., and ARCHIBALD GEIKIE, F.R.S. 8vo. with Portrait, 14s.

"*From the first page to the last the book claims careful reading, as being a full but not overcrowded rehearsal of a most instructive life, and the true picture of a mind that was rare in strength and beauty.*"—EXAMINER.

Freeman.—HISTORY OF FEDERAL GOVERNMENT, from the Foundation of the Achaian League to the Disruption of the United States. By EDWARD A. FREEMAN, M.A. Vol. I. General Introduction. History of the Greek Federations. 8vo. 21s.

"*The task Mr. Freeman has undertaken is one of great magnitude and importance. It is also a task of an almost entirely novel character. No other work professing to give the history of a political principle occurs to us, except the slight contributions to the history of representative government that is contained in a course of M. Guizot's lectures .... The history of the development of a principle is at least as important as the history of a dynasty, or of a race.*'—SATURDAY REVIEW.

OLD ENGLISH HISTORY FOR CHILDREN. By EDWARD A. FREEMAN, M.A., late Fellow of Trinity College, Oxford. With *Five Coloured Maps*. Extra fcap. 8vo., half-bound. 6s.

"*Its object is to show that clear, accurate, and scientific views of history, or indeed of any subject, may be easily given to children from the very first... I have, I hope, shown that it is perfectly easy to teach children, from the very first, to distinguish true history alike from legend and from wilful invention, and also to understand the nature of historical authorities, and to weigh one statement against another. . . . . I have throughout striven to connect the history of England with the general history of civilized Europe, and I have especially tried to make the book serve as an incentive to a more accurate study of historical geography."*—PREFACE.

French (George Russell).—SHAKSPEAREANA
GENEALOGICA. 8vo. cloth extra, 15s. Uniform with the "Cambridge Shakspeare."

Part I.—Identification of the dramatis personæ *in the historical plays, from King John to King Henry VIII.; Notes on Characters in Macbeth and Hamlet; Persons and Places belonging to Warwickshire alluded to. Part II.—The Shakspeare and Arden families and their connexions, with Tables of descent. The present is the first attempt to give a detailed description, in consecutive order, of each of the* dramatis personæ *in Shakspeare's immortal chronicle-histories, and some of the characters have been, it is believed, herein identified for the first time. A clue is furnished which, followed up with ordinary diligence, may enable any one, with a taste for the pursuit, to trace a distinguished Shakspearean worthy to his lineal representative in the present day.*

Galileo.—THE PRIVATE LIFE OF GALILEO. Compiled principally from his Correspondence and that of his eldest daughter, Sister Maria Celeste, Nun in the Franciscan Convent of S. Matthew, in Arcetri. With Portrait. Crown 8vo. 7s. 6d.

It has been the endeavour of the compiler to place before the reader a plain, ungarbled statement of facts; and as a means to this end, to allow Galileo, his friends, and his judges to speak for themselves as far as possible.

Gladstone (Right. Hon. W. E., M.P.).—JUVENTUS
MUNDI. The Gods and Men of the Heroic Age. Crown 8vo. cloth extra. With Map. 10s. 6d. Second Edition.

This new work of Mr. Gladstone deals especially with the historic element in Homer, expounding that element, and furnishing by its aid a full account of the Homeric men and the Homeric religion. It starts, after the introductory chapter, with a discussion of the several races then existing in Hellas, including the influence of the Phœnicians and Egyptians. It contains chapters on the Olympian system, with its several deities; on the Ethics and the Polity of the Heroic age; on the geography of Homer; on the characters of the Poems; presenting, in fine, a view of primitive life and primitive society as found in the poems of Homer.

"GLOBE" ATLAS OF EUROPE. Uniform in size with Macmillan's Globe Series, containing 45 Coloured Maps, on a uniform scale and projection; with Plans of London and Paris, and a copious Index. Strongly bound in half-morocco, with flexible back, 9s.

This Atlas includes all the countries of Europe in a series of 48 Maps, drawn on the same scale, with an Alphabetical Index to the situation of more than ten thousand places, and the relation of the various maps and countries to each other is defined in a general Key-map. All the maps being on a uniform scale facilitates the comparison of extent and distance, and conveys a just impression of the relative magnitude of different countries. The size suffices to show the provincial divisions, the railways and main roads, the principal rivers and mountain ranges. "This atlas," writes the British Quarterly, "will be an invaluable boon for the school, the desk, or the traveller's portmanteau."

Guizot.—(Author of "JOHN HALIFAX, GENTLEMAN.")—M. DE BARANTE, A Memoir, Biographical and Autobiographical. By M. GUIZOT. Translated by the Author of "JOHN HALIFAX, GENTLEMAN." Crown 8vo. 6s. 6d.

" *The highest purposes of both history and biography are answered by a memoir so lifelike, so faithful, and so philosophical.*"
BRITISH QUARTERLY REVIEW.

HISTORY, BIOGRAPHY, & TRAVELS.

HISTORICAL SELECTIONS. Readings from the best Authorities on English and European History. Selected and arranged by E. M. SEWELL and C. M. YONGE. Crown 8vo. 6s.

When young children have acquired the outlines of history from abridgements and catechisms, and it becomes .desirable to give a more enlarged view of the subject, in order to render it really useful and interesting, a difficulty often arises as to the choice of books. Two courses are open, either to take a general and consequently dry history of facts, such as Russell's Modern Europe, or to choose some work treating of a particular period or subject, such as the works of Macaulay and Froude. The former course usually renders history uninteresting; the latter is unsatisfactory, because it is not sufficiently comprehensive. To remedy this difficulty, selections, continuous and chronological, have in the present volume been taken from the larger works of Freeman, Milman, Palgrave, and others, which may serve as distinct landmarks of historical reading. "We know of scarcely anything," says the Guardian, *of this volume, "which is so likely to raise to a higher level the average standard of English education."*

Hole.—A GENEALOGICAL STEMMA OF THE KINGS OF ENGLAND AND FRANCE. By the Rev. C. HOLE, M.A., Trinity College, Cambridge. On Sheet, 1s.

The different families are printed in distinguishing colours, thus facilitating reference.

A BRIEF BIOGRAPHICAL DICTIONARY. Compiled and Arranged by the Rev. CHARLES HOLE, M.A. Second Edition. 18mo. neatly and strongly bound in cloth, 4s. 6d.

One of the most comprehensive and accurate Biographical Dictionaries in the world, containing more than 18,000 persons of all countries, with dates of birth and death, and what they were distinguished for. Extreme care has been bestowed on the verification of the dates; and thus numerous errors, current in previous works, have been corrected. Its size adapts it for the desk, portmanteau, or pocket.

"An invaluable addition to our manuals of reference, and, from its moderate price, cannot fail to become as popular as it is useful."—TIMES.

Hozier.—THE SEVEN WEEKS' WAR; Its Antecedents and its Incidents. By H. M. HOZIER. With Maps and Plans. Two vols. 8vo. 28s.

This work is based upon letters reprinted by permission from "The Times." For the most part it is a product of a personal eye-witness of some of the most interesting incidents of a war which, for rapidity and decisive results, may claim an almost unrivalled position in history.

THE BRITISH EXPEDITION TO ABYSSINIA. Compiled from Authentic Documents. By CAPTAIN HENRY M. HOZIER, late Assistant Military Secretary to Lord Napier of Magdala. 8vo. 9s.

"*Several accounts of the British Expedition have been published..... They have, however, been written by those who have not had access to those authentic documents, which cannot be collected directly after the termination of a campaign..... The endeavour of the author of this sketch has been to present to readers a succinct and impartial account of an enterprise which has rarely been equalled in the annals of war.*"—PREFACE.

Irving.—THE ANNALS OF OUR TIME. A Diurnal of Events, Social and Political, which have happened in or had relation to the Kingdom of Great Britain, from the Accession of Queen Victoria to the Opening of the present Parliament. By JOSEPH IRVING. 8vo. half-bound. 18s.

"*We have before us a trusty and ready guide to the events of the past thirty years, available equally for the statesman, the politician, the public writer, and the general reader. If Mr. Irving's object has been to bring before the reader all the most noteworthy occurrences which have happened since the beginning of Her Majesty's reign, he may justly claim the credit of having done so most briefly, succinctly, and simply, and in such a manner, too, as to furnish him with the details necessary in each case to comprehend the event of which he is in search in an intelligent manner. Reflection will serve to show the great value of such a work as this to the journalist and statesman, and indeed to every one who feels an interest in the progress of the age; and we may add that its value is considerably increased by the addition of that most important of all appendices, an accurate and instructive index.*"—TIMES.

HISTORY, BIOGRAPHY, & TRAVELS.

Kingsley (Canon).—ON THE ANCIEN REGIME as it Existed on the Continent before the FRENCH REVOLUTION. Three Lectures delivered at the Royal Institution. By the Rev. C. KINGSLEY, M.A., formerly Professor of Modern History in the University of Cambridge. Crown 8vo. 6s.

These three lectures discuss severally (1) Caste, (2) Centralization, (3) The Explosive Forces by which the Revolution was superinduced. The Preface deals at some length with certain political questions of the present day.

THE ROMAN AND THE TEUTON. A Series of Lectures delivered before the University of Cambridge. By Rev. C KINGSLEY, M.A. 8vo. 12s.

CONTENTS :—*Inaugural Lecture ; The Forest Children ; The Dying Empire ; The Human Deluge ; The Gothic Civilizer; Dietrich's End; The Nemesis of the Goths ; Paulus Diaconus ; The Clergy and the Heathen : The Monk a Civilizer ; The Lombard Laws ; The Popes and the Lombards ; The Strategy of Providence.*

Kingsley (Henry, F.R.G.S.).—TALES OF OLD TRAVEL. Re-narrated by HENRY KINGSLEY, F.R.G.S. With Eight Illustrations by HUARD. Crown 8vo. 6s.

CONTENTS :—*Marco Polo ; The Shipwreck of Pelsart ; The Wonderful Adventures of Andrew Battel ; The Wanderings of a Capuchin ; Peter Carder ; The Preservation of the "Terra Nova ;" Spitzbergen ; D'Ermenonville's Acclimatization Adventure ; The Old Slave Trade ; Miles Philips ; The Sufferings of Robert Everard ; John Fox ; Alvaro Nunez ; The Foundation of an Empire.*

Latham.—BLACK AND WHITE: A Journal of a Three Months' Tour in the United States. By HENRY LATHAM, M.A., Barrister-at-Law. 8vo. 10s. 6d.

" The spirit in which Mr. Latham has written about our brethren in America is commendable in high degree."—ATHENÆUM.

Law.—THE ALPS OF HANNIBAL. By WILLIAM JOHN LAW, M.A., formerly Student of Christ Church, Oxford. Two vols. 8vo. 21s.

"No one can read the work and not acquire a conviction that, in addition to a thorough grasp of a particular topic, its writer has at command a large store of reading and thought upon many cognate points of ancient history and geography."—QUARTERLY REVIEW.

Liverpool.—THE LIFE AND ADMINISTRATION OF ROBERT BANKS, SECOND EARL OF LIVERPOOL, K.G. Compiled from Original Family Documents by CHARLES DUKE YONGE, Regius Professor of History and English Literature in Queen's College, Belfast; and Author of "The History of the British Navy," "The History of France under the Bourbons," etc. Three vols. 8vo. 42s.

Since the time of Lord Burleigh no one, except the second Pitt, ever enjoyed so long a tenure of power; with the same exception, no one ever held office at so critical a time . . . . *Lord Liverpool is the very last minister who has been able fully to carry out his own political views; who has been so strong that in matters of general policy the Opposition could extort no concessions from him which were not sanctioned by his own deliberate judgment. The present work is founded almost entirely on the correspondence left behind him by Lord Liverpool, and now in the possession of Colonel and Lady Catherine Harcourt.*

"Full of information and instruction."—FORTNIGHTLY REVIEW.

Maclear.—*See Section,* "ECCLESIASTICAL HISTORY."

Macmillan (Rev. Hugh).—HOLIDAYS ON HIGH LANDS; or, Rambles and Incidents in search of Alpine Plants. By the Rev. HUGH MACMILLAN, Author of "Bible Teachings in Nature," etc. Crown 8vo. cloth. 6s.

"Botanical knowledge is blended with a love of nature, a pious enthusiasm, and a rich felicity of diction not to be met with in any works of kindred character, if we except those of Hugh Miller."—DAILY TELEGRAPH.

HISTORY, BIOGRAPHY, & TRAVELS.

Macmillan (Rev. Hugh), (*continued*)—

-FOOT-NOTES FROM THE PAGE OF NATURE. With numerous Illustrations. Fcap. 8vo. 5s.

"*Those who have derived pleasure and profit from the study of flowers and ferns—subjects, it is pleasing to find, now everywhere popular—by descending lower into the arcana of the vegetable kingdom, will find a still more interesting and delightful field of research in the objects brought under review in the following pages.*"—PREFACE.

BIBLE TEACHINGS IN NATURE. Fourth Edition. Fcap 8vo. 6s.—*See also* "SCIENTIFIC SECTION."

Martin (Frederick).—THE STATESMAN'S YEAR-BOOK: A Statistical and Historical Account of the States of the Civilised World. Manual for Politician and Merchants for the year 1870. By FREDERICK MARTIN. *Seventh Annual Publication.* Crown 8vo. 10s. 6d.

The new issue has been entirely re-written, revised, and corrected, on the basis of official reports received direct from the heads of the leading Governments of the World, in reply to letters sent to them by the Editor.

"*Everybody who knows this work is aware that it is a book that is indispensable to writers, financiers, politicians, statesmen, and all who are directly or indirectly interested in the political, social, industrial, commercial, and financial condition of their fellow-creatures at home and abroad. Mr. Martin deserves warm commendation for the care he takes in making 'The Statesman's Year Book' complete and correct.*"
STANDARD.

Martineau.—BIOGRAPHICAL SKETCHES, 1852—1868. By HARRIET MARTINEAU. Third Edition, with New Preface. Crown 8vo. 8s. 6d.

A Collection of Memoirs under these several sections:—(1) *Royal,* (2) *Politicians,* (3) *Professional,* (4) *Scientific,* (5) *Social,* (6) *Literary. These Memoirs appeared originally in the columns of the* "Daily News."

Masson (Professor).—ESSAYS, BIOGRAPHICAL AND CRITICAL. *See Section headed* "POETRY AND BELLES LETTRES."

LIFE OF JOHN MILTON. Narrated in connexion with the Political, Ecclesiastical, and Literary History of his Time. By DAVID MASSON, M.A., LL.D., Professor of Rhetoric at Edinburgh. Vol. I. with Portraits. 8vo. 18s. Vol. II. in the Press.

It is intended to exhibit Milton's life in its connexions with all the more notable phenomena of the period of British history in which it was cast—its state politics, its ecclesiastical variations, its literature and speculative thought. Commencing in 1608, the Life of Milton proceeds through the last sixteen years of the reign of James I., includes the whole of the reign of Charles I. and the subsequent years of the Commonwealth and the Protectorate, and then, passing the Restoration, extends itself to 1674, or through fourteen years of the new state of things under Charles II. The first volume deals with the life of Milton as extending from 1608 to 1640, which was the period of his education and of his minor poems.

Morison.—THE LIFE AND TIMES OF SAINT BERNARD, Abbot of Clairvaux. By JAMES COTTER MORISON, M.A. New Edition, revised. Crown 8vo. 7s. 6d.

"*One of the best contributions in our literature towards a vivid, intelligent, and worthy knowledge of European interests and thoughts and feelings during the twelfth century. A delightful and instructive volume, and one of the best products of the modern historic spirit.*"
PALL MALL GAZETTE.

Morley (John).—EDMUND BURKE, a Historical Study. By JOHN MORLEY, B.A. Oxon. Crown 8vo. 7s. 6d.

"*The style is terse and incisive, and brilliant with epigram and point. It contains pithy aphoristic sentences which Burke himself would not have disowned. But these are not its best features: its sustained power of reasoning, its wide sweep of observation and reflection, its elevated ethical and social tone, stamp it as a work of high excellence, and as such we cordially recommend it to our readers.*"—SATURDAY REVIEW.

HISTORY, BIOGRAPHY, & TRAVELS.

Mullinger.—CAMBRIDGE CHARACTERISTICS IN THE SEVENTEENTH CENTURY. By J. B. MULLINGER, B.A. Crown 8vo. 4s. 6d.

"*It is a very entertaining and readable book.*"—SATURDAY REVIEW.

"*The chapters on the Cartesian Philosophy and the Cambridge Platonists are admirable.*"—ATHENÆUM.

Palgrave.—HISTORY OF NORMANDY AND OF ENGLAND. By Sir FRANCIS PALGRAVE, Deputy Keeper of Her Majesty's Public Records. Completing the History to the Death of William Rufus. Four vols. 8vo. £4 4s.

Volume I. General Relations of Mediæval Europe—The Carlovingian Empire—The Danish Expeditions in the Gauls—And the Establishment of Rollo. Volume II. The Three First Dukes of Normandy; Rollo, Guillaume Longue-Épée, and Richard Sans-Peur—The Carlovingian line supplanted by the Capets. Volume III. Richard Sans-Peur—Richard Le-Bon—Richard III.—Robert Le Diable—William the Conqueror. Volume IV. William Rufus—Accession of Henry Beauclerc.

Palgrave (W. G.).—A NARRATIVE OF A YEAR'S JOURNEY THROUGH CENTRAL AND EASTERN ARABIA, 1862-3. By WILLIAM GIFFORD PALGRAVE, late of the Eighth Regiment Bombay N. I. Fifth and cheaper Edition. With Maps, Plans, and Portrait of Author, engraved on steel by Jeens. Crown 8vo. 6s.

"*Considering the extent of our previous ignorance, the amount of his achievements, and the importance of his contributions to our knowledge, we cannot say less of him than was once said of a far greater discoverer. Mr. Palgrave has indeed given a new world to Europe.*"—PALL MALL GAZETTE.

Parkes (Henry).—AUSTRALIAN VIEWS OF ENGLAND. By HENRY PARKES. Crown 8vo. cloth. 3s. 6d.

"*The following letters were written during a residence in England, in the years* 1861 *and* 1862, *and were published in the* Sydney Morning Herald *on the arrival of the monthly mails* . . . . *On re-perusal, these letters appear to contain views of English life and impressions of English notabilities which, as the views and impressions of an Englishman on his return to his native country after an absence of twenty years, may not be without interest to the English reader. The writer had opportunities of mixing with different classes of the British people, and of hearing opinions on passing events from opposite standpoints of observation.*"—AUTHOR'S PREFACE.

Prichard.—THE ADMINISTRATION OF INDIA. From 1859 to 1868. The First Ten Years of Administration under the Crown. By ILTUDUS THOMAS PRICHARD, Barrister-at-Law. Two vols. Demy 8vo. With Map. 21s.

In these volumes the author has aimed to supply a full, impartial, and independent account of British India between 1859 *and* 1868—*which is in many respects the most important epoch in the history of that country which the present century has seen.*

Ralegh.—THE LIFE OF SIR WALTER RALEGH, based upon Contemporary Documents. By EDWARD EDWARDS. Together with Ralegh's Letters, now first collected. With Portrait. Two vols. 8vo. 32s.

"*Mr. Edwards has certainly written the Life of Ralegh from fuller information than any previous biographer. He is intelligent, industrious, sympathetic: and the world has in his two volumes larger means afforded it of knowing Ralegh than it ever possessed before. The new letters and the newly-edited old letters are in themselves a boon.*"—PALL MALL GAZETTE.

HISTORY, BIOGRAPHY, & TRAVELS.

Robinson (Crabb).—DIARY, REMINISCENCES, AND CORRESPONDENCE OF CRABB ROBINSON. Selected and Edited by Dr. SADLER. With Portrait. Second Edition. Three vols. 8vo.cloth. 36s.

Mr. Crabb Robinson's Diary extends over the greater part of three-quarters of a century. It contains personal reminiscences of some of the most distinguished characters of that period, including Goethe, Wieland, De Quincey, Wordsworth (with whom Mr. Crabb Robinson was on terms of great intimacy), Madame de Staël, Lafayette, Coleridge, Lamb, Milman, &c. &c.: and includes a vast variety of subjects, political, literary, ecclesiastical, and miscellaneous.

Rogers (James E. Thorold).—HISTORICAL GLEANINGS : A Series of Sketches. Montague, Walpole, Adam Smith, Cobbett. By Rev. J. E. T. ROGERS. Crown 8vo. 4s. 6d.

Professor Rogers's object in the following sketches is to present a set of historical facts, grouped round a principal figure. The essays are in the form of lectures.

Smith (Professor Goldwin).—THREE ENGLISH STATESMEN : PYM, CROMWELL, PITT. A Course of Lectures on the Political History of England. By GOLDWIN SMITH, M.A. Extra fcap. 8vo. New and Cheaper Edition. 5s.

"A work which neither historian nor politician can safely afford to neglect."—SATURDAY REVIEW.

Tacitus.—THE HISTORY OF TACITUS, translated into English. By A. J. CHURCH, M.A. and W. J. BRODRIBB, M.A. With a Map and Notes. 8vo. 10s. 6d.

The translators have endeavoured to adhere as closely to the original as was thought consistent with a proper observance of English idiom. At the same time it has been their aim to reproduce the precise expressions of the author. This work is characterised by the Spectator *as "a scholarly and faithful translation."*

B

THE AGRICOLA AND GERMANIA. Translated into English by A. J. CHURCH, M.A. and W. J. BRODRIBB, M.A. With Maps and Notes. Extra fcap. 8vo. 2s. 6d.

The translators have sought to produce such a version as may satisfy scholars who demand a faithful rendering of the original, and English readers who are offended by the baldness and frigidity which commonly disfigure translations. The treatises are accompanied by introductions, notes, maps, and a chronological summary. The Athenæum *says of this work that it is "a version at once readable and exact, which may be perused with pleasure by all, and consulted with advantage by the classical student."*

Taylor (Rev. Isaac).—WORDS AND PLACES; or Etymological Illustrations of History, Etymology, and Geography. By the Rev. ISAAC TAYLOR. Second Edition. Crown 8vo. 12s. 6d.

"*Mr. Taylor has produced a really useful book, and one which stands alone in our language.*"—SATURDAY REVIEW.

Trench (Archbishop).—GUSTAVUS ADOLPHUS: Social Aspects of the Thirty Years' War. By R. CHENEVIX TRENCH, D.D., Archbishop of Dublin. Fcap. 8vo. 2s. 6d.

"*Clear and lucid in style, these lectures will be a treasure to many to whom the subject is unfamiliar.*"—DUBLIN EVENING MAIL.

Trench (Mrs. R.).—Edited by ARCHBISHOP TRENCH. Remains of the late MRS. RICHARD TRENCH. Being Selections from her Journals, Letters, and other Papers. New and Cheaper Issue, with Portrait, 8vo. 6s.

Contains notices and anecdotes illustrating the social life of the period —extending over a quarter of a century (1799—1827). It includes also poems and other miscellaneous pieces by Mrs. Trench.

HISTORY, BIOGRAPHY, & TRAVELS.

Trench (Capt. F., F.R.G.S.).—THE RUSSO-INDIAN QUESTION, Historically, Strategically, and Politically considered. By Capt. TRENCH, F.R.G.S. With a Sketch of Central Asiatic Politics and Map of Central Asia. Crown 8vo. 7s. 6d.

"*The Russo-Indian, or Central Asian question has for several obvious reasons been attracting much public attention in England, in Russia, and also on the Continent, within the last year or two. . . . I have thought that the present volume, giving a short sketch of the history of this question from its earliest origin, and condensing much of the most recent and interesting information on the subject, and on its collateral phases, might perhaps be acceptable to those who take an interest in it.*"—AUTHOR'S PREFACE.

Trevelyan (G.O., M.P.).—CAWNPORE. Illustrated with Plan. By G. O. TREVELYAN, M.P., Author of "The Competition Wallah." Second Edition. Crown 8vo. 6s.

"*In this book we are not spared one fact of the sad story; but our feelings are not harrowed by the recital of imaginary outrages. It is good for us at home that we have one who tells his tale so well as does Mr. Trevelyan.*"—PALL MALL GAZETTE.

THE COMPETITION WALLAH. New Edition. Crown 8vo. 6s.

"*The earlier letters are especially interesting for their racy descriptions of European life in India. . . . Those that follow are of more serious import, seeking to tell the truth about the Hindoo character and English influences, good and bad, upon it, as well as to suggest some better course of treatment than that hitherto adopted.*"—EXAMINER.

Vaughan (late Rev. Dr. Robert, of the British Quarterly).—MEMOIR OF ROBERT A. VAUGHAN. Author of "Hours with the Mystics." By ROBERT VAUGHAN, D.D. Second Edition, revised and enlarged. Extra fcap. 8vo. 5s.

"*It deserves a place on the same shelf with Stanley's 'Life of Arnold,' and Carlyle's 'Stirling.' Dr. Vaughan has performed his painful but not all unpleasing task with exquisite good taste and feeling.*"—NONCONFORMIST.

Wagner.—MEMOIR OF THE REV. GEORGE WAGNER, M.A., late Incumbent of St. Stephen's Church, Brighton. By the Rev. J. N. SIMPKINSON, M.A. Third and cheaper Edition, corrected and abridged. 5s.

"*A more edifying biography we have rarely met with.*"
LITERARY CHURCHMAN.

Wallace.—THE MALAY ARCHIPELAGO: the Land of the Orang Utan and the Bird of Paradise. A Narrative of Travels with Studies of Man and Nature. By ALFRED RUSSEL WALLACE. With Maps and Illustrations. Second Edition. Two vols. crown 8vo. 24s.

"*A carefully and deliberately composed narrative. . . . We advise our readers to do as we have done, read his book through.*"—TIMES.

Ward (Professor).—THE HOUSE OF AUSTRIA IN THE THIRTY YEARS' WAR. Two Lectures, with Notes and Illustrations. By ADOLPHUS W. WARD, M.A., Professor of History in Owens College, Manchester. Extra fcap. 8vo. 2s. 6d.

"*Very compact and instructive.*"—FORTNIGHTLY REVIEW.

Warren.—AN ESSAY ON GREEK FEDERAL COINAGE. By the Hon. J. LEICESTER WARREN, M.A. 8vo. 2s. 6d.

"*The present essay is an attempt to illustrate Mr. Freeman's Federal Government by evidence deduced from the coinage of the times and countries therein treated of.*"—PREFACE.

Wilson.—A MEMOIR OF GEORGE WILSON, M.D., F.R.S.E., Regius Professor of Technology in the University of Edinburgh. By his SISTER. New Edition. Crown 8vo. 6s.

"*An exquisite and touching portrait of a rare and beautiful spirit.*"
GUARDIAN.

HISTORY, BIOGRAPHY, & TRAVELS.

Wilson (Daniel, LL.D.).—PREHISTORIC ANNALS OF SCOTLAND. By DANIEL WILSON, LL.D., Professor of History and English Literature in University College, Toronto. New Edition, with numerous Illustrations. Two vols. demy 8vo. 36s.

This elaborate and learned work is divided into four Parts. Part I. deals with The Primeval or Stone Period : *Aboriginal Traces, Sepulchral Memorials, Dwellings, and Catacombs, Temples, Weapons, &c. &c. ; Part II.,* The Bronze Period : *The Metallurgic Transition, Primitive Bronze, Personal Ornaments, Religion, Arts, and Domestic Habits, with other topics ; Part III.,* The Iron Period : *The Introduction of Iron, The Roman Invasion, Strongholds, &c. &c.; Part IV.,* The Christian Period : *Historical Data, the Norrie's Law Relics, Primitive and Mediæval Ecclesiology, Ecclesiastical and Miscellaneous Antiquities. The work is furnished with an elaborate Index.*

PREHISTORIC MAN. New Edition, revised and partly re-written, with numerous Illustrations. One vol. 8vo. 21s.

This work, which carries out the principle of the preceding one, but with a wider scope, aims to " view Man, as far as possible, unaffected by those modifying influences which accompany the development of nations and the maturity of a true historic period, in order thereby to ascertain the sources from whence such development and maturity proceed." It contains, for example, chapters on the Primeval Transition ; Speech ; Metals ; the Mound-Builders ; Primitive Architecture ; the American Type ; the Red Blood of the West, &c. &c.

SECTION II.

POETRY AND BELLES LETTRES.

Allingham.—LAURENCE BLOOMFIELD IN IRELAND; or, the New Landlord. By WILLIAM ALLINGHAM. New and cheaper issue, with a Preface. Fcap. 8vo, cloth, 4s. 6d.

In the new Preface, the state of Ireland, with special reference to the Church measure, is discussed.

"*It is vital with the national character.* . . . *It has something of Pope's point and Goldsmith's simplicity, touched to a more modern issue.*"—ATHENÆUM.

Arnold (Matthew).—POEMS. By MATTHEW ARNOLD. Two vols. Extra fcap. 8vo. cloth. 12s. Also sold separately at 6s. each.

Volume I. contains Narrative and Elegiac Poems; Volume II. Dramatic and Lyric Poems. The two volumes comprehend the First and Second Series of the Poems, and the New Poems.

NEW POEMS. Extra fcap. 8vo. 6s. 6a.

In this volume will be found "Empedocles on Etna;" "Thyrsis" (written in commemoration of the late Professor Clough); "Epilogue to Lessing's Laocoön;" "Heine's Grave;" "Obermann once more." All these poems are also included in the Edition (two vols.) above-mentioned.

POETRY & BELLES LETTRES.

Arnold (Matthew), (*continued*)—

ESSAYS IN CRITICISM. New Edition, with Additions. Extra fcap. 8vo. 6s.

CONTENTS :—*Preface ; The Function of Criticism at the present time ; The Literary Influence of Academies ; Maurice de Guerin ; Eugenie de Guerin ; Heinrich Heine ; Pagan and Mediæval Religious Sentiment ; Joubert ; Spinoza and the Bible ; Marcus Aurelius.*

ASPROMONTE, AND OTHER POEMS. Fcap. 8vo. cloth extra. 4s. 6d.

CONTENTS :—*Poems for Italy ; Dramàtic Lyrics ; Miscellaneous.*

Barnes (Rev. W.).—POEMS OF RURAL LIFE IN COMMON ENGLISH. By the REV. W. BARNES, Author of "Poems of Rural Life in the Dorset Dialect." Fcap. 8vo. 6s.

"*In a high degree pleasant and novel. The book is by no means one which the lovers of descriptive poetry can afford to lose.*"—ATHENÆUM.

Bell.—ROMANCES AND MINOR POEMS. By HENRY GLASSFORD BELL. Fcap. 8vo. 6s.

"*Full of life and genius.*"—COURT CIRCULAR.

Besant.—STUDIES IN EARLY FRENCH POETRY. By WALTER BESANT, M.A. Crown. 8vo. 8s. 6d.

A sort of impression rests on most minds that French literature begins with the "siècle de Louis Quatorze;" any previous literature being for the most part unknown or ignored. Few know anything of the enormous literary activity that began in the thirteenth century, was carried on by Rulebeuf, Marie de France, Gaston de Foix, Thibault de Champagne, and Lorris ; was fostered by Charles of Orleans, by Margaret of Valois, by Francis the First ; that gave a crowd of versifiers to France, enriched, strengthened, developed, and fixed the French language, and prepared the way for Corneille and for Racine. The present work aims to afford information and direction touching the early efforts of France in poetical literature.

"In one moderately sized volume he has contrived to introduce us to the very best, if not to all of the early French poets."—ATHENÆUM.

Bradshaw.—AN ATTEMPT TO ASCERTAIN THE STATE OF CHAUCER'S WORKS, AS THEY WERE LEFT AT HIS DEATH. With some Notes of their Subsequent History. By HENRY BRADSHAW, of King's College, and the University Library, Cambridge. [*In the Press.*

Brimley.—ESSAYS BY THE LATE GEORGE BRIMLEY. M.A. Edited by the Rev. W. G. CLARK, M.A. With Portrait. Cheaper Edition. Fcap. 8vo. 3s. 6d.

Essays on literary topics, such as Tennyson's "Poems," Carlyle's "Life of Stirling," "Bleak House," &c., reprinted from Fraser, the Spectator, and like periodicals.

Broome.—THE STRANGER OF SERIPHOS. A Dramatic Poem. By FREDERICK NAPIER BROOME. Fcap. 8vo. 5s.

Founded on the Greek legend of Danae and Perseus.

Clough (Arthur Hugh).—THE POEMS AND PROSE REMAINS OF ARTHUR HUGH CLOUGH. With a Selection from his Letters and a Memoir. Edited by his Wife. With Portrait. Two vols. crown 8vo. 21s. Or Poems separately, as below.

The late Professor Clough is well known as a graceful, tender poet, and as the scholarly translator of Plutarch. The letters possess high interest, not biographical only, but literary—discussing, as they do, the most important questions of the time, always in a genial spirit. The "Remains" include papers on "Retrenchment at Oxford;" on Professor F. W. Newman's book " The Soul ;" on Wordsworth; on the Formation of Classical English ; on some Modern Poems (Matthew Arnold and the late Alexander Smith), &c. &c.

Clough (Arthur Hugh), *(continued)*—

THE POEMS OF ARTHUR HUGH CLOUGH, sometime Fellow of Oriel College, Oxford. With a Memoir by F. T. PALGRAVE. Second Edition. Fcap. 8vo. 6s.

"*From the higher mind of cultivated, all-questioning, but still conservative England, in this our puzzled generation, we do not know of any utterance in literature so characteristic as the poems of Arthur Hugh Clough.*"—FRASER'S MAGAZINE.

Dante.—DANTE'S COMEDY, THE HELL. Translated by W. M. ROSSETTI. Fcap. 8vo. cloth. 5s.

"*The aim of this translation of Dante may be summed up in one word —Literality. . . . To follow Dante sentence for sentence, line for line, word for word—neither more nor less—has been my strenuous endeavour.*" —AUTHOR'S PREFACE.

De Vere.—THE INFANT BRIDAL, and other Poems. By AUBREY DE VERE. Fcap. 8vo. 7s. 6d.

"*Mr. De Vere has taken his place among the poets of the day. Pure and tender feeling, and that polished restraint of style which is called classical, are the charms of the volume.*"—SPECTATOR.

Doyle (Sir F. H.).—Works by Sir FRANCIS HASTINGS DOYLE, Professor of Poetry in the University of Oxford :—

THE RETURN OF THE GUARDS, AND OTHER POEMS. Fcap. 8vo. 7s.

"*Good wine needs no bush, nor good verse a preface; and Sir Francis Doyle's verses run bright and clear, and smack of a classic vintage. . . . His chief characteristic, as it is his greatest charm, is the simple manliness which gives force to all he writes. It is a characteristic in these days rare enough.*"—EXAMINER.

Doyle (Sir F. H.), *(continued)*—

LECTURES ON POETRY, delivered before the University of Oxford in 1868. Extra crown 8vo. 3*s.* 6*d.*

THREE LECTURES :—(1) *Inaugural;* (2) *Provincial Poetry;* (3) *Dr. Newman's " Dream of Gerontius."*

" Full of thoughtful discrimination and fine insight: the lecture on 'Provincial Poetry' seems to us singularly true, eloquent, and instructive."
                                                                                                                SPECTATOR.

Evans.—BROTHER FABIAN'S MANUSCRIPT, AND OTHER POEMS. By SEBASTIAN EVANS. Fcap. 8vo. cloth. 6*s.*

" In this volume we have full assurance that he has ' the vision and the faculty divine.' . . . Clever and full of kindly humour."—GLOBE.

Furnivall.—LE MORTE D'ARTHUR. Edited from the *Harleian* M.S. 2252, in the British Museum. By F. J. FURNIVALL, M.A. With Essay by the late HERBERT COLERIDGE. Fcap. 8vo. 7*s.* 6*d.*

Looking to the interest shown by so many thousands in Mr. Tennyson's Arthurian poems, the editor and publishers have thought that the old version would possess considerable interest. It is a reprint of the celebrated Harleian copy; and is accompanied by index and glossary.

Garnett.—IDYLLS AND EPIGRAMS. Chiefly from the Greek Anthology. By RICHARD GARNETT. Fcap. 8vo. 2*s.* 6*d.*

" A charming little book. For English readers, Mr. Garnett's translations will open a new world of thought."—WESTMINSTER REVIEW.

GUESSES AT TRUTH. By TWO BROTHERS. With Vignette, Title, and Frontispiece. New Edition, with Memoir. Fcap. 8vo. 6*s.*

" The following year was memorable for the commencement of the 'Guesses at Truth.' He and his Oxford brother, living as they did in constant and free interchange of thought on questions of philosophy and

literature and art; delighting, each of them, in the epigrammatic terseness which is the charm of the 'Pensées' of Pascal, and the 'Caractères' of La Bruyère—agreed to utter themselves in this form, and the book appeared, anonymously, in two volumes, in 1827."—MEMOIR.

Hamerton.—A PAINTER'S CAMP. By PHILIP GILBERT HAMERTON. Second Edition, revised. Extra fcap. 8vo. 6s.

BOOK I. *In England;* BOOK II. *In Scotland;* BOOK III. *In France. This is the story of an Artist's encampments and adventures. The headings of a few chapters may serve to convey a notion of the character of the book: A Walk on the Lancashire Moors; the Author his own Housekeeper and Cook; Tents and Boats for the Highlands; The Author encamps on an uninhabited Island; A Lake Voyage; A Gipsy Journey to Glen Coe; Concerning Moonlight and Old Castles; A little French City; A Farm in the Autunois, &c. &c.*

"*His pages sparkle with happy turns of expression, not a few well-told anecdotes, and many observations which are the fruit of attentive study and wise reflection on the complicated phenomena of human life, as well as of unconscious nature.*"—WESTMINSTER REVIEW.

ETCHING AND ETCHERS. A Treatise Critical and Practical. By P. G. HAMERTON. With Original Plates by REMBRANDT, CALLOT, DUJARDIN, PAUL POTTER, &c. Royal 8vo. Half morocco. 31s. 6d.

"*It is a work of which author, printer, and publisher may alike feel proud. It is a work, too, of which none but a genuine artist could by possibility have been the author.*"—SATURDAY REVIEW.

Helps.—REALMAH. By ARTHUR HELPS. Cheap Edition. Crown 8vo. 6s.

Of this work, by the Author of "Friends in Council," the Saturday Review *says: "Underneath the form (that of dialogue) is so much shrewdness, fancy, and above all, so much wise kindliness, that we should think all the better of a man or woman who likes the book."*

Herschel.—THE ILIAD OF HOMER. Translated into English Hexameters. By Sir JOHN HERSCHEL, Bart. 8vo. 18s.

A version of the Iliad in English Hexameters. The question of Homeric translation is fully discussed in the Preface.

"*It is admirable, not only for many intrinsic merits, but as a great man's tribute to Genius.*"—ILLUSTRATED LONDON NEWS.

HIATUS : the Void in Modern Education. Its Cause and Antidote. By OUTIS. 8vo. 8s. 6d.

The main object of this Essay is to point out how the emotional element which underlies the Fine Arts is disregarded and undeveloped at this time so far as (despite a pretence at filling it up) to constitute an Educational Hiatus.

HYMNI ECCLESIÆ. *See* "THEOLOGICAL SECTION."

Kennedy.—LEGENDARY FICTIONS OF THE IRISH CELTS. Collected and Narrated by PATRICK KENNEDY. Crown 8vo. 7s. 6d.

"*A very admirable popular selection of the Irish fairy stories and legends, in which those who are familiar with Mr. Croker's, and other selections of the same kind, will find much that is fresh, and full of the peculiar vivacity and humour, and sometimes even of the ideal beauty, of the true Celtic Legend.*"—SPECTATOR.

Kingsley (Canon).—*See also* "HISTORIC SECTION," "WORKS OF FICTION," *and* "PHILOSOPHY;" *also* "JUVENILE BOOKS," *and* "THEOLOGY."

THE SAINTS' TRAGEDY: or, The True Story of Elizabeth of Hungary. By the Rev. CHARLES KINGSLEY. With a Preface by the Rev. F. D. MAURICE. Third Edition. Fcap. 8vo. 5s.

ANDROMEDA, AND OTHER POEMS. Third Edition. Fcap. 8vo. 5s.

POETRY & BELLES LETTRES.

Kingsley (Canon), (*continued*)—

PHAETHON; or, Loose Thoughts for Loose Thinkers. Third Edition. Crown 8vo. 2s.

Kingsley (Henry).—*See* "WORKS OF FICTION."

Lowell.—UNDER THE WILLOWS, AND OTHER POEMS By JAMES RUSSELL LOWELL. Fcap. 8vo. 6s.

"*Under the Willows is one of the most admirable bits of idyllic work, short as it is, or perhaps because it is short, that have been done in our generation.*"—SATURDAY REVIEW.

Masson (Professor).—ESSAYS, BIOGRAPHICAL AND CRITICAL. Chiefly on the British Poets. By DAVID MASSON, LL.D., Professor of Rhetoric in the University of Edinburgh. 8vo. 12s. 6d.

"*Distinguished by a remarkable power of analysis, a clear statement of the actual facts on which speculation is based, and an appropriate beauty of Language. These essays should be popular with serious men.*"
ATHENÆUM.

BRITISH NOVELISTS AND THEIR STYLES. Being a Critical Sketch of the History of British Prose Fiction. Crown 8vo. 7s. 6d.

"*Valuable for its lucid analysis of fundamental principles, its breadth of view, and sustained animation of style.*"—SPECTATOR.

MRS. JERNINGHAM'S JOURNAL. Extra fcap. 8vo. 3s. 6d. A Poem of the boudoir or domestic class, purporting to be the journal of a newly-married lady.

"*One quality in the piece, sufficient of itself to claim a moment's attention, is that it is unique—original, indeed, is not too strong a word—in the manner of its conception and execution.*"—PALL MALL GAZETTE.

Mistral (F.).—MIRELLE: a Pastoral Epic of Provence. Translated by H. CRICHTON. Extra fcap. 8vo. 6s.

"*This is a capital translation of the elegant and richly-coloured pastoral epic poem of M. Mistral which, in 1859, he dedicated in enthusiastic terms to Lamartine. . . . . . It would be hard to overpraise the sweetness and pleasing freshness of this charming epic.*"—ATHENÆUM.

Myers (Ernest).—THE PURITANS. By ERNEST MYERS. Extra fcap. 8vo. cloth. 2s. 6d.

"*It is not too much to call it a really grand poem, stately and dignified, and showing not only a high poetic mind, but also great power over poetic expression.*"—LITERARY CHURCHMAN.

Myers (F. W. H.)—ST. PAUL. A Poem. By F. W. H. MYERS. Second Edition. Extra fcap. 8vo. 2s. 6d.

"*It breathes throughout the spirit of St. Paul, and with a singular stately melody of verse.*"—FORTNIGHTLY REVIEW.

Nettleship.—ESSAYS ON ROBERT BROWNING'S POETRY. By JOHN T. NETTLESHIP. Extra fcap. 8vo. 6s. 6d.

Noel.—BEATRICE, AND OTHER POEMS. By the Hon. RODEN NOEL. Fcap. 8vo. 6s.

"*Beatrice is in many respects a noble poem; it displays a splendour of landscape painting, a strong definite precision of highly-coloured description, which has not often been surpassed.*"—PALL MALL GAZETTE.

Norton.—THE LADY OF LA GARAYE. By the HON. MRS NORTON. With Vignette and Frontispiece. Sixth Edition Fcap. 8vo. 4s. 6d.

"*There is no lack of vigour, no faltering of power, plenty of passion, much bright description, much musical verse. . . . Full of thoughts well-expressed, and may be classed among her best works.*"—TIMES.

POETRY & BELLES LETTRES. 31

Orwell.—THE BISHOP'S WALK AND THE BISHOP'S TIMES. Poems on the days of Archbishop Leighton and the Scottish Covenant. By ORWELL. Fcap. 8vo. 5*s*.

"*Pure taste and faultless precision of language, the fruits of deep thought, insight into human nature, and lively sympathy.*"—NONCONFORMIST.

Palgrave (Francis T.).—ESSAYS ON ART. By FRANCIS TURNER PALGRAVE, M.A., late Fellow of Exeter College, Oxford. Extra fcap. 8vo. 6*s*.

Mulready—Dyce—Holman Hunt—Herbert—Poetry, Prose, and Sensationalism in Art—Sculpture in England—The Albert Cross, &c.

SHAKESPEARE'S SONNETS AND SONGS. Edited by F. T. PALGRAVE. Gem Edition. With Vignette Title by JEENS. 3*s*. 6*d*.

"*For minute elegance no volume could possibly excel the 'Gem Edition.'*"—SCOTSMAN.

Patmore.—Works by COVENTRY PATMORE :—

THE ANGEL IN THE HOUSE.

BOOK I. *The Betrothal;* BOOK II. *The Espousals;* BOOK III. *Faithful for Ever. With Tamerton Church Tower.* Two vols. fcap. 8vo. 12*s*.

*** *A New and Cheap Edition in one vol.* 18mo., *beautifully printed on toned paper, price* 2*s*. 6*d*.

THE VICTORIES OF LOVE. Fcap. 8vo. 4*s*. 6*d*.

The intrinsic merit of his poem will secure it a permanent place in literature. . . . Mr. Patmore has fully earned a place in the catalogue of poets by the finished idealization of domestic life."—SATURDAY REVIEW.

Rossetti.—Works by CHRISTINA ROSSETTI :—

GOBLIN MARKET, AND OTHER POEMS. With two Designs by D. G. ROSSETTI. Second Edition. Fcap. 8vo. 5*s.*

"*She handles her little marvel with that rare poetic discrimination which neither exhausts it of its simple wonders by pushing symbolism too far, nor keeps those wonders in the merely fabulous and capricious stage. In fact she has produced a true children's poem, which is far more delightful to the mature than to children, though it would be delightful to all.*"— SPECTATOR.

THE PRINCE'S PROGRESS, AND OTHER POEMS. With two Designs by D. G. ROSSETTI. Fcap. 8vo. 6*s.*

"*Miss Rossetti's poems are of the kind which recalls Shelley's definition of Poetry as the record of the best and happiest moments of the best and happiest minds. . . . They are like the piping of a bird on the spray in the sunshine, or the quaint singing with which a child amuses itself when it forgets that anybody is listening.*"—SATURDAY REVIEW.

Rossetti (W. M.).—DANTE'S HELL. *See* "DANTE."

FINE ART, chiefly Contemporary. By WILLIAM M. ROSSETTI. Crown 8vo. 10*s.* 6*d.*

This volume consists of Criticism on Contemporary Art, reprinted from Fraser, The Saturday Review, The Pall Mall Gazette, *and other publications.*

Roby.—STORY OF A HOUSEHOLD, AND OTHER POEMS. By MARY K. ROBY. Fcap. 8vo. 5*s.*

Shairp (Principal).—KILMAHOE, a Highland Pastoral, with other Poems. By JOHN CAMPBELL SHAIRP. Fcap. 8vo. 5*s.*

"*Kilmahoe is a Highland Pastoral, redolent of the warm soft air of the Western Lochs and Moors, sketched out with remarkable grace and picturesqueness.*"—SATURDAY REVIEW.

POETRY & BELLES LETTRES.

Smith.—Works by ALEXANDER SMITH :—

A LIFE DRAMA, AND OTHER POEMS. Fcap. 8vo. 2s. 6d.

CITY POEMS. Fcap. 8vo. 5s.

EDWIN OF DEIRA. Second Edition. Fcap. 8vo. 5s.

"*A poem which is marked by the strength, sustained sweetness, and compact texture of real life.*"—NORTH BRITISH REVIEW.

Smith.—POEMS. By CATHERINE BARNARD SMITH. Fcap. 8vo. 5s.

"*Wealthy in feeling, meaning, finish, and grace; not without passion, which is suppressed, but the keener for that.*"—ATHENÆUM.

Smith (Rev. Walter).—HYMNS OF CHRIST AND THE CHRISTIAN LIFE. By the Rev. WALTER C. SMITH, M.A. Fcap. 8vo. 6s.

"*These are among the sweetest sacred poems we have read for a long time. With no profuse imagery, expressing a range of feeling and expression by no means uncommon, they are true and elevated, and their pathos is profound and simple.*"—NONCONFORMIST.

Stratford de Redcliffe (Viscount).—SHADOWS OF THE PAST, in Verse. By VISCOUNT STRATFORD DE REDCLIFFE. Crown 8vo. 10s. 6d.

"*The vigorous words of one who has acted vigorously. They combine the fervour of politician and poet.*"—GUARDIAN.

Trench.—Works by R. CHENEVIX TRENCH, D.D., Archbishop of Dublin. See also Sections "PHILOSOPHY," "THEOLOGY," &c.

POEMS. Collected and arranged anew. Fcap. 8vo. 7s. 6d.

ELEGIAC POEMS. Third Edition. Fcap. 8vo. 2s. 6d.

34   GENERAL CATALOGUE.

Trench (Archbishop), (*continued*)—

CALDERON'S LIFE'S A DREAM: The Great Theatre of the World. With an Essay on his Life and Genius. Fcap. 8vo. 4*s.* 6*d.*

HOUSEHOLD BOOK OF ENGLISH POETRY. Selected and arranged, with Notes, by R. C. TRENCH, D.D., Archbishop of Dublin. Extra fcap. 8vo. 5*s.* 6*d.*

This volume is called a " Household Book," by this name implying that it is a book for all—that there is nothing in it to prevent it from being confidently placed in the hands of every member of the household. Specimens of all classes of poetry are given, including selections from living authors. The Editor has aimed to produce a book "which the emigrant, finding room for little not absolutely necessary, might yet find room for in his trunk, and the traveller in his knapsack, and that on some narrow shelves where there are few books this might be one."

"*The Archbishop has conferred in this delightful volume an important gift on the whole English-speaking population of the world.*"—PALL MALL GAZETTE.

SACRED LATIN POETRY, Chiefly Lyrical. Selected and arranged for Use. Second Edition, Corrected and Improved. Fcap. 8vo. 7*s.*

"*The aim of the present volume is to offer to members of our English Church a collection of the best sacred Latin poetry, such as they shall be able entirely and heartily to accept and approve—a collection, that is, in which they shall not be evermore liable to be offended, and to have the current of their sympathies checked, by coming upon that which, however beautiful as poetry, out of higher respects they must reject and condemn—in which, too, they shall not fear that snares are being laid for them, to entangle them unawares in admiration for ought which is inconsistent with their faith and fealty to their own spiritual mother.*"—PREFACE.

Turner.—SONNETS. By the Rev. CHARLES TENNYSON TURNER. Dedicated to his brother, the Poet Laureate. Fcap. 8vo. 4s. 6d.

"*The Sonnets are dedicated to Mr. Tennyson by his brother, and have, independently of their merits, an interest of association. They both love to write in simple expressive Saxon; both love to touch their imagery in epithets rather than in formal similes; both have a delicate perception of rythmical movement, and thus Mr. Turner has occasional lines which, for phrase and music, might be ascribed to his brother. . . He knows the haunts of the wild rose, the shady nooks where light quivers through the leaves, the ruralities, in short, of the land of imagination.*"—ATHENÆUM.

SMALL TABLEAUX. Fcap. 8vo. 4s. 6d.

"*These brief poems have not only a peculiar kind of interest for the student of English poetry, but are intrinsically delightful, and will reward a careful and frequent perusal. Full of naïveté, piety, love, and knowledge of natural objects, and each expressing a single and generally a simple subject by means of minute and original pictorial touches, these sonnets have a place of their own.*"—PALL MALL GAZETTE.

Vittoria Colonna.—LIFE AND POEMS. By Mrs. HENRY ROSCOE. Crown 8vo. 9s.

The life of Vittoria Colonna, the celebrated Marchesa di Pescara, has received but cursory notice from any English writer, though in every history of Italy her name is mentioned with great honour among the poets of the sixteenth century. "In three hundred and fifty years," says her biographer Visconti, "there has been no other Italian lady who can be compared to her."

"*It is written with good taste, with quick and intelligent sympathy, occasionally with a real freshness and charm of style.*"—PALL MALL GAZETTE.

Webster.—Works by AUGUSTA WEBSTER :—
DRAMATIC STUDIES. Extra fcap. 8vo. 5s.

"*A volume as strongly marked by perfect taste as by poetic power.*"
NONCONFORMIST.

PROMETHEUS BOUND OF ÆSCHYLUS. Literally translated into English Verse. Extra fcap. 8vo. 3s. 6d.

"*Closeness and simplicity combined with literary skill.*"—ATHENÆUM.

MEDEA OF EURIPIDES. Literally translated into English Verse. Extra fcap. 8vo. 3s. 6d.

"*Mrs. Webster's translation surpasses our utmost expectations. It is a photograph of the original without any of that harshness which so often accompanies a photograph.*"—WESTMINSTER REVIEW.

A WOMAN SOLD, AND OTHER POEMS. Crown 8vo. 7s. 6d.

"*Mrs. Webster has shown us that she is able to draw admirably from the life; that she can observe with subtlety, and render her observations with delicacy; that she can impersonate complex conceptions, and venture into which few living writers can follow her.*"—GUARDIAN.

Woolner.—MY BEAUTIFUL LADY. By THOMAS WOOLNER. With a Vignette by ARTHUR HUGHES. *Third Edition.* Fcap. 8vo. 5s.

"*It is clearly the product of no idle hour, but a highly-conceived and faithfully-executed task, self-imposed, and prompted by that inward yearning to utter great thoughts, and a wealth of passionate feeling which is poetic genius. No man can read this poem without being struck by the fitness and finish of the workmanship, so to speak, as well as by the chastened and unpretending loftiness of thought which pervades the whole.*"
GLOBE.

WORDS FROM THE POETS. Selected by the Editor of "Rays of Sunlight." With a Vignette and Frontispiece. 18mo. Extra cloth gilt. 2s. 6d. *Cheaper Edition*, 18mo. limp., 1s.

GLOBE EDITIONS.

UNDER the title GLOBE EDITIONS, the Publishers are issuing a uniform Series of Standard English Authors, carefully edited, clearly and elegantly printed on toned paper, strongly bound, and at a small cost. The names of the Editors whom they have been fortunate enough to secure constitute an indisputable guarantee as to the character of the Series. The greatest care has been taken to ensure accuracy of text; adequate notes, elucidating historical, literary, and philological points, have been supplied; and, to the older Authors, glossaries are appended. The series is especially adapted to Students of our national Literature; while the small price places good editions of certain books, hitherto popularly inaccessible, within the reach of all.

Shakespeare.—THE COMPLETE WORKS OF WILLIAM SHAKESPEARE. Edited by W. G. CLARK and W. ALDIS WRIGHT. Ninety-first Thousand. Globe 8vo. 3s. 6d.

"A marvel of beauty, cheapness, and compactness. The whole works— plays, poems, and sonnets—are contained in one small volume: yet the page is perfectly clear and readable. .... For the busy man, above all for the working Student, the Globe Edition is the best of all existing Shakespeare books."—ATHENÆUM.

Morte D'Arthur.—SIR THOMAS MALORY'S BOOK OF KING ARTHUR AND OF HIS NOBLE KNIGHTS OF THE ROUND TABLE. The Edition of CAXTON, revised for Modern Use. With an Introduction by SIR EDWARD STRACHEY, Bart. Globe 8vo. 3s. 6d. Third Edition.

"*It is with the most perfect confidence that we recommend this edition of the old romance to every class of readers.*"—PALL MALL GAZETTE.

Scott.—THE POETICAL WORKS OF SIR WALTER SCOTT. With Biographical Essay, by F. T. PALGRAVE. Globe 8vo. 3s. 6d. New Edition.

"*As a popular edition it leaves nothing to be desired. The want of such an one has long been felt, combining real excellence with cheapness.*"
SPECTATOR.

Burns.—THE POETICAL WORKS AND LETTERS OF ROBERT BURNS. Edited, with Life, by ALEXANDER SMITH. Globe 8vo. 3s. 6d. Second Edition.

"*The works of the bard have never been offered in such a complete form in a single volume.*"—GLASGOW DAILY HERALD.
"*Admirable in all respects.*"—SPECTATOR.

Robinson Crusoe.—THE ADVENTURES OF ROBINSON CRUSOE. By DEFOE. Edited, from the Original Edition, by J. W. CLARK, M.A., Fellow of Trinity College, Cambridge. With Introduction by HENRY KINGSLEY. Globe 8vo. 3s. 6d.

"*The Globe Edition of Robinson Crusoe is a book to have and to keep. It is printed after the original editions, with the quaint old spelling, and is published in admirable style as regards type, paper, and binding. A well-written and genial biographical introduction, by Mr. Henry Kingsley, is likewise an attractive feature of this edition.*"—MORNING STAR.

Goldsmith.—GOLDSMITH'S MISCELLANEOUS WORKS. With Biographical Essay by Professor MASSON. Globe 8vo. 3s. 6d.

This edition includes the whole of Goldsmith's Miscellaneous Works— the Vicar of Wakefield, Plays, Poems, &c. Of the memoir the SCOTSMAN *newspaper writes:* "*Such an admirable compendium of the facts of Goldsmith's life, and so careful and minute a delineation of the mixed traits of his peculiar character, as to be a very model of a literary biography.*"

Pope.—THE POETICAL WORKS OF ALEXANDER POPE. Edited, with Memoir and Notes, by Professor WARD. Globe 8vo. 3s. 6d.

"*The book is handsome and handy. . . . The notes are many, and the matter of them is rich in interest.*"—ATHENÆUM.

Spenser.—THE COMPLETE WORKS OF EDMUND SPENSER. Edited from the Original Editions and Manuscripts, by R. MORRIS, Member of the Council of the Philological Society. With a Memoir by J. W. HALES, M.A., late Fellow of Christ's College, Cambridge, Member of the Council of the Philological Society. Globe 8vo. 3s. 6d.

"*A complete and clearly printed edition of the whole works of Spenser, carefully collated with the originals, with copious glossary, worthy—and higher praise it needs not—of the beautiful Globe Series. The work is edited with all the care so noble a poet deserves.*"—DAILY NEWS.

⁎⁎* Other Standard Works are in the Press.

⁎⁎* The Volumes of this Series may also be had in a variety of morocco and calf bindings at very moderate Prices.

GOLDEN TREASURY SERIES.

Uniformly printed in 18mo., with Vignette Titles by SIR NOEL PATON, T. WOOLNER, W. HOLMAN HUNT, J. E. MILLAIS, ARTHUR HUGHES, &c. Engraved on Steel by JEENS. Bound in extra cloth, 4s. 6d. each volume. Also kept in morocco.

"*Messrs. Macmillan have, in their Golden Treasury Series especially, provided editions of standard works, volumes of selected poetry, and original compositions, which entitle this series to be called classical. Nothing can be better than the literary execution, nothing more elegant than the material workmanship.*"—BRITISH QUARTERLY REVIEW.

THE GOLDEN TREASURY OF THE BEST SONGS AND LYRICAL POEMS IN THE ENGLISH LANGUAGE. Selected and arranged, with Notes, by FRANCIS TURNER PALGRAVE.

"*This delightful little volume, the Golden Treasury, which contains many of the best original lyrical pieces and songs in our language, grouped with care and skill, so as to illustrate each other like the pictures in a well-arranged gallery.*"—QUARTERLY REVIEW.

THE CHILDREN'S GARLAND FROM THE BEST POETS. Selected and arranged by COVENTRY PATMORE.

"*It includes specimens of all the great masters in the art of poetry, selected with the matured judgment of a man concentrated on obtaining insight into the feelings and tastes of childhood, and desirous to awaken its finest impulses, to cultivate its keenest sensibilities.*"—MORNING POST.

THE BOOK OF PRAISE. From the Best English Hymn Writers. Selected and arranged by Sir Roundell Palmer. *A New and Enlarged Edition.*

"*All previous compilations of this kind must undeniably for the present give place to the Book of Praise. . . . The selection has been made throughout with sound judgment and critical taste. The pains involved in this compilation must have been immense, embracing, as it does, every writer of note in this special province of English literature, and ranging over the most widely divergent tracts of religious thought.*"—Saturday Review.

THE FAIRY BOOK; the Best Popular Fairy Stories. Selected and rendered anew by the Author of "John Halifax, Gentleman."

"*A delightful selection, in a delightful external form; full of the physical splendour and vast opulence of proper fairy tales.*"—Spectator.

THE BALLAD BOOK. A Selection of the Choicest British Ballads. Edited by William Allingham.

"*His taste as a judge of old poetry will be found, by all acquainted with the various readings of old English ballads, true enough to justify his undertaking so critical a task.*"—Saturday Review.

THE JEST BOOK. The Choicest Anecdotes and Sayings. Selected and arranged by Mark Lemon.

"*The fullest and best jest book that has yet appeared.*"—Saturday Review.

BACON'S ESSAYS AND COLOURS OF GOOD AND EVIL. With Notes and Glossarial Index. By W. Aldis Wright, M.A.

"*The beautiful little edition of Bacon's Essays, now before us, does credit to the taste and scholarship of Mr. Aldis Wright. . . . It puts the reader in possession of all the essential literary facts and chronology necessary for reading the Essays in connexion with Bacon's life and times.*"—Spectator.

"*By far the most complete as well as the most elegant edition we possess.*"—Westminster Review.

D

THE PILGRIM'S PROGRESS from this World to that which is to come. By JOHN BUNYAN.

"*A beautiful and scholarly reprint.*"—SPECTATOR.

THE SUNDAY BOOK OF POETRY FOR THE YOUNG. Selected and arranged by C. F. ALEXANDER.

"*A well-selected volume of sacred poetry.*"—SPECTATOR.

A BOOK OF GOLDEN DEEDS of all Times and all Countries. Gathered and narrated anew. By the Author of "THE HEIR OF REDCLYFFE."

"*... To the young, for whom it is especially intended, as a most interesting collection of thrilling tales well told; and to their elders, as a useful handbook of reference, and a pleasant one to take up when their wish is to while away a weary half-hour. We have seen no prettier gift-book for a long time.*"—ATHENÆUM.

THE POETICAL WORKS OF ROBERT BURNS. Edited, with Biographical Memoir, Notes, and Glossary, by ALEXANDER SMITH. Two Vols.

"*Beyond all question this is the most beautiful edition of Burns yet out.*"—EDINBURGH DAILY REVIEW.

THE ADVENTURES OF ROBINSON CRUSOE. Edited from the Original Edition by J. W. CLARK, M.A., Fellow of Trinity College, Cambridge.

"*Mutilated and modified editions of this English classic are so much the rule, that a cheap and pretty copy of it, rigidly exact to the original, will be a prize to many book-buyers.*"—EXAMINER.

THE REPUBLIC OF PLATO. TRANSLATED into ENGLISH, with Notes, by J. Ll. DAVIES, M.A. and D. J. VAUGHAN, M.A.

"*A dainty and cheap little edition.*"—EXAMINER.

THE SONG BOOK. Words and Tunes from the best Poets and Musicians. Selected and arranged by JOHN HULLAH, Professor of Vocal Music in King's College, London.

"*A choice collection of the sterling songs of England, Scotland, and Ireland, with the music of each prefixed to the words. How much true wholesome pleasure such a book can diffuse, and will diffuse, we trust, through many thousand families.*"—EXAMINER.

LA LYRE FRANCAISE. Selected and arranged, with Notes, by GUSTAVE MASSON, French Master in Harrow School.

A selection of the best French songs and lyrical pieces.

TOM BROWN'S SCHOOL DAYS. By an OLD BOY.

"*A perfect gem of a book. The best and most healthy book about boys for boys that ever was written.*"—ILLUSTRATED TIMES.

A BOOK OF WORTHIES. Gathered from the Old Histories and written anew by the Author of "THE HEIR OF REDCLYFFE." With Vignette.

"*An admirable edition to an admirable series.*"
  WESTMINSTER REVIEW.

www.ingramcontent.com/pod-product-compliance
Lightning Source LLC
Chambersburg PA
CBHW032138230426
43672CB00011B/2383